Being Religious
Interreligiously

Being Religious Interreligiously

Asian Perspectives on Interfaith Dialogue

Peter C. Phan

ORBIS BOOKS

Maryknoll, New York 10545

Third Printing, February 2008

Founded in 1970, Orbis Books endeavors to publish works that enlighten the mind, nourish the spirit, and challenge the conscience. The publishing arm of the Maryknoll Fathers and Brothers, Orbis seeks to explore the global dimensions of the Christian faith and mission, to invite dialogue with diverse cultures and religious traditions, and to serve the cause of reconciliation and peace. The books published reflect the opinions of their authors and are not meant to represent the official position of the Maryknoll Society. To obtain more information about Maryknoll and Orbis Books, please visit our website at www.maryknoll.org.

Library of Congress Cataloging in Publication Data

Phan, Peter C., 1943–
  Being religious interreligiously : Asian perspectives on interfaith dialogue / Peter C. Phan.
    p. cm.
  ISBN 1–57075–565–5 (pbk.)
  1. Christianity and other religions. 2. Asia—Religion. I. Title.
  BR128.A77P48 2004
  261.2—dc22
                    2004006511

To
William R. Burrows, Ph.D.
Redattore straordinario
con amicizia e gratitudine

Contents

PART ONE

DOING THEOLOGY INTERRELIGIOUSLY IN THE POSTMODERN AGE

Preface

At Vatican II the Catholic church at last caught up with the modern world, whose "joy and hope" and "grief and anguish" it wanted to share. Ironically, in the meantime, the world had moved on to what is today called *postmodernity* and presents a different set of challenges to the church's mission, especially in terms of cultural and religious pluralism.

To meet these challenges the Asian bishops and theologians propose a new way of being church. This new way consists in a triple dialogue: with the Asian peoples, especially their poor (liberation); with their cultures (inculturation); and with their religions (interreligious dialogue).

Inspired by these Asian theologies I have offered some reflections on the first two dialogues in my earlier works *(Christianity with an Asian Face* and *In Our Own Tongues)*. In this book, which completes the trilogy, I broach the theme of the third dialogue, understood very broadly to include, besides interreligious dialogue as such, the task of faith seeking understanding and liturgical worship.

In the two above-mentioned works I attempted a Christology on the basis of the Confucian tradition of ancestor veneration and a Mariology based on the Buddhist tradition of the Buddha of Compassion. Here I extend further my theology of interreligious dialogue by reflecting on the challenges that interreligious dialogue in the postmodern age poses to the way of doing theology; by developing particular themes of Christian theology, especially in dialogue with Confucianism and Judaism; and by indicating how prayer and worship should be practiced in the postmodern, multicultural, and multi-religious age. Of course, interreligious dialogue in Asia should deal with other religions such as Taoism, Hinduism, Islam, Jainism, Sikhism, and tribal religions. My lack of expertise in these religious traditions is an implicit invitation to better qualified theologians to develop the comparative theology in these fields that is so necessary today.

Three volumes of about eight hundred pages take up a lot of space for three theological themes. Yet I must confess they have barely scratched the surface of these complex issues. A lot more could have been said, and more profoundly, at least by people wiser and more learned than I. In an autobiographical lapse I have publicly confessed that I am an "accidental theologian." Had South Vietnam not been defeated by the North and had I not been fortuitously brought to the United States as a refugee, I would have earned my daily rice by non-academic jobs in my native country and would have blissfully remained a theological ignoramus. But Divine Providence has planned otherwise, and along

with opportunities came responsibilities. I have tried to discharge these theological responsibilities by building bridges between East and West, and I am
sure Asian theologians of the next generation will construct better ones between
the two cultures.

Acknowledgments

It is my great pleasure to express my deepest thanks to the Louisville Institute for a generous grant and the Catholic University of America for a year-long sabbatical (2001–2002). It was only thanks to these two gifts that I was able to complete this trilogy with previously published essays and new ones. To Catholic University in particular, my academic home for fifteen years, I would like to express my profound gratitude for the many opportunities it offered me for professional advancement and the warm affection of many friends. Fortunately, Georgetown University is only a few miles away, and it is not difficult to return to the old home for occasional nostalgic visits. My new academic home, especially my colleagues in the Department of Theology, deserve my deep gratitude for their warm welcome and their collegial spirit.

I also give my heartfelt thanks to the family that generously endows the Ignacio Ellacuría, S.J., Chair in Catholic Social Thought, but wishes to remain anonymous, for the ample opportunities for study and research associated with the chair. May God's abundant blessings be on them!

As to the mechanics of the publication of this book, I owe thanks to Catherine Costello and Joan Laflamme, who have lavished abundant care on it as they have done on its two older siblings.

I would have been very fortunate if Orbis Books had published only one of my books. To have my trilogy (and other books) appear under its aegis is pure grace, and to the powers that be at Orbis, especially Michael Leach, Susan Perry, and Robert Ellsberg, thanks for the support and encouragement. But to Bill Burrows, editor *extraordinaire*, I owe a big debt, and this book is dedicated to him as a small token of friendship and gratitude. He knows why the dedication is written in Italian!

Some of the chapters of this book have appeared in earlier versions or were delivered in various venues. I am grateful to the editors and publishers for their permission to reprint them in revised forms. And I am grateful to those who have reacted to earlier versions of these ideas; they have helped me rethink and refine ideas that in some cases needed clarity and second thoughts to mature my thinking. In this regard, Chapter 1 appeared first in *Theological Studies* 62 (2001): 730–52; Chapter 2 in *Salesianum* 60 (1998): 125–45; Chapter 3 in *Horizons* 25/2 (1998): 159–89; Chapter 4 in *Theological Studies* 64 (2003): 495–519; Chapter 5 in *Indian Theological Studies* 31/1 (1994): 44–66; Chapter 6 in *Irish Theological Quarterly* 55 (1989), 277–90; Chapter 10 in Howard Clark Kee and Irvin L. Borovski, eds., *Removing Anti-Judaism from the Pulpit* (New York:

Continuum, 1996), 75–92; Chapter 11 in Michael Signer, ed., *Humanity at the Limit: The Impact of the Holocaust Experience on Jews and Christians* (Bloomington and Indianapolis: Indiana University Press, 2000), 112–37; Chapter 13 in Keith Pecklers, ed., *Liturgy in a Postmodern World* (New York: Continuum, 2003), 55–86; Chapter 14 in *Worship* 72/3 (1998): 192–210; Chapter 15 in Timothy Fitzgerald and David Lysik, eds., *Incongruities: Who We Are and How We Pray* (Chicago: Liturgy Training Publications, 2000), 5–33.

Abbreviations

AG	*Ad gentes (Decree on the Church's Missionary Activity)*
DI	*Dominus Iesus*
EA	*Ecclesia in Asia*
FABC	Federation of Asian Bishops' Conferences
GS	*Gaudium et spes (Pastoral Constitution on the Church in the Modern World)*
LG	*Lumen gentium (Dogmatic Constitution on the Church)*
NA	*Nostra aetate (Declaration on the Relation of the Church to Non-Christian Religions)*
NCCB	National Conference of Catholic Bishops (United States)
PO	*Presbyterorum ordinis (Decree on the Ministry and Life of Priests)*
RM	*Redemptoris missio*
SC	*Sacramentum concilium (Constitution on the Sacred Liturgy)*
UR	*Unitatis redintegratio (Decree on Ecumenism)*
USCC	United States Catholic Conference

Introduction

Theology and Interreligious Dialogue in the Postmodern Age

Contemporary cultural critics have long noted that the mood of our time is sharply different from that of the eighteenth and nineteenth centuries. While modernity is characterized by a belief in limitless progress achievable by universal rationality, technology, and individual freedoms, we are witnessing today a widespread critique of these ideals, at least in the forms espoused by the Enlightenment, as the result of an increasing awareness of their nefarious effects on society and the environment. In contrast to modernity, our age has been called, for lack of a better term, *postmodern.* Though the label is slippery and the contours of our age still remain hazy, there is little doubt that since the beginning of the twentieth century there has been, at least in the West, to use David Tracy's expression, a "disenchantment with disenchantment," that is, a radical critique of the Enlightenment's critique of premodern modes of thought and action.[1]

POSTMODERNISM AND ITS CHALLENGES TO CHURCH AND THEOLOGY

This contemporary disillusionment with modernity's championship of rationality, technology, and individual autonomy, however, is no call for a return to the paradise of premodern innocence. Rather, with the very weapons forged by the Enlightenment itself, postmodern thinkers direct their withering attacks against modernity's celebration of objective and universal reason, the benefits of technological achievements, and the liberation of the individual from institutional control. While recognizing the undeniable contributions of modernity in these three areas, postmodern critics have argued that philosophic reason is laden with vested interests, technology leads to the brink of annihilation for humanity and the ecology, and individual freedoms collude with the subjugation of the powerless and the voiceless. The horror and terror of history, rather than being tamed by modernity, have grown exponentially.

---

[1] See David Tracy, *Blessed Rage for Order: The New Pluralism in Theology* (New York: The Seabury Press, 1975), 10.

True to its underlying philosophical assumptions, postmodernism is a multivalent and even ambiguous phenomenon. Initiated in architecture and the arts, postmodernism rejects modernity's preference for stylistic integrity and purity and espouses instead heterogeneity and polyvalence, bricolage and pastiche, and an eclectic mixture of disjointed and contradictory elements. In theater, postmodernism celebrates transience instead of temporal permanence and experiments with improvisation, group authorship, and viewer participation rather than continuing the tradition of performing a ready-made script. In literature, the postmodern favorite genres are the spy novel and science fiction, the former juxtaposing a seemingly disjointed series of events and unconnected clues, the latter laying side by side two radically different worlds, the one real in appearance but turning out to be illusionary, and the other sinister in appearance but turning out to be more benign and real at the end. This phantasmagoria of the fictional and the real is further enhanced by the filmmaking technology that allows the viewer to perceive what transpires in the movies and on television, disjointed in time and space, as a unity in space and time. The unreality of the real and the reality of the unreal are made even more indistinguishable by means of advanced techniques of computer-generated images and special effects. Added to all this is the Internet world of "virtual reality," in which the screen of the personal computer both connects the surfer with the whole wide world of other surfers and chatters and at the same time shields him or her from the world of interpersonal, face-to-face relationships. In the virtual world there is neither objective reality "out there" nor subjective reality "in here"; rather, the events happen somewhere in between, blurring the distinction between subject and object, the very thing postmodernism says "reality" is.

Undergirding and perhaps also resulting from such a cultural outlook is the philosophical stance that despairs of achieving objective truth and absolute knowledge of reality. Instead of yielding universal, supra-cultural, and timeless truths about "reality," knowledge is viewed as an ever-shifting social construction made by a particular community in view of its own interests. The best that can be obtained in our knowledge of reality, according to postmodern epistemology, is a "useful fiction," not generalizing principles or overarching systems (metanarratives) that can be reasonably legitimated. In this view knowledge is inherently uncertain, incomplete, fragmented, interest-laden, relative, particular, and pluralistic.

Basic to the postmodernist epistemology is respect for and celebration of particularity and "otherness" in all dimensions of human life, from race and ethnicity to gender to religion to culture. Diversity and plurality, which otherness implies, are seen not as curses to human flourishing to be exorcised or as threats to human unity to be suppressed. Rather, they are to be vigorously promoted and joyously celebrated as natural endowments necessary for genuine peace and justice. Plurality and diversity are perceived to be the essential safeguards preventing life-affirming unity from degenerating into deadening uniformity or, worse, into an instrument for the powerful to homogenize those who are different and to deny them their basic right to be who and what they are.

Ironically, however, concomitant with this centrifugal celebration of plurality and otherness, there is also in postmodernity a centripetal movement toward universal unity, toward the construction of the "global village," under the pressure of the process of ever-widening globalization. Aided by the worldwide adoption of a single neo-capitalistic system of free enterprise, globalization has extended beyond the West not only the technological achievements but also the ideals of modernity to other parts of the world (globalization as *extension*). Thanks to communication technologies and ease of travel, geographical boundaries have now collapsed, and a person's identity is no longer defined by his or her place of birth. Even our sense of time is largely compressed, with the present dominating our temporal awareness and relentlessly pressing onto the future with ever "new and improved" versions of what is now technologically available (globalization as *compression*). As a result, there has emerged everywhere outside of the West, especially among youth, a homogenized "hyperculture" characterized by modern values (and vices) and consumption of Western goods.

But the movement is not unidirectional. On the contrary, the non-Western parts of the world, though technologically less developed (except Japan, South Korea, Singapore, Hong Kong, and Taiwan) have also transformed the cultural and religious landscape of the West, especially through immigration. As Diana Eck has convincingly demonstrated, thanks to the 1965 Hart-Celler Act, which abolished restrictive quotas on immigration from countries other than Europe, a record number of Asians, Africans, and Latin Americans have come to the United States, bringing with them their diverse cultural and religious traditions, so that the "Christian country" has become "the world's religiously most diverse nation," with Buddhist, Confucian, Taoist, Hindu, Jain, Sikh, Zoroastrian, Islamic, African, and Afro-Caribbean traditions well represented.[2] Cultural and religious diversity is increasingly true also of countries such as Britain, France, Germany, and Italy.

Needless to say, this new cultural, socio-political, and religious context—cultural diversity, economic globalization, and religious pluralism—presents difficult challenges to the church and theology. *Culturally*, how can the Catholic church purge its two-millennia-long tradition of Eurocentric elements so that its face is truly catholic, that is, universal? How can the Catholic church become a truly local church? *Socio-politically*, how can the church credibly preach Jesus' teaching on God's preferential love for the poor and the marginalized and act in solidarity with those crushed by the forces of globalization? *Religiously*, how can the church not only respect but also incorporate into its own life and worship the teachings and practices of other religions in order to be enriched and transformed by them?

Answers to these three questions based on any appeal to universal reason or sacred authority are unlikely to find a receptive ear, especially in the postmodern age. Any attempt to construct a metanarrative on the basis of either natural law

---

[2] See Diana Eck, *A New Religious America: How a "Christian Country" Has Become the World's Religiously Most Diverse Nation* (New York: HarperSanFrancisco, 2001).

or divine revelation that could claim universal validity and absolute normativeness, apart from particular social locations, is illusory; there is no acultural and
atemporal ground upon which to stand to render a verdict on the alleged universal validity and absolute normativeness of such a metanarrative. We are ineluc-
tably socially located and historically conditioned animals. There is no
Archimedean point from which to survey the whole of history, which is still
ongoing, or to intuit the unchangeable essence of things, which always exist in
time and space and therefore are in the process of continuous becoming. Both
the knower and the known are caught in a mutually conditioning nexus from
which neither can be extracted to be either the unbiased observer or the neutral
object of investigation. Apart from the object known there is no knower, and
without the knower there is no object known. This is all the more true in matters
religious, which are ultimately matters of life and death, where life-transform-
ing decisions are not amenable to explanations by means of a rational apologetics
and logical syllogisms.

All these considerations need not lead to skepticism, agnosticism, or relativism, as some postmodernist thinkers have argued. Rather, what these reflections imply and require is an epistemological modesty that accepts the finite
(and in the Christian view, fallen and benighted) intellects that we are. In addition, we have at our disposal modes of knowing that are not purely rational, that
appeal to the imagination and the heart, that do not make grandiose claims to
absolute validity and universal normativeness, that do not produce an infallible
certainty but anchor the mind and the soul in an unshakable *certitude*, the kind
of knowledge that is proper to interpersonal relationships, different from that of
mathematical equations and physical laws, the sort of knowing that leads to
decision and action.

Furthermore, human knowledge, at least of things that matter deeply, is not
obtained by means of meditation in a solitary cell or in boisterous, hard-ball talk
shows in which the sole purpose is to score rhetorical victories over one's opponents. Rather, it is gained in a serious and thoughtful give-and-take of mutual
learning and teaching, in a respectful and humble conversation with the tradition and the community of fellow seekers, in a word, in a genuine *dialogue* with
the other, in which one's own insights are humbly offered, the other's wisdom
gratefully appropriated, and the quest for truth is undertaken together in mutual
respect and love.

CHRISTIAN FAITH AND RELIGIOUS PLURALISM

It is in this spirit of dialogue that the church must engage with the other
religions. The church, which shares "the joy and hope, the grief and anguish of
people of our time, especially of those who are poor and afflicted in any way,"[3]
inevitably is enmeshed in the turmoil of our age. Ironically, the church, which

---

[3] Vatican II, *Pastoral Constitution on the Church in the Modern Word (Gaudium et spes)*, no. 1. Note the word *modern* in the title.

finally caught up with the *modern* world, as the title of *Gaudium et Spes* implies, after centuries of "kicking and screaming," is now being left behind as the world moves into *postmodernity*. The question now is whether, faced with the signs of the time, the church will repeat its mistakes, either indulging in a futile nostalgia for a vanishing golden age of order and uniformity by promoting a restorationist agenda, or succumbing to the songs of the postmodern sirens by swallowing postmodernism hook, line, and sinker.

Christian faith would, it seems, wholeheartedly welcome religious pluriformity and diversity as the fruits of God's creative act, reflecting God's own being. Indeed, the God Christians believe in is not a solitary monad but a *koinonia* of three divine persons, that is, of the eternal subsistent relations resulting from the Father "generating" the Son and "breathing forth" the Spirit through the Son; of the Son being "generated" by the Father and "breathing forth" the Spirit by the power of the Father; and of the Spirit "proceeding" from the Father through the Son and uniting them both in love. *Because of*—not in spite of—divine unity, plurality and diversity are inherent in God's Trinitarian life and being; conversely, *because of*—not in spite of—divine diversity and plurality, God is one. On the one hand, were it not for the plurality of the divine persons, there would not be the one God, since divine unity is constituted by the harmony of diverse eternal relations. On the other hand, were there many gods, there would not, paradoxically, be divine plurality, since they would be uniformly divine. In the divine Being, the more God is one, the more plural God is, and vice versa. God's oneness and plurality are in direct, not inverse proportion with each other. It is only because the Father and the Son and the Spirit are related in mutual *perichoresis* or *circumincessio* (or *circuminsessio*) that God is one, and God's oneness *necessarily* entails plurality. Divine unity does not consist in the one *nature* or *substance* but in the unity of the eternal threefold relations.

Furthermore, creation itself can be regarded as God's free and loving gift of God's otherness and plurality. Creation is not a mere prolongation of the same divine substance into time and space, as emanationists suggest. Rather, it consists in bringing into existence a genuine other, ontologically different from the divine, which reflects and embodies divine plurality in the variety and multiplicity of creation.

This same otherness is preserved in the incarnation. In the enfleshed Logos the divine nature and the human nature are, to use the expression of the Council of Chalcedon, "without confusion and change, without division and separation." Indeed, as the council teaches, "the distinction between the natures was never abolished by their union but rather the character proper to each of the two natures was preserved as they came together in one person *(prosōpon)* and one hypostasis."[4]

---

[4] For the English translation, see J. Neuner and J. Dupuis, eds., *The Christian Faith in the Doctrinal Documents of the Catholic Church* (New York: Alba House, 1982), 154–55. The quotations from Vatican II documents also are taken from this book.

Finally, grace or union with the divine is not an ontological dissolution of the human self into the divine being, like a drop of water falling into the ocean. Rather, it is a deification of the human person in which a real distinction remains between the divinized human being and the divinizing Holy Spirit.

This inherent bias of the Christian faith toward plurality and diversity, based on theological, christological, and pneumatological grounds, does not mean that Christianity itself in its past two millennia has always and everywhere accepted and fostered these two features of reality as divine blessings. It is true that the church has taken to heart the Pauline model of ecclesiology in which a variety of charisms is encouraged for the building up of the body of Christ (cf. 1 Cor 14) and has attempted at various times to be, like Paul, everything to everybody. Nevertheless, there is a well-nigh irresistible tendency in any organization with large-scale structures and well-defined canons, such as the Catholic church, to promote centralization and uniformity and to nip in the bud any centrifugal movement toward plurality and diversity as a threat to its institutional order and well-being.

The Catholic church's attitude toward followers of other religions and the religions themselves has followed an arduous and twisted path. Happily, it is now long past considering the followers of other religions as "infidels" or "pagans" and no longer teaches, as the Decree for the Jacobites of the Council of Florence did in 1442, on the basis of Matthew 25:41, that those who remain outside the Catholic church, including pagans, Jews, heretics, or schismatics, will go to the "eternal fire prepared for the devil and his angels," unless before their death they join the Catholic church. The Catholic church no longer holds Pius IX's teaching in his allocution *Singulari quadam* (1854) that "no one can be saved outside the apostolic Roman Church, that the Church is the only ark of salvation, and that whoever does not enter it will perish in the flood" and that they are exculpated only in virtue of their "invincible ignorance."[5]

On the contrary, in the *Dogmatic Constitution on the Church (Lumen gentium)* Vatican II affirms the possibility of salvation for Jews, Muslims, those "who without fault on their part do not know the Gospel of Christ and his Church, but seek God with a sincere heart, and under the influence of grace endeavor to do his will as recognized through the promptings of their conscience," and even for those "who, without fault on their part, have not yet reached an explicit knowledge of God, and yet endeavor, not without grace, to live a good life" (*LG*, no. 16). Furthermore, Vatican II in the *Decree on the Church's Missionary Activity (Ad gentes)* recognizes the presence of "elements of truth and of grace" (*AG*, no. 9) in non-Christian religions and acknowledges them as "seeds of the Word" implanted by God before the preaching of the Gospel that "may sometimes be taken as leading the way *(paedagogia)* to the true God and as a preparation for the Gospel" (*AG*, no. 3).

In the post-conciliar period Pope John Paul II, more than any of his predecessors, has made enormous contributions to interreligious dialogue, not only in

---

[5] For the English text, see Neuner and Dupuis, *The Christian Faith*, 423–24.

his extensive and ground-breaking writings on the subject, but also, and perhaps more significantly, through his numerous symbolic actions, such as his visits to places of worship of other religions and his several gatherings of leaders of various religions in Assisi for prayer.[6]

In spite of its positive evaluation of non-Christian religions in general and of Judaism in particular, Vatican II self-consciously refrains from affirming that these religions as such function as ways of salvation in a manner analogous, let alone parallel, to Christianity. In the last three decades, however, extensive reflections have been done on the relationship between Christianity, and by implication, Jesus Christ, on the one hand, and non-Christian religions, especially Judaism, on the other. A new theology of religions has reassessed the role of Christ as the unique and universal savior and the function of non-Christian religions themselves within God's plan of salvation. Several theologians—myself included—have argued that these religions may be said to be ways of salvation and that religious pluralism is part of God's providential plan.

Such a theologoumenon brings with it far-reaching and radical consequences for the practice of Christian mission and raises thorny questions regarding conversion and baptism as the primary goals of evangelization. Indeed, if religious pluralism belongs to divine providence and is not just the fruit of human sinfulness, then it may not and must not be abolished by converting all the followers of non-Christian religions, at least during our common journey in history. At any rate, from the purely pragmatic point of view, the disappearance of these religions is extremely unlikely, given the fact that after almost five hundred years of mission in Asia, only 3 percent of Asians (who constitute three-fourths of humanity) are Christian, not to mention the fact that new religions and religious movements are founded all the time.

One immediate requirement of this situation is for theology to rethink the relationship between Christianity and other religions. In a recent work Catholic theologian Paul F. Knitter, who has written extensively on religious pluralism, has helpfully categorized contemporary theologies of religions into four basic types, which he terms "replacement," "fulfillment," "mutuality," and

---

[6] Two recent statements of the Magisterium deserve special notice. In his 1990 encyclical on mission Pope John Paul II declares that the Holy Spirit is present "not only in individuals but also in society and history, peoples, cultures, and religions" (*Redemptoris missio*, no. 28). The 1991 document *Dialogue and Proclamation* of the Congregation for the Evangelization of Peoples and the Pontifical Council for Interreligious Dialogue says that because of "the active presence of God through his Word" and "the universal presence of the Spirit" not only in persons outside the church but also in their religions, it is "in the sincere practice of what is good in their own religious traditions . . . that the members of other religions correspond positively to God's invitation and receive salvation" (no. 29). Unfortunately, the 2000 declaration *Dominus Iesus* of the Congregation for the Doctrine of the Faith has dampened the efforts toward interreligious dialogue. For an evaluation of John Paul II's work for interreligious dialogue, see Byron L. Smith et al., eds., *John Paul II and Interreligious Dialogue* (Maryknoll, N.Y.: Orbis Books, 1999).

"acceptance" models.[7] The first affirms that Christianity is the one true religion and that it will replace, totally or partially, all other religions, which are considered basically humanity's sinful attempts at self-salvation. The second, while affirming Christianity as the one true religion, acknowledges the presence of elements of truth and grace in other religions and advocates a mutual, though not equal, complementarity between Christianity and other religions through dialogue. The third holds that there are many true religions, none necessarily superior to the others, which are all called to dialogue and collaborate with one another, especially in projects of liberation, in order to realize their true nature. The fourth stresses the diversity of religions and refuses to seek a common ground among them; rather, it urges each religion to foster its own aims and practices.

THEOLOGY, INTERRELIGIOUS DIALOGUE, AND WORSHIP

In light of the increasing importance of religious pluralism and interreligious dialogue in our postmodern age, the present book, the last of a trilogy, makes these topics its explicit theme; its two older siblings explored the themes of liberation and inculturation. Focusing on the issues of religious pluralism and interreligious dialogue seems to be called for by recent Roman interventions and documents. With regard to theology, not only have several theologians been under investigation by the Congregation for the Doctrine of the Faith (one of them, Tissa Balasuriya, a Sri Lankan Oblate of Mary Immaculate, was even excommunicated in 1997), but also Catholic theologians are now required to obtain a *mandatum* from their bishops to exercise their teaching function in Catholic colleges and universities. In matters of interreligious dialogue the recent years'-long trial of Jacques Dupuis, a Belgian Jesuit, and the declaration of the Congregation for the Doctrine of the Faith *Dominus Iesus* (June 2000) serve as a chilling warning to those engaged in this enterprise not to move beyond the pale of Roman orthodoxy. In liturgical matters the various instructions of the Congregation for Divine Worship and the Discipline of the Sacraments, in particular those regarding liturgical inculturation (*Varietates legitimae*, 1994) and the translation of liturgical texts (*Liturgiam authenticam*, 2001) raise serious questions about the autonomy of the local churches and the legitimacy of cultural differences.

Religious pluralism and interreligious dialogue in postmodernity present serious problems to Christianity in at least three areas, namely, the way of doing theology, the practice of interreligious dialogue, and the manner of worship. Hence the three parts of this book. The first part examines the challenges postmodernism poses to the task of faith seeking understanding. The first chapter confronts the postmodern suspicion against *mythos* and *logos* as ways to the knowledge of the truth and explores an alternative path to wisdom. It argues that the practice of foolish wisdom or wise foolishness, common to both

---

[7] See Paul F. Knitter, *Introducing Theologies of Religions* (Maryknoll, N.Y.: Orbis ɔks, 2002).

Christianity and non-Christian religions and celebrated by philosophers and theologians of East and West, may be, when coupled with personal holiness, the most potent antidote to the burning acids of postmodern skepticism and an appropriate pedagogue to the love of wisdom in postmodernity. In interreligious dialogue questions are often raised regarding the distinctiveness of the Christian faith and which Christian belief provides the Christian faith with its unity and cohesiveness.

Chapter 2 discusses the need for a central doctrine imparting not deadly uniformity but organic unity to the Christian theological edifice, especially to catechesis, and after reviewing several approaches in contemporary theology, the chapter suggests, on the basis of the *Catechism of the Catholic Church*, the doctrine of the Trinity as a viable candidate. The third chapter argues that in the post–Vatican II era, the identity of a Catholic has become blurred, especially in view of the emergence of what Andrew Greeley calls "the communal Catholic," and suggests the "indirect way" to strengthen the "deep structures" of Catholicity in shaping the Catholic identity, especially of youth.

Chapter 4 discusses one growing phenomenon in the West, namely, multiple religious belonging, which is often seen as a dangerous fruit of interreligious dialogue. It lays out the kind of theology of religion undergirding this practice and from the experiences of pioneers in multiple religious belonging, it draws lessons and warnings for a spiritually enriching practice for both church and theology.

The book moves on to examine specific themes of interreligious dialogue in its second part. The first issue to be considered, one that is often encountered as a block to interreligious understanding, is the claim of uniqueness and universality made for the founder of one's religious tradition and even for one's religion. Such a claim smacks of spiritual arrogance and historical blindness. Chapter 5 examines the logic of such a claim and contends that it should not be bracketed in interreligious dialogue and in fact should be made if it is part of one's core religious beliefs. Nevertheless, it is suggested that, at least with regard to Christianity, such a claim may be made only for Jesus Christ, which is an affirmation of faith and cannot be validated on the rational level, and not for Christianity as a historical institution. The next two chapters broach the fundamental theme in interfaith conversation, namely, God. Chapter 6 explores whether there are equivalents among the different ways religions refer to the deity, and on the basis of the German Jesuit theologian Karl Rahner's theology, suggests that the various divine names refer to the source and goal of human transcendence named Holy Mystery. Chapter 7 asks how to talk of God today in the poverty-stricken, multicultural, and multi-religious context of Asia and proposes God-talk that speaks of God taking the side of the poor, of God as universal harmony, and of the all-inclusive God.

The next two chapters discuss the figure of Jesus in the interreligious context. In dialogue with Buddhism, Chapter 8 presents Jesus as the buddha, that is, as the Enlightened One, and argues that Jesus is the Word of God that enlightens all humans precisely because he is the buddha, that is, the Enlightened One. In dialogue with Judaism, whose covenant with God remains eternally valid,

Chapter 9 attempts to interpret Jesus' role as the universal, unique, and absolute savior in a way that honors God's fidelity to God's covenant with Israel and is harmonious with the Christian faith in Jesus as the Christ and Lord.

Judaism and Christianity have been active partners in a vibrant dialogue, at least since the Second Vatican Council. Much progress has been made toward mutual reconciliation and understanding. One important post-conciliar document is the *Catechism of the Catholic Church,* which is intended to serve as the basis and guide for all national and local catechisms. Given the potentially enormous influence of this universal catechism, Chapter 10 examines its strengths and weaknesses with regard to Judaism and shows how the church's official statements should be pushed further toward a greater appreciation of Judaism and the Jewish people. Chapter 11 considers the Holocaust from the perspective of Asian liberation theology and reveals the hidden and unconscious anti-Judaism to which this theology is prone; at the same time it points forward to a continuing dialogue between Asian liberation theology and the theology of the Holocaust. The last chapter of the second part broaches the most urgent issue for contemporary interfaith dialogue, namely, the role and contribution of all religions in peacebuilding and reconciliation. It frankly and humbly recognizes the many ways all religions have fueled hatred and armed conflicts, but it also shows how religions, especially Confucianism and Buddhism, can offer helpful means for achieving justice, reconciliation, and peace.

Interreligious dialogue, as the Federation of Asian Bishops' Conferences (FABC) has repeatedly insisted, must consist not only in theological exchange but also in common life, common action, and the sharing of religious experiences among followers of diverse religions. The third part of this book focuses on prayer and worship in interreligious dialogue in the postmodern age. Chapter 13 analyzes the postmodern challenges to the understanding of culture and to inculturation, evaluates the responses of the Congregation of Worship and the Discipline of the Sacraments to postmodernity's challenges in its document *Varietates legitimae,* and suggests how the works of Filipino Benedictine liturgist Anscar Chupungco and the FABC can help achieve a more thorough liturgical inculturation. Chapter 14 discusses the difference between uniformity and unity and suggests ways to overcome the deep division between the so-called conservative and liberal wings in the church with regard to liturgical inculturation. The final chapter examines the possible pitfalls of the theological principle that the liturgy constitutes the summit and source of the church's life and activities. It relates the Eucharist to the liturgy of life and proposes that the latter be seen as the true summit and source of the former.

Dialogue with the poor and the marginalized people, dialogue with cultures, and dialogue with religions, this is the threefold way in which the church's mission, according to the FABC and Asian theologians, is to be carried out in Asia to promote the coming of God's reign. Of course, the church has been engaged in this threefold task ever since its birth: remembering "the poor" (Gal 2:10), becoming "all things to all people" (1 Cor 9:22), and recognizing in the "unknown God" that others worshiped "the God who made the world and everything in it, he who is the Lord of heaven and earth" (Acts 17:23–24).

But in the postmodern age the way of carrying out liberation, inculturation, and interreligious dialogue cannot be the same as in times past. In our time we need a new church and a new way of being church. Not a church allied with the rich and the powerful in their conquest of foreign lands and subjugation of peoples in order to save their souls and plant the church, but a church opting for and living in solidarity with the poor and the marginalized. Not a church associated with imperialism and colonialism, in a *mission civilisatrice*, exporting Western civilization to the "uncouth" natives of other continents, but a church willing to empty itself of its own cultural traditions and learn from the treasures of the more ancient cultures of these peoples in order to enrich its understanding of the gospel. Not a church proclaiming itself as the exclusive channel of God's grace and asserting its superiority over the religions of the "pagans" whom it comes to save from spiritual darkness and moral depravity, but a church humbly walking side by side with other seekers of God and God's reign, witnessing to them its faith in Jesus as God's gift of all-inclusive love to humanity and recognizing the presence of God's Spirit among them and learning from them ways of being more faithful to God's call.

Fortunately, these ways are by no means new and unheard of, for they are as old as Jesus' way with the people of his time and that of God with God's chosen people. Thus, ironically, the future of the church lies not in discovering new-fangled tricks from the world in order to fulfill the Lord Jesus' command "to make disciples of all nations" (Mt 28:19), but in returning to the past and gazing steadily on the face of Jesus and that of his God and trying to find the answer to the question: How did Jesus and how did his God act in history? Or, in a more theological formulation, How are the three divine persons related among themselves in their inner trinitarian life? The answers to these questions regarding God's action in history and God's eternal life may well contain the ultimate secret as to how the church must fulfill its mission in the twenty-first century and beyond.

Doing Theology Interreligiously in the Postmodern Age

1

The Wisdom of Holy Fools

A WAY TO THE LOVE OF TRUTH IN POSTMODERNITY

The way to wisdom for most people has often been through stories and reasoning. *Mythos*, especially in the form of dramatic narratives explaining the origin and operation of the universe and the place of humans within it, is, in the early stages of humanity, the widespread way of expressing the communal fund of wisdom that, together with rituals and ethics, shapes the social reality and is shaped by it. In addition, *logos*, particularly as practiced in philosophy, not only transmits the perennial truths of the community to successive generations but also inculcates the love of wisdom by which humans can live the good life.

However effective and reliable guides *mythos* and *logos* have been in showing the way to wisdom for past generations, they have lost much of their appeal in our postmodern age. Contemporary people, at least in the West, have become deeply disillusioned with modernity's myth of progress. The inhumanity displayed throughout history, which modernity claimed to exorcise by means of reason, especially instrumental reason, has not vanished. On the contrary, it has grown exponentially, as attested by the two world wars and the many genocides of the twentieth century. Thanks precisely to the technological innovations spawned by the Enlightenment's worship of reason and progress, our capacity for inhumanity has been refined to the extreme. While technological reason has no doubt improved the quality of life in many respects, the monumental failure of modernity's myth of progress has rendered any talk of moral progress through the application of universal reason a sick joke. At the dawn of the third Christian millennium, there is a widespread sense of hopelessness and fear due to reason's proven inability to predict and control the future. Humans are seen not as subjects but as objects of history, driven by an anonymous and despotic power whose intentions and direction are beyond their ken. Out of this rootlessness and despair is born a profound distrust of reason, both philosophic and instrumental, as a way to wisdom. Turned into a primarily deconstructive instrument to unmask oppressive structures, reason remains unable to offer a constructive vision of reality.

If Enlightenment's goddess of reason has been dethroned, *mythos* fares no better as a pedagogue of wisdom. Postmodernity has been characterized by

Jean-François Lyotard as "incredulity toward meta-narratives."[1] Whereas stories and storytelling only thrive when people preserve an appreciation for the past and the future, postmodernity, with the decline of the myth of progress, has lost a sense of history and is fixated on the present. The past is merely a theme park to visit occasionally for entertainment, and the future is reduced to being a momentary prolongation of the present without a meaningful direction. Not surprisingly, recent commentators speak of the "end of history" in our contemporary culture with its "compressed time."[2] Postmodernity's deconstruction of mimetic imagination leads not merely to the end of this or that metanarrative but to the end of story as such. Thus, in postmodernity, the royal road to wisdom by means of *mythos* and *logos* is barred, at least for those who have experienced the tragic consequences of the modern myth of progress. The question is whether there remains for them other ways to reach the same destination.

In this chapter I would like to explore what has been called "holy folly" or "crazy wisdom" or "foolish wisdom" as an alternative route to rekindle the love of wisdom in the hearts of contemporary people.[3] As is well known, the figure of the "wise fool"—alternatively, the paradoxical notion that the fool may be wise and that the wise may be foolish—has a long and distinguished pedigree, not only in the Christian tradition (for example, the fool in Christ or the fool for Christ's sake) but also in other religions (for example, the Sufi *majzub* and the Hindu *avadhuta*). In some religious traditions, Zen in particular, "holy madness" has been widely used by the *roshi* (teacher) as a shock technique to induce *satori* or enlightenment (for example, shout, koan, hand-clapping, and physical violence). In the political realm, the court fool or jester in his traditional costume of motley, cap, and bells was allowed to satirize the morals of the powerful and comment on the affairs of the state with impunity. In the West there exists a large body of writings by the learned and wise in praise of folly, among which Erasmus's *Moriae Encomium* is the most outstanding. Indeed, after the sixteenth century the figure of the wise fool had become so popular that he was an omnipresent fixture of Elizabethan drama, so much so that—it was once claimed—there was no play of any merit without a fool.

The purpose of this chapter is not to provide an account of how foolish wisdom or the wisdom of folly has functioned in diverse fields of human endeavor but to show how this peculiar way of knowing, which is distinct from *mythos* and *logos*, can, if properly practiced, lead to the recovery of the love of wisdom.

---

[1] Jean-François Lyotard, *The Postmodern Condition*, trans. G. Bennington and B. Massumi (Minneapolis: University of Minneapolis Press, 1984), xxiv.

[2] See, for instance, Francis Fukuyama, *The End of History and the Last Man* (London: Penguin, 1992).

[3] Note that by exploring this alternative road to wisdom rather than *mythos* and *logos*, I do not necessarily grant the essential point of postmodernism that there are no objective or universal norms that underlie, or ought to underlie, our judgments about what is true and good. For a possible way to overcome postmodern skepticism and nihilism on the basis of Bernard Lonergan's cognitional theory, see Hugo A. Meynell, *Postmodernism and the New Enlightenment* (Washington, D.C.: The Catholic University of America Press, 1999), 18–55.

More precisely, it argues that it is not just any kind of foolish wisdom but only the wisdom of the *holy* fool that will lead to the love of wisdom. Accordingly, though the approach is primarily epistemological, it will be necessary to describe in some detail the various characteristics that distinguish holy madness from its numerous counterfeits. The chapter first describes briefly the three paths to wisdom—*mythos, logos,* and if a neologism be permitted, *mōrosophia*—and compares their respective characteristics. Second, it explicates the epistemological process involved in foolish wisdom and the philosophical and theological foundation for this kind of wisdom. Third, it shows how this way of knowing is congenial to the postmodern ethos. It ends with the argument that for crazy wisdom to lead us to *philosophia*—the love of wisdom—in postmodernity, it has to be the wisdom of the *holy* fool.

FROM *MYTHOS* TO *LOGOS* TO *MŌROSOPHIA*

Mythos as an Imaginative Way to the Community's Wisdom

Almost every civilization and religion has stories about the origins of the universe and of the human race. These cosmogonic myths, usually involving supernatural beings, offer "explanations" of the natural order and cosmic forces. In addition, they convey in dramatic form the self-understanding of a particular group of persons bound together by a common race or language or political arrangement. Periodically reenacted through rituals, they reinforce the group's identity and social cohesiveness and, through further retelling, preserve and expand the wisdom of the community.[4] Moreover, these stories not only transmit a set of ideas clothed in metaphors and allegories but also make an implicit truth-claim about them as embodying the communal fund of wisdom and consequently prescribe behaviors that accord with the community's wisdom and proscribe those that contravene it. Thus, new members are socialized into the community by being told these myths, by taking part in their ritualistic enactments, and by observing the moral code they entail.[5]

---

[4] I prescind here from the debate about the priority of ritual over myth, as proposed, for example, by W. Robertson-Smith, *Lectures on the Religion of the Semites,* new ed. (London: A. & C. Black, 1914); and propagated by Jane Harrison, *Themis: A Study of the Social Origins of Greek Religion,* 2nd rev. ed. (Cambridge: Cambridge University Press, 1937); and Arthur M. Hocart, *The Progress of Man: A Short Survey of His Evolution, His Customs, and His Works* (London: Methuen, 1933).

[5] For studies on myth as a way to transmit the common wisdom of the group, see the classical works of Giambattista Vico, Max Müller, Andrew Lang, Carl Jung, Bronislaw Malinowski, Claude Lévi-Strauss, Mircea Eliade, and George Sorel. According to Vico, myths are neither false narratives nor allegories; they are rather the collective mentality of a given age ("The fables of the gods are true histories of customs."). His view went counter to the Enlightenment's (e.g., Herder's) generally negative view of myths commonly regarded as pardonably false beliefs. Müller interpreted mythologies as embodiments of the evolution of language. Lang rejected Müller's philological approach to myths and saw them as survivals of earlier social norms. Carl Jung's theory of the collective is well known. For Malinowski, myths express, enhance, and codify beliefs;

Myths, of course, are not concerned exclusively with the origination of the universe and the beginnings of a tribe or a nation, nor do they represent a "primitive," precritical, prescientific stage in the intellectual development of humankind, nor are they always connected with religion and rituals. *Mythos* can mean simply anything delivered by word of mouth, narrative, and conversation. In contemporary parlance it tends to signify a fiction, but a fiction that conveys a truth too deep to be communicated adequately by means of discursive reasoning.[6] It is this sense of *mythos* that is of interest to us here. It refers to storytelling not just as an art form but as epistemology and rhetoric, a way of knowing and communicating truths that affect human living so profoundly and extensively— philosophic and religious truths—that they cannot be fully known and conveyed by logic and concepts. It is the vehicle of ultimate meaning about the divine, the world, the self, and other selves. Rather than relying on discursive reason, *mythos* makes use of the imagination as a means of access to reality. Through its distinctive form, that is, narratives and symbols, it points to a reality beyond itself and thus contains in itself a "surplus of meaning."[7] Because myths are concerned with the fundamental symbols of human existence, and because their function is to "cosmicize" the world, that is, to make it understandable and livable, they are taken seriously. However, they are not to be understood literally, that is, not as reporting facts.

As a way of knowing, myth-making or storytelling presents the wisdom of the community not as a system of clearly and definitively formulated truths but

---

they safeguard and enforce morality; and they vouch for the efficacy of rituals. Lévi-Strauss placed myths in their social and economic contexts, with special reference to the groups' kinship systems. In his structuralist interpretation myths incorporate and exhibit the binary oppositions present in the structure of the society and overcome these oppositions by making them intellectually and socially tolerable. In contrast, Eliade relates the content of myths to general human religious interests rather than to their particular cultural and socio-economic contexts. Myth, for him, narrates sacred history; it relates events that took place *in illo tempore*. Sorel distinguished between the truth (or falsity) and effectiveness (or ineffectiveness) of myths and regarded them as beliefs about the future (not the past, like most other theorists of myth) that embody the deepest inclinations of some particular groups.

[6] Not all theorists of myth accept the explanatory function of myth. Whereas there are scholars who insist on the explanatory power of myth, though not in the literalist way, others prefer to emphasize the social and psychological functions of myth (e.g., B. Malinowski's functionalism), or to regard myth as a kind of language with a surface and deep structure composed by invariant features. E. Thomas Lawson groups recent explanatory approaches under four types, which he terms "the theory of formal continuity but idiomatic discontinuity," "the theory of conceptual relativism," "the theory of rational dualism," and "the theory of situational logic." See "The Explanation of Myth and Myth as Explanation," *Journal of the American Academy of Religion* 46/4 (1978): 507–23. See also Jack Carloye, "Myths as Religious Explanations," *Journal of the American Academy of Religion* 48/2 (1980): 175–89.

[7] For this concept, see the works of Paul Ricoeur, in particular *The Symbolism of Evil*, trans. Emerson Buchanan (Boston: Beacon Press, 1967), and *Hermeneutics and the Human Sciences*, ed. and trans. John B. Thompson (Cambridge: Cambridge University Press, 1981).

as a dance of metaphors that guide the community's thinking and acting. Storytelling resists all attempts to encapsulate wisdom in timeless propositions and freeze them in a fixed time and space. Storytellers do not prize uniformity, consistency, and linearity. No story is told the same way twice; rather, the shape of the story depends on the audience, the context, and the purposes for which the story is told. In some way the story is the common creation of its teller and listeners. The very act of storytelling and myth-making assumes that change, emendation, revision, expansion, and plurality are the stuff of life. Storytelling also presupposes that human beings are primarily agents or doers—story-making and storytelling—within the continuum of past, present, and future, and that who they are is revealed in the actions that make up their life stories. Moreover, storytelling posits that stories, even tragic or absurd ones, make sense; otherwise, they cannot be told with the hope that listeners will "get the point." Ultimately, it is assumed that the story of human history will make sense, that at the heart of reality there is wisdom, even though what the universal meaning will be cannot be known *now* but only at the end, since the story is ongoing.[8]

Logos as the Way to Wisdom through Printed Texts

If human beings are myth-making and myth-telling animals; if "the symbol gives rise to thought" (Paul Ricoeur); and if human understanding is inevitably an essentially *temporal* event, a dynamic and open-ended process of interpretation upon which history exercises its influence,[9] then what has brought about the depreciation of *mythos* as a way to wisdom in the West? Contrary to popular perception, the cause of the eclipse of myth as a way of knowing reality and hence as a path to wisdom is not the contrast between *mythos* and *logos* as epistemological instruments, the former allegedly naive and archaic and the latter critical and scientific. It is now widely recognized that the epistemology of empirical sciences, for all its vaunted claims to objectivity and exactness, is deeply metaphorical. Even the rise of Greek philosophy—the discovery of *logos*—did not come about by leaving *mythos* behind. Indeed, Greek myths such as those in Hesiod's *Theogony* already contain a striking degree of rationality, as is testified by the fact that among the gods there are personifications of concepts such as wisdom, right, lawfulness, justice, and peace. Whereas it is true that Heraclitus and Xenophanes explicitly attacked the accepted mythologies, Sophists such as Protagoras and Prodicus made use of myth as an

---

[8] On the art of storytelling, see John Navone and Thomas Cooper, *Tellers of the Word* (New York: Le Jacq, 1981); and Kevin M. Bradt, *Story as a Way of Knowing* (Kansas City: Sheed & Ward, 1996).

[9] For this notion of *Wirkungsgeschichte*, see the works of Hans-Georg Gadamer, especially *Truth and Method*, 2nd rev. ed., trans. Joel Weinsheimer and Donald G. Marshall (New York: Crossroad, 1989). For helpful general studies of Gadamer's hermeneutics, see *The Philosophy of Hans-Georg Gadamer* (Chicago: Open Court, 1997); Jean Grondin, *Introduction à Hans-Georg Gadamer* (Paris: Cerf, 1999); and Lawrence K. Schmidt, *The Epistemology of Hans-Georg Gadamer: An Analysis of the Legitimation of* Vorurteile (New York: Peter Lang, 1987).

explanatory tool.[10] Plato himself regarded myth as an ally in the working out of a philosophy. For him, myth not only offers illuminating insights into realities that elude precise explanations but also is particularly appropriate for expressing changing features of the world of becoming.[11]

It is true that the distinct form of *mythos* is narrative and that of *logos* is discursive reasoning. However, this difference did not by itself lead to the depreciation of *mythos* as a way of knowing. Rather, this was due primarily to the move from an oral mode to literacy. With the rise of writing and literacy, oral storytelling, through which myths and stories are transmitted, declined; as the result of this decline, thinking in abstract terms and the tendency to view the world in mutually exclusive terms increased substantially. The knower not only became separated from the known, but also the literate from the illiterate. With Gutenberg's invention of the printing press, this separation was exacerbated. As Walter Ong has shown, the printing press diffused knowledge as never before, set universal literacy as a serious goal, made possible the rise of modern science, and altered social and intellectual life.[12]

The invention of the printing press aided and abetted the rise of modernity. In return, modernity favored reading and writing over storytelling and listening; information and proofs over stories; texts, preferably portable (such as pocket editions and paperbacks), that can be read in private and controlled over the free and unpredictable to-and-fro of conversation; the written contract over the oral agreement. The printed text becomes the privileged path to knowledge and wisdom. The truth is now inscribed and located in the text, and because it is written down, the truth remains unchangeable and permanent. Indeed, unless recorded in texts, nothing is reliable, authoritative, and true, as the expression "as it is written" suggests. Furthermore, those who can read texts are "authorities" and have power over the illiterate. The latter are dependent on the former to know what the text says, or more precisely, what they *say* the text says.

In the process the written text itself becomes the channel of truth and wisdom and the source of power and privilege. Coming to know the truth is made possible only through an objective and scientific interpretation of the text, especially

---

[10] For studies of the Sophists' use of myth, see Heinrich Gomperz, *Sophistik und Rhetorik: Das Bildungsideal des eu legein in seinem Verhältnis zur Philosophie des 5. Jarhhunderts* (Stuttgart: Teubner, 1912); and Werner Jaeger, *Paidea: The Ideals of Greek Culture*, trans. Gilbert Highet (Oxford: Oxford University Press, 1939), vol. I, bk. 2, chap. 3.

[11] For Plato's use of myth, see Janet Smith, *Plato's Use of Myth as a Pedagogical Device* (Ottawa: National Library of Canada, 1985); and Nickolas Pappas, *Plato's Use of Myth: Myth and Its Audience* (Gambier, Ohio: s.n., 1981).

[12] See Walter Ong, *Orality and Literacy: The Technologizing of the Word* (London: Routledge, 1988), 117–18. See also his "Worship at the End of the Age of Literacy," in his *Faith and Contexts*, vol. 1, *Selected Essays and Studies 1952–1991* (Atlanta: Scholars Press, 1992), 175–88; "Writing, Technology, and the Evolution of Consciousness," in *Faith and Contexts*, vol. 3, *Further Essays* (Atlanta: Scholars Press, 1995), 202–14; *Interfaces of the Word: Studies in the Evolution of Consciousness and Culture* (Ithaca, N.Y.: Cornell University Press, 1982); and *The Presence of the Word: Some Prolegomena for Cultural and Religious History* (New Haven, Conn.: Yale University Press, 1967).

classics and sacred scriptures. As a consequence, truth becomes a commodity at the disposal of the intellectual elite and the powerful class, and *logos* is an instrument for reasoned and discursive argument. By the same token, oral myth-making and storytelling are considered inferior, imprecise, primitive guides to truth and wisdom. It is no accident that since the nineteenth century, myth has often been sharply distinguished from history, which alone is concerned with reality. Mythic consciousness is judged to represent an inferior and primitive stage of mental development incapable of expressing an abstract philosophical truth, which should now be made accessible by means of demythologization.[13]

Even though *logos* as a path to knowledge and wisdom is in practice reserved to a few, it is thought by modernity to be universal, at least potentially, since, in theory, everyone can be taught to read and hence have access to texts. Furthermore, when wedded to technology, *logos* became principally instrumental reason, and out of this marriage was born the myth of progress. But as hinted above, the child has become totally unruly and unpredictable, and its future, to judge from the havoc it has played on the human family in the twentieth century, remains under threat.

Mōrosophia: The Path of Foolish Wisdom

The paradoxical idea that the fool may be wise, even though it was not to achieve its fullest expression until the Renaissance, is as old as humanity itself; it is a common experience that the untutored and simpleminded, including children, can sometimes penetrate more profound truths than the lettered and the learned. Jesus alluded to this fact when he gave thanks and praise to God his Father for having hidden from the learned and the clever what was revealed to the merest children (see Mt 11:25). He himself at the age of twelve amazed the teachers in the Temple with his intelligence (Lk 2:46–47). Heraclitus also observed that much learning does not teach wisdom, implying therefore that wisdom can be possessed by the unlearned.[14]

It is important to note that the fool who is said to be wise is not the same as the empty-headed, the feebleminded, or the dull-witted, not an idiot, a simpleton, a buffoon, though in behavior the fool may resemble any one of these. Because of this similarity, the harmless fool is often tolerated by society, pitied or made fun of, and sometimes even venerated as under God's special protection. However, unlike other kinds of the mentally deficient, the "wise fool" is believed to possess a source of knowledge that is more akin to supernatural and inspired wisdom than to information accumulated through formal education.

---

[13] On demythologization, see Rudolf Bultmann, *Jesus Christ and Mythology* (London: SCM Press, 1966); and *New Testament and Mythology and Other Basic Writings*, ed. and trans. Schubert M. Ogden (Philadelphia: Fortress Press, 1984). See also Hans Werner Bartsch, ed., *Kerygma and Myth: A Theological Debate* (New York: Harper & Row, 1961).

[14] See Heraclitus of Ephesus, *Fragments* (Toronto: University of Toronto Press, 1991), *Fragment* 40.

Moreover, it is necessary to distinguish fools who are born that way (the "natural") from artificial or professional fools, such as court and dramatic fools who affect foolishness for the license to behave and speak as they please with impunity.

Despite all these differences, fools of various types have several things in common. First, fools are considered to lead carefree and even happy lives, since they are not intelligent enough to remember the past and to be tortured by the memory of faults and failures or to anticipate the future and suffer anxiety before the unknown. Ignorance is indeed bliss! Second, because fools are not supposed to possess intelligence, they are not expected to abide by the conventions and customs of society. They are allowed to say and do what they please without fear of consequences. Third, when their foolishness is extrapolated into a wider social context, their nonconformity can be turned into ideological iconoclasm, their naturalism into social anarchy, and their verbal inhibition into literary satire. Fourth, since the fool's wisdom is not derived from normal intelligence, much less formal education—from *mythos* and *logos*—it is assumed that the fool follows another path to wisdom or that the fool's wisdom is not something earned and learned but granted and revealed. More than anything else, foolish wisdom is seen as a gift of knowledge, a flash of intuition, an insight of revelation. To anticipate our discussion of Thomas à Kempis, Nicholas of Cusa, and Erasmus of Rotterdam, foolish wisdom is akin to "holy simplicity," "learned ignorance" or "stultitia." Foolish wisdom is not knowledge nourished by myths and stories or derived from printed texts and reasoned arguments. Rather, it is *sophia* or *sapientia* or illumination of the mind, singular and sudden and received, which stands in contrast to the common wisdom of the world, the laborious *scientia* of the learned and the technical expertise of the specialist.

FOOLISHNESS AS A WAY TO WISDOM

Folly as Virtue

The archetypal wise fool is Socrates, who explicitly claimed that his wisdom was derived from his awareness of his ignorance and whose distinctive teaching method consisted in exposing the foolishness of the wise.[15] Jesus, whom Christian tradition proclaims to be the Logos and the Wisdom of God, was regarded during his life as insane by his family and was deemed by his opponents to be possessed by Beelzebul.[16] Not only was his behavior scandalous to the religious

---

[15] On the Socratic method, see Rebecca B. Pagen, "Socratic Method and Self-Knowledge in Plato's Early Dialogues," Ph.D. diss., University of California, Santa Barbara, 1999; and Kenneth Seeskin, *Dialogue and Discovery: A Study in Socratic Method* (Albany, N.Y.: State University of New York Press, 1987).

[16] See Mk 3:21–22. I am grateful to my colleague Dr. Irwin Blank for drawing my attention to the Hebrew tradition of wisdom within which Jesus stood. Here, due to limitation of space, I will prescind from this tradition. Perhaps the fact that wisdom in the Hebrew tradition is often limned in female imagery was an ironic subversion of the androcentric custom of associating wisdom with male figures.

establishment but his teaching, from his beatitudes to his parables, challenged the sacred text and offended traditional wisdom.[17] Even Peter, who should have known better, was shocked by Jesus' prediction of his passion and death and had to be reminded that he was judging not by God's standards but by human standards (Mk 8:33), an anticipation of Paul's contrast between "God's folly" and the "wisdom of this world." Jesus' words to those who wish to follow him represent the height of folly: "If any want to become my followers, let them deny themselves and take up their cross and follow me" (Mt 16:24).[18]

The cross of Christ as the paradigm of God's folly—foolish wisdom and wise foolishness—is elaborated at length by Paul in his first letter to the Corinthians.[19] To these Christians who were attempting to reconcile their faith with the philosophies of the day, Paul said that he had been sent by Christ to preach the gospel, but "not the wisdom of discourse," that is, by employing the technique of the philosopher or the rules of studied eloquence and artificial rhetoric—the *mythos* and *logos* of our day—"lest the cross of Christ be rendered void of its meaning." Quoting Isaiah 29:14, Paul says that God will "destroy the wisdom of the wise and thwart the cleverness of the clever." In the absurdity of the cross, which is "a stumbling block for Jews and foolishness for Greeks," God's power has "turned the wisdom of this world into folly" since "God's foolishness is wiser than human wisdom." Paul urges the person who wants to become "wise in a worldly way" to "become a fool," so that he or she "will really be wise, for the wisdom of this world is foolishness with God" (1 Cor 3:18). Paul acknowledges that he himself has become "a fool for Christ's sake," so that the Corinthians can become "wise in Christ" (1 Cor 4:10).

This Pauline fool for Christ's sake tradition was later developed into a spiritual discipline and became an important feature of Christian monasticism.[20] The desert fathers of the third and fourth centuries were enthusiastic practitioners of the foolishness of God. While many of them were illiterate, a few were highly educated but in self-effacement pretended to be stupid or ignorant in order to learn humility from the contempt of others. This foolishness (Jesus' "deny themselves and take up their cross") was not limited to giving up family, material possessions, and career but also included the renunciation of the ego-personality,

---

[17] For portrayals of Jesus as a Cynic sage, see the works of Burton L. Mack and John Dominic Crossan, who attempt to portray Jesus as free of eschatology: Burton Mack, *A Myth of Innocence: Mark and Christian Origins* (Philadelphia: Fortress Press, 1988); and John Crossan, *The Historical Jesus: The Life of a Mediterranean Jewish Peasant* (San Francisco: HarperSanFrancisco, 1992).

[18] For a presentation of Jesus as Foolish Wisdom, see Elizabeth-Anne Stewart, *Jesus the Holy Fool* (Kansas City: Sheed & Ward, 1999).

[19] See 1 Cor 1:17–25. For studies of Pauline "foolish wisdom," see David R. Nichols, "The Strength of Weakness, the Wisdom of Foolishness: A Theological Study of Paul's Theologia Crucis," Ph.D. diss., Marquette University, 1992.

[20] For an account of this tradition in Christianity, see Jaroslav Pelikan, *Fools for Christ: Essays on the True, the Good, and the Beautiful* (Philadelphia: Muhlenberg Press, 1955); and John Saward, *Perfect Fools: Folly for Christ's Sake in Catholic and Orthodox Spirituality* (Oxford: Oxford University Press, 1980).

sometimes to such extremes that these practicing fools acquired the reputation of being mad. This spiritual practice of holy folly was continued in the Russian Orthodox Church by the *yurodive,* who were particularly prominent during the reign of Ivan the Terrible. After the seventeenth century, however, the figure of the holy fool vanished from the Russian religious scene, though he lingered on as a character in Russian literature, for example, in Dostoevsky's *The Idiot.*[21] Furthermore, with the dawning of the Age of Reason, holy fools virtually disappeared. As Michel Foucault has shown, this was the time of the "great confinement," in which mad people and vagrants were no longer allowed to roam freely but were publicly humiliated, beaten, and locked up in asylums or workhouses.[22]

Though so far we have discussed foolish wisdom in Christianity and in the West, it is not an exclusively Christian and Western phenomenon. It is also practiced in Sufism, where it is known as the path of blame. Some Sufi mystics are known for their strange behavior as well as for their heretical doctrine of identification with the divine. Like their Christian counterparts, Sufi practitioners of "crazy wisdom" pursued freedom and humility without concern for worldly opposition.[23]

In Hinduism, there is the figure called *avadhuta,* a Sanskrit term meaning literally "he who has cast off [all concerns]." The distinguishing characteristic of the *avadhuta,* as implied by the word, is total indifference to his fate in the world. He has no wife, children, home, job, social responsibility, or political obligation. As a symbol of his utter detachment, the Hindu renunciate, as some fools for Christ's sake did, would walk around naked. In addition to the *avadhuta,* there is the figure of the *mast,* a Hindi word meaning "numbskull." These are God-intoxicated individuals who roam the streets of India and whose behavior suggests psychotic disturbance. Lastly, there are the *baul,* a Bengali word meaning "mad" or "confused." The *bauls* are religious eccentrics whose quest for God on the path of devotion *(bhakti)* takes precedence over everything else.[24]

---

[21] See Fyodor Dostoevsky, *The Idiot,* trans. Constance Garnett, rev. Avrahm Yarmolinski (New York: Heritage Edition, 1966). For an insightful study of *The Idiot,* see Dennis P. Slattery, *The Idiot: Dostoevsky's Fantastic Prince: A Phenomenological Approach* (New York: Peter Lang, 1983).

[22] See Michel Foucault, *Madness and Civilization: A History of Insanity in the Age of Reason* (London: Tavistock, 1971).

[23] On Sufi mysticism, see the two helpful volumes *Islamic Spirituality: Foundations* and *Islamic Spirituality: Manifestations,* ed. Seyyed Hossein Nasr (New York: Crossroad, 1991), with an abundant bibliography on Sufism. See also Krishna Prakash Bahadur, *Sufi Mysticism* (New Delhi: Ess Ess Publications, 1999); H. Wilberforce Clarke, *An Account of Sufi Mysticism* (Edmonds, Wash.: Near Eastern Press, 1994); Muhammad Abdul Haq Ansari, *Sufism and Sharia* (Leicester: The Islamic Foundation, 1986); A. J. Arberry, *Sufism* (London: George Allen and Unwin, 1950); idem, *Muslim Saints and Mystics* (London: Routledge and Kegan Paul, 1966); and Reynold Nicholson, *Studies in Islamic Mysticism* (Cambridge: Cambridge University Press, 1921).

[24] For an informative exposition of the practice of crazy wisdom in non-Christian religions, see Georg Feuerstein, *Holy Madness: The Shock Tactics and Radical Teachings of Crazy-Wise Adepts, Holy Fools, and Rascal Gurus* (New York: Paragon House, 1991), 14–53. On the *avadhuta,* see Swami Dattatreya, ed., *Avadhuta Gita* [The Song of the Ever-Free] (Madras: Sri Ramakrishna Math, 1988); and Jaya Chamaraja Wadiyar, *Avadhuta: Reason and Reverence* (Bangalore: Indian Institute of World Culture, 1958).

Tibetan Buddhism also has its share of eccentric lamas (gurus) who use weird methods to initiate their disciples into enlightenment and of "mad lamas" *(smyon-pa)* with their rejection of the monastic tradition, ecclesiastical hierarchy, societal conventions, and book learning.[25] Finally, the adepts of Zen Buddhism make use of shock techniques such as sudden shouting, physical beatings, paradoxical verbal responses, and riddles to teach enlightenment.[26]

Foolishness as a Path to Wisdom

From what has been said above, it is clear that foolishness, as rejection of the world to concentrate solely on spiritual matters, is practiced as a means to cultivate humility, to imitate Christ, to unite oneself with the divine, or to reach enlightenment. But it is also a pedagogical device to lead others to wisdom. This aspect lays the stress on the second member of the oxymoron "foolish wisdom" and is more emphasized in Eastern than in Western religious tradition. There is no doubt that for the proponents of "foolish wisdom"—Paul; the "fools for Christ's sake"; the Sufi mystics; the Hindu *avadhutas, masts,* and *bauls;* the Tibetan adepts; and the Zen masters—foolishness is a path to true wisdom, however this is defined. What, then, epistemologically speaking, is so distinct about foolishness or madness or folly that it can lead to wisdom, just as *mythos* and *logos* claim to do?

In Christian theology, negative theology or apophatic theology emphasizes God's transcendence and our radical inability to know what God is.[27] Our knowledge of God is limited to what God is not, and therefore must end in ignorance and worshipful silence. This theology, first developed by the Cappadocians, in

---

[25] On Tibetan or VajrayAna Buddhism, see John Powers, *Introduction to Tibetan Buddhism* (Ithaca, N.Y.: Snow Lion Publications, 1995); Robert A. F. Thurman, *Essential Tibetan Buddhism* (San Francisco: HarperSanFrancisco, 1996); Surya Das, *Awakening the Buddha Within: Tibetan Wisdom for the Western World* (New York: Broadway Books, 1997); Geoffrey Samuel, *Civilized Shamans: Buddhism in Tibetan Societies* (Washington, D.C.: Smithsonian, 1995); and Austine Waddell, *Tibetan Buddhism, with Its Mystic Cults, Symbolism and Mythology, and in Its Relation to Indian Buddhism* (New York: Dover, 1972).

[26] For Zen Buddhism's techniques of enlightenment, see Garma Chen-chi Chang, *The Practice of Zen* (New York: Harper, 1959); Daisetz T. Suzuki, *The Awakening of Zen* (Boston: Shambhala, 1987); Dennis G. Merzel, *Beyond Sanity and Madness: The Way of Zen Master Dogen* (Boston: Charles E. Tuttle, 1994); Kazuaki T. Dogen, ed., *Enlightenment Unfolds: The Essential Teachings of Zen Master Dogen* (Boston: Shambhala, 1999).

[27] By taking negative theology as an example of "foolish wisdom" I do not intend to mean that the former is to be equated with the latter but only that there is in negative theology a conscious recognition, akin to wise foolishness, that human reason and discourse are ultimately incapable of knowing and speaking about God as God is. On negative theology, see Thomas Edwards, *Indiscretion: Finitude and the Naming of God* (Chicago: University of Chicago Press, 1999); Deirdre Carabine, *The Unknown God: Negative Theology in the Platonic Tradition: Plato to Eriugena* (Louvain: Peeters, 1995); Beverly Lanzetta, *The Other Side of Nothingness: Toward a Theology of Radical Openness* (Albany, N.Y.: State University of New York Press, 2001); and Willi Oelmüller, *Negative Theologie heute: Die Lage der Menschen vor Gott* (Munich: Fink, 1999).

particular Gregory of Nyssa, has always been a central feature of the mystical tradition.[28] For example, according to the sixth-century mystical theologian Dionysius the Pseudo-Areopagite, the union between the soul and God, its "deification," is achieved by a process of "unknowing," in which the soul leaves behind the perceptions of the senses as well as the reasoning of the intellect. The soul enters a darkness in which it will be increasingly illuminated by the "Ray of Divine Darkness" and brought ultimately to the knowledge of the ineffable Being that transcends affirmation and negation alike.[29] Similarly, according to the English mystical treatise *The Cloud of Unknowing*, human reason is radically incapable of knowing God. The "cloud of unknowing" that lies between God and the human intellect is not pierced by the intellect but by "a sharp dart of love."[30] Thus, there is an essential element of ignorance in our knowledge of God.

The philosophical and theological foundation for "foolish wisdom" was however laid by two men who were deeply indebted to the mystical tradition of the "Brethren of the Common Life" known as the *devotio moderna*, namely, Thomas à Kempis (c. 1380–1471) and Nicholas of Cusa (c. 1400–1464). Thomas is probably the author of the extremely influential spiritual manual *Imitatio Christi*, in which he urges Christians to emulate Christ the Fool through "holy simplicity."[31] The life of pietistic simplicity and humility recommended by Thomas is not very different from that of the "fools for Christ's sake" and the crazy-wise adepts of Eastern religions. Like them, he believes that nothing is more useful than self-knowledge and self-contempt.

Nicholas of Cusa is the author of *De Docta Ignorantia,* in which he defends two basic principles. First, *docta ignorantia* or "learned ignorance" is the highest

---

[28] See Jean Daniélou, *Platonisme et théologie mystique: Essai sur la doctrine spirituelle de saint Grégoire de Nysse* (Paris: Aubier, 1953); and Walther Völker, *Gregor von Nyssa als Mystiker* (Wiesbaden: F. Steiner, 1955).

[29] See Dionysius the Areopagite, *On the Divine Names and Mystical Theology*, trans. G. E. Rolt (New York: The Macmillan Co., 1920). For studies on Dionysius's negative theology, see Donald F. Duclow, "The Learned Ignorance: Its Symbolism, Logic and Foundations in Dionysius the Areopagite, John Scotus Eriugena and Nicholas of Cusa," Ph.D. diss., Bryn Mawr College, 1974; Walther Völker, *Kontemplation und Ekstase bei pseudo-Dionysius* (Wiesbaden: F. Steiner, 1958); and Edith Stein, *Wege der Gotteserkennis: Dionysius der Areopagit und sein Symbol* (Munich: Kaffke, 1979).

[30] See *The Cloud of Unknowing* (New York: Paulist Press, 1981). For studies on this work, see William Johnston, *The Mysticism of* The Cloud of Unknowing (New York: Fordham University Press, 1967); Constantino S. Nieva, *The Transcending God: The Teaching of the Author of* The Cloud of Unknowing (Greenwood, S.C.: Attic Press, 1969); and Bradley Holt, *The Wisdom of* The Cloud of Unknowing (Oxford: Lion, 1999).

[31] For an English translation, see Thomas à Kempis, *The Imitation of Christ*, trans. Ronald Knox (New York: Sheed & Ward, 1962). For studies on this work, see G. H. Preston, *Studies on Thomas à Kempis* (The Imitation of Christ) *in the Light of Today* (London: Mowbray, 1912); Anne C. Barlett, ed., *Vox Mystica: Essays in Medieval Mysticism in Honor of Professor Valerie M. Lagorio* (Rochester, N.Y.: D. S. Brewer, 1995); and William Meninger, *Bringing the Imitation of Christ into the Twenty-First Century* (New York: Continuum, 1998).

stage of intellectual understanding accessible to the human intellect, since Truth, which is one, absolute, and infinitely simple, is unknowable to humans. Knowledge, by contrast, is multiple, relative, and complex, and therefore is at best approximate. For Cusanus, the relationship of our intellect to Truth is like that of a polygon to a circle. The resemblance increases as we multiply the angles of the polygon, but no multiplication, even if it is infinite, will ever make the polygon equal to the circle. Therefore, the path to Truth leads beyond reason and the principle of noncontradiction. It is only by intuition that we can discover God, in whom there is *coincidentia oppositorum*, the unification of all contradictions, which is the second principle of Cusanus's philosophy. Human reason, confined by the principle of noncontradiction, is demonstrably incapable of giving rational expression to the Infinite, who is the unification of all contradictions. Herein lies our ignorance. But the fact that we are aware of our ignorance and the basic reason for it elevates our ignorance to the status of *docta ignorantia*. The more we learn this lesson of ignorance, the closer we draw to Truth itself.[32]

It is in these two paradoxical principles of Cusanus's philosophy, namely, the *docta ignorantia* and the *coincidentia oppositorum*, that the Renaissance elaboration of the wise fool, both substantively and stylistically, as we shall see, finds its chief inspiration. Cusanus's questioning of the possibility of knowledge, his antithesis between irrational absolute and logical reason, his affirmation of knowledge beyond reason through intuition, his insistence on the necessity of a conscious recognition of the limitations of our intellect as a condition for wisdom, and his unification of all contradictions in God, all of these elements pave the way for the "coincidence" of foolishness and wisdom, *ignorantia* and *scientia*, in *docta ignorantia*.

The work that embodies these ideas par excellence is Erasmus's *Moriae Encomium*, or *Laus Stultitiae*, which he wrote in 1509 and first published in 1511.[33] Foolishness, personified as Lady Stultitia, praises "foolish wisdom" or "wise foolishness" as a way to truth, because truth, which is never simple, cannot be known by either knowledge or ignorance alone, but only by a combination of both.

---

[32] For studies on Nicholas of Cusa, see Edmond Vansteenberghe, *Autour de la Docte Ignorance: Une controverse sur la théologie mystique au XVe siècle* (Münster: Aschendorff, 1915); Ulrich Offermann, *Christus, Wahrheit des Denkens: Eine Untersuchung zur Schrift "De Docta Ignorantia" des Nikolaus von Kues* (Münster: Aschendorff, 1991); Hans Joachim Ritter, *Docta ignorantia: Die Theorie des Nichtwissens bei Nicolaus Cusanus* (Leipzig: Teubner, 1927); and Joseph Lenz, *Die docta ignorantia oder die mystische Gotteserkennis des Nikolaus Cusanus in ihren philosophischen Grundlagen* (Würzburg: C. J. Becker, 1923).

[33] For an English translation, see *The Praise of Folly*, trans. Clarence H. Miller (New Haven, Conn.: Yale University Press, 1979). Critical studies include: Walter Kaiser, *Praisers of Folly: Erasmus, Rabelais, Shakespeare* (Cambridge, Mass.: Harvard University Press, 1963); Kathleen Williams, ed., *Twentieth Century Interpretations of The Praise of Folly* (Englewood Cliffs, N.J.: Prentice-Hall, 1969); and Michael A. Screech, *Ecstasy and the Praise of Folly* (London: Duckworth, 1980).

It is important to note that in *The Praise of Folly* it is not the learned and wise that praise foolishness but foolishness that praises foolishness. The subject and object of the encomium is the same. Hence, it is a *mock* encomium. Here lies the profound irony of Erasmus's work. If foolishness gives itself *mock* praise, then it censures itself. But if foolishness censures itself, it is really wise, because it recognizes foolishness for what it is, which is possible only to the wise. Thus, foolishness's mock praise of itself is really a praise of wisdom; the path to wisdom is foolishness mockingly praising itself. Irony is displayed again when at one point in her eulogy, Stultitia says that what she is saying may appear at first sight foolish or absurd, yet it is really profoundly true. But if this statement is true, then it cannot be said by a foolish person. However, if it is false, then it has been uttered truthfully and wisely by a foolish person. What is implied here is that a wise person may be foolish, and the fool may be wise, and hence foolishness may be a way to wisdom. Here, Cusanus's *docta ignorantia* and *coincidentia oppositorum* find a perfect literary embodiment. Like the professional fool, whose function is to make people laugh, and like the wise person, whose role is to teach the truth, Erasmus, by combining laughter with seriousness in his use of irony, develops the oxymoronic concept of the wise fool. Thus, folly is necessary to reach wisdom, and to be human is to play the fool, and to be wise is to acknowledge this truth.

Stultitia proceeds to apply this technique of reversal to all that society holds as true, noble, and beautiful. Not unlike the "fools for Christ's sake" and adepts of Eastern religions who use shock tactics to flout the conventions of society, Stultitia scorns the pretensions of learning, especially in its medieval and Scholastic forms, and shows the limitations of worldly wisdom. Thus she praises the drinking of wine and self-love; she attacks prudence, the enemy of foolishness; she appreciates experience as a mode of knowing and a path to wisdom; and she affirms that pleasure is virtue.

Finally, because Stultitia believes that Christians are fools for Christ's sake, she knows she is more than a fool. She knows that it is the wisdom of this world that is really folly and that her foolishness is wisdom. Indeed, she says that, for her, "the Christian religion taken all together has a certain affinity with some sort of folly and has little or nothing to do with wisdom."[34] The fool of fools is the pious Christian who imitates the folly of Christ by accepting the cross of Christ. The Christian is a fool because, in accepting the folly of Christ and in rejecting the wisdom of the world, the Christian accepts that "the foolishness of God is wiser than man."

FOOLISH WISDOM AS IRONY AND FANTASY IN THE POSTMODERN WORLD

Foolish Wisdom and the Postmodern World

If foolish wisdom brings about the *coincidentia oppositorum*, if it is rooted in the *docta ignorantia*, and if it flourishes only in the soil of paradox and irony,

---

[34] *The Praise of Folly*, 132.

then arguably it is the most congenial way to wisdom in the postmodern world. There are profound parallels between the age in which the notion of foolish wisdom was given full articulation and our own age. The Renaissance was a time of transition, when the Middle Ages were dying and modernity was struggling to be born. In such an in-between time, what is needed is the ability to hold tensions together—the *coincidentia oppositorum*—the ability to live between jest and earnestness, between wisdom and folly, between knowledge and ignorance, that is, the *docta ignorantia*. This interval is, to use the words of T. S. Eliot,

> between midnight and dawn, when the past is all
> deception,
> The future futureless.[35]

In a profound sense our postmodern age, like the Renaissance, is also "between midnight and dawn." We no longer trust the past because "the past is all deception." Hence, the postmodern incredulity toward metanarratives and the failure of *mythos* to be effective as a way to wisdom. On the other hand, we can no longer plan for the future because the future is futureless. Hence, the postmodern suspicion of rationality and instrumental reason and the rejection of *logos* as a reliable path to wisdom.[36]

Beside this general similarity between the Renaissance and postmodernity as transitional periods of history, there are also other more specific family resemblances. Both foolish wisdom and postmodernity reject rationality with its logical argumentation as the only or most perfect way of knowing reality. Instead, they place a premium on emotions and intuitions as conduits to knowledge. Furthermore, in the notion of *docta ignorantia* there is an undercurrent of skepticism and relativism that are the hallmarks of postmodern philosophers such as Jacques Derrida, Michel Foucault, and Richard Rorty.[37] In Stultitia's impassioned

---

[35] I am indebted to Walter Kaiser for the use of T. S. Eliot's verse to describe the Renaissance. See his *Praisers of Folly,* 24. The application of this description to postmodernity is mine.

[36] For a helpful introduction to postmodernism, see Stanley J. Grenz, *A Primer on Postmodernism* (Grand Rapids, Mich.: Eerdmans, 1996). It has an extensive bibliography on various aspects of postmodernism (197–202).

[37] See the main works of Jacques Derrida: *Of Grammatology,* trans. Gayatri Chakavorty Spivak (Baltimore: Johns Hopkins University Press, 1976); *Limited Inc.* (Baltimore: Johns Hopkins University Press, 1977); *Writing and Difference,* trans. Alan Bass (Chicago: University of Chicago Press, 1978); *Margins of Philosophy,* trans. Alan Bass (Chicago: University of Chicago Press, 1982); *The Post Card: From Socrates to Freud and Beyond,* trans. Alan Bass (Chicago: University of Chicago Press, 1987); *On the Name,* ed. Thomas Dutoit (Stanford, Calif.: Stanford University Press, 1995). Michel Foucault: *The Archaeology of Knowledge,* trans. A. M. Sheridan Smith (New York: Pantheon Books, 1972); *Discipline and Punish: The Birth of Prison,* trans. Alan Sheridan (New York: Vintage Press, 1975); *Critique and Power: Recasting the Foucault/Habermas Debate,* ed. Michael Kelly (Cambridge, Mass.: MIT Press, 1994); *Madness and Civilization; Language, Counter-Memory, Practice: Selected Essays and Interviews,* ed. Donald Bouchard, trans. Donald Bouchard and Sherry Simon (Ithaca, N.Y.: Cornell University

attacks against metaphysics (albeit of the Scholastic kind) we hear echoes of Derrida's call for abandonment of both "onto-theology" and the "metaphysics of presence." Her derision of wisdom is similar to Michel Foucault's attempt to unmask human "discourse" as a form of will to power. Even behind the concept of *coincidentia oppositorum* there lurks the postmodern celebration of pluralism and diversity, since the *coincidentia* of differences and contradictions occurs only in God and not in humans. Finally, irony, which is the favorite literary weapon of *The Praise of Folly,* recalls Derrida's mastery of double-coding and the hidden meanings of the text.

If postmodernity rejects *mythos* and *logos* as ways to knowledge, there remains, I submit, another way to wisdom, and that is *mōrosophia,* the way of foolish wisdom.[38] As has been shown above, this path has an ancient and distinguished pedigree—from Socrates to Jesus to Paul to the Cappadocian theologians to Dionysius to Nicholas of Cusa to Erasmus of Rotterdam, as well as adepts of Eastern religions and contemporary philosophers and theologians. The philosophical and theological basis of foolish wisdom has been expounded above. It remains to see briefly how it can function as a literary form. Here the concepts of irony and fantasy prove helpful.

Irony as a Topsy-turvy Way of Knowing

It has been said above that *The Praise of Folly* is an ironic encomium to folly because what is intended is the praise of true wisdom, the wisdom of the fool. Clearly, then, irony plays a central role in foolish wisdom. It is no accident that the prototypical wise fool, Socrates, is best known for his irony (Socratic irony). Taking the role of the *eirōn* or "dissembler," Socrates feigns ignorance and foolishness, asks seemingly innocuous and naive questions, gradually undermines the interlocutor's confidence in his knowledge and wisdom, and finally brings him to seeing the truth. More than a pedagogical device, however, irony, as Kierkegaard has shown in *The Concept of Irony* (1841), is a mode of seeing things, a way of viewing existence. Irony springs from a perception of the absurdity of life in spite of its apparent reasonableness.[39] It is a perception of a

---

Press, 1977); *Power/Knowledge* (New York: Pantheon Books, 1987); *Politics, Philosophy, Culture: Interviews and Other Writings,* ed. Lawrence D. Kritzman, trans. Alan Sheridan (New York: Routledge, 1988). Richard Rorty: *Philosophy and the Mirror of Nature* (Princeton, N.J.: Princeton University Press, 1979); *Objectivity, Relativism, and Truth* (Cambridge: Cambridge University Press, 1991).

[38] I am aware that Stultitia coins the word *morosophoi* and uses it in the pejorative sense to refer to learned men who parade their knowledge and who are in fact fools. I am using the term *mōrosophia* in the positive sense to refer to foolish wisdom.

[39] See John Lippitt, *Humour and Irony in Kierkegaard's Thought* (New York: St. Martin's Press, 2000); Michael Strawser, *Both/And: Reading Kierkegaard from Irony to Edification* (New York: Fordham University Press, 1997); Theresa Sandok, "Kierkegaard on Irony and Humor," Ph.D. diss. (University of Notre Dame, 1975; and Peter D. Suber, "Kierkegaard's Concept of Irony Especially in Relation to Freedom, Personality and Dialectic," Ph.D. diss., Northwestern University, 1978.

discrepancy or incongruity between words and their meanings, between actions and their results, between appearance and reality. At the heart of irony is the paradoxical, or to put it in the favorite language of postmodern thinkers, the *other* or *alterity.*

Because reality is paradoxical, the only way to attain it is through irony, or foolish wisdom. Irony is often the witting or unwitting instrument of truth. As an intrinsic part of foolish wisdom and, like the fools for Christ's sake and the crazy-wise adepts of Eastern religions, it turns the world upside down; challenges the received wisdom; chides, irritates, deflates, scorns, or inspires, uplifts, affirms the listeners and readers. In a word, like shock tactics used by Zen masters, it brings about enlightenment, but always as *docta ignorantia.*

Foolish Wisdom as Fantasy

Another way to illustrate how foolish wisdom can be a path to truth in the postmodern age is to consider another literary genre called fantasy.[40] Different from the "marvelous," which creates an entirely alternative world, coherent in its own right, and also totally different from this world, fantasy, as part of the logic of the imagination, starts from the data of the world as we know it but deliberately breaches the principle of analogy by which we know things that are different from one another, and construes events and states of affairs that, on the basis of the accumulated wisdom of human experience, will be judged not only improbable but outrageous, nonsensical, foolish. The fantasist lives in the everyday world but finds it too confining and therefore seeks to modify it by deliberately flouting conventions and subverting dominant construals of the real and the possible.[41] Fantasy, in the words of Rosemary Jackson, "takes the real and breaks it."[42] Its basic trope is oxymoron, the juxtaposition of contradictory elements without pretension to synthesis, in other words, the *coincidentia oppositorum.* Fantasy belongs to the "rhetoric of the unsayable."[43]

Like irony, fantasy is an essential part of foolish wisdom. As fantasy is rooted in the real world, so foolish wisdom is part of the world of the wise. But, like fantasy, foolish wisdom breaks the real and creates not an alternative world but *another* world by turning our view of reality upside down and inside out. It asks us to imagine otherwise by considering the possibility that the wisdom of the world may be folly and that the folly of God may be wisdom.

---

[40] See Ceri Sullivan and Barbara White, eds., *Writing and Fantasy* (New York: Longman, 1998); Colin N. Manlove, *Christian Fantasy: From 1200 to the Present* (Notre Dame, Ind.: University of Notre Dame Press, 1992); and Stephen Prickett, *Victorian Fantasy* (Bloomington, Ind.: Indiana University Press, 1979).

[41] The difference between the marvelous and the fantastic is well explained in Richard Bauckham and Trevor Hart, *Hope against Hope: Christian Eschatology at the Turn of the Millennium* (Grand Rapids, Mich.: Eerdmans, 1991), 89–95.

[42] Rosemary Jackson, *Fantasy: The Literature of Subversion* (London: Methuen, 1981), 33.

[43] See J. Bellemin-Noel, "Des formes fantastiques aux thèmes fantasmatiques," *Littérature* 2 (May 1971): 112.

The Wisdom of the Holy Fool

The history of spirituality in all religions has shown that crazy wisdom or foolish wisdom is a two-edged sword, to be handled with extreme caution. The dividing line between wisdom and foolishness is very thin, and it is not possible to say with certainty when a fool is just a fool, or a psychopath, or a fool graced by wisdom, or a wise person touched by foolishness.

Analogously, postmodernity is also a two-headed beast. On the one hand, its critique of the Enlightenment assumption that knowledge is always certain, objective, and inherently good is well taken.[44] With postmoderns we have to deny that the scientific method is the only path to truth. With them we also have to affirm that no observer can stand outside the historical process and take an absolutely objective and morally neutral standpoint. Furthermore, the experiences of the twentieth century have taught us that knowledge can be put to terrible use. On the other hand, we cannot subscribe to the postmodern proposition that since *mythos* and *logos* have failed us in our quest for truth and wisdom, we are condemned to despair about ever reaching wisdom and truth. Nor should we suspect that the only purpose in seeking wisdom is to deceive others or exercise power over them.[45]

For postmoderns there is still, as has been argued, the way of *mōrosophia*—foolish wisdom or wise folly. But crazy wisdom is an ambiguous thing, liable to abuse and self-deception, as the history of Christian and non-Christian spirituality has proved beyond a shadow of doubt. Because the line between foolish wisdom and insanity, between genuine quest for enlightenment and spiritual arrogance, is very thin, wise folly needs another force to foster its authenticity and to keep it on the narrow path toward true knowledge, namely, love, which is the hallmark of holiness.

Love, as Karl Rahner has argued, functions as the "light of knowledge." Because the contingent is freely created by God's love, that is, God's "luminous will

---

[44] Hugo Meynell argues that modernity (he terms it "the Old Enlightenment") has spawned four "monsters": scientism, utilitarianism, a naive attitude toward the darker human passions, and an uncritical contempt for traditional ways of thinking, speaking, and acting. See his *Postmodernism and the New Enlightenment,* 184.

[45] For an effective refutation of Nietzsche's claim that knowledge is nothing but "the will to power," see Meynell, *Postmodernism and the New Enlightenment,* 7–8. It is interesting to note that the writings of Nietzsche lie behind not only Barthes, Derrida, and Foucault, but also Lacan, Deleuze, Baudrillard, and Lyotard. Meynell bases his argument against Nietzsche and indirectly against postmodernists on Bernard Lonergan's transcendental precepts: "Be attentive, be intelligent, be reasonable, be responsible," which, if practiced consistently, will, Meynell claims, lead to the knowledge of truth. In Meynell's view, "the fundamental defect of the Old Enlightenment [modernity] is not excess of rationality, but the fact that it was not quite rational enough" (186). Because of this diagnosis, his prescription for postmodernity is a better use of reason. My own remedy for postmodern skepticism and despair about the attainment of truth differs from Meynell's inasmuch as I would recommend not more rationality by means of Lonergan's cognitional theory, but the practice of foolish wisdom animated by love.

willing the person" *(gelichtete Wille zur Person)*, the human person and other creatures can be understood only in the light of God's free act of love. Finite creatures become luminous in God's free act of love for God's self and for God's creatures. Conversely, a knowledge of finite realities that is not fulfilled in love for them, Rahner goes on to say, turns into darkness, because it will erroneously assume that they are necessary and not contingent, insofar as they come into being in virtue of God's creative freedom and love. Moreover, according to Rahner, we must ratify and appropriate *(nachvollziehen)* this divine love in our love for it, experiencing it as it were in its origin and its creative act. In this way, "love is the light of knowledge of the finite and since we know the infinite only through the finite, it is also the light of the whole of our knowledge. In the final analysis, knowledge is but the luminous radiance of love. . . . Only in the logic of love does logic reach the understanding of free being."[46]

If behind issues of truth lurks, as postmodernists claim, nothing but the will-to-power, manipulation, domination, and rhetoric, and therefore all truth-claims, especially as embodied in metanarratives, must be unmasked for what they are by means of suspicion and distrust, then foolish wisdom animated by selfless and non-manipulative love is the way to counter the will-to-knowledge as the will-to-power with the will-to-knowledge as the will-to-love. Or, as Rahner thinks, it must be shown that love, not power, is the light of knowledge. As Anthony C. Thiselton puts it, "A love in which a self genuinely *gives* itself to the Other *in the interests of the Other* dissolves the acids of suspicion and deception."[47] In Christian terms, foolish wisdom animated by love is realized in a paradigmatic way in Jesus' death on the cross. It was in his total self-emptying love and utter powerlessness on the cross that Jesus destroyed the powers dividing humanity from divinity and Jews from Gentiles, and revealed God as all-embracing Love calling us to love God and to love one another as God has loved us. Without love, and hence holiness, foolishness is just foolishness, and wisdom mere inflated knowledge. Ultimately, foolish wisdom is a *gift*, a

---

[46] Karl Rahner, *Hearer of the Word*, trans. Joseph Donceel (New York: Continuum, 1994), 81. Because of the reciprocal implication of human intellect and will, so that "knowledge and love constitute originally the one basic stance of the one human being" (83), Rahner argues that just as humans as spirits have a necessary transcendental knowledge of God as the horizon of being and truth toward which they reach out and anticipate *(vorgreiffen)*, so too in willing any finite object whatever humans necessarily tend toward God as the horizon of goodness, and in this sense are said to have a transcendental love for God: "Our self-actualizing [*sich vollziehende*] standing before God through knowledge (which constitutes our nature as spirit) possesses, as an intrinsic element of this knowledge, a love of God: our love of God is not something that may or not happen, once we have come to know God. As an intrinsic element of knowledge it is both its condition and its ground" (82).

[47] Anthony C. Thiselton, *Interpreting God and the Postmodern Self: On Meaning, Manipulation and Promise* (Grand Rapids, Mich.: Eerdmans, 1995), 160.

revelation, received in humility of mind and simplicity of heart.[48] Only then has it the power to convince and transform more effectively than the sword and rhetoric. It is no accident that Saint Francis of Assisi, a prototype of foolish wisdom, who regarded himself as a *frater minor*, a fool deserving nothing but contempt and dishonor, is also celebrated for his tender love for God and for God's creatures, great and small.[49]

---

[48] Jean-Luc Marion argues that in what he calls the "saturated phenomenon," such as intensely packed and vivid historical events, events of great personal significance, like birth and death, love and betrayal, persons can experience the sense of "gift" or better still "givenness" *(die Gegebenheit)*, or the "possibility of the impossible." In such experience of experiences, the experience of the impossible par excellence, one encounters, according to Marion, *id quo major nequit cogitari*, God without being, as testified to in mystical theology. See "In the Name: How to Avoid Speaking of 'Negative Theology,'" in *God, the Gift, and Postmodernism*, ed. John D. Caputo and Michael J. Scanlon, 20–53 (Bloomington and Indianapolis: Indiana University Press, 1999). See also his earlier work *God without Being*, trans. Thomas A. Carlson (Chicago: University of Chicago Press, 1991).

[49] Perhaps no other work has shaped the figure of Saint Francis as a holy fool better than Ugolino di Monte Santa Maria's *Actus Beati Francisci et sociorum ejus*, popularly known as the *Fioretti* or *The Little Flowers of St. Francis*. See *The Little Flowers of St. Francis*, trans. Raphael Brown (Garden City, N.Y.: Image Books, 1958). Along with Saint Francis, mention should be made of one of his followers, Brother Juniper, whose antics embodied the tradition of being a "fool for Christ's sake." I am grateful to my colleague Dr. Berard Marthaler, O.F.M., for drawing my attention to Brother Juniper and the Franciscan tradition of foolish wisdom.

2

Now That I Know How to Teach, What Do I Teach?

IN SEARCH OF THE UNITY OF FAITH

The 1971 *Directorium Catechisticum Generale* of the Sacred Congregation for the Clergy dedicates two of its six parts to expounding the Christian message (part three) and catechetical methodology (part four).[1] Though treated in different parts, the content and the method by which that content is communicated cannot be considered independently, because to be effective, the method must be tailored to what it is supposed to convey. Hence, the title of this chapter is not intended to suggest a dichotomy between content and method in religious education, as if the content of faith does not determine the way in which it should be transmitted in catechesis.

Nevertheless, if by *method* we mean merely the techniques of communication derived from psychological, sociological, and pedagogical sciences,[2] it is possible to be an expert in the use of the inductive and deductive methods, learning activities, group dynamics, and audiovisual aids and still be at a loss to know what to teach. Indeed, one sometimes admires the wizardry of rhetorical tricks and technical gadgets of a lecture or a homily and still wonders whether what has been served is "lean cuisine" or hearty fare.

Beside this jejune understanding of method as technique, which separates it from content, there is another difficulty peculiar to the teaching of Christian doctrines. As anyone who has made use of the *Catechism of the Catholic Church*

---

[1] For the English translation of this document, see *General Catechetical Directory* (Washington, D.C.: Publications Office, United States Catholic Conference, 1971).

[2] The *General Catechetical Directory* does treat, besides method, catechesis according to age levels (part five) and catechetical aids such as catechetical directories, programs, catechisms, textbooks, and audiovisuals (chapter 4 of part six). By method is meant, as Lonergan puts it, "a normative pattern of recurrent and related operations yielding cumulative and progressive results" (*Method in Theology* [New York: Herder and Herder, 1972], 4). Method in religious education is determined by four elements: the person to be formed religiously; the triune God; the end of religious education, which is the loving union between the person and God; and the means whereby this union is achieved, such as prayer, doctrine, liturgy, and ethical practice.

with its 2,865 paragraphs in religious education is painfully aware, one can be overwhelmed by the sheer number of beliefs and practices to be taught and of formulas to be memorized. Wandering among these doctrinal trees, one runs the risk of missing the proverbial forest. The question facing the religious educator, then, is how to present the Christian faith in such a way that the learner can perceive it not as a confusing aggregation of disparate beliefs and practices but as a living unity with a central core giving these beliefs and practices cohesiveness and consistency.

To achieve this goal two complementary approaches may be adopted. One is methodological, focusing on *how* to present the Christian faith in a unitary way; the other is substantive, selecting a particular *doctrine* as the central truth to which all other truths are related. In this chapter, after a review of the first approach, I explore how the doctrine of the Trinity can function as the architectonic principle with which to build the cathedral of faith, or, to vary the metaphor, as the thread to weave all the Christian doctrines into a patterned tapestry.

METHODOLOGICAL APPROACHES
TO THE UNITY OF FAITH

In a sense the message of Jesus' preaching has already been given a unifying core by the synoptic Gospels when they make the kingdom/reign of God/heaven its central theme (Mt 4:17; Mk 1:14; Lk 4:43).[3] Jesus' life and death, his preaching (in particular his parables), and his miracles can all be understood as a prophetic proclamation and realization of the imminent coming of the kingdom of God.

This concern for the unity and cohesiveness of the Christian message was also evident in the early church's formulation of the "canon of truth" or "rule of faith" *(regula fidei)*. The purpose of the rule of faith is not to offer a compelling list of the tenets of the Christian faith propositionally formulated but rather to show the contents of the faith as an ordered understanding of God's dealing with humanity as Creator, Savior, and Sanctifier of the whole creation.[4]

Among contemporary theologians several ways have been proposed to achieve a unified presentation of the contents of the faith. The first is by means of short credal formulas. It is well known that creeds or symbols serve a multiplicity of functions in the life of the church. Originally a baptismal formula (either in the

---

[3] For the theme of the kingdom of God in the New Testament, see Wendel Willis, ed., *The Kingdom of God in Twentieth-Century Interpretation* (Peaboby, Mass.: Hendrickson, 1987); and Bruce Chilton, ed., *The Kingdom of God in the Teaching of Jesus* (Philadelphia: Fortress Press, 1984). For a brief history of the development of the symbol of kingdom of God, see Benedict T. Viviano, *The Kingdom of God in History* (Wilmington, Del.: Michael Glazier, 1988).

[4] For the concept of the rule of faith, see D. Van Den Eynde, *Les normes de l'enseignement chrétiens dans la littérature patristique des trois premiers siècles* (Paris: Grembloux, 1933); and B. Hägglund, "Die Bedeutung der regula fidei als Grundlage theologischer Aussagen," *Studia theologica* 12 (1958): 1–44.

interrogative or declarative form), the creed tended to become an elaborate norm of orthodoxy and a means of *communio* among the churches. Despite its growing complexity, however, the unity of the creed was never lost sight of. Thomas Aquinas insisted that all the diverse articles should be seen as implicitly contained in the primordial truths of God's existence and providence.[5] As faith's fundamental tenets are explicated, the number of the articles of beliefs naturally increases, but Thomas argues that the ultimate object of faith is not the multitude of the articles but God as the *prima Veritas*.[6]

Nevertheless, as the language and categories of the creed have become unfamiliar and its complexity forbidding to most contemporary Christians, several theologians, foremost among them Karl Rahner, have argued for a simpler and shorter version, focusing on the essentials of the Christian faith and highlighting their unity. As Rahner puts it, "Without this kind of a creed the fullness of Christian faith very quickly becomes amorphous, or a believer very easily places too much value in his religious practice on things which are only secondary."[7] Rahner suggests that, given the theological and cultural pluralistic situation of our times, there should be several different formulations of this brief creed that would "only have to contain what is of fundamental importance and what provides a basic starting point for reaching the whole of the faith" and "has to have an explicit Christological structure in this profession."[8] Rahner attempted a brief three-part formulation of his own on the basis of his transcendental theology: a theological, anthropological, and future-oriented creed.[9]

The second approach, intimately connected with the project of formulating a shorter creed, is dictated by the hierarchy-of-truths doctrine. As Vatican II puts it in *Unitatis redintegratio*, "In Catholic doctrine there exists an order or 'hierarchy' of truths, since they vary in their relation to the foundation of the Christian faith" (no. 11).[10] Though all dogmas are true and binding, their importance and relevance vary according to how close their contents are to the trinitarian

---

[5] Thomas Aquinas, *Summa Theologiae* II-II, q.1, a.7. Thomas makes it clear that the "act of the believer does not terminate in a proposition but in a thing" (actus autem credentis non terminatur ad enuntiabilem sed ad rem) (ibid., q.1, a.2, ad.2).

[6] See ibid., q.1, a.1.; Thomas Aquinas, *De veritate* q.14, a.8, ad 5, ad 12.

[7] Karl Rahner, *Foundations of Christian Faith*, trans. William Dych (New York: The Seabury Press, 1978), 448. See also, idem, *Theological Investigations*, vol. 9, trans. Graham Harrison (New York: Herder and Herder, 1972), 117–22; and idem, *Theological Investigations*, vol. 11, trans. David Bourke (New York: The Seabury Press, 1970), 230–44.

[8] Rahner, *Foundations of Christian Faith*, 452, 453.

[9] For Rahner's brief creed, see *Foundations Christian Faith*, 454, 456, and 457. The search for a common creed is also important for ecumenical dialogue. See Mark Heim, ed., *Faith to Creed: Ecumenical Perspectives on the Affirmation of the Apostolic Faith in the Fourth Century* (Grand Rapids, Mich.: Eerdmans, 1991).

[10] English translation from Austin Flannery, ed., *Vatican Council II: The Conciliar and Post Conciliar Documents* (Collegeville, Minn.: Liturgical Press, 1984). No. 12 of the same decree mentions the trinitarian and christological dogmas as the foundation of the Christian faith.

and christological foundation of the Christian faith.[11] Needless to say, the principle of hierarchy of truths proves a helpful tool not only in understanding the development of dogmas, in ecumenical and interreligious dialogue, and in evangelization and inculturation, but also in catechesis.

With respect to the handing on of the faith in religious education, the issue is twofold: first, objectively, the revealed truths are seen in their varying relations to the core truths, thus highlighting their intrinsic unity; and secondly, subjectively, the ordered relationships among God's revealed truths are seen in the context of the faith of the individual and the community as an existential response to God's self-communication. The question in religious education is how, granted the legitimate possibility that an individual or a community may choose to focus on a particular truth in living out its faith, the teacher can enable the students' subjective faith to be guided by the objective nexus of the doctrines so that the students should not place at the center of their faith something that is objectively peripheral. The *Catechism of the Catholic Church* emphasizes the hierarchy of truths by affirming the "organic connection between our spiritual life and the dogmas" (no. 89) and "the mutual connections between dogmas, and their coherence . . . in the whole of the Revelation of the mystery of Christ" (no. 90).[12]

A third way to achieve the unity of the Christian faith is by way of narrative theology. This theology, of recent vintage, privileges *narratio* over *appellatio* and *argumentatio* as a mode, though not an exclusive mode, of theological discourse. It views Jesus as primarily Storyteller and the kerygma as the proclamation of lived events and experiences. Indeed, for narrative theologians, the core of the faith of the apostolic church, namely, that Jesus is risen, is basically a story. Doing theology in this vein is not primarily arguing doctrinal conclusions (for example, in the mode of neo-Scholastic theology) or making moral exhortations but retelling and recreating by means of narratives the events of God's intervention in history, especially in Jesus' life, for contemporary listeners. The memory, at times "dangerous," of these events will call forth responses of faith from the hearers, who become personally involved as actors in these stories.[13]

---

[11] For studies on the hierarchy of truths, see Heribert Mühlen, "Die Lehre des Vatikanum II: Über die Hierarchia veritatum und ihre Bedeutung für den ökumenischen Dialog," *Theologie und Glaube* 57 (1966): 303–35; Ulrich Valeske, *Hierarchia veritatum: Theologiegeschichte Hintergründe und mögliche Konzequenzen eines Hinweises im Ökumenismusdekret des II Vatikanischen Konzils zum Zwischenkirlichen Gespräch* (Munich: Claudius, 1968); and William Henn, "The Hierarchy of Truths Twenty Years Later," *Theological Studies* 48 (1987): 439–71. It is to be noted that the point of the doctrine of the hierarchy of truths is not to *rank* the dogmas according to their importance but to create a substantial unity among the Christian doctrines by imparting to them a rational *structure* with a core or center.

[12] See also no. 234 for the assertion that "the mystery of the Most Holy Trinity is the central mystery of Christian faith and life."

[13] For expositions on narrative theology, see John Navone, *Gospel Love: A Narrative Theology* (Wilmington, Del.: Michael Glazier, 1984); John Navone and Thomas Cooper, *Tellers of the Word* (New York: Le Jacq, 1981); John Baptist Metz, "A Short Apology of

In narrative theology, catechesis is made to assume a mainly narrative form and structure. Its overriding purpose is to arouse, by means of narratives, faith or conversion in the listeners in the form of memory of past events, awareness of God's present summons and demands, and anticipation of God's future total redemption. What gives unity and consistency to catechesis is the story proclaimed, celebrated, lived, and prayed.[14]

A fourth way to give coherence and cohesiveness to the Christian doctrines is to present them as divine answers to human questions. This method of correlation, popularized by Paul Tillich,[15] need not be conceived merely in the question-and-answer mode, with God's revelation serving as the response to humanity's existential questions. It may and must also be practiced as a critical correlation and confrontation between the two poles of Christian theology and catechesis, namely, Christian experience and present-day experience.

In Edward Schillebeeckx's formulation, the first pole (Christian experience) includes four structural principles: the theological-anthropological principle (God wills the salvation of all), the christological mediation (Jesus is the definitive self-disclosure of God), the ecclesial mediation (Jesus' story and message continue in the church), and the eschatological dimension (the story of salvation cannot be fulfilled within time and space). The second pole (contemporary experience) includes the two contrasting elements of Western utilitarian individualism: an excess of suffering and injustice, and a hopeful tension toward the future. The purpose of the correlation and confrontation between the first and the second poles is to enable the Christian experience with its four basic structures to bear on the present experience of suffering

---

Narrative," *Concilium* 85 (1973): 84–96; and Kevin Bradt, *Story as a Way of Knowing* (Kansas City: Sheed & Ward, 1996). It is to be noted that narrative theology makes use of historical science and its critical methods and therefore has passed from the first naivete of subjectivism and arbitrariness to the critical stance of the second naivete. In a certain sense the theology of Metz can be described as narrative theology. For Metz, there are three hermeneutical principles in theology: first, narrative, in that Christian faith is based not on an idea but on the story of Jesus; second, memory, in that the church remembers the story of God's identification with the victims of history in the story of Jesus and in the light of this "dangerous memory" criticizes existing unjust structures; and third, solidarity, in that the Christian basis for society is founded on solidarity rather on the principle of exchange of modernity. On the basis of his first two hermeneutical principles Metz is aligned with narrative theology, whereas the third principle groups him with political and liberation theologians. See John Baptist Metz, *Theology of the World*, trans. William Glenn-Doepel (New York: Herder and Herder, 1969); and idem, *Faith in History and Society*, trans. David Smith (New York: The Seabury Press, 1980).

[14] For a catechetical method in which story plays a central role, see Thomas Groome, *Christian Religious Education: Sharing Our Story and Vision* (San Francisco: Harper & Row, 1980).

[15] See Paul Tillich, *Systematic Theology*, vol. 1 (Chicago: Chicago University Press, 1951), 59–66; and John P. Clayton, *The Concept of Correlation: Paul Tillich and the Possibility of Mediating Theology* (New York: De Gruyters, 1980).

and hope. In so doing theology and catechesis achieve a certain unity between Christian truths and contemporary experience.[16]

Whereas the first four approaches attempt to create the unity of the faith by focusing primarily, though not exclusively, on the objective doctrines, the fifth approach does so by concentrating on the internal dispositions of the students. Transcendental theology, as proposed by Karl Rahner and Bernard Lonergan, seeks to identify and facilitate the existential conditions of possibility for Christian faith. For Rahner, such conditions are the person's "transcendental experience," that is, the subjective, unthematic, and necessary consciousness of God as the Absolute and Holy Mystery in each of his or her particular or categorical acts of knowledge and freedom.[17] For Lonergan, it is the experience of "being-in-love" with God unrestrictedly as a result of God's pouring God's Spirit into our hearts.[18] With this experience comes a threefold conversion that Lonergan describes as intellectual, moral, and religious and that sets up a new horizon "in which the love of God will transvalue our values and the eyes of that love will transform our knowing."[19]

In this transcendental approach, catechesis seeks to produce a unified understanding of the Christian faith on the basis of the interior experiences of faith in the students either by unveiling the dynamic tension toward and anticipation of God in all our acts of knowledge and love (Rahner's notion of *Vorgriff* and mystagogical method) or by disclosing the reality of conversion brought about by divine grace by which we experience, understand, judge, and decide about the data of our consciousness (Lonergan's explication of the four levels of consciousness or intentional operations).

A sixth approach to achieve unity in the teaching of Christian doctrines consists in linking them with practice. The starting point of catechesis is not scripture or doctrines but a "praxis," that is, a personal commitment to and struggle with those who are poor, oppressed, and marginalized for their liberation. The sought-after unity is not the intrinsic coherence among the various doctrines demonstrated intellectually but the subjective coherence in the *believer* between his or her knowing and doing, faith and life, prayer and socio-political action. Religious education in liberation theologies is not primarily a communication of doctrines but a conscientization of the poor and the oppressed about their

---

[16] See Edward Schillebeeckx, *Interim Report on the Books "Jesus" and "Christ,"* trans. John Bowden (New York: Crossroad, 1981), 50–63. This method of critical correlation is further elaborated by David Tracy in *Blessed Rage for Order* (New York: Crossroad, 1975). For Tracy the two "sources" to be critically correlated are "Christian texts" and "common human experience and language." To investigate the religious dimension present in the common human experience and language the method to be used is phenomenology, whereas the method to be used in the investigation of the Christian texts is historical and hermeneutical analysis. Finally, to determine the truth of the results of one's investigations into both common human experience and Christian texts, Tracy suggests that an explicit metaphysics be employed.

[17] See Rahner, *Foundations of Christian Faith*, 20–23.

[18] See Lonergan, *Method in Theology*, 105–7.

[19] Ibid., 106. For Lonergan's description of conversion, see ibid., 237–44.

being exploited and discriminated against and an interpretation of the scripture and tradition in light of this situation. In this process, religious education involves a critique of ideology ("hermeneutics of suspicion"), a rediscovery of forgotten or suppressed religious doctrines and practices ("hermeneutics of retrieval"), and an elaboration of different formulations and practices ("hermeneutics of reconstruction") to achieve an integral liberation.[20]

Each of these six methodological approaches to achieve the unity of faith has its own strengths and weaknesses.[21] Fortunately, it is not necessary in catechesis to choose one of them to the exclusion of the others, since they all can be helpful in achieving unity and coherence in the presentation of the Christian faith. Moreover, besides methodological approaches, there have also been attempts at creating unity and cohesiveness by focusing on a particular *doctrine* or *belief* as a fulcrum around which catechesis is organized and the contents of faith are presented. To some of these I now turn.

PARTICULAR DOCTRINES AS FOCI TO ACHIEVE UNITY IN CATECHESIS

Vatican I (1869–70) indicated three ways in which a fruitful understanding of the Christian doctrines can be achieved: by elaborating the analogy between the mysteries of faith and natural things, by connecting these mysteries with each other, and by highlighting the connections of these mysteries with our ultimate end.[22] While not explicitly following the method recommended by Vatican I, some contemporary Catholic theologians have sought a unified understanding of the Christian faith by focusing on a particular doctrine and making it the linchpin of their theologies. The choice of this doctrine is often dictated by the objective centrality of the doctrine itself or by its immediate relevance to the needs and demands of a particular age and situation.

Most prominent among twentieth-century theologians, Karl Rahner seeks to unify Christian theology with the concept of divine grace as God's self-communication. Starting from a transcendental anthropology,[23] Rahner shows that at the center of Christian faith is the event of God the Father's self-communication in grace to humans in two unified and complementary modalities: on the

---

[20] See Paolo Freire, *Pedagogy of the Oppressed* (New York: The Seabury Press, 1970). For an exposition of the method of liberation theology, see Clodovis Boff, *Theology and Praxis: Epistemological Foundations*, trans. Robert Barr (Maryknoll, N.Y.: Orbis Books, 1987).

[21] For a critique of some of these approaches, see Francis Schüssler Fiorenza, "Systematic Theology: Task and Methods," in *Systematic Theology*, vol. 1, ed. Francis Schüssler Fiorenza and John Galvin, 35–65 (Minneapolis: Fortress Press, 1991).

[22] See Vatican I's dogmatic constitution *Dei Filius* in Denzinger-Schönmetzer, *Enchiridion Symbolorum* (Rome: Herder, 1976), no. 3016: "Ac ratio quidem, fide illustra, cum sedulo, pie et sobrie quaerit, aliquam Deo dante mysteriorum intelligentiam eamque fructuosissimam assequitur tum ex eorum, quae naturaliter cognoscit, analogia, tum e mysteriorum ipsorum nexu inter se et cum fine hominis ultimo."

[23] For Rahner's reflections on his theological method, see "Reflections on Methodology in Theology," in *Theological Investigations*, 11:68–114.

one hand, as origin, history, invitation, and knowledge in Jesus; and on the other hand, as future, transcendence, acceptance, and love in the Spirit.[24] For Rahner, there are not, strictly speaking, many mysteries but only one, namely, God as Absolute and Holy Mystery, who communicates the divine self to us in the Incarnation (the Son) and in Grace (the Holy Spirit).[25] The task of theology and catechesis, as Rahner conceives it, is a "mystagogy," that is, a leading of the persons back to the Mystery, a *reductio in mysterium*. It is the doctrine of God as Mystery-that-communicates-self-as-grace-in-Word-and-Spirit that provides cohesiveness and unity to Christian doctrines.

For Hans Urs von Balthasar, another prominent contemporary theologian, the central Christian doctrine is God as Supreme Beauty, which is dramatically revealed in the cross of Jesus. In this event Divine Beauty manifests itself as self-emptying Love. Thus Being is not self-consciousness but ecstatic love, or more precisely, the trinitarian love between the Father and the Son in the Spirit. In response to this self-revelation of Divine Beauty, faith is an *aesthetic* contemplation of and grasp by this Beauty in the form *(Gestalt)* of the crucified Jesus.[26] But beauty is also goodness, and under this transcendental von Balthasar discusses the historical drama of the interplay between divine and human freedom.[27] Finally, beauty is also truth, and in this context von Balthasar focuses on the nature of truth, Jesus' claim to be the truth in person, and the role of the Holy Spirit as leading us into the truth of Christ.[28]

In von Balthasar's theological aesthetics,[29] catechesis is primarily the process whereby persons are shaped into the form *(Gestalt)* of Jesus' obedient self-surrender to his Father through their participation in the Paschal Mystery. The central doctrine that confers unity and cohesiveness to the catechetical enterprise is that of God as Beauty revealed in the form of the crucified Jesus.[30]

---

[24] See Karl Rahner, *The Trinity*, trans. Thomas O'Meara (New York: Herder and Herder, 1970), 87–99.

[25] See "The Concept of Mystery in Catholic Theology," in *Theological Investigations*, vol. 4, trans. Kevin Smyth (New York: Crossroad, 1966), 36–73; and "The Theology of Symbol," in ibid., 221–45.

[26] Von Balthasar treats Divine Beauty in the seven volumes of the first part of his trilogy, *Herrlichkeit: Eine Theologische Ästhetik* (Einsiedeln: Johannes Verlag, 1961–69).

[27] See the five volumes of the second part of his trilogy, *Theodramatik* (Einsiedeln: Johannes Verlag, 1973–83).

[28] See the three volumes of the third part of his trilogy, *Theologik* (Einsiedeln: Johannes Verlag, 1985–87).

[29] It is to be noted that von Balthasar contrasts theological aesthetics with aesthetic theology. The latter uses secular standards of beauty to judge the manifestation of the divine, e.g., when one evaluates the Bible as a great work of literature, whereas the former judges God's self-revelation in the light of faith itself. In theological aesthetics the object of faith itself provides light and the conditions of possibility of its knowledge.

[30] For excellent and readable presentations of von Balthasar's theology, see John O'Donnell, *Hans Urs von Balthasar* (Collegeville, Minn.: Liturgical Press, 1992); and Edward T. Oakes, *Pattern of Redemption: The Theology of Hans Urs von Balthasar* (New York: Continuum, 1994).

Among most liberation theologians,[31] the key doctrine around which other Christian beliefs are organized is the eschatological symbol of the kingdom of God. As Jon Sobrino has argued, whereas liberation as the liberation of the poor obtains "primacy" in reality in liberation theology, the kingdom of God (and not the resurrection of Jesus) is its "theological ultimate," "the organizing and ranking principle of everything else."[32] The reason why the doctrine of the kingdom of God can function as the pivot of liberation theology is threefold: first, it corresponds to the nature of liberation theology as a historical, prophetical, praxic, and popular theology; second, it is capable of unifying, without either separation or confusion, transcendence and history; and third, it lays the emphasis on praxis as the matrix of doing theology, which is the second act following the first act of the struggle for liberation.[33]

Sobrino uses three ways to determine the meaning of the symbol of the kingdom of God: first, by analyzing the biblical notion of the kingdom of God as understood by the Old Testament, by John the Baptist, and by Jesus (for example, by Jesus as being "at hand" purely as God's gift, as good news); second, by looking at its addressees, that is, the "poor" in the economical and sociological sense, and finding that God is partial to them; and third, by examining the practice of Jesus, especially his miracles, his casting out devils, his welcoming sinners, his preaching in parables, and his celebrations of the coming of the kingdom of God.[34]

Around this concept of the kingdom of God derived from its use in the Bible, its addressees, and the practice of Jesus, Sobrino develops not only the basic premise of the Christian faith, that is, the option for the poor, but also the dual principle of hope and praxis for interpreting the Bible.[35] Furthermore, Sobrino organizes the whole content of theology around the concept of the kingdom of God: God as the God jealous of other "idols" and the God of the poor and oppressed; Christ as truly divine and truly human and as the proclaimer and

---

[31] Liberation theologians include not only Latin American liberation theologians but also African, Asian, black, and feminist theologians who make praxis—that is, reflected-upon action and acted-upon reflection—with and for the oppressed and the poor an essential part of their theological method.

[32] Jon Sobrino, *Jesus the Liberator: A Historical-Theological View*, trans. Paul Burns and Francis McDonagh (Maryknoll, N.Y.: Orbis Books, 1993), 122. See also his "Central Position of the Reign of God in Liberation Theology," in *Mysterium Liberationis: Fundamental Concepts of Liberation*, ed. Jon Sobrino and Ignacio Ellacuría, 350–51 (Maryknoll, N.Y.: Orbis Books, 1993). In the latter work Sobrino argues that the eschatological symbol of the kingdom of God rather than the resurrection of Jesus offers the point of view from which "to impose a qualitative, ordered organization of the entire content of theology" (351). The theme of the kingdom of God is only implicit in Gustavo Gutiérrez's first work, *A Theology of Liberation*, rev. ed., trans. Caridad Inda and John Eagleson (Maryknoll, N.Y.: Orbis Books, 1988). It is treated at length in his *The God of Life*, trans. Matthew J. O'Connell (Maryknoll, N.Y.: Orbis Books, 1991), 65–139.

[33] See Sobrino, "Central Position," 352–57.

[34] See Sobrino, *Jesus the Liberator*, 70–104; Sobrino, "Central Position," 358–71.

[35] See Sobrino, "Central Position," 374–79.

eschatological mediator of the reign of God; the church as not identical with the reign of God but as commissioned to serve the kingdom by evangelization and denunciation, proclamation of the word, and historical realization of liberation; and spirituality as contemplation in action for justice.[36]

So far the survey of how a particular doctrine can be made to unify Christian doctrines has been limited to Roman Catholic theologians. The scope of this chapter does not include a discussion of non–Roman Catholic theologians. However, it is important to note that the attempt to give cohesiveness to Christian faith by means of a particular doctrine has also been made by Protestant theologians. Suffice it to mention here Karl Barth's doctrine of the Word of God[37] and Jürgen Moltmann's doctrine of the crucified God.[38]

Whatever doctrine is selected to order the presentation of the Christian faith,[39] it is important to observe the principles enunciated by the *General Catechetical Directory* with regard to catechesis. The document lists nine norms or criteria according to which the presentation of Christian doctrines should be made (nos. 37–45). Of particular interest for our theme are what may be called the principles of totality, organicity, and hierarchical structuration. Totality means that the *entire* structure of the Christian message must be presented at every level of catechesis in a way appropriate to the various cultural and spiritual conditions of the students. Organicity means that catechesis must demonstrate the *harmony* and *interrelation* among the objects of faith. Finally, hierarchical structuration means that catechesis must show how certain truths function as the *basis* upon which other truths, no less pertaining to faith itself, are built. In the light of these principles an attempt will be made in the last section of this chapter to show how the doctrine of the Trinity can serve as the pivot for a unified and coherent presentation of the Christian doctrines.

THE TRINITY AS THE CENTER OF THE CHRISTIAN FAITH AND CATECHESIS

One of the encouraging signs in contemporary theology is that the doctrine of the Trinity, after having been relegated to the role of a mere appendix in dogmatic theology since Friedrich Schleiermacher,[40] has recently made a dramatic

---

[36] See ibid., 382–86. See also Peter C. Phan, "Peacemaking in Latin American Liberation Theology," *Église et Théologie* 24 (1993): 25–41.

[37] It may be plausibly argued that the doctrine of the Word of God as God's self-revelation in Christ through scripture is the undergirding structure of Barth's *Church Dogmatics* (1936–69).

[38] See Jürgen Moltmann, *The Crucified God*, trans. R. A. Wilson and John Bowden (New York: Harper & Row, 1974); and idem, *The Trinity and the Kingdom*, trans. Margaret Kohl (New York: Harper & Row, 1981).

[39] Aidan Nichols rightly suggests that the most important question that can be put about any theologian is this: "What overall perspective on Christian faith did revelation suggest to this person?" (*The Shape of Catholic Theology* [Collegeville, Minn.: Liturgical Press, 1991], 352).

[40] Starting from the human experience of absolute dependence, Schleiermacher argues that the primary utterances of the Christian faith refer us to the one God (monotheism),

comeback to center stage in both Catholic and Protestant theology.[41] My intention here is not to review and critique contemporary developments in trinitarian theology;[42] rather, it is to examine how the doctrine of the Trinity as elaborated by contemporary theologians can be used to order a unified presentation of the Christian faith.

Ever since Karl Rahner's trailblazing recovery of trinitarian doctrine for theology,[43] it is axiomatic to anchor theological reflections on the Trinity in the experiences of salvation history and to affirm the identity between the "economic Trinity" and the "immanent Trinity."[44] With this background in mind, we may begin our exploration into unifying catechesis by means of the trinitarian doctrine with an examination of how the *Catechism of the Catholic Church* is structured around this basic Christian doctrine.[45]

Catechism builds its presentation of the Christian faith on four "pillars": the profession of faith, the celebration of faith, the life of faith, and prayer. It is intended to be *"an organic presentation* of the Catholic faith in its entirety. It should be seen as a unified whole" (no. 18). To achieve this organic unity, *Catechism*, I suggest, self-consciously makes use of the trinitarian doctrine as the thread linking its four parts together into a coherent whole. This trinitarian

---

and that the trinitarian discourse is secondary. Consequently, he places the doctrine of the Trinity as an appendix at the end of his systematic theology (*The Christian Faith* [Edinburgh: T&T Clark, 1928, 1960]). Carol Voisin, however, argues that the doctrine of the Trinity is central to Schleiermacher (see "A Reconsideration of Friedrich Schleiermacher's Treatment of the Doctrine of the Trinity," Th.D. diss., Graduate Theological Union, 1980).

[41] Among Protestants, see the works of Karl Barth, Eberhard Jüngel, Jürgen Moltmann, Robert Jensen, Wolfhart Pannenberg, Ted Peters, Peter C. Hodgson, and Michael Welker; among Catholics, see the works of Karl Rahner, Yves Congar, Heribert Mühlen, Walter Kasper, William Hill, Anthony Kelly, John J. O'Donnell, Leonardo Boff, Joseph Bracken, Catherine LaCugna, and Elizabeth Johnson.

[42] For an useful survey of recent developments in trinitarian theology, see Joseph Bracken, *What Are They Saying about the Trinity?* (New York: Paulist Press, 1979); and Ted Peters, *God as Trinity: Relationality and Temporality in Divine Life* (Louisville, Ky.: Westminster, 1993), 27–145.

[43] See Karl Rahner, *The Trinity*, trans. Thomas O'Meara (New York: Herder & Herder, 1970).

[44] See Catherine LaCugna, *God for Us: The Trinity and Christian Life* (San Francisco: HarperSanFrancisco, 1991), 209–32. Rahner's "axiom" that the economic Trinity is the immanent Trinity and vice versa is widely accepted by both Catholic and Protestant theologians.

[45] The official English translation of this catechism for the United States of America is copyrighted by the United States Catholic Conference and published by Paulist Press (1994). The unnecessarily exclusive language of this translation is to be deplored. Henceforth, *Catechism*. For an introduction and critique of the *Catechism*, see Berard Marthaler, ed., *Introducing the Catechism of the Catholic Church: Traditional Themes and Contemporary Issues* (New York: Paulist Press, 1994); and Michael Walsh, ed., *Commentary on the Catechism of the Catholic Church* (Collegeville, Minn.: Liturgical Press, 1994). For an assessment of *Catechism*'s presentation of the Trinity, see the excellent essay by Catherine LaCugna, "The Doctrine of the Trinity," in Walsh, *Commentary on the Catechism of the Catholic Church*, 66–80.

leitmotif, I hope to show, resounds loud and clear in each part of *Catechism*. *Catechism* itself states most explicitly:

> The mystery of the Most Holy Trinity is the central mystery of Christian faith and life. It is the mystery of God in himself. It is therefore the source of all the other mysteries of faith, the light that enlightens them. It is the most fundamental and essential teaching in the "hierarchy of the truths of faith." The whole history of salvation is identical with the history of the way and the means by which the one true God, Father, Son, and Holy Spirit, reveals himself to men "and reconciles and unites with himself those who turn away from sin" (no. 234).[46]

In the first part of *Catechism* "the profession of faith summarizes the gifts that God gives man: as the Author of all that is good; as Redeemer; and as Sanctifier. It develops these in the three chapters on our baptismal faith in the one God: the almighty *Father*, the Creator; his *Son* Jesus Christ, our Lord and Savior; and the *Holy Spirit*, the Sanctifier, in the Holy Church" (no. 14; see also no. 190). The second part "explains how God's salvation, accomplished once for all through Christ Jesus and the Holy Spirit, is made present in the sacred action of the Church's liturgy, especially in the seven sacraments" (no. 15). The third part explicates Christian life as a life "in the sight of the Father" (no. 1693); a life in which "incorporated into *Christ* by Baptism, Christians are 'dead to sin and alive to God in Christ Jesus' and so participate in the life of the Risen Lord" (no. 1694), and a life in which "the Holy Spirit renews us interiorly through a spiritual transformation" (no. 1695). The last part presents Christian prayer as "a covenant relationship between God and man in Christ. It is the action of God and of man, springing forth from both the Holy Spirit and ourselves, wholly directed to the Father, in union with the human will of the Son of God made man" (no. 2564). In summary, for *Catechism*, "the ultimate end of the whole divine economy is the entry of God's creatures into the perfect unity of the Blessed Trinity. But even now we are called to be a dwelling for the Most Holy Trinity" (no. 260).

In addition to ordering each of its four parts on the basis of the trinitarian doctrine, *Catechism* also explicitly relates the main Christian doctrines to it. It is, of course, impossible to show here how *Catechism* does this for each doctrine; suffice it to give a few key examples. In its exposition of the creed, *Catechism* emphasizes the role of the Trinity in divine revelation,[47] and stresses the nature of faith as the human person's response to each of the three divine

---

[46] In speaking of the heart of catechesis, *Catechism* also emphasizes the centrality of the Trinity: "Catechesis aims at putting 'people . . . in communion . . . with Jesus Christ: only he can lead us to the Father in the Spirit and make us share in the life of the Trinity'" (no. 426).

[47] See no. 50: "God has fully revealed this plan by sending us his beloved Son, our Lord Jesus Christ, and the Holy Spirit."

persons.[48] Creation is presented as "the work of the Holy Trinity" and not of the divine essence.[49] In Christ's transfiguration *Catechism* sees the revelation of the Trinity.[50] Jesus' resurrection is described as the "work of the Holy Trinity."[51] The trinitarian structure of the church is made clear when it is said to be "a plan born in the Father's heart," "instituted by Christ Jesus," and "revealed by the Holy Spirit" (nos. 759, 763, 767). The church is also described with a triple image as "the people of God," the "body of Christ," and the "temple of the Holy Spirit" (nos. 781–98). Our own resurrection is said to be "the work of the Most Holy Trinity" (no. 989). Heaven is defined as the "perfect life with the Most Holy Trinity" (no. 1023).

In its elaboration of the Christian celebration of faith, *Catechism* stresses that the liturgy is "the work of the Holy Trinity": the Father is the "source and goal of the liturgy";[52] "in the liturgy of the Church, it is principally his own Paschal mystery that Christ signifies and makes present" (no. 1085); and, in the sacramental economy "the Holy Spirit prepares for the reception of Christ" (no. 1093), "recalls the mystery of Christ" (no. 1093), and "makes present the mystery of Christ" (no. 1104). In particular, the trinitarian nature of the Eucharist is emphasized: it is considered as "thanksgiving and praise to the *Father*; the sacrificial memorial of *Christ* and his Body; the presence of Christ by the power of his word and of his *Spirit*" (no. 1358).

In its exposition of our life in Christ, *Catechism* is less explicit on its trinitarian structure, though by describing it as "life in the Spirit" (no. 1699),[53] *Catechism* implies that it is a participation in the life of the Trinity. This aspect is made clear when *Catechism* explains justification and grace: "Grace is a *participation in the life of God.* It introduces us into the intimacy of trinitarian life: by Baptism the Christian participates in the grace of Christ, the Head of his Body. As an 'adopted son' he can henceforth call God 'Father,' in union with the only Son. He receives the life of the Spirit who breathes charity into him and who forms the Church" (no. 1997).

---

[48] See nos. 150, 151, and 152. "Faith is first of all a personal adherence of man to God. . . . For a Christian, believing in God cannot be separated from believing in the One he sent, his 'beloved Son.' . . . One cannot believe in Jesus Christ without sharing his Spirit. It is the Holy Spirit who reveals to men who Jesus is."

[49] See no. 291: "The Old Testament suggests and the New Covenant reveals the creative action of the Son and the Spirit, inseparably one with that of the Father."

[50] See no. 555: "Christ's Passion is the will of the Father: the Son acts as God's servant; the cloud radiates the presence of the Holy Spirit. 'The whole Trinity appeared: the Father in the voice; the Son in the man; the Spirit in the shining cloud.'"

[51] See no. 648: "Christ's Resurrection is an object of faith in that it is a transcendent intervention of God himself in creation and history. In it the three divine persons act together as one, and manifest their own proper characteristics."

[52] See no. 1082: "In the Church's liturgy the divine blessing is fully revealed and communicated. The Father is acknowledged and adored as the source and end of all the blessings of creation and salvation. In his Word who became incarnate, died, and rose for us, he fills us with his blessings. Through his Word, he pours into our hearts the Gift that contains all gifts, the Holy Spirit."

[53] See also nos. 1830–1832 for discussion on the gifts and fruits of the Holy Spirit.

Last, in the *Catechism*'s teaching on prayer, the trinitarian emphasis returns powerfully. First, Jesus' own prayer is described as a *"filial prayer*, which the Father awaits from his children" (no. 2599) and which Jesus performed in "the action of the Holy Spirit" (no. 2600). Second, the prayer of the church, especially that of blessing and adoration, is said to have a double movement: " our prayer *ascends* in the Holy Spirit through Christ to the Father—we bless him for having blessed us; it implores the grace of the Holy Spirit that *descends* through Christ from the Father—he blesses us" (no. 2727). Third, it is said that we address the Lord's Prayer to the Father but "by so doing we do not divide the Godhead. . . . The *Holy Trinity* is consubstantial and indivisible. When we pray to the Father, we adore and glorify him together with the Son and the Holy Spirit" (no. 2789).

From the above cursory survey of both the structure of *Catechism* and the way it elaborates certain key Christian doctrines, it is abundantly clear that *Catechism* has used the doctrine of the Holy Trinity as the architectonic principle to give catechesis unity and coherence. In this way it may be said that *Catechism* has incorporated (consciously or not, it is impossible to tell) the insights on trinitarian theology of contemporary Catholic theologians such as Karl Rahner and Hans Urs von Balthasar, to name only two of the most influential thinkers. Rahner's lament that Christians are "monotheists" has become something of a mantra among theologians writing on the Trinity, and *Catechism*'s attempt to place the Trinity at the center of the Christian faith and to use it as the link to unify catechesis can be regarded as a long overdue corrective.

This does not mean that *Catechism*'s own exposition of the doctrine of the Trinity is beyond criticism.[54] In at least two respects it needs improvement. First, while it is undeniable that *Catechism* anchors its teaching on the Trinity in the experiences and events of the history of salvation,[55] its placing of the exposition

---

[54] LaCugna's overall assessment of *Catechism*'s presentation of the Trinity in terms of contemporary ways of thinking is accurate: "On this score, the *Catechism* mostly fails because its main thrust seems to be the repetition of conciliar statements, rather than a dynamic, vital restatement of what the doctrine of the Trinity really seeks to affirm, namely, that both God and human beings, and indeed all of creation, find their fulfilment in communion rather than solitariness" ("The Doctrine of the Trinity," 71).

[55] To put it in technical terms, *Catechism* begins with the "economic Trinity" rather than the "immanent Trinity," and roots its *theologia* in the *oikonomia*. *Catechism* explains the mutual dependence between *theologia* and *oikonomia* in no. 236: "Through the *oikonomia* the *theologia* is revealed to us; but conversely, the *theologia* illuminates the whole *oikonomia*. God's works reveal who he is in himself; the mystery of his inmost being enlightens our understanding of all his works." This statement, though helpful, is ambiguous, because it does not say explicitly that we do not have any epistemological access to the *theologia* except through the *oikonomia*, or to God's "inmost being" except through "God's works." This does not mean that we should not undertake a reflection on the "intra-trinitarian" relations among the Father and the Son and the Holy Spirit with the help of various analogies and metaphors beyond the (mostly narrative) biblical categories. Such a reflection is necessary not so much in order to gain a deeper understanding of a Trinity allegedly lying beyond or behind the Trinity we have experienced in the history of salvation (the so-called immanent Trinity, a kind of double of the economic Trinity) but to ward off misunderstandings of the Trinity as it has given itself to us, such as tritheism, Arianism, and modalism.

on the Trinity right after its exposition on the one God and the Father[56] under-cuts its rootedness in the history of revelation and salvation. Such a presentation of the Trinity would be more understandable *after* the works of Jesus and the Holy Spirit in history have been considered.[57]

Second, though *Catechism* is aware of the *development* of the doctrine of the Trinity, its actual exposition of it exclusively follows that of the Western church with all its mind-numbing metaphysical vocabulary. One shudders at the thought of how to make such concepts as substance, essence, nature, person, hypostasis, relation, and real distinction as applied to the Trinity understandable to even highly educated Catholics![58] Fortunately, *Catechism* does speak of the "missions" of the Trinity, and though it affirms that "the whole divine economy is the common work of the three divine persons," it clearly emphasizes that "each divine person performs the common work according to his unique personal property" (no. 258). Hence, it can make the enormously important affirmation that "the whole Christian life is a communion with each of the divine persons, without in any way separating them" (no. 259). But even this statement is incomprehensible without an explicit acknowledgment that the doctrine of the Trinity can and perhaps should be formulated in terms other than those of Greek metaphysics.

In the remaining pages I shall attempt to suggest (and no more than suggest!) how insights from contemporary theology of the Trinity can enrich *Catechism*'s presentation of the Trinity, and more important, how they can be related to other Christian doctrines.

1. In the first place, it is useful to summarize the universally agreed principles of contemporary theology of the Trinity, the *terra firma,* as it were, in our voyage of exploration into the mystery of the Triune God, in addition to the classical rejection of tritheism, subordinationism, and modalism: (1) The theology of the Trinity must begin with and be rooted in the Trinity's self-communication to humans in the history of revelation and salvation (the *oikonomia*).[59] (2) The incarnation of the Word and the gift of the Holy Spirit in grace are two distinct, related, and mutually interdependent ways of the one self-communication of God the Father to us.[60] (3) There is an identity between the "economic

---

[56] *Catechism* discusses the one God in nos. 200–227. It is to be noted with commendation that its treatment of the one God is not the usual treatise *De Deo Uno*. It is not based on the philosophy of the divine essence; rather, it is deeply rooted in the biblical revelation of the divine name.

[57] *Catechism* tries to make up for the absence of a thorough presentation of the works of the Trinity in the history of salvation with a brief description of how the Father was revealed by the Son and how the Father and the Son were revealed by the Spirit (nos. 238–48).

[58] *Catechism* explicates all these intricate concepts in two short paragraphs, nos. 251 and 252.

[59] This point is forcefully argued by Catherine LaCugna (*God for Us*, 209–32). I disagree, however, with her collapsing the immanent Trinity into the economic Trinity (she prefers the use of *theologia* and *economia* respectively), by dispensing with the distinction between God's life *ad intra* and *ad extra*.

[60] Rahner argues convincingly for his point in *The Trinity*, 83–99.

Trinity" and the "immanent Trinity" and vice versa ("Rahner's Rule").[61] (4) In knowledge and love humans have a specifically different relation to each of the three divine persons and not to the divine essence or nature or substance.[62] (5) The doctrine of the Trinity must be related to each and every important theme of Christian theology, from systematic to moral to pastoral theology.

2. With regard to the structure of our treatise on the Trinity, I suggest that we reverse its traditional order. Rather than beginning with the Father, then moving to the Son, and ending with the Holy Spirit, given the principle that we should root our trinitarian theology in our experiences of salvation, we should begin with our present-day experiences of the Holy Spirit, and then show how this Spirit is the Spirit of Jesus, and end with Jesus' revelation of the mystery of God the Father.[63] This procedure has several advantages: (1) It shows convincingly that the Trinity is a mystery of salvation for us *today*. (2) It incorporates into trinitarian theology not only charismatic but also ordinary, daily experiences of grace. (3) It highlights the indispensable role of the Holy Spirit in Christian life, thus making pneumatology, long lamented to be neglected in Western theology, a central theme of Christian theology, and opening a venue for a dialogue with Orthodox theology.[64] (4) It shows that the experiences of the Trinity are not limited to Christians but can also be found outside of Christianity and hence can promote interreligious dialogue. (5) It confirms the way we have access to God: from the Spirit, through the Son, to the Father.[65]

---

[61] Walter Kasper remarks that "what Rahner sets down as a basic principle reflects a broad consensus among the theologians of the various churches." See his *The God of Jesus Christ*, trans. Matthew O'Connell (New York: Crossroad, 1984), 274. Kasper then offers some useful warnings against misinterpreting "Rahner's Rule" (275–77). For a Protestant perspective on Rahner's Rule, see Eberhard Jüngel, *The Doctrine of the Trinity: God's Being in Becoming* (Grand Rapids, Mich.: Eerdmans, 1976) with his "principle of correspondence."

[62] For insightful reflections on the implications of the doctrine of the Trinity for prayer and worship, see LaCugna, *God for Us*, 321–68.

[63] For kinds of experiences of the Holy Spirit today, see Karl Rahner, *The Spirit in the Church* (New York: The Seabury Press, 1979).

[64] For an excellent essay on the role of the Holy Spirit in the life of the Christian, see J. H. P. Wong, "The Holy Spirit in the Life of Jesus and of the Christian," *Gregorianum* 73/1 (1992): 57–95. For recent important studies on the Spirit, see Yves Congar, *I Believe in the Holy Spirit*, 3 vols., trans. David Smith (New York: The Seabury Press, 1983); José Comblin, *The Holy Spirit and Liberation*, trans. Paul Burns (Maryknoll, N.Y.: Orbis Books, 1989); and Michael Welker, *God the Spirit*, trans. John Hoffmeyer (Minneapolis: Fortress Press, 1994).

[65] I am aware that the placement of the doctrine of the Trinity in systematic theology presents a thorny problem. While most theologians would abandon the traditional division of the treatise of God into two parts, *De Deo Uno* and *De Deo Trino*, some (e.g., Karl Barth) would begin the whole dogmatics with the doctrine of the Trinity, while others would not give a particular treatment to it but would make it the overall structuring principle, the inner rationale of all theology (e.g., the so-called Dutch Catechism). My suggestion here is that at least as a *catechetical* strategy, it would be better to place the doctrine of the Trinity after Christology and pneumatology and to reverse the order Father-Son-Spirit to Spirit-Son-Father.

3. Besides the many themes that *Catechism* has already related to the doctrine of the Trinity, as mentioned above, others must be brought into its orbit. First of all, the paschal mystery, in particular the event of Jesus' cross, must be brought into relation with the life of the Trinity. Among Protestant theologians, Jürgen Moltmann has offered bold speculations on the cross as an intra-trinitarian event in which the Son offers himself to but is abandoned by the Father and in which the Father leaves the Son, offers him up, and suffers the death of the Son in the pain of love and in which the Father and the Son are reconciled by the Spirit.[66] Among Catholics, von Balthasar suggests that the cross is the manifestation of trinitarian love[67] and that Holy Saturday represents the mystery of the Son's descent into hell in obedience to the Father to experience the full weight of abandonment and rejection by the Father in solidarity with sinners.[68] Even if one finds Moltmann's and von Balthasar's reflections on the Trinity and the cross of Jesus too adventuresome, especially for catechesis, their insight that the cross is a trinitarian event deserves serious consideration and further development.

4. In anthropology, the classical concept of person as "individual substance of a rational nature" (Boethius) and the modern understanding of person as autonomy and self-consciousness (Descartes' *cogito ergo sum*) must be corrected and enriched by the notion of "person" in the Trinity as *relationality* and *mutuality*.[69] In this way God is seen to be personal only through one or another of the three hypostases, not as a single ineffable entity or self-conscious subject.[70] Furthermore, God's *unity* is seen to consist in the unification of the relationships among the three divine persons or their communion in love rather than in the abstract oneness of a single divine substance.[71]

---

[66] See Moltmann, *The Crucified God*, 235–49; and Moltmann, *The Trinity and the Kingdom*, 75–83.

[67] See Hans Urs von Balthasar, *Mysterium Paschale*, trans. Aidan Nichols (Grand Rapids, Mich.: Eerdmans, 1993), 140: "The Son's Cross is the revelation of the Father's love (Romans 8:32; John 3:16), and the bloody outpouring of that love comes to its inner fulfilment in the shedding abroad of their common Spirit in the hearts of men (Romans 5:5)."

[68] See von Balthasar, *Mysterium Paschale*, 174–76. In his speculations on the meaning of the cross and Holy Saturday von Balthasar was heavily indebted to the mystical experiences of Adrienne von Speyr. For an exposition of von Balthasar's theology of the Trinity and the cross, see Gerald F. O'Hanlon, *The Immutability of God in the Theology of Hans Urs von Balthasar* (Cambridge: Cambridge University Press, 1990), 110–30.

[69] The notion of person as relationality is well developed by LaCugna (*God for Us*, 243–305). Influences on her in this respect include philosopher John Macmurray and Orthodox theologian John Zizioulas. For Macmurray, see *The Self as Agent* (New York: Harper & Brothers, 1957) and *Persons in Relation* (New York: Harper & Brothers, 1961); for Zizioulas, see *Being as Communion* (Crestwood, N.Y.: St. Vladimir's Seminary Press, 1985).

[70] This idea is developed by Wolfhart Pannenberg in *Systematic Theology*, vol. 1 (Grand Rapids, Mich.: Eerdmans, 1991), 259–336.

[71] For reflections on the unity of God as communion in love, see Walter Kasper, *The God of Jesus Christ*, 290–99; and Leonardo Boff, *Trinity and Society* (Maryknoll, N.Y.: Orbis Books, 1988).

5. Another theme connected with anthropology is gender. Whatever validity is to be attached to the claim that the classical trinitarian doctrine fomented patriarchy and androcentrism, it is undeniable that contemporary trinitarian theology cannot evade the issues of exclusive language and sexism, both inside and outside the church. Contemporary trinitarian theology offers opportunities to reflect on the analogical and pluralistic character of our language about God and the affirmation of basic equality and mutuality inherent in the doctrine of the Trinity.[72]

6. This last point brings us to the implication and relevance of the Trinity as a model for church and society. While concrete ecclesiastical, socio-political, and economic policies cannot be directly derived from the doctrine of the Trinity, it contradicts any system or policy that jeopardizes the equality, freedom, and full participation of all members of the ecclesial and political communities.[73] The Trinity shapes as well the forms of ministry in the church.[74]

7. As mentioned above, pneumatology brings us into dialogue with other religions. Moreover, the whole Christian doctrine of the Trinity must be brought into conversation with beliefs of other religions in such a way that the divine triunity is seen to undergird reality as such.[75]

8. Finally, eschatology and ecology must be correlated with the doctrine of the Trinity. Heaven is not an individual's beatific vision of the divine essence but the entire human history and the cosmos brought into eternal communion with the Trinity. It is time made eternity and eternity realized in time. It is the kingdom or rule of God in which the material universe is not destroyed, human history not abolished, but both the cosmos and humanity assumed into the life of the Trinity.[76]

---

[72] See Elizabeth Johnson, *She Who Is: The Mystery of God in Feminist Theological Discourse* (New York: Crossroad, 1993); Leonardo Boff, *The Maternal Face of God: The Feminine and Its Religious Expressions*, trans. Robert Barr and John Diercksmeier (Maryknoll, N.Y.: Orbis Books, 1987); and Donald Gelpi, *The Divine Mother: A Trinitarian Theology of the Holy Spirit* (Lanham, Md.: University Press of America, 1984).

[73] See Moltmann, *The Trinity and the Kingdom*, 191–222; and Boff, *Trinity and Society*, 123–54. Ted Peters objects to using the doctrine of the Trinity as a model for society; he proposes the symbol of the kingdom of God instead (see his *God as Trinity*, 184–86).

[74] See Peter Drilling, *Trinity and Ministry* (Minneapolis: Fortress Press, 1991).

[75] See Raymond Panikkar, *The Trinity and World Religions* (Madras: The Christian Literature Society, 1970); Michael von Brück, *The Unity of Reality* (New York: Paulist Press, 1991); and Roger Corless and Paul Knitter, eds., *Buddhist Emptiness and Christian Trinity: Essays and Explorations* (New York: Paulist Press, 1990).

[76] This thesis is forcefully argued by Ted Peters, in the wake of Pannenberg, in *God as Trinity*, 146–87. I am in agreement with Peters' basic thesis regarding the eschatological incorporation of human history into the trinitarian life, though I question the validity of the Moltmann-Pannenberg-Jenson-Peters conclusion that the immanent Trinity is therefore "open" and that "God's self-definition through the economy of salvation will become the immanent Trinity when God's work of creation and reconciliation is finally consummated" (144) and that "God is in the process of constituting himself as a God

In these ways, in addition to those described by *Catechism*, catechesis can bring unity and cohesiveness to the presentation of the Christian faith. It aims not at a static and permanent unity but at a dynamic and ongoing unity of both doctrine and personal appropriation of the Christian faith.

---

who is in relationship with what is other than God" (145). For an alternative view that also takes God's becoming seriously but does not collapse the immanent into the economic Trinity, see John J. O'Donnell, *The Mystery of the Triune God* (New York: Paulist Press, 1989), 159–72.

3

To Be or Not to Be Catholic?
Is It Still the Question?

CATHOLIC IDENTITY AMID RELIGIOUS PLURALISM

In the culture of religious pluralism, guaranteed in the United States by the constitutional right to freedom *for* and *from* the exercise of religion, a serious concern is often voiced, especially by religious educators, about the possible loss of denominational or even religious identity. Not only does the importance of the differences among Christian denominations seem to have lessened, but there also has been growing phenomena, especially among youth, of being "spiritual but not religious" and of multiple religious belonging.[1] Religious boundaries and identity markers have become porous, and exclusive membership in a particular religious community no longer seems to be an intrinsic element of one's religious identity.

For Catholic educators, the issue of religious identity is taking on an added note of urgency, both because the new posture seems to reject the traditional belief that Catholic identity is shaped by an explicit adherence to defined doctrines and a faithful observance of prescribed practices and because the Vatican has recently insisted on the necessity of preserving the Catholic identity of Catholic colleges and universities.[2]

---

[1] On multiple religious belonging, see Chapter 4 herein.

[2] Recent publications have taken up the question of Catholic identity, both on the scholarly and popular levels. To be noted are the following: Francis J. Butler, *American Catholic Identity* (Kansas City: Sheed & Ward, 1994); William V. D'Antonio, et al., *Laity: American and Catholic* (Kansas City: Sheed & Ward, 1996); James D. Davidson, et al., *The Search for Common Ground: What Unites and Divides American Catholics* (Huntington, Ind.: Our Sunday Visitor, 1997); Daniel Donovan, *Distinctively Catholic: An Exploration of Catholic Identity* (New York: Paulist Press, 1997); Andrew Greeley, *The Catholic Myth: The Behavior and Beliefs of American Catholics* (New York: Simon and Schuster, 1990); John A. Grindel, *Whither the U.S. Church?* (Maryknoll, N.Y.: Orbis Books, 1991); Robert A. Ludwig, *Reconstructing Catholicism for a New Generation* (New York: Crossroad, 1996); Timothy G. McCarthy, *The Catholic Tradition before and after Vatican II: 1878–1993* (Chicago: Loyola University Press, 1994); Patrick H. McNamarra, *Conscience First, Tradition Second: A Study of Young Catholics* (Albany, N.Y.: State University of New York Press, 1992); Richard Rohr and Joseph Martos,

It is interesting to note that of the four marks of the church—unity, holiness, apostolicity, and catholicity—only the last has acquired the status of a theological and sociological label to identify a group of Christians, in contradistinction to others such as Anglicans, Orthodox, and Protestants. These latter groups, of course, have not given up their claim to catholicity, but it is a significant fact that a large, indeed the largest group of Christians has self-consciously adopted the word *catholic* to denote its distinctive identity, and had, until recently, made an exclusive claim to it. Of late, however, for reasons that will be made clear shortly, the understanding of what constitutes catholicity and Catholicism, by no means synonymous words, has undergone drastic changes so that questions have been raised as to what it means to be a Catholic today and by implication what Catholic identity is.

In this chapter I first examine how the changing meanings of the word *catholic* have created an identity crisis for Roman Catholics. Second, I explore the problems as well as the challenges these permutations pose for the ministry of religious education and catechesis. I conclude with some suggestions as to how these challenges can be fruitfully met.

CATHOLIC OR NOT CATHOLIC—HOW CAN ONE TELL?

The word *catholic,* from the Greek adverb *kath' holon,* or the later adjective *katholikos,* usually translated into Latin as *universalis* or *catholicus,* means "referring to or directed toward the whole, the general, the universal," as opposed to the partial or the particular. Though never used in the New Testament to describe the church, the term became an official description of the church in the Apostles' Creed and the so-called Nicene Creed.

Hans Küng has helpfully listed the six meanings that have been successively attached to the term *catholic:* (1) the whole church, in contrast to the local churches, as in Ignatius of Antioch's statement "Where the bishop is, there his people should be, just as, where Jesus Christ is, there is the Catholic Church" (*Smyrn.* 8:2); this is the original ecclesiological meaning; (2) the orthodox, doctrinally pure church as opposed to heretical or schismatic or apostate groups; this polemical meaning became popular after the edicts of Constantine (312) and of Theodosius (380); (3) the church spread throughout the whole world (geographical catholicity); (4) the church larger in number than any other (numerical or

Why Be Catholics? Understanding Our Experience and Tradition (Cincinnati: St. Anthony Messenger Press, 1989); David L. Schindler, *Catholicism and Secularization in American Culture* (Huntington, Ind.: Our Sunday Visitor, 1990); Paul Wilkes, *The Good Enough Catholic: Guide for the Perplexed* (New York: Ballantine, 1996); William O'Malley, *Why Be Catholic?* (New York: Crossroad, 1994); and Cassian Yuhaus, ed., *The Catholic Church and American Culture: Reciprocity and Challenge* (New York: Paulist Press, 1990). I am grateful to my colleague William Dinges for information on this bibliography.

There is also a plethora of recent publications on *Ex corde ecclesiae* as well as on the nature of the Catholic identity of Catholic educational institutions, academic freedom, and ecclesiastical *mandatum* required for teaching theological disciplines.

statistical catholicity); (5) the church that has always existed (temporal or historical catholicity); and (6) the church that is open to all cultures as opposed to being ethnically or culturally exclusive (sociological or cultural catholicity).[3]

More recently, another distinguished ecclesiologist, Avery Dulles, has also studied the various meanings of the term *catholic*, with or without an initial capital. In his influential book *The Catholicity of the Church* he enumerates five usages of *catholic* to denote: (1) sharing in the universal Christian community that transcends the barriers of time and space, as opposed to sectarian; (2) universal, as opposed to particular or local; (3) true or authentic, as opposed to false or heretical; (4) emphasizing visible continuity in space and time and visible mediation by means of social and institutional structures such as creeds, sacraments, and the historical episcopate, as opposed to Protestant (in this sense, *Catholic* with a capital C); and (5) describing the Catholic church, which is governed by the bishop of Rome as the successor of Peter. In this sense, *Catholic* is often preceded by the word *Roman*.[4]

The *Catechism of the Catholic Church* takes *catholic* to mean "universal," in the sense of "according to the totality" or "in keeping with the whole." It explains that the church is catholic for two reasons: first, "because Christ is present in her," and second, "because she has been sent out by Christ on a mission to the whole of the human race" (nos. 830–31).[5] Because of Christ's presence in it, the church possesses "correct and complete confession of faith, full sacramental life, and ordained ministry in apostolic succession (no. 830), and because of Christ's missionary charge, it possesses the character of universality.

Given the various meanings of the word *catholic,* it is only to be expected that the question of the identity of the Roman Catholic Church in general, and of Roman Catholics in particular, as distinct from other Christians, defies easy and clear-cut answers.

1. One way to get a handle on this issue is to describe *philosophically* and *theologically* what is distinctive about Catholicism. Richard McBrien, for instance, suggests that, although the doctrine of the papacy might be regarded as the distinctive element of Roman Catholicism, the Roman Catholic Church is distinguished from the other Christian confessions by the particular *configuration* of the philosophical position of critical realism (as expounded, for example, by Bernard Lonergan in opposition to naive realism, empiricism, and idealism) and of the theological focus on sacramentality, mediation, and communion.[6]

---

[3] See Hans Küng, *The Church*, trans. Ray and Rosaleen Ockenden (New York: Sheed & Ward, 1967), 296–300.

[4] See Avery Dulles, *The Catholicity of the Church* (Oxford: Clarendon Press, 1985), 185. See also his essay "The Meaning of Catholicism: Adventures of an Idea," in his *The Reshaping of Catholicism: Current Challenges in the Theology of Church* (San Francisco: Harper & Row, 1988), 51–74.

[5] *The Catechism of the Catholic Church* (Mahwah, N.J.: Paulist Press, 1994).

[6] See Richard McBrien, *Catholicism* (Minneapolis: Winston Press, 1981), 1171–84. McBrien makes a distinction between *characteristic* and *distinctive*. What is *characteristic* may also be found in others, but what is *distinctive* is found in oneself alone. *Characteristic* of Catholicism is the insistence on the triumph of grace over sin, tradition and

Robert Imbelli offers a similar characterization of Catholicism. According to him, the Catholic church is distinguished by five foundational sensitivities, namely, to the corporeal, the communal, the universal, the cosmic, and the transformational.[7] For both McBrien and Imbelli, the Catholic church promotes and sustains the creative tension between "both-and" rather than succumbing to the reductionistic "either-or."

Avery Dulles, while expressing agreement with the two theologians mentioned above, goes on to explore four dimensions of catholicity. Catholicity "from above" is God's gift and is grounded in the triune God's self-communication in the incarnation of the Son and the sanctification of the Holy Spirit. Catholicity "from below" acknowledges the pervasive presence of God's grace in all things despite sin. Whereas these first two dimensions of catholicity may be called qualitative or vertical, the last two refer to its quantitative or horizontal aspects. Catholicity "in breadth" seeks to expand the universality of the church by means of missionary activities. Last, catholicity "in length" seeks both to preserve and to transform the tradition of the church until the end of time.[8]

While these theological reflections on catholicity are helpful and indeed profound and must be kept in mind as we discuss the issue of Catholic identity, they cannot be readily translated into a set of criteria to settle the question of who is a Roman Catholic today. There are several reasons why this is so. First, the characteristics alleged to be distinctive of Roman Catholicism are not uniformly understood, even by Catholic theologians, nor are their actual embodiments in the Catholic church evaluated in the same way. For instance, with regard to sacramentality and mediation, while there is near-unanimous agreement that they are distinctive, though not exclusive, of Catholicism, there is no accord on the kinds of institutional structures (for example, doctrines, sacraments, and ministries) by which they are actualized in the church. To take an ecumenically sensitive issue, how is the papacy to be exercised so that it functions in fact as an organ for catholicity? Much less is there a common view on which of these structures individual Catholics must minimally accept in order to retain their Catholic identity.

Second, it is necessary to distinguish between the question of the distinctiveness of Roman Catholicism and that of the identity of a Roman Catholic. While these two issues are intimately intertwined and must be considered together, the question of the identity of a Roman Catholic is narrower in scope than that of

---

continuity, community, sacramentality, and mediation. *Distinctive* of Catholicism is its teaching on the Petrine office. Also *distinctive* is the particular *configuration* of the various characteristics mentioned above (see ibid., 722–23). For older works by McBrien on catholicity, see *Who Is a Catholic?* (Denville: N.J.: Dimension Books, 1971); *Church: The Continuing Quest* (New York: Newman Press, 1970); and *Do We Need the Church?* (New York: Harper & Row, 1969).

[7] See Robert Imbelli, "Vatican II: Twenty Years Later," *Commonweal* 109/17 (1982): 522–26.

[8] See Avery Dulles, *The Catholicity of the Church*, 30–105. See also his essay "Changing Concepts of Church Membership" in his *The Resilient Church: The Necessity and Limits of Adaptation* (New York: Doubleday, 1977), 133–51.

the distinctiveness of the Catholic church. The latter is of a universal and theological nature, whereas the former, though theological, refers to particular individuals and admits of sociological and even canonical considerations.

Thirdly, while church authorities and theologians can in principle spell out theological and canonical criteria for Catholic identity, it is quite another question whether persons, already baptized into the Catholic church, either as infants or adults, correctly understand them and fulfill them in their lives, even though, sociologically at least, they regard themselves and are regarded by others as Catholics.

2. A second helpful guide through this labyrinth of the distinctiveness of Catholicism and Catholic identity is provided by recent conciliar teachings and canonical determination. In *Lumen gentium* Vatican II describes a Catholic Christian as follows:

> Fully incorporated into the Church are those who, possessing the Spirit of Christ, accept all the means of salvation given to the Church together with her entire organization, and who—by the bonds constituted by the profession of faith, the sacraments, ecclesiastical government, and communion—are joined in the visible structure of the Church of Christ, who rules her through the Supreme Pontiff and the bishops (no. 14).[9]

As is widely known, the 1917 Code of Canon Law presumed that the church of Christ is the Catholic church and determined that baptism into this church constitutes one a person in the church with all the rights and duties of a Christian. Pius XII in his encyclical *Mystici corporis* (1943) also identified the church of Christ with the Catholic church and added the profession of true faith to the 1917 code's two requirements for one to be truly *(reapse)* a member of the church, namely, baptism and good standing.

Vatican II modified Pius XII's teaching by introducing a distinction between the church of Christ and the Catholic church and taught that the church of Christ, "constituted and organized as a society in the present world, subsists in the Catholic church, which is governed by the successor of Peter and by the bishops in communion with him" (*LG*, no. 8). Furthermore, the council distinguished between "incorporation" into the church as the effect of baptism and "full incorporation" into the church (canon 205 of the 1983 Code of Canon Law uses the expression "fully in communion") as the result of the following four elements: (1) possession of the Spirit of Christ; (2) personal adhesion to the entire system and all the means of salvation of the church; (3) union to Christ through the church's visible structure described as the bonds of professed faith, the sacraments, and ecclesiastical government; and (4) communion.

---

[9] English translation from Austin Flannery, ed., *Vatican Council II: The Conciliar and Post Conciliar Documents* (Collegeville, Minn.: Liturgical Press, 1984). For the canons on the identity of the Christian faithful and those fully in communion with the Catholic church, see canons 204 and 205; see also the very helpful commentary by James Provost in *The Code of Canon Law: A Text and Commentary* (New York: Paulist Press, 1985), 119–29.

Taxonomic as Vatican II's description of full incorporation into the church is, it is far from being helpful in answering the question of Catholic identity. Whereas acceptance of the second and third elements is verifiable, at least in principle, it is not at all clear how the presence of the first and fourth elements can be accurately gauged. By their nature possession of the Holy Spirit and communion are of an internal and spiritual order and evade empirical measurement.

Interestingly enough, the canon that enumerates the conditions for "full communion" of the baptized with the church mentions only those visible bonds and omits the possession of the Holy Spirit and communion.[10] In so doing the code makes the issue of Catholic identity much less messy than it actually is, and people desirous of conceptual clarity may welcome this restriction to empirically verifiable criteria. However, the price for canonical neatness is unacceptably high, since what is at the heart of Catholic reality, namely, union with Christ and other Christians in the Holy Spirit, is left aside. Indeed, Vatican II felt obligated to add to its description of Catholic identity the warning that "even though incorporated into the Church, one who does not however persevere in charity is not saved. He remains indeed in the bosom of the Church, but 'in body' not 'in heart'" (*LG*, no. 14).[11] Clearly, for Vatican II, the spiritual conditions for full incorporation into the church obtains primacy over the visible ones.

3. So far our examination of theological, conciliar, and canonical writings has not yielded a helpful set of criteria to determine who is Catholic. A third way to help settle this question is religious sociology. It may be said that Catholics are baptized persons who actually describe themselves as Catholic and behave externally as Catholics. This is in fact the usual way pastors determine who is a Catholic in their parishes. They simply count (more or less accurately) the number of people who are registered in their parishes and/or who attend various liturgical functions and report to the chancery the number of Catholics in their districts. Though placing great importance on the conditions for full incorporation into the church, pastors do not explicitly inquire whether their parishioners possess the Spirit of Christ, accept all the means of salvation given to the church, internalize the three bonds of union with Christ, and live out communion with God and others.

This statistical method may be useful in determining the size of the Catholic population and the amount of diocesan tax the parish owes (for this reason pastors may be excused for regularly underestimating the number of Catholics in their parishes!), but it is far from satisfactory theologically. It does not tell us what constitutes the heart of being Catholic. Most important, this sociological approach highlights a severe challenge for people engaged in the ministry of religious education, especially with regard to the issue of Catholic identity. Sociologist Andrew Greeley has been arguing for over two decades in his many

---

[10] Canon 205 reads: "Those baptized are fully in communion with the Catholic Church on this earth who are joined with Christ in its visible structure by the bonds of profession of faith, of the sacraments and of ecclesiastical governance."

[11] The quoted expressions "in body" and "in heart" are taken from Augustine.

publications that his research has revealed a new kind of Catholic that he calls a "communal Catholic":

> What is a communal Catholic? I would suggest that a communal Catholic is one committed to Catholicism and self-conscious in his attempt to understand the Catholic experience in the United States. He does not care much what the church as an institution says or does not say, does or does not do. He is committed to Catholicism as a collectivity and as a world view (though he reserves the right to interpret that world view to meet his own needs). But his expectations of the church as an ecclesiastical institution are minimal. Unlike some of his predecessors, he does not grow irate when the church fails to take a stand on the latest fashionable social issue, he doesn't much care because he isn't very confident that church leaders are well informed about such issues. Even if they did take a stand, he would not listen very seriously to what they say. However, he will turn to the church for sacramental ministry when it is needed, and he may deem that ministry to be needed very frequently in his life. He will not expect religious, social, moral, or human guidance from the church.[12]

Greeley goes on to say that communal Catholics like being Catholic, though not militantly or belligerently so. Moreover, though not well versed in Catholic doctrines, they do have opinions about church issues: they tend to be in favor of optional celibacy for the clergy and of birth control, and they are generally opposed to abortion and sexual permissiveness. Furthermore, according to Greeley, communal Catholics tend to demand professional competence, both of themselves and church leaders:

> They are professionally competent. . . . The professionalism of these communal Catholics is so much a part of their lives that they simply cannot understand how it could be otherwise. They are offended by Sunday sermons, not so much because the content is either too radical or conservative, but because they are so bad. . . .
>
> Despite their lack of interest in internal affairs, internal politics, and internal debates of the organizational church, the communal Catholics are each profoundly and deeply involved in a search for understanding what it means to be Catholic in America. Their search is open minded, open ended, respectful, sympathetic, and critical. . . .
>
> While they are very self-conscious in their search for insight and understanding, the communal Catholics have yet to emerge as a self-conscious, collective group in the church, and they may never do so.[13]

---

[12] Andrew Greeley, *The Communal Catholic* (New York: The Seabury Press, 1976), 9–10.

[13] Ibid., 13–14. I give this long quotation to give the reader a concrete feel of the "communal Catholic." Greeley has given a schematic definition of the communal Catholic:

In a later work Greeley traced the rise of this "selective Catholicism" or "do-it-yourself Catholicism" or "Catholicism on your own terms" or "cafeteria Catholicism" to the reforms of Vatican II; Paul VI's encyclical *Humanae vitae;* the emergence of Catholics as a well-educated, suburban, and professional group in the early seventies; and the failure of leadership of the American Catholic hierarchy.[14] Finally, Greeley insists that "while as an institution the Catholic Church is in terrible condition, the Catholic community prospers—precisely because Catholics like being Catholic" and that therefore "Catholicism is reshaping itself into new and intriguing forms for the next century and the next millennium."[15]

How many communal Catholics are there in the American Catholic Church? Greeley has not, to my knowledge, provided a precise number, but from his comments on the rate of non-reception of *Humanae vitae*[16] and about how the Catholic church would lose four-fifths of its communicants were communal Catholics forced to leave,[17] it can be presumed that the number of communal Catholics is rather high, among both the laity and the lower clergy.

Even if one finds Greeley's strident and arrogant voice distasteful and disagrees with some or most of the remedies he recommends for curing the ills he diagnosed in the church,[18] one can hardly ignore the sociological data regarding a new kind of American Catholics that his research has unearthed. Combined with the theological uncertainties concerning the identity of a Catholic discussed above, the recent emergence of the "communal Catholic" clearly poses a tremendous challenge for religious educators; it touches the very heart of their enterprise, which is the formation and shaping of a Catholic identity and life. We now turn to these challenges.

"1. The communal Catholic is loyal to Catholicism. It is his religious self-definition. He will have no other. 2. The communal Catholic is not angry at the ecclesiastical structure. 3. He does not expect to receive important instruction from that structure on any issue, ranging from sexuality to international economics. 4. Nevertheless, he is interested in and fascinated by the Catholic tradition to which he is loyal, and wishes to understand it better. 5. The communal Catholic seeks sacramental ministry from the church at such times in his life when such ministry seems appropriate and necessary—for some, every day, for others, only at rites of passage like baptism, marriage, and death." Greeley points out that items 1, 3, and 5 have been present with American Catholicism almost since its beginning, whereas items 2 and 4 are new and are promising venues for the church to reach communal Catholics (see ibid., 181–82).

[14] See Andrew M. Greeley and Mary Greeley Durkin, *How to Save the Catholic Church* (New York: Viking Penguin, 1984), 3–17. See also Andrew Greeley, *American Catholics since the Council: An Unauthorized Report* (Chicago: St. Thomas More Press, 1985).

[15] Greeley, *The Catholic Myth*, 4.

[16] See ibid., 90–96.

[17] See Greeley and Durkin, *How to Save the Catholic Church*, 8.

[18] Greeley's solutions include presentation of sex as sacramental experience, understanding woman as analog of God, a positive assessment of marriage and family as "cosmic story," restoration of the parish as "organic community," revitalization of worship, fostering of popular devotions, and strengthening of Catholic schools (see, in particular, Greeley and Durkin, *How to Save the Catholic Church*, 105–248).

CATHOLIC IDENTITY AND ITS CHALLENGES TO RELIGIOUS EDUCATION

Identity, both of the individual and of the group, is usually defined by delineating differences and drawing clear boundaries between oneself and others and between one group and other groups, respectively. The sharper the differences between individuals, the stronger is the consciousness of one's identity. Similarly, the more numerous are the boundaries making the crossing of a member of one group over to another group impossible or at least costly, both materially and psychologically, the deeper and the more permanent is the esprit de corps and the cohesiveness of the group. In short, the identity both of the individual and of the group is defined and maintained over *against* that of others. Furthermore, to function as effective determinants of the identity of either the individual or the group, differences and boundaries must be highly visible and easily verifiable. Differences, even though profound and numerous, that remain at the invisible or spiritual level, and therefore not amenable to empirical verification, do not serve well to define and maintain personal and social identity.

In light of these considerations on the formation of individual and social identity it is clear that recent developments in the Catholic church and its ecclesiology have conspired to corrode the identity of both the individual Catholic and the church as a whole. As summarized above, etymologically, the word *catholic* has lost much of its geographical, temporal, numerical, and doctrinal connotations—dimensions that are visible and readily verifiable. It is now predominantly taken to refer to "wholeness," a much richer concept but somewhat vague and therefore less capable of defining boundaries and differences.[19]

Theologically, Vatican II's refusal to identify the Catholic church with the church of Christ, as Pius XII had done in *Mystici corporis*, had the unintended effect of blurring the defining characteristics of the Catholic church as the true church. Vatican II's non-use of the adjective *Roman* to describe the Catholic church, as Vatican I had done,[20] added to the confusion. Furthermore, the portrait of a Catholic was made fuzzy when Vatican II privileged spiritual conditions for full incorporation into the church, that is, possession of the Spirit and communion, over the acceptance of the visible bonds of profession of faith, sacraments, and hierarchical structure. In addition, Vatican II's description of the various ways in which non-Catholic Christians are "joined" to the Catholic church, non-Christian believers are "related" to it, and nonbelievers can be saved

---

[19] This is true also of Protestants. Evaluating the report of the Fourth Assembly of the World Council of Churches (Uppsala, 1968), Avery Dulles writes: "The concept of catholicity in this document may be described as qualitative rather then quantitative. Gone is the traditional stress on geographical extension.... No effort, moreover, is made to exploit catholicity as a visible mark of the true Church. (see *The Catholicity of the Church*, 26).

[20] See Vatican I's dogmatic constitution on the Catholic faith *(Dei Filius)*, which speaks of "the holy, catholic, apostolic, and Roman Church." Since the nineteenth century, *romanitas* has been sometimes treated as if it were the fifth mark of the church.

often prompts the question of why one should be a Catholic at all (see *LG*, nos. 15–16).

Sociologically, the identity of the Catholic has been further eroded by the presence of "communal Catholics." If Greeley's characterization of these Catholics is correct, and there is no reason to question its accuracy,[21] the boundaries separating Catholics and non-Catholic Christians have been stretched beyond tolerable limits.

With all these developments, it is not surprising that religious education is faced with a host of challenges, since its goals include fostering understanding of the Catholic faith and inculcating Catholic practices with a view to deepening Catholic identity. These challenges can be summarized as follows, though the list is by no means exhaustive:

1. Accepting Vatican II's recognition of the ecclesial nature of non-Catholic denominations, which it calls "churches" and "ecclesial communities" (see *UR*, nos. 14–24), and their positive relationships to the Catholic church, and accepting the necessity of ecumenical dialogue and practices, how can one impress upon Catholics the same council's teaching that "it is through Christ's Catholic Church *alone*, which is the universal help towards salvation, that the *fullness* of the means of salvation can be obtained"? (*UR*, no. 3, emphasis added). The challenge is not to *prove* to Catholics the truth of this teaching, since presumably, being Catholic, they have already accepted it. Rather, it is how to *strengthen* and *deepen* this conviction in their consciousness by means of various "structures of plausibility," to use the expression of sociologist Peter Berger.

2. In view of Vatican II's call for dialogue with non-Christian religions, and given the existence of various religious movements, such as New Age, that appropriate a host of beliefs and practices of Eastern religions, how can the distinctly Catholic beliefs and practices be maintained? Again, the challenge is not to *prove* to Catholics that Christian beliefs and practices are better than those of non-Christian religions, because presumably, being Christian, they are already convinced of their truth and values. Rather, it is to help them *understand* and *live* the Christian truths and practices in the context of religious pluralism of the American society.

3. With regard to communal Catholics, while pointing out their doctrinal inconsistencies and lamenting their lack of interest in the institutional aspects of the church, how can we respond to their abiding love for Catholicism and the Catholic symbolic system? Is there a way, *in* and *through* the

---

[21] See Stanley Presser and Linda Stinson, "Data Collection Mode and Social Desirability Bias in Self-Reported Religious Attendance," *American Sociological Review* 63/1 (1900): 137–45. The authors conclude that "respondents in conventional surveys substantially overreport their religious attendance. Apparently, misreporting error is caused mainly by social desirability pressures associated with interviewer-administration. The error can be minimized through either self-administration or asking about time-use" (144–45). I am grateful to Dr. Stinson for drawing my attention to this fact.

Catholic symbolic system itself, to reconnect them to the "full incorporation" into the Catholic church as Vatican II describes it?

4. In meeting these challenges, can we gain a new understanding of the Catholic identity itself, one that keeps in creative tension the spiritual and institutional, the invisible and visible elements? Should this new concept of catholicity inform and shape the goal and practice of religious education?

SHAPING THE CATHOLIC IDENTITY AS A TASK OF RELIGIOUS EDUCATION

In this last part I make a few suggestions as to how the above-mentioned challenges can be met in religious education. Since these challenges overlap with each other, I will not deal with them individually but will treat them *in globo*.

It may be helpful, however, to preface this discussion with two observations. First, while intra-Christian and interreligious dialogue is imperative for contemporary Christian theology and practice, it is neither feasible nor productive in religious education to aim at the formation of a generically Christian attitude and identity, since it is only through a particular community of faith, with its own beliefs, rituals, and ethical and spiritual practices that a person gains access to and is socialized into the common Christian heritage. Of course, such a community of faith must be able to acknowledge the religious traditions of communities other than itself and critically appropriate their positive aspects to enrich its own self-understanding and religious practices. Nevertheless, members of a particular religious community cannot do so effectively unless they are already well established in their own tradition. To put it differently, in ecumenical and interreligious dialogue, one cannot "cross over" and "come back" unless one already is familiar with and dwells comfortably in the home from which one ventures forth into other faith communities and to which one returns, strengthened in one's own religious identity.

Second, I am aware that Catholic identity is shaped not by doctrines alone but also by other means, such as worship and prayer. Indeed, the most effective catechesis is one that is built on all four pillars of religious education, namely, doctrine, liturgy, ethical praxis, and prayer.[22] In this part I focus only on doctrine, while not denying the greater importance of the other three elements in shaping the Catholic identity. The reason for this narrow concentration is that according to the findings of a project currently directed by a research team

---

[22] See the structure of the *Catechism of the Catholic Church* and Congregation for the Clergy, *General Directory for Catechesis* (The Vatican: Libreria Editrice Vaticana, 1997), no. 85. The *General Directory for Catechesis* lists four fundamental tasks of catechesis: promoting knowledge of the faith, liturgical celebration, moral formation, and teaching to pray. For a brief discussion of religious education after Vatican II, see Gabriel Moran, "Religious Education after Vatican II," in *Open Catholicism: The Tradition at Its Best, Essays in Honor of Gerard Sloyan*, ed. David Efroymson and John Raines, 151–66 (Collegeville, Minn.: Liturgical Press, 1997). Moran singles out three elements of religious education: catechetics, worship, and service.

composed of Dean Hoge, William Dinges, Mary Johnson, and Juan Gonzalez at the Catholic University of America, the elements that rank lowest in the American youth's estimation of what constitute Catholic identity are specific moral teachings.[23]

Perhaps it is necessary and proper to acknowledge at the outset that the issue of the identity of the Catholic church and of Catholics and the alleged "identity crisis" cannot be resolved by religious education alone. These issues are much larger than religious education, and it is unfair to lay the confusion about Catholic identity at the doorsteps of religious educators exclusively. Measures other than religious education have been suggested by both "liberals" and "conservatives" to restore Catholic identity to the American church.[24]

As far as religious education is concerned, it has been suggested that the most effective means to restore and strengthen Catholic identity are a faithful presentation of Catholic doctrines and a fervent promotion of Catholic practices, preferably by means of a common catechism, such as the *Catechism of the Catholic Church*. On the face of it, it is hard to see how anyone can disagree with this proposal in its general thrust.

However, in my judgment the problem is *not* that the Catholic faithful do not *know* what the official church teaches. Except in arcane matters such as trinitarian theology, rare indeed is the Catholic who is ignorant of church teachings on issues such as sexual morality (for example, masturbation, premarital and extramarital intercourse, artificial contraception, and homosexuality), priestly celibacy, and the exclusion of women from the hierarchical priesthood. The Magisterium has repeatedly proclaimed its teachings on these issues, *opportune et inopportune*. Any Catholic still ignorant of church teachings on these issues can easily remedy his or her lack of knowledge by picking up any official catechism. Ironically, it is often thanks to the public media, the bête noire of conservatives, that church teachings on controversial issues are made known to a wide public (which is not to say that the media agree with them).

The real problem in religious education lies, then, not in the ignorance of church teachings but in presenting the *reasons* that the official church uses to

---

[23] I am grateful to my colleague William Dinges for sharing with me the results of the research project (see Dean Hoge, William Dinges, Mary Johnson, and Juan Gonzales Jr., *Young Adult Catholics: Religion in the Culture of Choice* [Notre Dame, Ind.: University of Notre Dame Press, 2001]). According to the survey, religious identity for young-adult Catholics is shaped by three basic elements: belief in God's presence in the sacraments, including the "real presence" in the Eucharist; social action to help the poor; and devotion to Mary. Least important are specific moral teachings and specific rules about the priesthood. Patrick H. McNamara, in his 1992 study of young American Catholics, found that "for the remaining two-thirds, 'being Catholic' was simply a matter of choice. Sometimes coming across as choosing specific teachings while rejecting others. This mode of choosing lies at the heart of the contemporary form, for younger Catholics, of Catholic self-identification." See *Conscience First, Tradition Second* (Albany, N.Y.: State University of New York Press, 1992), 158.

[24] For recommendations from the conservative side, see George A. Kelly, *Keeping the Church Catholic with John Paul II* (New York: Doubleday, 1990), 261–85.

justify its teachings.[25] To take two examples: presumably no Catholic is ignorant of the church's ban on artificial contraception and on the ordination of women; the problem is that the reasons for the church's positions do not appear reasonable and convincing, to judge from polls, to many Catholics, even devout ones.

The religious educator must, of course, present the reasons fully, competently, sympathetically, and clearly. But no amount of rhetoric, persuasion, pedagogy, repetition, or even threat can augment one bit the objective force and logic that these reasons possess in themselves. The teacher will rightfully appeal to faith and respect for the teaching church, but he or she cannot urge obedience to church authorities against the negative assessment of the logic of certain church teachings. One of the hallmarks of the Catholic church is a profound respect for human reason and freedom as authentic ways to know God. Unless the student accepts and internalizes the reasons given in support of church teachings, and not just the teachings themselves; unless he or she perceives the *reasonableness* of the teachings (which is not the same as their purely *rational* grounds), the Catholic identity, which these teachings and religious education intend to maintain and develop, remains very weak.

What is one to do when reasons for church teachings fail to convince? Rather than repeating the same arguments (the weaker the arguments, the louder the voice and the more strident the appeal to authority) or concocting more and more arguments in *direct* support of church teachings, I suggest an indirect approach.[26] The indirect approach does not seek to prove the validity and truth of a particular teaching by examining its intrinsic evidence but by investigating and appealing to the ontological and existential conditions in the hearer that make the acceptance of the teaching possible. This approach is particularly helpful when the objective proofs are too many and too complex for the average mind to be able to grasp in all their individual specificities. Indeed, in my judgment, this indirect rather than direct approach is the common one by which people reasonably arrive at certitude in matters that profoundly affect their lives, such as ethics and religion.[27]

---

[25] I prescind here from the possibility and legitimacy of "dissent" from the teaching of the Magisterium in non-infallible teachings. For helpful discussions of this issue, see André Naud, *Un Aggiornamento et son éclipse: La liberté de la pensée dans la foi et dans l'Église* (Québec: Fides, 1996); Richard R. Gaillardetz, *Teaching with Authority: A Theology of the Magisterium in the Church* (Collegeville, Minn.: Liturgical Press, 1997); and Francis A. Sullivan, *Magisterium: Teaching Authority in the Catholic Church* (New York: Paulist Press, 1983) and *Creative Fidelity: Weighing and Interpreting Documents of the Magisterium* (New York: Paulist Press, 1996).

[26] I am inspired by Karl Rahner's "indirect method" as it is deployed in his *Foundations of Christian Faith*, trans. William Dych (New York: Crossroad, 1982). See my "Cultural Pluralism and the Unity of the Sciences: Karl Rahner's Transcendental Theology as a Test Case," *Salesianum* 51 (1989): 785–809.

[27] I am indebted to Cardinal John Henry Newman's *An Essay in Aid of a Grammar of Assent*, first published in 1870. For a recent edition, see *An Essay in Aid of a Grammar of Assent* (Westminster, Md.: Christian Classics, 1973). Studies on Newman's epistemology are abundant. For recent studies, note the following: Gerard Magill, "Interpreting Moral

With regard to the question of Catholic identity, this approach is predicated upon the conviction that personal identity and social identity are shaped and maintained not primarily by the specific differences that an individual or a society possesses over *against* others, which may be many but superficial, but by what might be called "deep structures," which may be few and common to others. For example, my cultural identity as a Vietnamese is defined less by my particularities of birth, educational achievements, social status, and material acquisitions than by such long-lasting and pervasive factors as the language and culture that I have in common with other Vietnamese.

Analogously, what constitutes a person a Catholic and defines his or her Catholic identity is not so much what differentiates the person from a Protestant, Orthodox, or Anglican (for example, acceptance of the Petrine office) but the fundamental and deep structures, even though these may be common to others. Such deep structures may include doctrines but are by no means limited to them. Religion, as anthropologists have pointed out, is a system of symbols that includes not only doctrines but rituals, institutions, art, and behaviors.[28] Thus, a Catholic's identity is shaped not only by doctrines, but as much as (if not more) by sacramental celebrations (though sacraments are common to the Orthodox, the Anglicans, and most Protestants), by devotions to Mary and the saints (common to the Orthodox), by episcopal structures (common to the Orthodox and the Anglicans), and by artistic monuments such as architecture, the visual arts, and music.

These deep structures have been variously identified as sacramentality, mediation, communion, and the "analogical imagination."[29] My intention here is not to add other candidates to the list but to argue that to form the Catholic identity of their students, religious educators should attend to these deep structures, especially when the reasons for the official doctrines fail to carry weight with the audience. Indeed, unless these structures are shaped, cultivated, and

---

Doctrine: Newman on Conscience and Law," *Horizons* 20/1 (1993): 7–22; Jeffrey D. Marlett, "Conversion Methodology and the Case of Cardinal Newman," *Theological Studies* 58 (1997): 669–85; Linda L. Stinson, *Process and Conscience: Toward a Theology of Human Emergence* (Lanham, Md.: University Press of America, 1986); and Gerard Casey, *Natural Reason: A Study of the Notions of Inference, Assent, Intuition, and First Principles in the Philosophy of John Henry Cardinal Newman* (New York: Peter Lang, 1984).

[28] I am in broad agreement with George Lindbeck's view of religion as a cultural-linguistic system, though I think he unduly underestimates the cognitive and expressive dimensions of doctrines. See his *The Nature of Doctrine: Religion and Theology in a Postliberal Age* (Philadelphia: Westminster, 1984).

[29] Greeley speaks of four basic elements of the Catholic heritage: sacramental experience, the analogical imagination, the cosmic story, and organic community (see Greeley and Durkin, *How to Save the Catholic Church*, 33–102). With regard to the analogical imagination, see also Greeley, *The Catholic Myth*, esp. chap. 3 (pp. 34–64) entitled "Do Catholics Imagine Differently?" Greeley takes the analogical imagination as the root characteristic of Catholics. I agree with Greeley that Catholics tend to imagine "analogously," but I do not think that this is specific to Catholics. The analogical imagination works as powerfully among the Orthodox and the Anglicans, for example, as among

nurtured with care, most of the reasons for the church's controversial teachings, especially those that contradict popular trends, are not readily understandable.

It is commonly admitted that in moral and religious matters, besides the knowledge derived from formal inference and logical deduction, there is a knowledge through "connaturality," by "instinct," as it were. Though not opposed to the knowledge acquired through philosophical reasoning, this knowledge through connaturality is gained not so much from the technical accumulation of data and their logical ordering but from a personal, deep, and prolonged familiarity with the subject matter. This familiarity, which is often a product of technical expertise but far exceeds it, gives the individual an uncanny ability to see a pattern among the disparate data, to intuit a *Gestalt* in the disconnected parts, to anticipate the conclusion before the reasoning process is completed, to predict the outcome of an experiment, to tell true from false, right from wrong, from the "feel" of the thing. In short, it is a kind of the sixth sense, the knowledge of what Blaise Pascal calls the "heart." This is the ability, for example, of the detective to figure out the culprit despite confusing clues, of the archeologist to reconstruct bygone cities from bits and pieces of pottery, of the historian to interpret the meanings of events from conflicting records, of the artist to see beauty amid what appears to be disharmony and ugliness, of the virtuous person to discern with ease what is good and evil on the basis of his or her experience.

This ability Cardinal Newman calls the "illative sense," that is, the ability of the practical reason (akin to Aristotle's *phronesis*) to arrive at certitude in practical matters, particularly in matters concerning Christianity, which is, according to Newman, addressed to both intellect and imagination, "creating a certitude of its truth by arguments too various for direct enumeration, too personal and deep for words, too powerful and concurrent for refutation."[30]

Catholics, it may be argued, cultivate a special illative sense with which they grasp and assent to the Christian faith. It is characterized by the inclusiveness of "both-and" rather than "either-or" thinking, a positive appreciation of created realities as mediation and sacrament of their divine Creator, a high regard for the community as the locus of God's self-communication, and a basically optimistic attitude of hope for the redemption of everything. Prior to the explicit acceptance of each and every Christian belief and practice, there are these deep structures of the Catholic identity that function as both the religious context and the epistemological warrants for these beliefs and practices. These structures do not per se provide specific justifications for a particular belief or practice, which needs to be justified on its own merits, but they offer the context in which these arguments, "too various for direct enumeration, too personal and deep for words,"

Catholics; by the same token, the "dialectical imagination" is no less in use among Catholics than among Protestants. My point that Catholic identity is formed not by Catholics' differences from others, as long as these remain superficial, but by their deep structures, even though these may be shared extensively by others. This is not an idle point, since it allows Catholics to strengthen and nourish their own identity in a truly ecumenical way. In this way, ecumenical dialogue is seen not as diluting Catholic identity but as fortifying it.

[30] Newman, *An Essay in Aid of a Grammar of Assent*, 492.

and perhaps, we must add, not strong enough to convince, can acquire a certain plausibility and *invite* a faithful acceptance. Religious educators cannot and should not expect immediate acquiescence on the part of the listeners to the church teachings presented, but they must explain how these teachings can make sense within the whole complex of the fundamental options of Catholicism and hope that the listeners will give, eventually, a sympathetic consideration to perplexing church teachings. As Catholic religious educators, they can do no more— but also no less.

An example will clarify the role these deep structures perform in the acceptance of a particular belief or practice. It is a well-known fact that Paul VI's teaching that every act of sexual intercourse must be open to the transmission of life and that therefore artificial contraception is morally wrong encounters much resistance among Catholics. A religious educator may decide to defend this papal teaching directly with an array of arguments derived from natural law, often with very mixed results (and perhaps without full-throated conviction). Rather than ignoring the papal teaching altogether or dismissing it out of hand, the religious educator may want to try an alternative approach, which is to show its plausibility indirectly, in a circuitous way, as it were. He or she may appeal, for instance, to the fecund nature of God's love, both in the Trinity and for us, and to the belief that a Catholic should imitate this divine modus operandi as much as possible, sex being a sacrament of the divine.[31] Admittedly, these broad reflections do not prove that every act of sexual intercourse must be open to procreation, but they provide the theological context in which Pope Paul VI's teaching might make sense and deserves a serious hearing. More important, this teaching's connections with a central Christian doctrine and a deep structure of Christian identity (the analogical imagination) are made manifest, and even though its philosophical arguments may not gain greater persuasiveness, it gathers support from a fundamental principle of Christian faith and the challenge of *imitatio Dei*. In this way the Catholic identity of the student is not minimized but rather maintained and fostered.

There are at least five advantages in this indirect approach to shape the Catholic identity. First, by attending to the conditions of possibility for faith, it highlights the subjective aspects of faith, not only the objective motives of credibility. Second, the indirect approach shifts the emphasis from information and reasoning in religious education to formation of the *habitus mentis*, the illative sense, the intellectual and moral virtues of the individual, which mark the identity of a Catholic. Third, the indirect method spares the Magisterium the practice of attributing to the reasons justifying its teachings more weight they they can bear, thus risking the danger that Saint Thomas alluded to when he refused to prove by rational arguments the truth of creation, that is, exposing Catholic truths to the ridicule by nonbelievers who are led to think that Christians believe such truths on flimsy grounds. In other words, this method permits church teachers to affirm Christian truths with courage but also with humility and honesty. Fourth,

---

[31] For an attempt to understand how the doctrine of the Trinity can confer unity to Christian doctrine, see Chapter 2 herein.

by distinguishing the deep structures of Catholic identity from particular doctrines, the indirect method encourages the observance of the "hierarchy of truths," which is recommended by Vatican II (*UR*, no. 11). Fifth, with regard to communal Catholics, the indirect method appeals to their loyalty to Catholicism, and by attending to the deep structures of the Catholic identity, it exploits their interest in sacramental celebrations and devotional practices. It is to be hoped that through this "back door" they will be led to appreciate the importance and relevance of the Magisterium's teachings and the hierarchical structure of the church.

Finally, in light of these methodological considerations, it is clear that the question of the Catholic identity will have to be renegotiated. In *Catholic Identity after Vatican II* Frans Jozef van Beeck argues that Catholic identity has usually been defined by two experiences, which he calls "pistic" and "charismatic."[32] In pistic experiences Catholic life is defined by precepts and commandments and Catholic worship by rules and obligations and rubrics derived from the feudal shape of the Latin Church and the hardening of boundaries and definitions consequent upon the Counter Reformation. The pistic experiences are marked by four unacceptable characteristics: inappropriate dependency of the laity, totalitarianism and clericalism, inhospitable structures, and a judgmental attitude toward the outside world.[33]

By charismatic experiences van Beeck refers to those Christians who in virtue of their *charismata* exercise their ministries without dependence upon the hierarchy; are motivated by the situations in which they live; emphasize integrity, authenticity, and personal responsibility; and prefer pluriformity and differentiation of ministries. These charismatic experiences, though positive, are marked, according to van Beeck, by four weaknesses: diffuseness and compromise; loss of tradition; dissipation and even some mild, mostly unintentional heresy; and a completely moralistic version of the Catholic faith and identity experience.[34]

Given the inadequacy of pistic and charismatic experiences to define the Catholic identity, van Beeck suggests that they must be corrected and complemented by what he calls the "mystical" experience, which is based upon the resurrection of Jesus. This mystical experience consists of two aspects: worship and witness. At the heart of both is the person of Jesus: "*The person of Jesus Christ alive in the Spirit is the source of the Christian identity-experience as well as the Christian experience of openness to the world.*"[35] As worship and witness, mystical experience defines the Catholic identity by its liturgical spirituality, its insistence on personal and communal prayer, and its commitment to ecumenism and evangelization.[36]

Though in basic agreement with van Beeck's proposals, I prefer to speak of the Catholic identity not in terms of defining and emphasizing boundaries and

---

[32] Frans Jozef van Beeck, *Catholic Identity after Vatican II: Three Types of Faith in the One Church* (Chicago: Loyola University Press, 1983).

[33] Ibid., 24–34.

[34] Ibid., 34–45.

[35] Van Beeck, *Catholic Identity After Vatican II*, 57. Original italics.

[36] Ibid., 61–71. Daniel Donovan, in *Distinctively Catholic: An Exploration of Catholic Identity* (New York: Paulist Press, 1997), devotes the last chapter to the theme of being a Catholic today. As to what makes a Catholic today, Donovan singles out our common

differences that distinguish Catholics from other Christian and non-Christian believers. This approach concentrates on the characteristics that Catholics (allegedly) alone possess. It is a self-identity over *against* the others. It is "us versus them." Given the recent remarkable progress in ecumenical dialogue, doctrines and structures that at one time were regarded as exclusive properties of the Catholic church (for example, the Eucharist and the Petrine ministry) are today fast becoming common possessions of all mainline Christian churches.[37]

Rather than *differentiation* and *exclusiveness*, I conceive Catholic identity as *intensification* and *deepening* of those deep structures that are pervasive in the Catholic church's faith and practice and that are possessed in common with other Christians and even with non-Christian believers. In this way, ecumenical and interreligious dialogues do not constitute a threat to the preservation of the Catholic identity; rather, they provide necessary means and opportunities for deepening and intensifying the Catholic identity, not over against the others but with them.[38] This way of perceiving and forming the Catholic identity offers the means to maintain a healthy and creative tension between the four sets of apparently self-contradictory elements described at the end of the last section of this chapter: between the Vatican's recognition of the ecclesial nature of non-Catholic Christian denominations and its affirmation of the dynamic fullness of the Catholic church as a community of salvation; between Vatican II's call for dialogue with other world religions in the context of religious pluralism and its profession in the truth of the Christian faith; between recognizing the valid concerns of communal Catholics and insisting on the necessity of full and active participation in the life of the Catholic community; between the spiritual and institutional, the invisible and visible aspects of the church.[39]

Religious educators, needless to say, are privileged to participate in the task of forming and nurturing this kind of Catholic identity in an age when it is increasingly common to encounter a self-proclaimed Catholic-Protestant-Orthodox-Jewish-Buddhist-Hindu-Muslim-New Age.

---

humanity, which is shared with others; an affirmation of the presence and action of God in the life and destiny of Jesus; living in the presence of God; participating actively in the life of the church, especially its sacramental and eucharistic life; giving priority to grace; living a vocation of discipleship; celebrating forgiveness and reconciliation; and practicing the virtue of hope. However, for Donovan, "what is perhaps most distinctive of us as Catholics is our membership in the church with everything that it involves in terms of liturgy and sacraments, of mutual help and support" (210).

[37] See the ground-breaking Lima document *Baptism, Eucharist, and Ministry* (Geneva: World Council of Churches, 1982).

[38] For a discussion of the logic of interreligious dialogue that is open to the truths and values of other religions and remains faithful to the claims of one's faith, see Chapter 5 herein; see also Peter C. Phan, "Are There Other 'Saviors' for Other People? A Discussion of the Problem of the Universal Significance and Uniqueness of Jesus the Christ," in *Christianity and the Wider Ecumenism*, ed. Peter C. Phan, 163–80 (New York: Paragon House, 1990).

[39] For a discussion of the tension between religious pluralism and theology and religious education, see Chapter 1 herein; see also Peter C. Phan, "Multiculturalism, Church, and the University," *Religious Education* 90/1 (1994): 8–29.

4

Multiple Religious Belonging

OPPORTUNITIES AND CHALLENGES FOR THEOLOGY AND CHURCH

It is a telling sign of the times that a recent American college graduate, when asked about her religious identity, gave the following answer with an easy laugh: "Methodist, Taoist, Native American, Quaker, Russian Orthodox, and Jew."[1] Whether her "multiple religious belonging" or "hyphenated religious identity" is a thoughtful and coherent response to the contemporary situation of religious pluralism or a self-indulgent, free-floating, cafeteria-style potpourri of mutually incompatible spiritualities, there is no doubt that multiple religious belonging is no longer a rare phenomenon in the West and that it brings serious challenges as well as enriching opportunities not only to Christian identity but also to interreligious dialogue and Christian mission in general.[2]

In this chapter I first examine the phenomenon of multiple religious belonging and its underlying theological presuppositions. Second, I delineate some of the features that have accompanied such multiple religious belonging and that make it fruitful for contemporary church life. Finally, I highlight a few implications that multiple religious belonging will have on theological education.[3]

MULTIPLE RELIGIOUS BELONGING
AND A THEOLOGY OF RELIGIOUS PLURALISM

Before examining the phenomenon of multiple religious belonging and its undergirding theological principles, it is helpful to state briefly what is meant by this expression. The phenomenon under review does not refer simply to the process known today as inculturation, whereby the gospel, or more concretely, a particular form of Christianity (usually the Western one, not some pure,

---

[1] Diane Winston, "Campuses Are a Bellwether for Society's Religious Revival," *The Chronicle of Higher Education* (January 16, 1998), A60.

[2] On the implications of multiple religious belonging for Catholic identity, see Chapter 3 herein.

[3] Among recent literature on multiple religious belonging, one work in particular deserves mention: Catherine Cornille, ed., *Many Mansions? Multiple Religious Belonging and Christian Identity* (Maryknoll, N.Y.: Orbis Books, 2002).

acultural Christianity that of course does not exist) encounters a particular group
of people, assumes their language and culture as its modes of self-realization
and expression, transforming and, when necessary, correcting them with Christian beliefs and values, and at the same time is enriched in turn by them. Such a
process, explicitly endorsed by the Roman Magisterium in our days, is unavoidable and should not be considered controversial, at least in principle. Historically, it has taken place in different ways ever since Christianity moved out of
its Jewish matrix into the Hellenistic, Roman, and Teutonic worlds, or into what
is commonly designated by the general term *Western world*. Today this process
of inculturation is extended, as a matter of principle, to cultures other than Western, in particular African and Asian. In this sense one may and must be both
Christian and Vietnamese, for example, or whatever cultural group one belongs
to. In other words, a person need not and must not renounce his or her cultural
identity and traditions upon becoming a Christian.

Nor does multiple religious belonging refer to interreligious dialogue in which
one engages not only in theological discussion with the followers of other religions but also in sharing life with them in an open and neighborly spirit, collaborating with them in works for integral development and liberation, and participating in religious experiences of prayer and contemplation.[4] Indeed,
interreligious dialogue, even in that form, militates against multiple religious
belonging because it requires as a matter of methodology that participants in
interreligious or interfaith dialogue preserve their distinctive religious doctrines
and practices and show how these are not only similar to but also different from
those of other religions.

Going beyond inculturation and interreligious dialogue, albeit intimately related to these two activities, multiple religious belonging or hyphenated religious identity refers to the fact that some Christians believe that it is possible
and even necessary not only to accept in theory certain doctrines or practices of
other religions and to incorporate them, perhaps in modified form, into Christianity, but also to adopt and live in their personal lives the beliefs, moral rules,
rituals, and monastic practices of religious traditions other than Christianity,
perhaps even in the midst of the community of the devotees of other religions.

The question about multiple religious belonging is twofold. First, must one
abandon altogether the practice of one's former religion when becoming a Christian, supposing that one was a devotee of such religion, and if not, why not and
to what purposes? Second, if one is already a Christian, is it theologically possible to adopt the beliefs and practices of other religions in one's life? In other
words, as Catherine Cornille puts it, "A heightened and widespread consciousness of religious pluralism has presently left the religious person with the choice

---

[4] For this fourfold dialogue of life, action, theological exchange, and religious experience, see the Pontifical Council for Inter-Religious Dialogue and the Congregation for
the Evangelization of Peoples, *Dialogue and Proclamation* (May 19, 1991), no. 42. The
English text is available in *Redemption and Dialogue: Reading* Redemptoris Missio
and Dialogue and Proclamation, ed. William Burrows (Maryknoll, N.Y.: Orbis Books,
1993).

not only of *which* religion, but also of *how many* religions she or he might belong to. More and more individuals confess to being partly Jewish and partly Buddhist, or partly Christian and partly Hindu, or fully Christian and fully Buddhist."[5]

Two further remarks on multiple religious belonging are in order. First, it may be helpful to distinguish, as Claude Jeffré does, between "multiple belonging" and "double belonging."[6] In contrast to the latter, which is the fruit of a paradigmatic shift in the theology of religions and of inculturation, the former is a contemporary, postmodern form of syncretism in which a person looks upon various religions as a supermarket from which, like a consumer, one selects at one's discretion and pleasure whatever myth and doctrine, ethical practice and ritual, and meditation and healing technique best suits the temperament and needs of one's body and mind, without regard to their truth values and mutual compatibilities.

While such a spirituality must be respected as a serious personal quest for meaning in a secular world and a challenging question to the continuing relevance and credibility of Christianity as a religion, it must be admitted that too often this New Age movement represents the unbridled consumerism, excessive individualism, and the loss of the collective memory that are characteristic of modernity and its twin, globalization. Though I use the two expressions *multiple belonging* and *double belonging* in this chapter interchangeably, I reject as incompatible with the Christian faith the kind of New Age syncretism described above, which has justly been called "believing without belonging" (Grace Davie), "nebulous esoteric mysticism" (François Champion), and "Nietzschean neo-paganism" (Claude Geffré).

Second, multiple religious belonging emerges as a theological *problem* only in religions that demand an absolute and exclusive commitment on the part of their adherents to their founders and/or faiths. This seems to be the case with the so-called religions of the Book, namely, Judaism, Christianity, and Islam. These three religions consider themselves not only mutually incompatible but also irreconcilable with any other religion whatsoever, so that "conversion" to any one of them is often celebrated with an external ritual signaling a total abjuration of all previous religious allegiances.

Not so with most other religions, particularly in Asia. In Asian countries such as China, Japan, Korea, Vietnam, India, Nepal, and Sri Lanka, multiple religious belonging is the rule rather than the exception, at least on the popular level. Indeed, the very expression *multiple religious belonging* as understood in the West, that is, as two or more memberships in particular systems of beliefs and practices within bounded communities, is a misnomer in Asia, where religions are considered not as mutually exclusive religious organizations but as having specialized functions responding, according to a division of labor as it

---

[5] Catherine Cornille, "Introduction: The Dynamics of Multiple Belonging," in Cornille, *Many Mansions?* 1.

[6] See Claude Jeffré, "Double Belonging and the Originality of Christianity as a Religion," in Cornille, *Many Mansions?* 93–94.

were, to the different needs and circumstances in the course of a person's life. Such is the case, for instance, with Shinto and Buddhism in Japan.[7] Thus, Asian people may well go to pray and worship in pagodas, temples, and shrines, without much consideration to what religions these sacred places belong, but depending on whether the local deity or spirit is reputed to grant a favor tailored to one's particular needs and circumstances. Furthermore, at times a religion that is not by nature exclusive becomes so in reaction to the claims of superiority made by Christianity, as happened to Buddhism in Sri Lanka in the nineteenth century, and then the relationship between the two religions becomes one of competition rather than peaceful coexistence.[8]

In sum, according to Catherine Cornille, "a rough-and-ready axiom" in matters of religious belonging can be formulated as follows: "The more encompassing a religion's claim to efficacy and truth, the more problematic the possibility of multiple religious belonging. Conversely, it thus seems that the idea of belonging to more than one religion can be tolerated only when and where a religion has accepted the complementarity of religions."[9]

The question then arises whether there is a theology of religions that justifies the possibility of multiple religious belonging for Christians. Such a theology

---

[7] See Jan Van Bragt, "Multiple Religious Belonging of the Japanese People," in Cornille, *Many Mansions?* 7–19. Van Bragt shows that "for most Japanese in history the allegiance to the Buddhist-Shinto conglomerate—and thus, in a sense, to both Buddhism and Shinto—did not have to be accompanied by a sense of multiple belonging. The composite religious system in which they were born and which served equally the legitimation of the political system and the social integration of the nation did not present them with a real choice entailing the rejecting of an alternative. If choice there was, it was rather in the sense of the possibility of different *specializations* on the basis of the acceptance of the system as a whole" (13). This does not mean that in Japan there has been no religious movement with exclusivist claims. For example, as Van Bragt notes, the school of Nichiren (1222–82) insists on the sole worship of the perennial Buddha Sakyamuni, as embodied in the *Lotus Sutra*, and on the sole practice of the *daikimu*, that is, the recitation of the title of the *Lotus Sutra*, "Namu myoho renge kyo," while the True Pure Land school of Shinran (1173–1262) chooses the Buddha Amida as the exclusive object of worship and reliance and advocates the *nembutsu*, that is, the recitation of Amida's name (*Namu Amida Butsu*) as the only practice leading to salvation (see 13–15).

[8] See Elisabeth J. Harris, "Double Belonging in Sri Lanka: Illusion or Liberating Path?" in Cornille, *Many Mansions?* 76–80. Harris points out that Protestant missionaries to Sri Lanka in the nineteenth century found that dual religious belonging posed no problem to the native Buddhists, for whom "being half Christian and half Buddhist is far better than being either decidedly Christian or Buddhist" (77). It was only after Buddhism was attacked by Protestant missionaries as nihilistic atheism and as a false religion that Sri Lankan Buddhists decreed that one could not be Buddhist and Christian at the same time. This Buddhist Revival became known as "Protestant Buddhism" because it was a protest against Christianity and appropriated from Protestant Christianity several of its forms and practices, in particular its claim of superiority and exclusivism: "Buddhism was pictured by later revivalists as irretrievably different from Christianity and irrevocably superior to it because of its non-theistic nature, its compatibility with science, its rationality, its optimism, and its ethics, each assertion being a direct challenge to one of the accusations made by the missionaries" (80).

[9] Cornille, "Introduction, 2.

must on the one hand maintain the *uniqueness* and *universality* of Jesus Christ as savior and the *singularity* of Christianity, as these truths are confessed by the Christian faith, and on the other hand offer an acceptable account for the complementarity and convergence of all religions, including Christianity.[10] It is neither necessary nor possible to give a detailed exposition of such a theology here. Suffice it to say that for Christians the possibility of a hyphenated religious identity would seem to depend on the acceptability of at least the following assertions.[11]

1. That Jesus is the unique and universal savior does not exclude the possibility of non-Christians being saved.[12]

2. Nor does this fact exclude the possibility of non-Christian religions functioning as "ways of salvation" insofar as they contain "elements of truth and of grace."[13]

---

[10] The terms *uniqueness*, *universality*, and *singularity* are emphasized here because they need to be interpreted very carefully so as not to connote exclusivism, as will be seen below.

[11] One very helpful presentation of contemporary theologies of religions is Paul Knitter, *Introducing Theologies of Religions* (Maryknoll, N.Y.: Orbis Books, 2002). Knitter divides them into four models, which he labels "replacement," "fulfillment," "mutuality," and "acceptance." The first three models correspond roughly to the older, more common categories of exclusivism, inclusivism, and pluralism popularized by Alan Race. The lines of the theology of religions I present here crisscross over the last three models described by Knitter and have much in common with Jacques Dupuis's *Toward a Christian Theology of Religious Pluralism* (Maryknoll, N.Y.: Orbis Books, 1977) and *Christianity and the Religions: From Confrontation to Dialogue* (Maryknoll, N.Y.: Orbis Books, 2002). For a brief and lucid summary of his view, with particular application to the issue of multiple religious belonging, see Jacques Dupuis, "Christianity and Religions: Complementarity and Convergence," in Cornille, *Many Mansions?* 61–75.

[12] The possibility of salvation for non-Christian believers and nonbelievers, with requisite conditions, is explicitly affirmed by Vatican II (*LG*, no. 16).

[13] *AG,* no. 9. Whether Vatican II affirmed that non-Christian religions are "ways of salvation" is a matter of debate. Karl Rahner and Gavin D'Costa held that Vatican II left the issue open. For Bishop Piero Rossano, who for years worked in the Secretariat for Non-Christian Religions, Vatican II did affirm that salvation reaches men and women in and through their religions, and not in spite of them. It may be noted that Karl Rahner himself subscribed to this opinion. His basic argument is that humans are historical, embodied, and social beings who are necessarily conditioned and influenced by their environments, among which religions play a key role. If Christians need the embodiments of God's grace in sacraments to be saved, so do non-Christians, and these embodiments are found in their religions. Two recent statements of the Magisterium deserve special notice. Pope John Paul II declares that the Holy Spirit is present "not only in individuals but also in society and history, peoples, cultures, and religions" (*Redemptoris Missio* [*RM*], no. 28). *Dialogue and Proclamation* says that because of "the active presence of God through his Word" and "the universal presence of the Spirit" not only in persons outside the church but also in their religions, it is "in the sincere practice of what is good in their own religious traditions . . . that the members of other religions correspond positively to God's invitation and receive salvation" (no. 29). It must be pointed out the theory that non-Christian religions are "ways of salvation" cannot be taught as Christian doctrine, but it is at least a *sententia communis* and *theologice certa*, and certainly not *temeraria* and *scandalosa*.

3. These two possibilities are realized by the activities of both the Logos and the Holy Spirit. The Logos, though identical with Jesus of Nazareth, is not exhaustively embodied in Jesus of Nazareth, who was spatially and temporally limited and therefore could not exhaustively express the divine saving reality in his human words and deeds. There is a "distinction-in-identity" or "identity-in-distinction" between the unincarnate *(asarkos)* Logos and Jesus Christ. Hence, the activities of the Logos, though inseparable from those of Jesus, are also distinct from and go beyond Jesus' activities, before, during, and after the incarnation.[14]

In addition, the Holy Spirit, though intimately united with the Logos, is distinct from him and operates salvifically beyond him and "blows where he wills" (Jn 3:8).Thus, God's saving presence through God's Word and Spirit is not limited to Judeo-Christian history but is extended to the whole of human history and may be seen especially in the sacred books, rituals, moral teachings, and spiritual practices of all religions. In this way what the Holy Spirit says and does may be truly different from, though not contradictory to, what the Logos says and does, and what the Logos and the Spirit do and say in non-Christian religions may be truly different from, though not contradictory to, what Jesus said and did.[15]

4. Religious pluralism, then, is not just a matter of fact but also a matter of principle.[16] That is, non-Christian religions may be seen as part of the plan of divine providence and endowed with a particular role in the history of salvation. They are not merely a "preparation" for, "stepping stones" toward, or "seeds" of Christianity and destined to be "fulfilled" by it. Rather, they have their own

---

[14] This thesis is not the same as the one rejected by *Dominus Iesus* (*DI*) (August 2000), namely, "the theory of the limited, incomplete, or imperfect character of the revelation of Jesus Christ, which would be complementary to that found in other religions" (no. 6). It does not claim "the truth about God cannot be grasped and manifested in its globality and completeness by any historical religion, neither by Christianity nor by Jesus Christ" (no. 6). Rather, it says that God, being Absolute Mystery, cannot by definition be exhaustively manifested and grasped by any human and therefore finite means, be these means used by Jesus or Christianity or any other religion. Otherwise the God who is revealed by Jesus or Christianity or any other religion would not be God but an idol. This point seems to be conceded by *DI* itself, when it says that "they [the words, deeds, and entire historical event of Jesus] possess in themselves the definitiveness and completeness of the revelation of God's salvific ways, *even if the depth of the divine mystery in itself remains transcendent and inexhaustible*" (no. 6, emphasis added). For a critical evaluation of *DI*, see Stephen J. Pope and Charles Helfling, eds., *Sic et Non: Encountering* Dominus Iesus (Maryknoll, N.Y.: Orbis Books, 2002), which also contains the English text of the declaration.

[15] Jacques Dupuis suggests that both a trinitarian Christology and a Spirit Christology are needed to explicate the mutual complementarity and convergence among all religions.

[16] It is to be noted that the expression "matter of fact" (*de facto*) and "matter of principle" (*de iure*) are not used in the sense rejected by *DI*, no. 4. Here, by "matter of principle" is meant simply the intrinsic value of non-Christian religions as ways of salvation in the one plan of God. It does not question any of the Christian claims listed in *DI*, no. 4.

autonomy and their proper roles as ways of salvation, at least for their adherents.

5. This autonomy of non-Christian religions detracts nothing from either the role of Jesus as the unique and universal savior or the Christian church as the sacrament of Christ's salvation. On the one hand, Christ's uniqueness is not exclusive or absolute but *constitutive* and *relational*.[17] That is, because the Christ-event belongs to and is the climax of God's plan of salvation, Christ is uniquely constitutive of salvation. Jesus' "constitutive uniqueness" means that he and only he "opens access to God for all people."[18] Moreover, because the non-Christian religions themselves are a part of God's plan of salvation, of which Christ is the culminating point, Christ and the non-Christian religions are related to one another. On the other hand, because the non-Christian religions possess an autonomous function in the history of salvation, different from that of Christianity, they and Christianity cannot be reduced to each other. However, being ways of salvation in God's plan, they are related to each other. Autonomy and relatedness are not mutually contradictory.

6. There is then a *reciprocal* relationship between Christianity and the other religions. Not only are the non-Christian religions complemented by Christianity, but Christianity is complemented by the other religions. In other words, the process of complementation, enrichment, and even correction is *two-way* or reciprocal. This reciprocity in no way endangers the faith confession that the church has received from Christ the fullness of revelation, since it is one thing to receive a perfect and unsurpassable gift and quite another to *understand* it fully and to *live* it completely. It is therefore only in dialogue with other religions that Christianity can come to a fuller realization of its own identity and mission and a better understanding of the unique revelation that it has received from Christ, and vice versa, other religions can achieve their full potential only in dialogue with one another and with Christianity.[19]

7. Furthermore, despite the fact that Christian faith proclaims that Jesus Christ is the fullness of revelation and the unique and universal savior, there is also a reciprocal relationship between him and other "savior figures" and non-Christian religions, since Jesus' uniqueness is not absolute but relational. In this sense Jesus' revelation and salvation are also "complemented" by God's self-revelation and

---

[17] *DI* makes a confusing statement that on the one hand recognizes the inclusiveness of Christ's saving work and on the other hand affirms that "Jesus Christ has a significance and a value for the human race and its history, which are unique and singular, proper to him alone, *exclusive*, universal, and absolute (no. 15, emphasis added). How can Jesus' significance and value be inclusive and exclusive at the same time?

[18] Dupuis, *Toward a Christian Theology of Religious Pluralism*, 387.

[19] This proposition is not contrary to the statement of *DI:* "It would be contrary to the faith to consider the Church as *one* way of salvation alongside those constituted by the other religions, seen as complementary to the Church or substantially equivalent to her, even if these are said to be converging with the Church toward the eschatological kingdom of God" (no. 21). The complementarity asserted here is placed in the context of the "asymmetrical" nature of the relationship between Christianity and the other religions as explained in thesis 8 below.

redemption manifested in other savior figures and non-Christian religions. In this context it is useful to remember that Jesus did not and could not reveal everything to his disciples and that it is the Holy Spirit that will lead them to "the complete truth" (Jn 16:12–13). There is nothing to prevent one from thinking that the Holy Spirit will lead the church to the complete truth through the dialogue with other religions in which the Spirit is actively present.[20]

8. Finally, from what has been said about the Christian claim that Jesus is the unique and universal savior and about the church as the sacrament of salvation, it is clear that the complementarity between them and other savior figures and religions, though complementary, is, to use Dupuis's expression, "asymmetrical."[21] This asymmetricality is required by the claim of the Christian faith that Jesus is the Logos made flesh and represents the climax or the decisive moment of God's dealings with humankind. What this asymmetricality intends to affirm is that according to the Christian faith, Jesus mediates God's gift of salvation to humanity in an overt, explicit, and fully visible way, which is now continued in Christianity, whereas other savior figures and religions, insofar as they mediate God's salvation to their followers, do so through the power of the Logos and the Spirit. In this sense Jesus may be said to be the "one mediator" and the other savior figures and non-Christian religions participating mediators or "participated mediations."[22]

THE DYNAMICS OF MULTIPLE RELIGIOUS BELONGING

Given this model of theology of religions (inclusive pluralism[23]), which is gaining widespread acceptance, it is not difficult to see why multiple religious belonging is not only possible but also desirable. If non-Christian religions contain "elements of truth and of grace" and if they may be considered ways of salvation from whose doctrinal teachings, sacred texts, moral practices, monastic traditions, and rituals and worship Christianity can and should benefit through dialogue, then there should be no theological objection and canonical censure against someone wishing to be a Christian and at same time to follow some doctrinal teachings and religious practices of, for example, Buddhism or Confucianism or Hinduism, as long as these are not patently contradictory to Christian faith

---

[20] Of course, this thesis does not affirm that there are two different "economies of salvation," that of Christ and that of the Spirit, which *DI* rightly rejects (see nos. 9–12). But affirming "the unicity of the salvific economy willed by the One and Triune God" (no. 11) does not prevent one from saying that Jesus and the Spirit can and do work in different ways and in different times and places.

[21] Dupuis, "Christianity and Religions," 65; Dupuis, *Christianity and the Religions*, 257–58.

[22] The language of "participated mediation" is used in *RM,* no. 5: "Although participated forms of mediation of different kinds and degrees are not excluded, they acquire meaning and value *only* from Christ's own mediation, and they cannot be understood as parallel or complementary to his." For further reflections on mediated participation, see Dupuis, *Christianity and the Religions*, 163–94.

[23] "Inclusive pluralism" or "pluralistic inclusivism" is the expression used by Jacques Dupuis to describe his theology of religions.

and morals. Whether that person should describe himself or herself as a Buddhist Christian, or Confucian Christian, or Hindu Christian, with *Buddhist, Confucian,* or *Hindu* functioning as a qualifier modifying the primary Christian identity rather than the other way around, is a matter for discussion below.

Before elaborating on the dynamics of multiple religious belonging and on its challenges and opportunities for the church, three observations are in order. First, it must be acknowledged that, historically, double religious belonging was the common form of life of the earliest Christians. As is evidenced from the book of Acts, they maintained both their newfound faith in the lordship of the risen Christ and their inherited Jewish beliefs and practices: "They went to the temple area together every day, while in their homes they broke bread" (Acts 3:46). Apparently, such double religious belonging did not cause any anxious soul-searching or theological qualms. It was only when some people came from Judea to Antioch with the teaching that unless circumcision is practiced, salvation is impossible (see Acts 15:1) that the problem of being a Jew and a Christian at the same time was broached. But even the so-called Council of Jerusalem did not rule out the possibility of a Jewish Christian/Christian Jew continuing to practice Judaism; it only refused to impose the Mosaic law on the Gentile Christians. It was only toward the end of the first century that, for a number of reasons, both theological and non-theological, Christianity had to define itself as a religious entity distinct and separate from and even superior to Judaism. In turn, Judaism rejected its younger sibling as an acceptable sect within itself. Then the possibility of being both Jew and Christian at the same time became a less likely option, and as converts to Christianity came almost exclusively from the Greco-Roman world, that option vanished.

In hindsight, the disappearance of Jewish Christianity/Christian Judaism proved to be a tragic loss to both Judaism and Christianity, as the subsequent history of bitter hatred and the "teaching of contempt"—mainly on the part of Christianity—is a sad proof. Perhaps a retrieval of the earliest form of Christianity, prior to the mutual condemnation and diatribe between Judaism and Christianity, will prove helpful in delineating a possible form of double religious identity not only between Judaism and Christianity but also in general.[24]

Second, in this chapter I leave aside the efforts of non-Christians to acknowledge the moral excellence of Jesus and the relevance of his teachings for their lives either without a personal commitment to him (for example, Mohandas K. Gandhi [1869–1948][25] or the Vietnamese Buddhist monk Thich Nhat Hanh [1926–][26]) or with a personal commitment to Christ but without accepting the

---

[24] On Jewish Christianity, the best evidence is the *Pseudo-Clementines*, a fourth-century work with second-century sources.

[25] See M. K. Gandhi, *Christian Missions* (Ahmedabad: Navajivan Publishing House, 1941); idem, *The Message of Jesus Christ* (Bombay: Bharatiya Vidya Bhawan, 1963). It is well known that Gandhi was much impressed by Jesus' teaching in the Sermon on the Mount.

[26] See Thich Nhat Hanh, *Living Buddha, Living Christ* (New York: Riverhead Books, 1995). He writes: "Jesus is not only our Lord, but He is also our Father, our Teacher, our Brother, and our Self" (44). However, he objects to John Paul II's statement that "Christ is absolutely original and absolutely unique": "The idea behind the statement, however,

church (for example, Keshub Chunder Sen [1838–84],[27] Sarvepalli Radhakrishnan [1888–1975],[28] or Swami Akhilananda [1894–1962][29]), since these are not, strictly speaking, instances of multiple religious belonging. Nor shall I consider the attempts of converts from non-Christian religions to Christianity to retain their former religious identity (for example, Manilal C. Parekh [1885–1967][30] or Brahmabandhav Upadhyaya [1861–1907][31]), since even in these cases there was only a weak or highly critical association with Christianity as an institution.[32] Rather, in discussing the dynamics of multiple religious belonging I focus on the

---

is the notion that Christianity provides the only way of salvation and all other religious traditions are of no use. This attitude excludes dialogue and fosters religious intolerance and discrimination" (193). For an introduction to Thich Nhat Hanh, see Sister Annabel Laity, "If You Want Peace, You Can Have Peace," in *Thich Nhat Hanh: Essential Writings*, ed. Robert Ellsberg, 1–16 (Maryknoll, N.Y.: Orbis Books, 2001).

[27] See Keshub Chunder Sen, *Lectures in India*, 2 vols. (London: Cassell, 1901–04). Keshub had a deep personal feeling for Christ and sometimes called himself *Jesus Das* (slave of Jesus), though he never converted. In his famous lecture "That Marvelous Mystery—The Trinity" (1882) Keshub gave an original interpretation of the Trinity, which is, however, basically modalist.

[28] See S. Radhakrishnan, *The Hindu View of Life* (London: Allen and Unwin, 1926); idem, *An Idealist View of Life* (London: Allen and Unwin, 1937); and idem, *Eastern Religions and Western Thought* (London: Allen and Unwin, 1939).

[29] See Swami Akhilananda, *The Hindu View of Christ* (New York: Philosophical Library, 1949). For Akhilananda, Christ is primarily an *avatara*, that is, an utterly illuminated soul with a full awareness of its divinity and therefore realizing in his life the two great aphorisms of Hinduism: *Aham brahmasmi* ("I am the Brahman") and *Tattvamasi* ("You are That [the Brahman]").

[30] See M. C. Parekh, *A Hindu's Portrait of Jesus* (Rajkot, Gujarat: 1953). Parekh came under the influence of Keshub Chunder Sen and was baptized in the Anglican Church in Bombay in 1918. For Parekh, Jesus announced a spiritual rather than secular kingdom and now dwells in us in spirit, leading us to God. A Hindu can have such a spiritual experience while remaining a Hindu, without a need to become a Christian.

[31] Brahmabandhav Upadhyaya, whose birth name is Bhavani Charan Bannerjee, was first baptized into the Anglican Church in 1891 but later became a Roman Catholic. He espoused a high Christology, confessing that Jesus is the very incarnation of God and not just an *avatar*. He promoted the use of the philosophy of Sankara to express the Christian faith, the recognition of the Vedas as the Indian Old Testament, and the establishment of an Indian monastic order. He edited a journal, *Sophia*, to disseminate his proposals. In 1902 he went to the Vatican to promote his views but was unsuccessful. After his return he moved away from active contact with the church and became more active in the national movement for political freedom. See B. Animananda, *The Blade: Life and Work of Brahmabandhav Upadhyaya* (Calcutta: Roy and Son, 1947).

[32] For the acknowledgment of Christ by the Indian Renaissance or Neo-Hinduism, see M. M. Thomas, *The Acknowledged Christ of the Indian Renaissance* (London: SCM Press, 1969) and Stanley Samartha, *The Hindu Response to the Unbound Christ* (Madras: Christian Literature Society, 1974). Jacques Dupuis discerns six different types of Christology among these figures of the Indian Renaissance: the *ethical* model of Jesus as the perfect symbol of nonviolence (Gandhi), the *devotional* model of Jesus as the perfect union between humanity and God (K. C. Sen), the *philosophical* model of Jesus as the highest stage of humanity's evolution toward its self-realization (S. Radhakrishnan), the *theological* model of Jesus as an *avatara* or a manifestation of the supreme Brahman (Swami Akhilananda), the *ascetical* model of Jesus as the extraordinary yogi (M. C. Parekh), and the *mystical* model of Jesus as a guru and friend. See Jacques Dupuis, *Jesus Christ at the Encounter of World Religions* (Maryknoll, N.Y.: Orbis Books, 1991), 18–45.

efforts of Christians to "go over" to other religions while keeping and even deepening their Christian identity. Or, to use the famous self-describing words of Raimon Panikkar: "I 'left' as a Christian, 'found myself' a Hindu, and I 'return' as a Buddhist, without having ceased to be a Christian."[33]

Third, a productive way to discuss the dynamics of multiple religious belonging is to start neither from an abstract consideration of the doctrinal compatibility or lack of it between the various doctrines and practices of Christianity and those of other religions nor from sociological and psychological investigations of the phenomenon of double religious identity, useful though these may be. Rather, as Jacques Dupuis has pointed out, a fruitful method would be to reflect "on the concrete experience of the pioneers who have relentlessly endeavored to combine in their own life their Christian commitment and another faith experience."[34]

Space does not permit a detailed recounting of the experiences of the Christian pioneers of multiple religious belonging, among whom the names of individuals such as French Benedictine Henri Le Saux, also known as Swami Abhishiktananda (1910–73),[35] German Japanese Jesuit Hugo M. Enomiya-Lassalle (1898–1990),[36] American Cistercian Thomas Merton (1915–68),[37] English Benedictine Bede Griffiths (1906–93),[38] Spanish Indian priest Raimon Panikkar (1918–),[39] and more recently, Sri Lankan Oblate Michael Rodrigo

---

[33] Raimon Panikkar, *The Intra-religious Dialogue* (New York: Paulist Press, 1978), 2.

[34] Dupuis, "Christianity and Religions," 69.

[35] The following works by Abhishiktananda may be noted: *Prayer* (Delhi: ISPCK, 1972); *Guru and Disciple* (London: SPCK, 1974); *Saccidananda: A Christian Approach to Advaitic Experience* (Delhi: ISPCK, 1974; rev. ed., 1984); *Hindu-Christian Meeting-Point* (Delhi: ISPCK, 1976); *The Secret of Arunachala* (Delhi: ISPCK, 1979); *Intériorité et révélation: Essais théologiques* (Sisteron: Editions Présence, 1982); *The Eyes of Light* (Denville, N.J.: Dimension Books, 1983); *The Further Shore* (Delhi: ISPCK, 1984); *La montée au fond du coeur: Le journal intime du moine chrétien-sannyasi hindou* (Paris: Oeil, 1986).

[36] Enomiya-Lassalle's most famous book is *Zen—Weg zur Erleuchtung: Einführung und Anleitung* (Freiburg im Briesgau: Herder Taschenbuch, 1992 [1960]). On Enomiya-Lassalle, see Werner G. Jeanrond, "Belonging or Identity? Christian Faith in a Multi-Religious World," in Cornille, *Many Mansions?* 111–15; and Ursula Baartz, *Hugo M. Enomiya-Lassalle: Ein Leben zwischen den Welten* (Zurich and Düssendorf: Benziger Verlag, 1998).

[37] Of Thomas Merton's numerous works, see *The Asian Journal of Thomas Merton* (New York: New Directions, 1975) and *Thoughts on the East* (New York: New Directions, 1995).

[38] Bede Griffiths's important books include *The Golden String* (Springfield, Ill.: Templegate Publishers, 1980 [1954]); *Vedanta and Christian Faith* (London: Dawn Horse Press, 1973); *Return to the Center* (London: Collins, 1976); *The Marriage of East and West: A Sequel to the Golden String* (London: Collins, 1982); *The Cosmic Revelation* (Bangalore: Asian Trading Company, 1985); *Christ in India* (Bangalore: Asian Trading Company, 1986); *A New Vision of Reality: Western Science, Eastern Mysticism and Christian Faith* (London: Collins, 1989).

[39] Of Raimon Panikkar's numerous publications, see *The Unknown Christ of Hinduism* (London: Darton, Longman and Todd, 1964); *Religionen und die Religion* (Munich:

(1927–87)[40] and Sri Lankan Jesuit Aloysius Pieris (1934–)[41] figure prominently. The religions that these practitioners of double religious belonging attempted to learn from and practice are predominantly Hinduism (Abhishikananda, Griffiths, and Panikkar), Zen Buddhism (Enomiya-Lassalle and Merton), and Theravada Buddhism (Rodrigo and Pieris). Of course, they did not espouse the same method of interreligious sharing, and the measure in which each immersed himself in these religions varied widely.

What is being attempted here is to create a composite sketch out of these divergent experiences of multiple religious belonging and to discern therein the challenges and opportunities that it poses for the church. The intention is not to derive from these experiences some kind of a normative pattern to serve as a model for an ideal multiple religious identity. Despite their variety and richness, these experiences are, as will be noted below, still too limited and even narrow to accommodate the wide-ranging and diverse forms of multiple religious belonging available today.

1. The first common element in these experiences of multiple religious belonging is that they did not originate in some kind of uncertainty about Christian identity or spiritual crisis or even discontent with the Catholic Church, much less in ignorance of the Christian tradition. On the contrary, all of the

---

Hüber Verlag, 1965); *L'homme qui deviant Dieu* (Paris: Aubier, 1969); *Le mystère du culte dans l'hindouisme et le christianisme* (Paris: Cerf, 1970); *Salvation in Christ: Concreteness and Universality. The Supername* (Santa Barbara, Calif.: University of California Press, 1972); *The Trinity and the Religious Experience of Man* (London: Darton, Longman and Todd, 1973); *The Intrareligious Dialogue* (New York: Paulist Press, 1978); *Myth, Faith and Hermeneutics: Cross-Cultural Studies* (New York: Paulist Press, 1979); *The Unknown Christ of Hinduism: Towards an Ecumenical Christophany*, rev., enl. ed. (Maryknoll, N.Y.: Orbis Books, 1981); *The Silence of God: The Answer of the Buddha* (Maryknoll, N.Y.: Orbis Books, 1989); *The Cosmotheandric Experience: Emerging Religious Consciousness* (Maryknoll, N.Y.: Orbis Books, 1993). For a critical study of Panikkar, see Joseph Brabhu, ed., *The Intercultural Challenge of Raimon Panikkar* (Maryknoll, N.Y.: Orbis Books, 1996).

[40] See Michael Rodrigo, *Fr. Mike and His Thought*, vol. 1, *The Moral Passover from Selfishness to Selflessness in Christianity and the Other Religions in Sri Lanka (Ceylon)*, ed. Sr. Milburga Fernando, *Logos* 27/3 (September 1988); *Tissues of Life and Death: Selected Poems of Fr. Michael Rodrigo O.M.I.*, ed. Elisabeth J. Harris, *Quest* 95 (June 1988).

[41] Aloysius Pieris's works include *An Asian Theology of Liberation* (Maryknoll, N.Y.: Orbis Books, 1988); *Love Meets Wisdom: A Christian Experience of Buddhism* (Maryknoll, N.Y.: Orbis Books, 1988); *Fire and Water: Basic Issues in Asian Buddhism and Christianity* (Maryknoll, N.Y.: Orbis Books, 1996); *God's Reign for God's Poor: A Return to the Jesus Formula: A Critical Evaluation of Contemporary Reformulations of the Mission Manifestation in Roman Catholic Theology in Recent Jesuit Documents* (Kelaniya: Tulana Research Centre, 1999); *Mysticism of Service: A Short Treatise on Spirituality with a Pauline-Ignatian Focus on the Prayer-Life of Christian Activists* (Kelaniya: Tulana Research Centre, 2000). On Michael Rodrigo and Aloysius Pieris, see Elisabeth J. Harris, "Double Belonging in Sri Lanka: Illusion or Liberating Path?" in Cornille, *Many Mansions?* 76–92.

protagonists were well versed in Christian tradition, and several of them held doctorates in theology and were also prolific authors.[42]

Furthermore, none of them went in search of the spiritual riches of non-Christian religions because of doubts about the unique and universal role of Christ as the savior understood inclusively as explained above.[43] Rather, all were deeply committed to Jesus Christ as the person in whom God's salvation was mediated to them. Nor did they reject the church as an institution in which this divine salvation is sacramentalized, even though some of them, in particular Pieris, were critical of some of the church's teachings and practices.[44] Indeed, their love and loyalty to the church were unquestioned, and out of this love and loyalty they undertook interreligious sharing in order to enrich the church with the spiritual resources of other religions and in this way help it achieve its full self-realization. In sum, their religious quest was deeply rooted in their Christian faith; indeed, their Christian conviction that revelation and salvation, brought about by Jesus, are somehow present in other religious traditions set them on their journey of multiple religious belonging.

2. Because of this fundamental and prior commitment to the Christian faith, it seems that the primary identity of these practitioners of double belonging is Christian. In other words, they are Hindu Christians or Buddhist Christians, with *Christian* functioning as a substantive and the other religious specification as a qualifier, rather than the reverse. This is due to the fact that none of them was a convert from a non-Christian faith to Christianity; they were "born" Christian to begin with, though some of them, such as Griffiths and Merton, "rediscovered" Christianity after a period of staying away from it.

---

[42] This is in stark contrast to a great number of contemporary young Catholics who appear to be innocent of an accurate knowledge of even the basic beliefs of the Christian faith. Professors of theology in Catholic colleges and universities can readily testify to this lamentable condition.

[43] A statement by Abhishiktananda may be taken as representative: "Willy-nilly, I am profoundly attached to Christ Jesus, and hence to ecclesial *koinônia*. It is in him that 'mystery' has discovered itself to me since my awakening to myself and to the world. It is under his *image*, his *symbol*, that I know God, and that I know myself and the world of men. . . . For me, Jesus is my *Sadguru* [true Guru]. It is in him that God has appeared to me" (see Le Saux, *La montée au fond du coeur* [July 24, 1970], 385, quoted in Dupuis, *Jesus Christ at the Encounter of World Religions*, 7–80). Again, this is much at variance with the attitude of those who dabble in various religions because they believe that all religions express the same core religious experiences or are simply different paths to the same goal of self-realization.

[44] A statement by Bede Griffiths may be taken as representative: "For the divine mystery can only be approached by faith, and the dogmas and sacraments of the Church are the walls in which the gate of faith, which is 'heaven's gate,' is to be found. The moment we attempt to enter ourselves, to do without the Church, we shut ourselves out of the City. But when we learn to accept the dogmas and sacraments of the Church, then we can enter by faith into the heart of the mystery; we can pass through the sign to the thing signified, through the image to the reality" (*The Golden String*, 186). Once more, this ecclesial dimension is contrary to the "believing without belonging" posture that sociologists of religion have noted among a number of contemporary practitioners of multiple religious belonging in the West.

This is not to deny the possibility that converts from other religions may also define themselves primarily as Christian and secondarily as Hindu or Buddhist or Confucian or whatever. However, it is often the case that when conversions occur not as the result of a deep personal choice but because of nonreligious factors (for example, marriage or tribal allegiance), and where religion is deeply intertwined with culture, as is true of most Asian religions,[45] many converts would define themselves and, more important, think and behave primarily as Hindu, or Buddhist, or Confucian, or whatever, and only secondarily as Christian.

Furthermore, the question of the primacy of one religious tradition over another is not a matter that is settled once and for all; it continually fluctuates, depending on circumstances. Some of those mentioned above were more Christian when they lived in or returned to the West, while being more Hindu or Buddhist when they lived in Asia. Or they tended to represent the Christian tradition when in dialogue with non-Christians, and vice versa, they appeared more Hindu and Buddhist when explaining their experiences to Christians. Sometimes it is simply a matter of mutual complementarity. Joseph S. O'Leary mentions the fascinating case of the late Winston and Jocelyn King, who meditated together every morning, he as a Buddhist Christian, she as a Christian Buddhist.[46] Above all, as will be explained below, the double identity is an irreducible and unresolvable tension that must be held together throughout a person's life until, in the evocative words of Abhishiktananda, "dawn may arise."[47]

---

[45] Claude Geffré has offered a forceful reminder of this fact: "We are familiar enough with the official discourses proclaiming a plural identity simultaneously both fully Christian and wholly Indian, Chinese, or Japanese. But what would the Indian identity consist of outside of Hinduism? What would comprise the Chinese identity without the complex religious mixture of Taoism, Confucianism, and Buddhism? What is the Japanese identity apart from Zen Buddhism and the Shinto tradition?" ("Double Belonging and the Originality of Christianity as a Religion," 96). While fully agreeing with Geffré's remark on the inextricable union between religion and culture, especially in Asia, and hence on the person's identity as comprising both religion and culture, I resist identifying the Indian identity with Hinduism because this fails to recognize the presence of other religions in these countries and their oppression by the religion of the majority.

[46] See J. S. O'Leary, "Toward a Buddhist Interpretation of Christian Truth," in Cornille, *Many Mansions?* 29. Perhaps this fluctuation in religious identity may be illustrated by a comparison with a person who holds two passports or speaks two languages. One is born a citizen of a country (one's primary nationality), but by acquiring another passport one also acquires a secondary nationality and a set of other rights and privileges that one may or must exercise (for example, vote) depending on where one lives. Similarly, if a person is multilingual, one language may be considered the "mother tongue" (one's primary linguistic competence), which one speaks with greater fluency, while, if one lives abroad, one is constrained to speak a "foreign language" (one's secondary linguistic competence), which, if one's sojourn is long enough, one may know better and speak with greater fluency than the mother tongue.

[47] Abhishiktananda noted on December 5, 1970: "The best thing is, I think, to hold, even if in extreme tension, these two forms of a unique 'faith,' till dawn may arise." See his *Ascent to the Depth of the Heart: The Spiritual Diary (1948–73) of Swami Abhishiktananda (dom Henri Le Saux)* (Delhi: ISPCK, 1998), 19.

3. As will be seen below, while insisting that their interreligious sharing must occur predominantly in the areas of ethical and monastic practices and prayer and even mysticism, none of these pioneers belittled the necessity of an intellectual mastery of the intricate doctrines and histories of non-Christian religions. Indeed, several of them were highly competent in the classical languages of these religions and intimately familiar with their sacred texts and even held a doctorate in Hinduism or Buddhism (for example, Rodrigo and Pieris). Many if not all of them were authoritative exponents of these religions, recognized as such by their Hindu or Buddhist peers.[48] Needless to say, without this hard and patient intellectual work, multiple religious belonging runs the risk of shallowness and trendiness.

4. In spite of their academic achievements, one common thread that links these pioneers of multiple religious belonging is their emphasis on the absolute necessity of what Panikkar calls the "intra-religious dialogue,"[49] or what Pieris terms "communicatio in sacris" or "to be baptized by its [the church's] precursors in the Jordan of Asian religion."[50] By this is meant an interior experience of the encounter of two or more religious traditions, allowing them to interact with one another while remaining fundamentally open to the unexpected and unforeseeable transformation that such an encounter may produce in oneself. In other words, the interreligious dialogue must go beyond the theological exchange of concepts and beyond the efforts at inculturating the Christian faith in the philosophical and religious categories of the culture to which the gospel is proclaimed, important and necessary though these two activities may be.

To achieve this intra-religious dialogue it is necessary that one step into the shoes, as it were, of a devotee of another religion and try to acquire, as far as possible, the religious experience of that devotee, most often in a monastic setting. To do so, however, the guidance of a master of that religious tradition is necessary. Abhishiktananda required the direction of Sri Ramana Maharshi and Swami Gnanananda, and Pieris prostrated himself at the feet of a learned Buddhist monk, begging him to accept him as his disciple and to be admitted into the Buddhist monastery.

5. This religious experience in terms of the teachings, rituals, prayers, and spiritual and monastic practices of a non-Christian religion and not in terms of those of the Christian tradition—while faithfully carrying out those of the Christian tradition at the same time—is, needless to say, profoundly unsettling and even threatening and remains ultimately inexpressible. Here a reference—albeit very brief—to the *advaita* experience of Abhishiktananda may be illuminating.[51] *Advaita* or non-dual mystical experience is briefly summarized by Jacques Dupuis:

---

[48] This intellectual competence also seems to be lacking in many contemporary Western practitioners of multiple religious belonging.

[49] See Raimon Panikkar, *The Intra-religious Dialogue* (New York: Paulist Press, 1978).

[50] Pieris, *Love Meets Wisdom*, 41.

[51] For a detailed study of this experience, see Dupuis, *Jesus Christ at the Encounter of World Religions*, 69–81; idem, "Christianity and Religions," 69–72.

Advaita experience may be described, it would seem, as an entry, or better as assumption, into the knowledge that the Absolute has of itself, and thus as a view of reality literally from the viewpoint of the Absolute. From the special viewpoint of this absolute awareness, all duality *(dvaita)* vanishes, since the Absolute alone is absolute, is One-without-a-second *(ekam advitiyam)*. From this viewpoint the universe, and history have no absolute meaning *(paramartha);* their existence pertains to the domain of the relative *(vyavahara)*, God's *lila* (God's play in creation). At the awakening of the experience of *advaita*, the ontological density of the finite seer itself vanishes. The awakening of absolute awareness leaves no room for a subjective awareness of self as a finite subject of cognition: there remains only the *aham*-("I") awareness of the Absolute in the epiphenomenon of the body *(satiram): Aham brahmasmi*. The experience of *advaita* thus implies a radical disappearance of all that is not the Absolute. . . . What abides is the awakening of the one who knows to the subjective consciousness of the Absolute itself. And it is not an objective knowledge of the Absolute by a finite me. In the process of illumination the human "me" gives way to the divine *Aham*. Such is the radical demand of *advaita*.[52]

This *advaita* experience, which implies the supreme renunciation of oneself and the even more radical renunciation of the divine "Thou" encountered in prayer, seems to run counter to the Christian doctrines of the triune God, creation, and prayer, and would make the double belonging to Christianity and Hinduism problematic if not impossible. As he noted in his journal, Abhishiktananda himself experienced acutely the antinomy between the Hindu and the Christian conceptions of reality and the painful push-and-pull of his double identity as a Hindu-Christian monk. He lived this anguish for nearly twenty-five years, never fully able to reconcile the two apparently opposing conceptions on the theoretical levels. As quoted above, he counseled acceptance of the unresolvable tension without attempting at harmonizing them: "The best thing is, I think, to hold, even in extreme tension, these two forms of a unique 'faith,' till dawn may arise."[53]

And yet this inability to reconcile theologically the *advaita* experience with various Christian doctrines did not diminish Abhishiktananda's certitude of the reality and validity of his experience. He noted, not without enthusiasm: "The experience of the *Upanishads* is true—I *know!*"[54] Hence, multiple religious belonging or double religious identity is by no means a facile compromise or a painless feat of intellectual balancing between two opposing world views and ways of life. Rather, it is a lived drama of tension, never fully resolved on the theoretical level but affirmed at the existential plane, a continuing quest for

[52] Dupuis, "Christianity and Religions," 70.

[53] Abhishiktananda, *Ascent to the Depth of the Heart,* 19.

[54] Le Saux, *La montée au fond du coeur* (May 11, 1972), 425, quoted in Dupuis, *Jesus Christ at the Encounter of World Religions,* 73.

harmony amid dissonance, ever elusive, provisional, and unfinished, to be heard fully only on the "other shore."

6. In concomitance with the intra-religious dialogue of the encounter of religions within oneself and the interreligious dialogue of sharing prayer and religious experiences with followers of other religions, multiple religious belonging must also be expressed in mutual collaboration among various religions for the defense and emancipation of the poor and the marginalized. Without a deep commitment to and struggle for justice, withdrawal into ashrams for prayer and contemplation and interreligious dialogue run the risk of spiritual escapism and bourgeois leisure life.

Aloysius Pieris is perhaps the most vocal proponent of a double baptism for the church in Asia: baptism by its precursors in the Jordan of Asian religion and by oppressive systems on the cross of Asian poverty. For Pieris, every religion is composed of three elements: core experience, collective memory, and interpretation. For example, Christianity and Buddhism both originated from a core experience: Jesus' proclamation of the reign of God and the enlightenment of the Buddha, respectively. Pieris calls the former "agape" and the latter "gnosis." The collective memory of each religion is made up of narratives, sacred texts, liturgy, songs, drama, and structural organization. The interpretation is constituted by the way in which the core experience is understood, explained, and transmitted throughout the history of each religion. Interreligious dialogue, which is not a luxury but a necessity, must be carried out on all the three elements, because the languages of love (agape) and wisdom (gnosis) need each other to achieve their fullness.

According to Pieris, each religion constitutes a unique and unrepeatable identity, but various religions can be seen as representing mutually corrective instincts of the human spirit and therefore must be brought into dialogue with one another. Thus, agape and gnosis, though pointing to different core experiences, are mutually complementary because neither is in itself an adequate medium to experience or to express our experiences of the divine.

Because of irreducible differences among religions, the goal of such dialogue is neither syncretism nor synthesis but rather symbiosis.[55] Syncretism and synthesis violate the unique identity of each religion. Pieris is opposed to the way many postmodern religious seekers pick and choose elements of various religions to suit their personal needs and to create a new religious entity unrecognizable to the followers of religions from which these elements were selected. By contrast, symbiosis is a movement in which members of different religious traditions live and work together in basic human communities (not just base Christian communities), especially in favor of and with the poor; in the process all are taught by the "other" more about what is unique and significant in their own faith. In other words, Buddhists, through collaborating with Christians, learn more about what is uniquely valuable in Buddhist gnosis, while Christians learn more about what is uniquely valuable in Christian agape. In so doing, both Buddhists and Christians must be joined by a common commitment to the poor,

---

[55] See Pieris, *Fire and Water*, 154–61.

a sensitivity to the Unspoken Speaker, that is, to the Spirit, who is not tied down to any dogma, rite, or law, and to the Word, which is uttered beyond the confines of any religious organization and hierarchy.[56]

From this analysis of the dynamics of multiple religious belonging as exhibited by some of its key pioneers, it is clear that this phenomenon both poses challenges and offers opportunities for the church. While it has been made more acceptable by recent theologies of religions, its practice by people, especially the young, who do not possess the necessary qualifications that were present, to an eminent degree, in those pioneers, can easily lead to the "nebulous esoteric mysticism" and "Nietzschean neo-paganism" that we have been warned against.[57] Among those qualifications especially important are a deep commitment to Jesus as the "unique" and "universal" savior (as interpreted inclusively), a firm rootedness in the Christian community, a competent knowledge of the doctrinal and religious traditions of both Christianity and the non-Christian religions, docility to the guidance of a trustworthy teacher/director, a genuine and sincere quest for communion with God, and an effective commitment to the work for justice.

Needless to say, how to make these conditions widely accessible is a tall order. However, given the significant rise of multiple religious belonging in the West (not to mention the emergence of new religious movements and sects), particularly among youth, the need to make multiple religious belonging spiritually fruitful for both the individual and the church is more urgent than ever. In the last part of this chapter I make a few modest suggestions as to how education for multiple religious belonging can be begun.

Multiple religious belonging not only poses challenges but also offers opportunities as well. We have already seen how pioneers in multiple religious belonging have enriched our understanding of Christianity itself. Among its many benefits, John B. Cobb Jr. highlights the opportunity for reconciliation between Christianity and other religions, in particular Judaism, Islam, and the Native American religions. For him, multiple religious belonging may be a useful means to purge Christianity of its long-lasting anti-Judaism, its crimes against Islam, and its injustices against Native Americans.[58]

---

[56] Ibid., 133.

[57] *DI* warns against the following dangers of interreligious encounter: "the difficulty in understanding and accepting the presence of definitive and eschatological events in history; the metaphysical emptying of the historical incarnation of the Eternal Logos, reduced to a mere appearing of God in history; the eclecticism of those who, in theological research, uncritically absorb ideas from a variety of philosophical and theological contexts without regard for consistency, systematic connection, or compatibility with Christian truth; finally, the tendency to read and to interpret Sacred Scripture outside the Tradition and Magisterium of the Church" (no. 4).

[58] See John B. Cobb Jr., "Multiple Religious Belonging and Reconciliation," in Cornille, *Many Mansions?* 20–28. Cobb frankly acknowledges, "I do not see multiple religious belonging as the primary way into the future. The primary way is the transformation of the particular religious traditions, at least in the Christian case, through their new encounter with other traditions" (27). He admits, however, that multiple belongers can contribute to this transformation.

Joseph S. O'Leary, while recognizing the validity of the warnings of *DI* against the dangers of interreligious encounter, argues that these dangers, even though unavoidable, are salutary, at least with regard to Buddhism: "The encounter of Christianity and Buddhism of its very nature puts a question mark against definitive eschatological events, demands a less substantialist ontology of the Incarnation, sets up a play of ideas that cannot be reduced to systematic connections, and uncovers meanings in scripture that are thinly represented in traditional church teaching."[59]

THEOLOGICAL EDUCATION TOWARD MULTIPLE RELIGIOUS BELONGING

As has been noted above, one of the conditions for fruitful multiple religious belonging is a competent knowledge of the doctrines and practices of non-Christian religions. In his most recent book, *Introducing Theologies of Religions*, Paul Knitter rings two bells, an alarm bell and an invitation bell, the former to alert Americans to the fact of religious pluralism in their midst, and the latter to urge them to take that fact seriously, not only *de facto* but also *de iure*, that is, to inquire into its possible significance for Christianity. The two bells need to be heeded because in our present age religious people, in Knitter's felicitous phrase, have "to be religious interreligiously."[60]

First, then, there is an urgent need to sensitize Catholic candidates for ordained ministry to the fact of religious diversity. This call seems at first to be a redundancy, yet on second thoughts, it is very much needed. Many seminaries are located far from urban centers, often shielded not only from racial, ethnic, and cultural diversity but also from religious diversity. Furthermore, candidates to the ministerial priesthood and seminary faculty tend to focus on training for pastoral ministry to parishes, which of course does not take non-Catholics, let alone non-Christians, into account. There is also the fact, often acknowledged by seminary faculty *sub rosa*, that there is a disturbing number of "conservative" and downright "right-wing" seminarians who would create trouble for the institution if there were any talk about the uniqueness and universality of Christ as savior in the inclusive sense or about non-Christian religions as possible ways of salvation.

---

[59] O'Leary, "Toward a Buddhist Interpretation of Christian Truth," 30. In O'Leary's view the contribution of Buddhism to Christianity is not in terms of this or that doctrine but in the way it helps cure the "sickness" of Christianity: "One way in which Buddhism may fall within the divine plan is as a pharmacopeia of antidotes for the sickness of religion. . . . Buddhism tempers the elements of fixation, irrationality, emotivity, and violence in Christian thinking and presents a peaceful, reasonable, wholesome mode of being present religiously to the contemporary world. . . . In an age when religious fundamentalism and sectarian strife are more virulent than ever, the healing critique of Buddhism has perhaps a more central role to play than the classical dogma of Christianity, at least at the forefront of history, whatever the ultimate shape of 'the divine plan of salvation'" (41–42).

[60] Knitter, *Introducing Theologies of Religions*, xi.

Second, a cursory examination of the academic programs offered in Catholic seminaries shows that little if any attention is devoted to missiology and interreligious dialogue. The lion's share of theological courses is given to basic courses in Catholic doctrine, often because candidates who come to the seminary do not possess the requisite undergraduate training in philosophy and theology and therefore require additional study of the Catholic tradition. And, if the truth be told, few seminary professors are well equipped to teach courses in non-Christian religions; courses on interreligious dialogue and religious pluralism are at best offered as electives and often are looked upon with suspicion. The Vatican's "examination" of theological works on religious pluralism—such as Jacques Dupuis's *Toward a Christian Theology of Religious Pluralism* and Roger Haight's *Jesus the Symbol of God*—and declarations such as *Dominus Iesus* do not help matters.

Third, theological education to religious pluralism and multiple religious belonging is nonetheless more urgent than ever. To begin with, not only must awareness of racial, ethnic, cultural, and religious diversity be raised, and to this effect courses on black, Hispanic/Latino, and Asian American theologies be made available, but also a course on religious pluralism, at a minimum, should be made mandatory for all ministerial students, who should be required to read (though not of course necessarily agree with) important works on the subject.[61]

Fourth, besides readings on theologies of religions, there is also the need to show how Catholic theology today must and can be done from an interreligious perspective. This is the emerging comparative theology, offered not as an alternative to the theology of religions but as a way of understanding one's own *Christian* theology better through a better understanding of *others*. That is, one tries not only to understand non-Christian religions through the Christian lens (Christian theology of religions) but also to understand Christian faith through the non-Christian lens (comparative theology).[62] Concrete examples of comparative

---

[61] Besides Dupuis's other work, I stronlgy recommend his latest book, *Christianity and the Religions: From Confrontation to Dialogue*. For a magisterial and even-handed introduction to the theologies of religions, Paul Knitter's *Introducing Theologies of Religions* is also highly recommended. Needless to say, documents of the Magisterium must also form required readings, especially the various documents of Pope John Paul II and the Federation of Asian Bishops' Conferences.

[62] On comparative theology, see John Renard, "Comparative Theology: Definition and Method," *Religious Studies and Theology* 17 (1998): 3–18; Francis Clooney, *Theology after Vedanta: An Experiment in Comparative Theology* (Albany, N.Y.: SUNY Press, 1993); idem, *Seeing through Texts* (Albany, N.Y.: SUNY Press, 1996); idem, "Comparative Theology: A Review of Recent Books (1989–1995)," *Theological Studies* 56 (1995): 521–50; James Fredericks, *Faith among Faiths: Christian Theology and Non-Christian Religions* (New York: Paulist Press, 1999); idem, "A Universal Religious Experience? Comparative Theology as an Alternative to a Theology of Religions," *Horizons* 22 (1995): 67–87; Peter C. Phan, "Doing Theology in the Context of Mission: Lessons from Alexandre de Rhodes," *Gregorianum* 81/4 (2000): 723–49; idem, "Doing Theology in the Context of Cultural and Religious Pluralism: An Asian Perspective," *Louvain Studies* 27 (2002): 39–68.

theology, though still few, should be offered as possible models for theologizing in the context of religious pluralism.[63]

Fifth, theological studies should not be divorced from spirituality. Consequently, theological reflections on religious pluralism should be accompanied by multi-faith worship and prayer in which sacred scriptures as well as prayers and rituals of non-Christian religions are used not as a substitute for but as a complement to the Christian Bible, prayers, and rituals. Furthermore, students should also be introduced to non-Christian monastic practices and meditation techniques to enrich their spiritual lives.[64]

Sixth, theological studies and spirituality should not be divorced from the work with and for the poor and the marginalized. Interreligious dialogue in the forms of sharing life and collaborating with people of non-Christian faiths should be strongly encouraged. Nothing can change a person's negative view about the possibility of salvation outside Christianity and about the positive values of non-Christian religions more quickly and effectively than an actual and prolonged encounter with non-Christians who are prayerful and holy. Interreligious dialogue is never carried out with religions as such but with flesh-and-blood believers and practitioners of other faiths.

This leads to my seventh and last suggestion, which has been eloquently and convincingly made by James Fredericks, who proposes that Christians engaged in interreligious dialogue and comparative theology should develop not only love (agape) but also friendship *(philia)* with non-Christians.[65] Love is a command of Jesus and is obligatory for all Christians; it is unconditional and must be given to all, one's enemies included. By contrast, friendship is optional and preferential; it is given only to people for whom one feels a certain attraction because of qualities in them one finds admirable and pleasing or because of mutual interests. Thus, Christians may become friends with non-Christians because of the beauty and value of their beliefs and practices.

---

[63] See, for instance, Francis Clooney, "God for Us: Multiple Religious Identities as a Human and Divine Prospect," in Cornille, *Many Mansions?* 44–60; John Keenan, *The Meaning of Christ: A Mahayana Reading* (Maryknoll, N.Y.: Orbis Books, 1989); idem, *The Gospel of Mark: A Mahayana Reading* (Maryknoll, N.Y.: Orbis Books, 1995); Peter C. Phan, "The Christ of Asia: An Essay on Jesus as the Eldest Son and Ancestor," *Studia Missionalia* 45 (1996): 25–55; idem, "Mary in Vietnamese Piety and Theology: A Contemporary Perspective," *Ephemerides Mariologicae* 51/4 (2001): 457–71; David Burrell, *Knowing the Unknowable God: Ibn-Sina, Maimonides, Aquinas* (Notre Dame, Ind.: University of Notre Dame Press, 1986); idem, *Freedom and Creation in Three Conditions* (Notre Dame, Ind.: University of Notre Dame Press, 1993); Donald Mitchell, *Spirituality and Emptiness* (New York: Paulist Press, 1991); Leo Lefebure, *The Buddha and the Christ: Explorations in Buddhist-Christian Dialogue* (Maryknoll, N.Y.: Orbis Books, 1993); David Carpenter, *Revelation, History, and the Dialogue of Religions: A Comparative Study of Bhartrhari and Bonaventure* (Maryknoll, N.Y.: Orbis Books, 1995); John Berthrong, *All under Heaven: Transforming Paradigms in Confucian-Christian Dialogue* (Albany, N.Y.: SUNY Press, 1994).

[64] For a helpful work on how to make use of Zen meditation in the Christian and Ignatian context, see Kakichi Kadowaki, *Zen and the Bible*, trans. Joan Rieck (Maryknoll, N.Y.: Orbis Books, 2002). Originally published in Japanese (1977).

[65] See Fredericks, *Faith among Faiths*, 173–77.

Furthermore, friends are at first strangers. Strangers are initially always strange and foreign and threatening to our sense of belonging and familiarity. By accepting the stranger as friend, we allow his or her "otherness" to confront us radically, challenging us with stories we have never heard, questions we have never raised, beliefs we have never entertained, and practices we have never imagined. By welcoming and learning to appreciate these new religious realities, we gradually adopt them as our own because our friends have them and share them with us, and thus we begin to acquire, perhaps without being aware of it, multiple religious belonging or double religious identity.

A final word of caution: Multiple religious belonging is not for the faint-hearted or the dilettante. As the life of Abhishiktananda has shown, it is a demanding vocation, a special call to holiness, which up till now God has granted only to a few. It is not unlike martyrdom. Ultimately it is not something one looks for or demands at will. It is a gift to be received in fear and trembling and in gratitude and joy.

PART TWO

Christianity
in Dialogue
with Other Religions

5

The Claim of Uniqueness and Universality

THE LOGIC OF INTERRELIGIOUS DIALOGUE

Among the many theological issues that may deter adherents of a particular religious tradition from participating in interreligious dialogue is the question of whether such a dialogue would require as a condition of possibility a renunciation or at least a bracketing *(epoche)* of their belief in the uniqueness and universality both of the founder(s) of their religion and of their religion itself.

Understandably, such a question is of utmost importance for people whose central beliefs include the conviction that their religious founder is the only and universal savior and whose fundamental duty is to convert others to their religion through missionary activities. Christians and Muslims, for example, clearly number among these, the former professing that there is no salvation under any name other than that of Jesus (Acts 4:12; Jn 14:6), the latter that "Muhammad is the apostle of God" (the *shahadah*). And, for both Christians and Muslims, the mission to convert other people to their faith is an essential obligation. But it is not only Christianity and Islam that make claims to uniqueness and universality. Among Eastern religions, Pure Land Buddhism also claims that salvation is obtained by placing absolute trust in the Amida Buddha and his merits.

But even religions that do not claim uniqueness and universality for their founders or for themselves as social institutions and do not make mission a basic task for their adherents still affirm that the truth they teach and the way of life they prescribe (for example, the Vedas, the Four Noble Truths, the Torah, and so on) are necessary for salvation or enlightenment or liberation, however these realities are understood. Hence, the question remains whether this more limited claim can and should still be made in interreligious dialogue.

In this chapter I examine (1) whether interreligious dialogue demands a recantation or at least a bracketing of the claim of religious uniqueness and universality; (2) what the nature of that claim is, if such a claim must be maintained; and (3) how such a claim should be defended without jeopardizing the purposes of interreligious dialogue.

THE CLAIM OF UNIQUENESS AND UNIVERSALITY
IN INTERRELIGIOUS DIALOGUE

For clarity's sake, a few preliminary observations on the meanings of the key terms in our discussion are in order.

By *unique* one can mean "having no like," as in the claim that every human being is unique. Though all human persons belong to the same species, and therefore are similar in this sense, each of them is so distinct as a particular individual that no one else can be said to be the same. In this sense everyone, Gautama or Jesus or Muhammad, is unique.

Unique can also mean "being the only one of its sort." So when some Christians claim that Jesus is the unique savior, they mean that Jesus is the only one who saves and that no one else can be said in any way to be a savior. Christians who make such a claim are called exclusivists.

Finally, *unique* can mean "having no equal or equivalent." To claim that Jesus is the unique savior in this sense does not *ipso facto* rule out the possibility of saviors other than Jesus; such a claim, however, entails that these saviors, if there be such, are either inferior to or dependent on Jesus. Christians who make this claim for Jesus are called inclusivists. There are also Christians who affirm that Jesus is unique in the first sense but deny that Jesus is unique in the second and third senses of the term; in their view, Jesus is simply one of the many saviors in the history of the world. They are called pluralists.[1]

The claim of universality for a religious figure, if it is made at all, is understood differently depending on the stance one takes with regard to the uniqueness of the religious figure in question. For pluralists, no savior can be said to be universal in the strict sense of the term because a savior's salvific influence is limited to his or her followers. Exclusivists, on the contrary, would maintain that their religion's founder is the universal savior in the sense that all salvation comes from that person alone and that, unless one explicitly acknowledges in faith their religion's founder as one's personal savior, accepts his or her teachings, and follows the way of life he or she prescribes, one cannot be saved. Inclusivists would also affirm the universality of the founder of their religion but, unlike the exclusivists, would recognize that the founders of other religions can exercise a saving role in the salvation of their adherents and that therefore these religions can be said to be ways of salvation, though, the inclusivists would add, these founders and their religions can only do so in dependence on their unique savior. Thus, the inclusivists' claim of the universality of their savior, compared with the claim of the exclusivists, is a qualified one. Nevertheless, both exclusivists and inclusivists agree that their savior, being universal, is definitive, absolute, normative, and superior to the founders of other religions.

---

[1] For the use of these categories of exclusivism, inclusivism, and pluralism, see Alan Race, *Christians and Religious Pluralism: Patterns in the Christian Theology of Religions* (Maryknoll, N.Y.: Orbis Books, 1983); and Gavin D'Costa, *Theology and Religious Pluralism* (Oxford: Basil Blackwell, 1986).

Two other observations are necessary to clarify our discussion of the claim of uniqueness and universality in interreligious dialogue. First, I suggest that a clear distinction be made between the claim of uniqueness and universality for a particular religious founder (such as Jesus or Muhammad) and for the institution of his or her adherents (such as Christianity or Islam). These two claims, though mutually connected, are, as will be argued later, different as to their theology, history, epistemology, and sociology. Second, one should also distinguish between a claim and its justification. A claim is as good as its supporting reasons; however, not every reason needs to be of a rational type. A claim (especially a religious one) should not be rejected simply because it does not or cannot offer strictly rational evidences for itself.

After these preliminary remarks we can now address the problem at hand, which can be broken down into two distinct questions. First, is the claim of the uniqueness and universality of a particular religious figure and/or a particular religion epistemologically, theologically, and ethically justified? Second, if justified, should it be made in the context of interreligious dialogue?

The Claim of Uniqueness and Universality

With regard to the first question, at this point I do not as yet apply the distinction mentioned above between the religious founder and the social institution that is formed as the result of his or her teachings and actions. Such a distinction is not yet relevant here because the focus is on the claim of uniqueness and universality as such. Proponents of the pluralistic thesis argue that such a claim (in this case the claim for Christianity) is rendered impossible by an epistemology that is conscious of the historico-cultural conditioning of all human knowledge, a theology guided by the conviction that God is Absolute Mystery, and by an ethics concerned with promoting social justice.[2]

Gordon Kaufman, John Hick, and Langdon Gilkey argue that the modern awareness of the historico-cultural limitation of all knowledge and religious beliefs and of the impossibility of judging the truth claim of another culture has rendered the claim of uniqueness and universality of a particular religious tradition no longer credible. Kaufmann suggests that any religious world view is an imaginative construction around four structural categories, namely, God, world, humanity, and Christ, and that no one imaginative construction can claim to be uniquely authorized or divinely warranted. Rather, it is to be regarded merely as a human attempt at finding orientation for life in a particular historical condition. Hick argues that any claim of uniqueness and superiority for a particular religious institution must be settled by an examination of facts, but of course, he

---

[2] See John Hick and Paul F. Knitter, eds., *The Myth of Christian Uniqueness: Toward a Pluralistic Theology of Religions* (Maryknoll, N.Y.: Orbis Books, 1987). For a comprehensive presentation of Hick's theology of religion, see his *An Interpretation of Religion* (New Haven, Conn.: Yale University Press, 1989). For Knitter's, see his *No Other Name? A Critical Survey of Christian Attitudes Toward World Religions* (Maryknoll, N.Y.: Orbis Books, 1985).

points out, such an examination is impossible or at best inconclusive. Gilkey maintains that given the plurality of competing world views it is impossible to claim that a particular religious tradition is universal or normative for the others.[3]

From the theological standpoint, the doctrine of God as Absolute Mystery who can never be adequately represented by any religion or any theological system is also said to militate against the claim of uniqueness and universality for a particular religion. Wilfred Cantwell Smith suggests that each religion is an "idol" (that is, image) of God and that if an "idol" is elevated to the status of uniqueness and exclusiveness, it is turned into an "idolatry." Stanley Samartha affirms that the nature of God as Mystery forbids any claim of uniqueness and finality for any religion. Raimundo Panikkar maintains that there is an all-embracing myth, a mystery called the Christ or the Christic principle, which is expressed in various religions so that no one religion can make an exclusive claim for itself. Seiichi Yagi denies that there is any fundamental difference between Jesus and us. Rather, the difference is only a matter of degree, because Jesus as the risen Christ or the Son of God was awakened to the presence of God in him in a way more thorough than we are. In this sense he can be said to be the model for others.[4]

Lastly, the claim of uniqueness and universality for any religious founder and/or religion must be rejected because it is alleged to lead to oppression and injustice. Rosemary Radford Ruether and Marjorie Hewitt Suchocki draw a parallel between this claim, on the one hand, and sexism and patriarchalism, on the other; in both there is the imperialistic attempt to impose one dimension of reality as normative for others. Aloysius Pieris argues that the claim of uniqueness and universality is a claim of faith and can be defended not by rational arguments but by action in favor of the poor. In the same vein Paul Knitter suggests that the claim of uniqueness and universality for a particular religious figure and religion can be settled only by examining how much religious figures and religions contribute to the liberation of the poor and "non-persons."[5]

---

[3] See these essays in Hick and Knitter, *The Myth of Christian Uniqueness:* Gordon Kaufman, "Religious Diversity, Historical Consciousness and Christian Theology," 3–15; John Hick, "The Non-Absoluteness of Christianity," 16–36; Langdon Gilkey, "Plurality and Its Theological Implications," 37–50.

[4] See these essays in Hick and Knitter, *The Myth of Christian Uniqueness:* Wilfred Cantwell Smith, "Idolatry in Comparative Perspective," 53–68; Stanley J. Samartha, "The Crow and the Rainbow: Christ in a Multireligious Culture," 69–88; Raimundo Panikkar, "The Jordan, the Tiber, and the Ganges: Three Kairological Moments of Christic Self-Consciousness," 89–116; Seiichi Yagi, "'I' in the Words of Jesus," 117–34.

[5] See these essays in Hick and Knitter, *The Myth of Christian Uniqueness:* Rosemary Radford Ruether, "Feminism and Jewish-Christian Dialogue: Particularism and Universalism in the Search for Religious Truth," 137–48; Marjorie Hewitt Suchocki, "In Search of Justice: Religious Pluralism from a Feminist Perspective," 149–61; Aloysius Pieris, "The Buddha and the Christ: Mediators of Liberation," 162–77; Paul F. Knitter, "Toward a Liberation Theology of Religions," 178–200.

This is not the place to respond in detail to all the three arguments against the possibility of the claim of uniqueness and universality for a religious founder and/or religion. I have already done so elsewhere.[6] Suffice it here to say that the three arguments, taken either singly or in combination, do not offer convincing reasons for rejecting the possibility of the claim of uniqueness and universality. For the sake of argument, let us take the stronger version of the claim, namely, exclusivism, and apply it to Christianity. Suppose that a claim is made that Jesus the Christ is the unique and universal savior, that there is no one else in human history that can legitimately be called savior, and that in order to be saved everyone must explicitly acknowledge Jesus as her or his personal savior. Is this claim logically invalidated by the three arguments advanced by the pluralists mentioned above, that is, historical consciousness, the nature of God as Absolute Mystery, and the ethical duty of promoting justice and peace?

First, that humans are historically and culturally conditioned in all their activities, including their knowledge and language about God, is a truth that modernity rightly drives home to us. But does this conditioning rule out the possibility of affirming something as universally true as distinct from the different ways of formulating this truth in various grammatical and linguistic sentences?[7] It seems not. For even the pluralists must concede that the proposition that historical consciousness rules out the possibility of the claim of uniqueness and universality is universally true, independently of its historico-cultural context, if it is to be taken seriously. This counter-argument, of course, does not settle the truth or falsity of the claim itself which still has to be evaluated on its own merits, but it is illogical to reject it a priori on the ground of its historico-cultural conditioning. Here the distinction mentioned earlier between a claim and its justification applies. The claim itself is logically possible; its veracity may or may not be validated, depending on the strength of the arguments offered in its defense.[8]

Second, that God is the incomprehensible and ineffable Mystery is the constant teaching of mystics, both Eastern and Western, and of the *theologia*

---

[6] See Peter C. Phan, "Are There Other 'Saviors' for other Peoples? A Discussion of the Problem of the Universal Significance and Uniqueness of Jesus the Christ," in *Christianity and the Wider Ecumenism,* ed. Peter C. Phan, 163–80 (New York: Paragon House, 1990). See also the critique of the pluralistic theology of religions in Gavin D'Costa, ed., *Christian Uniqueness Reconsidered: The Myth of a Pluralistic Theology of Religions* (Maryknoll, N.Y.: Orbis Books, 1990).

[7] A common distinction is made between a sentence and a statement or proposition, between what is used to say what is said and what is said. Thomas Aquinas points out the difference between the *res significata* (what is affirmed) and the *modus significandi* (the way of affirming something) in our language about God. The *res significata*, that is, the perfection affirmed of God, belongs to God in an eminent manner and can be truly affirmed of God, whereas the *modus significandi*, that is, our way of speaking of God, is necessarily inadequate. See *Summa contra gentiles* 1.30, and *Summa theologiae* I, 13, 3.

[8] For a defense of the possibility of affirming truth in a proposition, see Harold A. Netland, *Dissonant Voices: Religious Pluralism and the Question of Truth* (Grand Rapids, Mich.: Eerdmanns, 1991), 115–33.

negativa.[9] But does the ineffability of God preclude the possibility of affirming that some historical figure is the unique and universal savior? It does not seem so. Suppose that one affirms that there is no god but Allah and that Muhammad is the messenger of God, and that unless one accepts this twofold truth, one is not saved. There is nothing in this affirmation that *prima facie* contradicts the ineffability of God. The first part of the *shahadah* simply affirms monotheism, and, one may add, the ineffability of God as Absolute Reality; the second asserts that Muhammad is the person in whom Allah has revealed himself. That Allah may reveal himself in a created medium is not excluded a priori by his ineffability, since the doctrine of divine ineffability only denies the possibility of expressing God in an exhaustive way by means of a concept and not of God's self-expression in a finite reality. Of course, the claim that God makes Muhammad his messenger must be substantiated, and the merits of the arguments in its favor must be evaluated, but the claim itself is not invalidated by the ineffability of God.

Third, it would seem that the argument that the commitment to peace and justice requires the rejection of or at least the bracketing of the claim of uniqueness and universality is the least convincing. That believers have been responsible for various acts of injustice and oppression is hardly to be denied, but it is far from evident that the source of their arrogance and malfeasance vis-à-vis adherents of other religions is to be traced to their claim of uniqueness and universality for their religious founders and/or religions. For one thing, believers who do not make such a claim are not innocent of oppressing other believers. Moreover, there are believers who find in the claim of the uniqueness and universality of their savior the moral encouragement to work for the liberation and well-being of others. One may want to argue that to derive from such a claim the motivation to do good is misguided or that there are better ways of arousing oneself for the good, but one cannot deny that in fact such a claim has been a cause for benevolence. The point, it would seem, is not whether such a claim should be made or not, but rather the manner in which it is made.

Besides failing to be apodictic, the pluralists' arguments against the claim of uniqueness and universality suffer from internal inconsistency and other fallacies. It has been argued that, first, the pluralists are as intellectually imperialistic as the exclusivists and the inclusivists whom they castigate because pluralists too impose their (Western) notions of religion, dialogue, social justice, and so on on other religionists. Hence the pluralists' thesis is logically incoherent.[10] Second, the pluralists wrongly presume that there is such a thing as a common core of religious experience that functions as a genus embracing the different

---

[9] Among contemporary Roman Catholic theologians, Karl Rahner (1904–84) is to be counted among the most eloquent exponents of the incomprehensibility of God. On this theme, see Chapter 6 herein.

[10] See these essays in D'Costa, *Christian Uniqueness Reconsidered:* Gavin D'Costa, "Christ, the Trinity, and Religious Plurality," 16–29; Lesslie Newbigin, "Religion for the Marketplace," 135–48; Paul Griffiths, "The Uniqueness of Christian Doctrine Defended," 156–73.

species of religions.[11] Third, the pluralists neglect the social and historical particularities of each religion and therefore fail to take its distinct doctrines, texts, and practices seriously.[12] Fourth, the pluralists fail to consider the aims and forms of life of religious communities[13] and the different functions of doctrines.[14] Fifth, the pluralists' appeal to praxis inevitably leads to relativism and the rejection of the truth-claim inherent in doctrines.[15] Sixth, the pluralists do injustice to the meaning and practical import of some vital Christian doctrines such as the Trinity and Christology.[16] Finally, the pluralists misunderstand the nature and purpose of interreligious dialogue. They seem to regard it as a means to construct a universal theology of religions or to achieve social agenda of peace and justice.[17]

The Claim of Uniqueness and Universality in Interreligious Dialogue

The last point brings us to the second issue: If the claim of the uniqueness and universality of one's savior and/or religion is not ruled out on epistemological, theological, and ethical grounds, should it be made in interreligious dialogue? Is not the goal of interreligious dialogue thwarted by such an apparently exclusivistic claim? Here I would argue, along with Raimundo Panikkar, that it is impossible to avoid introducing the claim of uniqueness and universality for one's religious founder, if such a claim is made at all, into the interreligious conversation. Panikkar refers to the proposal that one should temporarily suspend one's judgment about the truth of one's fundamental beliefs and bracket one's faith in interreligious dialogue so as not to impose it on one's dialogue partners or at least not to influence them regarding the contents of the dialogue as "phenomenological *epoche.*" In discussing the merits of this proposal, Panikkar argues that transferring the *epoche* to a field not its own, like that of ultimate

---

[11] See these essays in D'Costa, *Christian Uniqueness Reconsidered:* John Milbank, "The End of Dialogue," 174–91; John Cobb Jr., "Beyond 'Pluralism,'" 81–95; and Newbigin, "Religion for the Marketplace."

[12] See these essays in D'Costa, *Christian Uniqueness Reconsidered:* Francis X. Clooney, "Reading the Word in Christ: From Comparison to Inclusivism," 63–80; J. A. DiNoia, "Pluralist Theology of Religions: Pluralistic or Non-Pluralistic?" 119–34; Kenneth Surin, "A 'Politics of Speech': Religious Pluralism in the Age of the McDonald's Hamburger," 192–212.

[13] See DiNoia, "Pluralist Theology of Religions."

[14] See Griffiths, "The Uniqueness of Christian Doctrine Defended."

[15] See Wolfhart Pannenberg, "Religious Pluralism and Conflicting Truth Claims: The Problem of a Theology of the World Religions," in D'Costa, *Christian Uniqueness Reconsidered*, 96–106.

[16] See these essays in D'Costa, *Christian Uniqueness Reconsidered:* Monika Hellwig, "Christology in the Wider Ecumenism," 107–16; M. M. Thomas, "A Christ-Centred Humanist Approach to Other Religions in the Indian Pluralist Context," 49–62. See also Newbigin, "Religion for the Marketplace"; Cobb, "Beyond 'Pluralism'"; and Pannenberg, "Religious Pluralism and Conflicting Truth Claims."

[17] See these essays in D'Costa, *Christian Uniqueness Reconsidered:* Jürgen Moltmann, "Is 'Pluralistic Theology' Useful for the Dialogue of World Religions?" 149–56; Milbank, "The End of Dialogue"; and Surin, "A 'Politics of Speech.'"

convictions in the interreligious dialogue, is "psychologically impracticable, phenomenologically inappropriate, philosophically defective, theologically weak and religiously barren."[18]

The *epoche* is psychologically impossible because interreligious dialogue is more than just doctrinal discussion; it is a personal encounter with the whole human person in which it would be a sham to affirm that one does not know or is not convinced of one's certainties. It is phenomenologically inappropriate for several reasons. First, dialogue presupposes and follows the use of transcendental-phenomenological reduction in which the *epoche* is practiced; hence, the *epoche* has its place in the study of religious phenomena and not in the actual performance of dialogue. Second, the phenomenological *epoche* per se does not require that one bracket one's convictions and the claim to truth but only the external "existence" of the object under investigation outside the mind. Third, there are cultures in which the basic presuppositions of *epoche*, namely, the distinction between truth and belief, between *noesis* and *noema*, between the formulated thing and the formula, and so on, are not accepted, and hence the performance of *epoche* is not possible. Furthermore, the *epoche* is philosophically defective because if philosophy requires an unconditional and sincere search for truth, such a quest is rendered otiose from the outset were the searchers to bracket their own ultimate and deepest convictions. The *epoche* is also theologically weak because were one to bracket one's faith and still be able to encounter the partners in interreligious dialogue religiously, humanly, and meaningfully, then faith would be something quite supererogatory and not something that embraces one's entire life. Finally, the *epoche* is religiously barren because with the bracketing of one's deepest religious convictions, interreligious dialogue becomes nothing more than empty chatter about trivia and bagatelles.[19]

WHAT SHOULD BE CLAIMED IN INTERRELIGIOUS DIALOGUE IN TERMS OF UNIQUENESS AND UNIVERSALITY?

Granted that one's basic religious convictions should be maintained in interreligious dialogue, what exactly can be claimed in terms of the uniqueness and universality of one's religious affiliation? Here I would like to explore the implications of the distinction I suggested earlier. There are, I submit, important differences between claiming uniqueness and universality for one's religious founder and claiming them for one's religion. The two claims differ, as I pointed out above, epistemologically, sociologically, historically, and theologically. Failure to maintain this difference has given rise to equivocation in much of current discussions on the claim of uniqueness and universality.

To elucidate this distinction and to make it concrete, I consider the claim made for Christianity as an example. I believe this instance is particularly instructive both because historically it is Christians who have made a most vigorous

---

[18] Raimon Panikkar, *The Intra-Religious Dialogue* (New York: Paulist Press, 1978).
[19] See Panikkar, *The Intra-Religious Dialogue*, 40–50.

claim of uniqueness and universality for themselves and because the difference between Jesus and Christianity is easily demonstrable. What exactly is meant by *Christian uniqueness,* an expression often invoked in interreligious dialogue? The adjective *Christian* can refer to Jesus as the Christ and to the Christian church as a religious institution. Thus uniqueness is claimed both for Jesus and the church. But to say that Jesus is unique and universal is one thing, and to say that the Christian church is unique and universal is quite another. Clearly, there is an intimate connection between them, but no less clearly Jesus the Christ is not the Christian church and vice versa. There are four grounds for this difference.

Theological Grounds

First of all, theologically, there is a fundamental difference between Jesus and the church. To blur this distinction would lead to idolatry. This difference is expressed in diverse ways by the New Testament. The synoptic Gospels attribute to Jesus various titles such as prophet, messiah, Son of God, Son of man, and charismatic holy man; the Johannine Gospel speaks of him as the divine incarnate Logos. Other New Testament writings, especially the Pauline letters, elaborate different aspects of this Christology.[20] The church, on the other hand, is described in relation to Jesus as the bride to the bridegroom, the body to the head, the branches to the vine, the flock to the shepherd, the people to their leader.[21] From these images it is clear that the church and Jesus are intimately intertwined; indeed, one may and should speak even of an ontological unity between the two. In the history of Christian theology Christ and the church are at times spoken of as one. Nevertheless, they have never been identified with each other, nor should the identification ever be made. In the language of the Second Vatican Council, the church, in relation to Christ, is said to be his "sacrament," that is, a sign and instrument of communion with God and of unity among human beings (*LG*, nos. 1, 9, 48). But the church should not be identified with the kingdom of God, much less with Christ himself (*LG*, no. 5).

I alluded above to the danger of idolatry if the theological difference between Jesus and the church is not clearly maintained. Indeed, Christians believe in and worship Jesus, but they do not believe in Christianity, much less worship it. It may be objected that some ancient creeds, such as the Nicene Creed and the Apostles' Creed, state that "I believe in the Holy Spirit . . . one, holy, catholic, and apostolic church." It seems that the church is the object of Christian faith. Three remarks should be made in this regard. First, the third article of the Creed intends to affirm faith in the Holy Spirit as the Spirit is in his inner reality and as the Spirit is active in the church, making it one, holy, catholic, and apostolic.

---

[20] Recent important studies on Christology include the multi-volume works of John Meier, James D. G. Dunn, N. T. Wright, and Larry Hurtado.

[21] For a systematic ecclesiology, see Hans Küng, *The Church,* trans. Ray and Rosaleen Ockenden (New York: Sheed & Ward, 1967); and Peter C. Phan, ed., *The Gift of the Church: A Textbook on Ecclesiology in Honor of Patrick Granfield* (Collegeville, Minn.: Liturgical Press, 2000).

Thus, given the tripartite structure of the Creed, the church is not a separate object of faith but is included in the faith in the Holy Spirit. Second, grammatically, as Tyrannius Rufinus (c. 345–410) pointed out, the preposition "in" properly goes with the first clause, "the Holy Spirit," only. It is reasonable to say, he contends, "we believe in" when the object of belief is a divine reality, whereas if the object of belief is a creature or a mystery of the Christian religion, it is more appropriate to say we believe it rather than we believe "in" it.[22] Thus, the object of the theological virtue of faith can only be a divine reality, not a created thing, in this case, the church. Third, the four marks of the church (unity, holiness, catholicity, and apostolicity) are understood as visible distinguishing character-istics of the true church and not merely invisible realities to believe in. Conse-quently, there must be ways by which such marks can be empirically verified. Ultimately, the distinction between Jesus and the church lies in the Christian belief that Jesus is God in the flesh whereas the church, however intimately united it is with its divine head and despite its divine origin, is human. Hence, whatever is claimed for both of them cannot be understood in the same meaning and to the same extent.

Sociological Grounds

Moreover, from the sociological standpoint, the identification of the church with Jesus is also impossible. Jesus is a historical individual with a determinate identity located in a particular space and time. And even if, according to the Christian faith, he is risen and continues to be salvifically effective in contem-porary history, he is not a social institution composed of many individuals called the church, however intimate the union between him and the members of this church may be. Contrary to Jesus, the church is an ongoing corporate entity with its organizational structures, its dogmas, its liturgy, its discipline, and so on. As historical and social entities, then, Jesus and the church should not be identified with each other.

---

[22] See his *Commentary on the Apostles' Creed*, 35; 39. Similarly, Faustus of Riez (c. 408–90) says that, properly speaking, we do not believe in the church: "All that in the creed follows 'the Holy Spirit' is to be construed without reference to the preposi-tion 'in,' so that our belief concerning the holy Church, the communion of saints, etc., is stated with reference to God, i.e. we confess that these things have been ordered by God and maintain their existence by Him" (*On the Holy Spirit*, 1, 2). Quoted in J. N. D. Kelly, *Early Christian Creeds* (New York: Longmans, Green and Co., 1950), 153. In a similar vein, the *Catechism of the Council of Trent* (1566) teaches: "With regard to the Three Persons of the Holy Trinity, the Father, the Son and the Holy Ghost we do not only believe them, but also believe in them. But here we make use of a different form of expression, professing to believe in the holy, not in the holy Catholic Church. By this difference of expression, we distinguish God, the author of all things, from His works, and acknowledge that all the exalted benefits bestowed on the Church are due to God's bounty" (*Catechism of the Council of Trent for Parish Priests*, trans. John McHugh and Charles Callan [New York: Joseph F. Wagner, 1937], 108–9). See also J. P. L. Oulton, "The Apostles' Creed and Belief Concerning the Church," *Journal of Theological Stud-ies* 39 (1938): 239–43.

Historical Grounds

If Jesus and the church cannot be identified with each other, whatever is claimed for one needs not and cannot be *ipso facto* claimed for the other. In particular, the claim of uniqueness and universality, if claimed at all for either, must be understood differently. From the historical point of view, in my judgment, it is the claim of uniqueness and universality of the Christian church that is most problematic, and not the claim of uniqueness and universality for Jesus. Indeed, once the divinity of Jesus is accepted, his uniqueness and universality, at least as understood by the inclusivists, seem to be a matter of course. The question is not whether or not this belief should be affirmed in interreligious dialogue (indeed it should, as I have argued above) but how to substantiate the faith in Jesus' divinity, especially in interreligious dialogue, and to this I will return in the epistemological grounds below.

On the other hand, what arouses much skepticism and even outrage is that a human institution such as the Christian church, with a history of light and darkness, a mixture of good and evil, claims to be the exclusive vessel of divine grace while there is plenty of evidence that other religious institutions, no less than the church, have been instrumental in achieving good (and, of course, evil as well). Here the pluralists' charge that the Christian claim of uniqueness has produced much suffering and oppression (the third argument discussed above) has some merit, though, in fairness, it must be said that such a charge should not be pressed too far, since religions (or more precisely, religious people) that make no claim to uniqueness and universality are no less guilty of oppression and injustice than Christians. Clearly, then, the claim of uniqueness and universality of Jesus and that of Christianity must be approached differently.

Epistemological Grounds

This brings me to the epistemological issue. How are the two claims to be substantiated, especially in the context of interreligious dialogue? First of all, it is to be noted that the claim that Jesus the Christ is the unique and universal savior, both in the exclusivistic and inclusivistic sense, is grounded in the more fundamental belief that he is no other than God incarnate, or more exactly, God the Son made flesh.[23] Thus, both assertions—that Jesus is God and that he is the

---

[23] It is no accident that pluralists who deny the uniqueness and universality of Jesus also question the traditional understanding of Jesus' divinity. For example, John Hick with his "inspiration Christology" holds that Jesus is not really God incarnate but rather simply a human being who was open to the presence and reality of God to such an unprecedented degree that he dramatically influenced everyone with whom he came into contact. See John Hick, ed., *The Myth of God Incarnate*, (London: SCM, 1977); and idem, "Rethinking Christian Doctrine in the Light of Religious Pluralism," in *Christianity and the Wider Ecumenism*, ed. Peter C. Phan, 89–102 (New York: Paragon House, 1990).

unique savior—are faith statements. As faith statements, they intend to affirm something true about Jesus and at the same time express his followers' loving commitment and devotion to him.[24]

But how do Christians go about proving the truth of their claim that Jesus is God and hence the unique and universal savior? Indeed, can this claim be proved at all? It is impossible to examine in detail the nature and scope of religious epistemology here, but at least the following observations should be made. First, there is a basic epistemological difference between the statement that, for instance, I am a Vietnamese, and the statement that Jesus is God. The former can be directly verified by examining my genetic roots, whereas the second cannot be so proved or disproved because one of the terms of the proposition is by definition not amenable to empirical verification. The two statements belong to two distinct orders of knowledge. As the First Vatican Council put it, "There is a twofold order of knowledge, distinct not only in its principle but also in its object; in its principle, because apart from what natural reason can attain, there are proposed to our belief mysteries revealed by God."[25]

Second, this impossibility of empirical verification does not entail that faith statements are untrue or meaningless.[26] Indeed, with regard to the claim that Jesus is God, there are reasonable grounds for it. One can appeal, for instance, to Jesus' teaching and behavior to vindicate his divinity. Of course, for non-Christians, such arguments do not amount to convincing proofs. But Christians themselves would readily acknowledge that fact, otherwise the claim of Jesus' uniqueness and universality would no longer be a faith affirmation but a logical conclusion drawn from evident premises, which would go against the very nature of the Christian faith.

Saint Thomas's well-known distinction between faith, on the one hand, and doubt, opinion, intuition, and knowledge, on the other, is helpful here. Doubt occurs when there is lack of evidence or when there is an apparent equality of the motives for both sides of the issue in question. Opinion occurs when the understanding tends more to one side than the other but the evidence is not strong enough to determine the assent fully. Intuition occurs when the understanding assents immediately because the objects adhered to are first principles which are known as soon as their terms are known. Knowledge (*scientia*) occurs when the understanding assents immediately because the conclusions are

---

[24] Paul Knitter's interpretation of the Christians' affirmation that Jesus is the "one and only" savior as a "love language" describing what Jesus does for Christians and their commitment to him is true but insufficient. It is true that the language of some of the New Testament texts belongs to this genre of "confessional" or "love language," but to say that they only affirm that Jesus is the savior of Christians and of not others is to fly in the face of their universalistic intent. See Knitter, *No Other Name?* 184–86.

[25] See Vatican I's dogmatic constitution *Dei Filius*. For the English translation, see Joseph Neuner and Jacques Dupuis, ed., *The Christian Faith in the Doctrinal Documents of the Catholic Church* (New York: Alba House, 1982), 45.

[26] 1 assume that it is agreed that the sort of "verification principle" proposed by Alfred Julius Ayer is self-contradictory.

demonstrated to have been correctly drawn from self-evident principles. Faith shares the characteristics of both doubt and opinion, on the one hand, and intuition and knowledge, on the other. Like intuition and knowledge, faith adheres firmly to one side; like doubt and opinion, it lacks the perfection of clear sight. What makes faith possible is the will (and Christians add that their will is moved by divine grace) that chooses to assent to one side because it sees this assent as a good. In the words of Thomas Aquinas:

> Sometimes, however, the understanding can be determined to one side of a contradictory proposition neither immediately through the definition of the terms, as is the case with principles, nor yet in virtue of principles, as is the case with conclusions from a demonstration. And in this situation our understanding is determined by the will, which chooses to assent to one side definitely and precisely because of something which is enough to move the will, though not enough to move the understanding, namely, since it seems good or fitting to assent to this side. And this is the state of one who believes.[27]

John Henry Newman offers a more phenomenological account of how one arrives at an assent. Making a distinction between "notional" and "real" assents (the former to ideas and remaining abstract, the latter to things and affecting one's behavior) and a distinction between "formal" and "informal" inferences (the former by means of deduction, the latter through the imagination) Newman argues that assent in faith is made possible by the "illative sense," that is, the ability through the imagination to bring together various disparate arguments and probabilities in such a way as to produce in the knower an unshakable certitude about a particular state of affairs, even though there is no objective certainty.

> Christianity is addressed, both as regards its evidences and its contents, to minds which are in the normal condition of human nature, as believing in God and in a future judgment. Such minds it addresses both through the intellect and through the imagination; creating a certitude of its truth by arguments too various for direct enumeration, too personal and deep for words, too powerful and concurrent for refutation.[28]

An objection may be entered here: What has been said for Jesus can, on this epistemological principle, be said for Gautama or Muhammad or any other religious figure as well. The answer, in my judgment, must be, yes, indeed, because

---

[27] *De Veritate*, q. 14, a. 1, reply. For the English translation, see *Truth*, trans. James V. McGlynn (Chicago: Henry Regnery Co., 1953), 210. See also *Summa theologiae* II-II, q. 2, a. 1.

[28] John Henry Newman, *An Essay in Aid of a Grammar of Assent* (Notre Dame, Ind.: University of Notre Dame Press, 1979), 379. The work was first published in 1870.

the claim of uniqueness and universality understood in the strong sense is a faith-claim and therefore operates with the same logic.

THE CLAIM OF UNIQUENESS AND UNIVERSALITY AND THE AIMS OF INTERRELIGIOUS DIALOGUE

But does this logic not make interreligious dialogue an endless monologue among the deaf, with each partner making a claim of uniqueness and universality for his or her religious founder without ever being able to settle the truth? The answer to this query brings us to the last issue of our discussion, which has to do with the purpose of interreligious dialogue. Four forms of interreligious dialogue have been distinguished, each with its own aim: the "dialogue of life," in which people of diverse faiths live together, sharing their everyday joys and sorrow; the "dialogue of action," in which they collaborate for justice, peace, and the integral development of all peoples; the "dialogue of religious experience," in which they, rooted in their own religious traditions, share their spiritual riches in forms of common prayer, worship, asceticisrn, and so on; and the "dialogue of theological exchange," in which scholars of one faith seek to deepen their understanding of the religious traditions of another faith and, when necessary, to correct the misunderstandings of their own faith.[29]

Only the fourth form of dialogue interests us here. The question is whether, on the epistemological principles adduced above, it would be condemned to being nothing more than the participants' endless and irrefutable profession of faith in dialogue in the uniqueness and universality of their own religious founders. It would seem that such a conversation will never lead to a consensus capable of producing a sort of ecumenical esperanto with which to construct a "universal theology of religion."[30] In reply, it should be noted, first of all, that the goal of theological interreligious dialogue is not to construe a universal theology of religion whose possibility is predicated upon a core religious experience. The existence of this common religious experience has been proved to be highly improbable; at any rate, there is no scholarly agreement as to the essential features of such alleged common experience. Rather, the goal of the "dialogue of theological exchange" is seeking understanding of the other faiths

---

[29] See *Dialogue and Proclamation,* jointly issued by the Pontifical Council for Interreligious Dialogue and the Congregation for the Evangelization of Peoples (June 20, 1991). The English text of *DP* is available in William Burrows, ed., *Redemption and Dialogue: Reading* Redemptoris Missio *and* Dialogue and Proclamation (Maryknoll, N.Y.: Orbis Books, 1993), 3–55.

[30] The project of constructing a universal theology of religion seems to be proposed by those who hold that there is a common core of religious experience in all religions, such as Leonard Swidler and Wilfred Cantwell Smith. See their essays in Leonard Swidler, ed., *Toward a Universal Theology of Religion* (Maryknoll, N.Y.: Orbis Books, 1987), 5–72. For a critique of this proposal of a common religious core, see George Lindbeck, *The Nature of Doctrine* (Philadelphia: Westminster, 1984); and Peter C. Phan, "Gott als Heiliges Mysterium und die Suche nach 'Gottes-Äquivalenten' im Interreligiosen Dialog," *Zeitschrift für Missionswissenschaft und Religionswissenschaft* 3 (1990): 161–75.

and one's own faith in the light of other faiths. Such understanding may and should lead to the other three forms of dialogue, without having to postulate the existence of a core religious experience.

Second, the practice of interreligious dialogue can indeed focus on the issue of uniqueness and universality without being bogged down in interminable protestations of faith. An example will clarify this point. It is well known that in Mahayana Buddhism Gautama, who in the *Tripikata* did not claim to be identical with the Saving Truth or the Liberating Path but only to be the Path-finder and Truth-discoverer, was gradually transformed into the eternal Truth that preexists Gautama (the *Dharma*), the Lord of the Cosmos *(lokanatha)*, the Knower of the World *(lokavidu)*, the Great Being *(mahasatta)*, the Lord *(bhagavan)* to be worshiped and praised.[31] In the history of Christian thought a similar process can be discerned in the development of Christology, for instance, from the Suffering Servant of Markan Christology to the Incarnate Logos of Johannine Christology. There has been a transformation of Jesus as the preacher of the kingdom of God into the Christ preached as the embodiment of the kingdom, of the Son of God into God the Son to be worshiped and praised.[32]

Suppose now that a Buddhist (mahayanist and not theravadin) believes that Gautama is the unique savior and that a Christian believes that Jesus is the unique savior (either in the exclusivistic or inclusivistic sense). Imagine that these two believers meet for an interreligious dialogue. Rather than bracketing those beliefs, they should express their claims as accurately as possible and present as clearly as they can the arguments that undergird them. It is hoped that the partners in dialogue go away from this intellectual exchange with a better understanding of the nature and scope of the claim of uniqueness and universality, of the reasons for which Christians and Buddhists make such a claim for their respective founders, and of the historical development of such a claim. Presumably they will have understood that the claim of uniqueness and universality is a faith-claim, that as such it has its own criteria of verification, that it should not be confused with the claim of uniqueness and universality of the social institutions that these founders have spawned (the *sangha* or the church), and that there is a homology between the development of Buddhology and Christology.[33]

---

[31] See David Kalupahana, *Buddhist Philosophy: A Historical Analysis* (Honolulu: University of Hawaii Press, 1976), 112–26.

[32] The bibliography on the development of New Testament Christology is huge. Important works include Reginald H. Fuller, *The Foundations of New Testament Christology* (New York: Charles Scribner's Sons, 1965); James D. G. Dunn, *Unity and Diversity in the New Testament*, rev. ed. (London: SCM Press, 1990); and idem, *Christology in the Making*, 2d ed. (London: SCM Press, 1989).

[33] For a discussion of the parallels between Buddhology and Christology, see Pieris, "The Buddha and the Christ," 162–77. Pieris points out that, corresponding to Christology, there is an "ascending Buddhology" (in Southeast Asia) and a "descending Buddhology" (in Northern Asia). He also notes, rightly to my mind, that the claim of uniqueness for one's religious founder is a faith-claim (he calls it "kerygmatic affirmation"), but I do not agree with him that "the only convincing proof it adduces is martyrdom," that is, liberation (174). The criterion of truth cannot be merely or only praxis.

Such an understanding should be a more-than-satisfactory result of interreligious dialogue. Of course, it is quite possible that as the result of the conversation the Christian and the Buddhist will be more convinced of the grounds of their respective claims, or that one is persuaded by the arguments of the other and so decides to convert to the other's faith. At any rate, they are urged to move beyond the dialogue of "theological exchange" to undertake the other forms of dialogue of "life," "action," and "religious experience."

Finally, what about the claim of the uniqueness and universality of the religious institutions founded by or at least somehow connected with religious charismatic figures, or to continue with our example, Christianity? I propose that it should be abandoned altogether in the context of interreligious dialogue. There are four reasons for this. First, historically, this claim has always been presented as an empirical claim, at least by the Roman Catholic Church. Vatican I declared: "To the sole Catholic Church belong all the manifold and wonderful endowments which by divine disposition are meant to put into light the credibility of the Christian faith. Nay more, the Church by herself, with her marvelous propagation, eminent holiness and inexhaustible fruitfulness in everything that is good, with her Catholic unity and invincible stability, is a great and perpetual motive of credibility and an irrefutable testimony of her divine mission."[34] As an empirical claim, its validity must be tested by an examination of the facts. And it is quite unlikely that such a sweeping claim can be borne out by the facts.

Second, this claim has often been associated in the past with colonialism and religious imperialism. The history of Christian mission furnishes ample evidence of this.[35] It is the triumphalistic claim for Christianity as a social organization, and not the claim of the uniqueness and universality of Jesus as the crucified Christ, that produced in Christians self-righteousness, contempt for other religions, and lust for domination.

Third, this claim, often encapsulated in the formula "extra ecclesiam nulla salus" (No salvation outside the church) has been shown to be historically and culturally dependent. Historically, Christians who made this claim were convinced that the only world that existed was Christian Europe. This conviction was shattered by Columbus's "discovery" of the New World. Culturally, Christians' limited grasp of human psychology led them to think that those who refused to accept the gospel were guilty of sinning against the truth. Contemporary psychology allows us to understand the various factors that influence a person's decision, and of those factors he or she may not be conscious and therefore not responsible.[36]

---

[34] Vatican I, *Dei Filius*, chap. III.

[35] For a history and theology of mission, see David J. Bosch, *Transforming Mission: Paradigm Shifts in Theology of Mission* (Maryknoll, N.Y.: Orbis Books, 1991); and Stephen Bevans and Roger P. Schroeder, *Constants in Contexts: Theology of Mission for Today* (Maryknoll, N.Y.: Orbis Books, 2004).

[36] For a study of the doctrine "no salvation outside the Church," see Francis A. Sullivan, *Salvation Outside the Church? Tracing the History of the Catholic Response* (New York: Paulist Press, 1992).

Fourth, in recent Catholic theology there has been a widespread consciousness of and theological reflection on the "sinfulness" of the church.[37] Vatican II speaks of the "Church, clasping sinners to her bosom, at once holy and in need of purification" (*LG*, no. 8). The empirical claim of uniqueness and universality of the church must be abandoned, or at least severely curtailed, in view of this renewed sense of the church's imperfections.[38]

In conclusion, here, in brief, are my proposals with regard to the claim of uniqueness and universality in interreligious dialogue:

1. Such a claim, if it is a fundamental article of faith of one's religious tradition, must be maintained in interreligious dialogue. The pluralist thesis is therefore rejected.

2. A distinction must be made between the claim of uniqueness and universality of one's religious founder and that of uniqueness and universality of one's religion as a social organization. The former claim is an affirmation of faith; the latter is an empirical statement. Different epistemologies and criteria of verification obtain in each case.

3. Whereas the faith-claim of the uniqueness and universality of one's religious founder must be clearly maintained and defended, the empirical claim of uniqueness and universality of one's institutional religion must be abandoned or at least extensively qualified in the context of interreligious dialogue. In other words, in interreligious dialogue it is possible and necessary to combine a "high" Christology (or Buddhology) with a "low" ecclesiology (or *sanghology*).[39]

4. Finally, a "high" Christology need not adopt the exclusivist thesis but is compatible with a Christian inclusivist theology of religions.

---

[37] See Karl Rahner, "The Church of Sinners," *Theological Investigations* (New York: Crossroad, 1982), 6:253–69. Originally written in 1947, the essay argues that one should speak not only of the "Church of sinners" but also of the "sinfulness of the church."

[38] In this respect the difference between the claim of Jesus' uniqueness and universality and that of the church's uniqueness and universality is clear. Whereas there has been an explicit acknowledgment of the sinfulness of the church, the sinlessness of Jesus has been affirmed from the very beginning (see, e.g., 2 Cor 5:21; Heb 4:15; 1 Pt 2:22; Jn 8:46; 1 Jn 3:5) and has never been questioned. Furthermore, it seems that only one who is sinless can be said to be the universal savior, for, were he or she saved by someone else, that someone else is the ultimate savior. From a practical standpoint, this acknowledgment of the sinfulness of the church allows the possibility of "loyal opposition" to and constructive critique of the church whereby the claim of its uniqueness and universality is rendered more credible.

[39] It is obvious that there is no opposition between a "high" Christology (or "descending Christology") and a "low" Christology (or "ascending Christology"), just as there is no contradiction between a "high" ecclesiology and a "low" ecclesiology.

6

God as Holy Mystery

THE QUEST FOR GOD-EQUIVALENTS
IN INTERRELIGIOUS DIALOGUE

One obvious thing about matters divine in religion is that believers, at least in monotheistic faiths, apply different names to the one and same God they worship and that different religions employ different names to designate the divine. The burden of this chapter is not to investigate how a particular religion uses different names for the one God in whom it professes its faith, whether these names say anything positive about that deity, and whether they are simply synonyms describing the selfsame deity. Rather, my question is whether the different names that different religions use to designate God are totally dissimilar or whether there exist some similarities among them so that these names can be termed *God-equivalents*, and, if the second alternative is granted, whether it is worthwhile in interreligious dialogue to identify them and how to do so.

Note that by different divine names I do not refer to the banal fact that the word *God* is said differently in different cognate languages (Theos, Deus, Dieu, Dio, Gott, God, etc.), but to the fact that at first sight the divine names in different religions seem to reflect different experiences and conceptual articulations of God. The issue under consideration is whether there is a parallel or equivalence among them.

THE NAMES OF GOD AND GOD-EQUIVALENTS

To the question of whether divine names used by different religions are equivalent, the following answers are possible:[1]

1. All religions are the same because they originate from a common experience of the divine being, so that their conceptual framework and categories, though expressed in different languages and cultural modes, are basically identical. On

---

[1] The following four positions are presented as ideal types rather than exact descriptions of theories of religion proposed by particular scholars.

the basis of this common core of religious experience a universal religion may be founded and a kind of "theological esperanto" can be devised.[2]

2. Each religion embodies a totally unique experience of the divine being and expresses this experience in a totally unique conceptual framework with distinctive categories so that no equivalence exists among different names employed by different religions to designate divinity. Religions are totally incommensurable with each other. To compare them would be tantamount to comparing apples with oranges.[3]

3. All religions are categorical expressions of a transcendental experience of the divine which is the condition of possibility for such categorical expressions. These expressions, whether rituals, sacrifices, behaviors, or doctrines, are not identical in their meanings because of their diverse cultural matrixes. What is common to all religions is the transcendental experience of the Absolute. This transcendental experience occurs in the inescapable drive of the human mind and will in acts of knowing and loving toward Absolute Truth/Absolute Value, which can never be grasped as an object but remains the ever-elusive goal of human anticipation. Since this experience is expressed in culturally diverse symbols, it is not possible to construct a universal religion, nor is it feasible to devise a sort of theological esperanto common to all religions. At best some of the doctrines formulated by these religions can be regarded as analogous or equivalent categorical expressions of the transcendental experience.[4]

4. Religions do not originate from some alleged common experience of the divine, transcendental or categorical. Religious doctrines are neither propositional nor symbolic expressions of an inner experience of God. Rather, religions are a complex of social constructs of various kinds—rituals, ethical prescriptions, doctrines, and so on—that mold a person's thinking and behavior, and the meaning of their doctrinal assertions can be gauged only in the context of their functions and uses. Religious doctrines, in other words, function as rules or grammar governing the religious speech and activities of the individual or community of believers. If there are equivalents among the doctrines of various religions, the equivalence does not reside in what they teach, which is more often than not impossible to determine with precision because of their radically diverse cultural contexts, but in the functions and uses they have in shaping the faith and practice of the community.[5]

---

[2] This appears to be the position of Leonard Swidler. He speaks of an "ecumenical esperanto" in interreligious and inter-ideological dialogue. See Leonard Swidler, ed., *Toward a Universal Theology of Religion* (Maryknoll, N.Y.: Orbis Books, 1987), 32–46.

[3] This is a possible conclusion for those who follow Wittgenstein in holding that religions are like tools or games that have different uses or rules.

[4] This is the position of so-called transcendental Thomism, especially as expounded by Karl Rahner.

[5] This is the position of George Lindbeck in *The Nature of Doctrine: Religion and Theology in a Postliberal Age* (Philadelphia: Westminster, 1984). Lindbeck describes his own position as a "cultural-linguistic" approach to religion and a "regulative" or "use" theory of doctrine.

In this chapter I shall reject the first and second positions and argue for some combination of the third and fourth. Specifically, I hold that the quest for God-equivalents in religious doctrines is best carried out if, negatively, it is not conceived as a search for and comparison between divine names that are regarded at the outset as culturally different expressions, but ultimately possessing an identical meaning in their affirmations about God; in other words, the search for a universal religion and a common theological language is ill-advised and futile.

Nevertheless, I do not think that religions are totally strangers to one another; after all, they are human activities vis-à-vis Ultimate Reality, and there is therefore a common basis among them, at least insofar as they are human activities. Hence, a quest for equivalences is possible and useful for interreligious dialogue. However, this quest is predicated upon a distinction between what Karl Rahner calls a transcendental religious experience and a categorical religious experience. Transcendental religious experience, however, should not be understood as some pre-linguistic, vague, internal experience that is at some later date articulated in various symbols.[6] Rather, transcendental experience is the condition of possibility of categorical religious experiences. There are no pre-linguistic transcendental experiences apart from particular, historical categorical experiences, nor are there categorical experiences without the conditions that make them possible, which are called transcendental experiences.

Moreover, religious doctrines and symbols are not like mathematical signs or theorems. Their main function is not to inform but to form. As religious language (that is, the first-order language that includes myths, stories, songs, bodily gestures, rituals, works of art, and so on) they perform specific tasks in arousing and fostering acts of worship, praise, thanksgiving, penance, proclamation, exhortation, and so forth. In other words, religious doctrines are not primarily interpretations of a world view but truths people live and are transformed by. The quest for God-equivalents on this level must therefore be conceived as an inquiry into the equivalent functions that this first-order language performs in and for the community of believers.

Beside this first-order language there is also a second-order language, that of theology and religious philosophy, which defines, describes, analyzes, explains, systematizes, and justifies in a reflective and critical fashion what the first-order religious language proclaims and prescribes. Second-order language tends to be more abstract and denotative than symbolic and connotative; it aims at promoting understanding rather than faith. It is, in Anselm's words, the language of *fides quaerens intellectum*. At this level the quest for God-equivalents will be most fruitful if attention is focused on the grammatical structure of such

---

[6] Lindbeck seriously misrepresented Rahner's position by including him in the experiential-expressive group. This prevented him from taking advantage of Rahner's insights in developing his cultural-linguistic approach to religion and regulative theory of doctrine. This is what I attempt to do in this chapter. For an evaluation of Lindbeck in the context of narrative theology, see Gary L. Comstock, "Two Types of Narrative Theology," *Journal of the American Academy of Religion* 55 (Winter 1987): 687–717.

God-talk, its vocabulary, its syntax, and its kinds. In what follows I attempt to provide some reasons for the proposals I have made; I close these considerations with a caveat that all religious language, both first order and second order, is an essentially analogous discourse about God as Holy Mystery.

RELIGIOUS EXPERIENCE AND RELIGIOUS LANGUAGE

It was fashionable among philosophers and historians of religions, especially after Kant's and Hume's attacks against rational arguments for God's existence, and under the influence of the Romantic movement's new concern for subjectivity and the life of emotions and intuitions of the individual, to identify one particular religious experience as either the source or the essence of religion. This attempt gave rise to what may be called a genetic or experiential-expressive theory of religions. In this view different religions are considered diverse expressions or objectifications of a common core experience that serves as the source or norm of all these religions.

This common core religious experience has been variously described. Friedrich Schleiermacher speaks of "the feeling of an absolute dependence";[7] Julian Huxley of "man's capacity for awe and reverence";[8] A. W. Hayden of "the outreach of man, the social animal, for the values of the satisfying life";[9] and Rudolf Otto of the "*sensus numinis*," that is, the feeling of awe and fascination vis-à-vis the "*mysterium tremendum et fascinans*."[10] Contemporary thinkers, though not of the experiential-expressive school in the strict sense, have analyzed various human situations from which a religious experience can arise or with which it can be identified. Paul Tillich speaks of human existence as estrangement from Being.[11] Langdon Gilkey deals with the experience of contingency, relativity, temporality, and freedom.[12] John Macquarrie highlights the tension between the polarities of human existence: possibility and facticity, rationality and irrationality, responsibility and impotence, anxiety and hope, individual and community.[13] Bernard Lonergan speaks of the experience of being in love without any restriction.[14] David Tracy analyzes limit-questions in science and morality and limit-situations in the everyday world.[15] John Dunne describes

---

[7] See his *On Religion*, trans. John Oman (New York: Harper & Row, 1958); and idem, *The Christian Faith*, trans. H. R. Mackintosh (New York: Harper & Row, 1956).

[8] See his *Religion without Revelation* (New York: New American Library, 1958).

[9] See his *Man's Search for the Good Life: An Inquiry into the Nature of Religions* (New York: Harper Brothers, 1937).

[10] See his *The Idea of the Holy*, trans. John W. Harvey (New York: Oxford University Press, 1958).

[11] See his *Systematic Theology*, 3 vols. (New York: Harper & Row, 1951, 1957, 1963); and idem, *The Courage to Be* (New Haven, Conn.: Yale University Press, 1952).

[12] See his *Naming the Whirlwind: The Renewal of God-Language* (New York: Bobbs-Merrill, 1969).

[13] See his *Principles of Christian Theology* (New York: Scribner's, 1977).

[14] See his *Method in Theology* (New York: Herder and Herder, 1972).

[15] See his *Blessed Rage for Order* (New York: The Seabury Press, 1975).

renunciation, death, time, and love.[16] Peter Berger examines the significance of play, hope, humor, and the propensity for order.[17] Edward Schillebeeckx refers to the quest for the *humanum*.[18] Hans Küng analyzes basic trust in reality.[19] Illtyd Trethowan speaks of the moral experience of absolute value.[20]

Furthermore, comparative studies of religions in all their dimensions— ritual, experience, narrative, doctrine, ethics, institution, art[21]—have shown that for many elements regarding which the claim of uniqueness has been made by a particular religion, parallels in other religions could be exhibited. Examples abound in each dimension mentioned above and can be cited almost endlessly. Most religions have some rituals and sacrifices (for example, baptismal rites, sacred meals, sacrifices); mystical and emotional experiences are highly prized and encouraged (for example, trance, *bhakti*, *dhvana*, beatific vision, supreme bliss and insight of nirvana); myths and stories are transmitted orally or in writing (such as the theogonic, anthropogonic, and cosmogonic myths as well as stories of founders of religions); similar doctrines are taught (e.g. the uniqueness and personality of God, incarnation, and *avatar*); ethical and legal rules are prescribed (such as the Torah, the Shari'a, the Eightfold Path, the Tao); similar social institutions and structures are erected to maintain religions (such as monasteries and *sangha*, priests and brahmins, prophets and gurus); holy places and artistic works are made for worship (for example, temple, church, images, relics).

Attempts have also been made to identify what Joachim Wach has called "universals in religion." After defining religious experience as the human person's "total," "most intense," and "practical" response to what is experienced as "ultimate reality," Wach proceeds to argue that religious experience is "universal" and universally "tends towards expression" on three levels: "theoretical expression, practical expression, and sociological expression." After a detailed analysis of these expressions, he concludes:

> Here, then, are some universals in religion: man relating himself in the experience which we call religious to ultimate reality. This experience, which is had within the limitations of time and space, tends to be expressed theoretically, practically and sociologically. The forms of this

---

[16] See his *The Way of All the Earth* (Notre Dame, Ind.: University of Notre Dame Press, 1978).

[17] See his *A Rumor of Angels: Modern Society and the Rediscovery of the Supernatural* (New York: Doubleday, 1969).

[18] See his *The Understanding of Faith: Interpretation and Criticism*, trans. N. D. Smith (New York: The Seabury Press, 1974).

[19] See his *Does God Exist? An Answer For Today*, trans. Edward Quinn (New York: Doubleday, 1978).

[20] See his *Absolute Value: A Study in Christian Theism* (New York: Humanities Press, 1970).

[21] These are the seven dimensions around which Ninian Smart organizes his descriptions of religions. See his *The World's Religions* (Englewood Cliffs, N.J.: Prentice Hall, 1989).

expression, though conditioned by the environment within which it originated, show similarities in structure; there are universal themes in religious thought, the universal is always embedded in the particular. Though
the differences and conflicts arise from particular loyalties, these cannot
simply be left out (as the Enlightenment would have it). They are the
arteries through which the life-blood of religious experience flows. But
they have constantly to be checked and purified.[22]

Both from the unity of religious experience and from the similarity of religious
expressions it is tempting (a temptation to which Enlightenment thinkers frequently succumbed) to conclude that different religions are fundamentally identical and that one religion is as good as another. This identity is especially affirmed at the level of doctrine, since of all seven dimensions of religion described
above, doctrine is the most abstract and the least subject to cultural vagaries and
hence the most universalizable. Among the doctrines, moreover, theology, that
is the doctrine of God, receives particular attention because religion by definition has to do with the divine or the transcendent, or to use Tillich's expression,
it is a matter of ultimate concern.

Not infrequently, therefore, it is asserted, at least on the popular level, that
the divine names and doctrines lying behind such names as El, Zeus, Yahweh,
the Father of Jesus Christ, Allah, Brahman, Vishnu, T'ien, Kami, Ta'aroa, Ahura
Mazda, Olorun, Kwoth, or any other names for the supreme god, designate the
Ultimate Reality called God.

Such facile identification has been rejected by a careful study of the contexts
in which these names originate and are used. It may be true that these names
may designate a supreme, personal deity and creator; nevertheless, their cultural contexts (Canaanite, Greek, Jewish, Christian, Muslim, Brahmanist [of
the *Upanishads*], Hindu [of the *Bhagavadgita*], Chinese, Japanese, Polynesian,
Zoroastrian, Yoruba, Nuer, respectively) are so diverse that the alleged similarities among them have to be whittled down so drastically that they die "the
death by a thousand qualifications."

Antony Flew's famous dictum intimates another challenge to the thesis that
all divine names used by different religions are identical, namely, analytic philosophy, especially as it was developed by Ludwig Wittgenstein in his *Philosophical Investigations*. In this posthumous work Wittgenstein abandoned his
earlier picture theory of language as proposed in his *Tractatus Logico-
Philosophicus,* according to which just as a picture gives knowledge of a scene,
so language gives knowledge of reality. Instead, he suggested the models of
tools and games for understanding language. As tools in a toolbox have different uses for different purposes, so the functions of language are numerous. As
the value of a tool lies in its function, so the value of a sentence, its meaning, is
a function of its use: who is using it, to whom it is addressed, in what context,

---

[22] Joachim Wach, *Types of Religious Experience: Christian and Non-Christian* (Chicago: University of Chicago Press, 1951), 47.

and to attain what purpose. To see language on the model of tools is to put aside the search for a common nature of all languages and to look instead for the concrete, specific uses to which a sentence might be put.

Games provide another model to understand language. Just as there are no universal rules applicable to all kinds of games (football, baseball, cricket, soccer, tennis, squash, chess, bridge, etc.), so the meaning of language can be learned only by examining the rules governing a particular language-game and not some general rule that supposedly covers all different kinds of languages. Such a general rule, were it to exist, would not tell us anything about a particular language. Each language-game is a "form of life," to be understood on its own merits and in terms of its individual characteristics.

What is said about language in general on the model of tool and game can be said *mutatis mutandis* about religious language. Far from being meaningless or noncognitive, as logical positivists maintain on the basis of the verification principle, religious language must be examined in the total context in which it operates. The meaning of a religious belief can be ascertained, Wittgenstein suggests, by asking what consequences the belief might have, by analyzing what the believer opposes to this belief, or by discovering what is connected with it. The meaning of a religious statement is seen in the use that is made of it in a particular situation. To identify its meaning, therefore, one must describe its functions, purposes, and uses, and its relationship to the other language-games.[23]

Wittgenstein's theory of religious language is often welcomed by theistic thinkers as an effective antidote to the reductionistic attacks against it by the earlier analytical tradition, which interpreted it as incompatible with any falsification whatever (Anthony Flew), as inherently incomprehensible (Bernard Williams), as "blik," that is, an attitude or framework for evaluation or explanation (Richard M. Hare), as moral assertions (Richard B. Braithwaite), and as emotive language (A. J. Ayer).

On the other hand, Wittgenstein's theory could be interpreted as adverse to religious language and interreligious dialogue. If religious language is compared to a tool or a game rule, and if one tool cannot be used to perform a job for which it is not intended, and if rules for one kind of game cannot be applied to another, then religion and its language remain totally private, cut off from other areas of human life, and incomprehensible to an outsider. Though they cannot be dismissed as meaningless, they are totally irrelevant to anyone except believers, and the practical effects are not very different from holding that they are meaningless. Furthermore, the various religions themselves would not be able to communicate with one another, especially if one holds that each religion embodies a radically diverse and totally inexpressible mystical experience. Wittgenstein's earlier dictum, "What can be said at all can be said clearly; and whereof one cannot speak thereof one must be silent," may be applicable here. Even if one does not go to the extreme of apophaticism, still it is conceivable

---

[23] For a short and clear presentation of Wittgenstein's theories of religious language, see Norman Malcolm, "Wittgenstein," in *The Encyclopedia of Philosophy*, vol. 8, ed. Paul Edwards (New York: Macmillan, 1967), 327–39.

that religious expressions are so culturally conditioned and distinct that no equivalencies among them are possible.

Wittgenstein himself did not draw such negative conclusions from his theory of religious language. In *Philosophical Investigations* and in his lectures he recognized that it is probable that the language of religion is similar in some respects to other language-games, though not reducible to them. These common elements, he granted, may be combined in a unique way in religious language. Furthermore, he noted that it is possible that religious language is a collection or "family" of languages. That is, it may include ethical language, the language of attitude formation and expression, the language of personal commitment, and others, and these may have various importance in the life of believers.

UNITY OF THE GOD EXPERIENCE AND GOD-EQUIVALENTS

If one grants with Wittgenstein that there are family resemblances not only between religious language and other language-games but also and a fortiori among different religious languages, how are these resemblances, especially in their doctrines of God (God-equivalents), to be determined? I have already said above that to hold the divine names found in different religions to be identical in meaning is to do injustice to their socio-cultural contexts and their diverse functions. Without presupposing that there exists an identical core of religious experience of which various religions are culturally diverse expressions, I suggest that the most fruitful strategy to discern possible God-equivalents is an investigation into (1) the conditions of possibility of categorical religious experiences, (2) the functions of first-order religious language, and (3) the grammar of second-order theological and doctrinal language. The rest of this chapter explores this three-pronged approach.

Among Roman Catholic theologians, Karl Rahner has offered an elaborate analysis of what he terms "the transcendental experience," by which he means

> the subjective, unthematic, necessary and unfailing consciousness of the knowing subject that is co-present in every spiritual act of knowledge, and the subject's openness to the unlimited expanse of all possible reality. It is an experience because this knowledge, unthematic but ever-present, is a moment within and a condition of possibility for every concrete experience of any and every object. This experience is called transcendental experience because it belongs to the necessary and inalienable structures of the knowing subject itself, and because it consists precisely in the transcendence beyond any particular group of possible objects or of categories. Transcendental experience is the experience of transcendence, in which experience the structure of the subject and therefore also the ultimate structure of every conceivable object of knowledge are present together and in identity.[24]

---

[24] Karl Rahner, *Foundations of Christian Faith: An Introduction to the Idea of Christianity*, trans. William Dych (New York: The Seabury Press, 1978), 20. For an excellent

In every act of knowledge and, in an analogous way, of love and freedom of a particular object (for example, a tree or a human person), not only is something known (and therefore there is an explicit relationship between the knowing subject and the object known), but also the subject's knowing is co-known, so that the subject is *ipso facto* conscious of itself, though not explicitly and thematically. This implicit, unthematic, and unobjective presence of the knowing and loving subject to self (that is, knowledge is always self-presence) is, as it were, the luminous zone or horizon within which an individual object upon which attention is focused can become manifest. It is the condition of possibility for such a categorical act of knowing and loving.

It is important to note that for Rahner this self-presence of the subject is not a separate experience in and by itself available apart from concrete acts of knowing and loving. Rather, it is given in and through categorical experiences as their condition of possibility and exists only with, in, and through language. Rahner points out that a tension between original self-consciousness and its conceptualization (which can never *totally* mediate it) is dialectical. On the one hand, the unthematic self-presence of the subject tends toward greater conceptualization, toward language, toward communication. On the other hand, reflection, conceptualization, and language have a necessary orientation to that original knowledge, to that original experience in which what is meant and the experience of what is meant are still one.

If one grants that there is such an original self-presence that functions as an a priori, an antecedent law governing what and how something can become manifest to the subject, a keyhole determining in advance what key fits, as it were, what does it say about the subject? Insofar as the subject is an intelligent and free spirit who can question being in general, it is "fundamentally and by its very nature pure openness for absolutely everything, for being as such."[25] Even a denial of such an unlimited openness of the human spirit implicitly and necessarily affirms it, for a subject that knows itself to be finite (and the human person is such a finite subject) has already transcended its finiteness. It has differentiated itself as finite from "a subjectively and unthematically given horizon of possible objects that is of infinite breadth."[26] The human person has therefore an anticipation *(Vorgriff)*, which has no intrinsic limit, toward being as such, because even the suspicion of such an intrinsic limitation of the subject posits this anticipation itself as going beyond the suspicion.[27]

Several features of this *Vorgriff* must be carefully noted. First, though it is called an "experience" of transcendence, it is not given by itself apart from other categorical experiences as a kind of common core experience of which

---

exposition of Rahner's transcendental philosophy, see Thomas Sheehan, *Karl Rahner: The Philosophical Foundations* (Athens, Ohio: Ohio University Press, 1987). For a short presentation, see Peter C. Phan, *Eternity in Time: A Study of Karl Rahner's Eschatology* (Selinsgrove, Pa.: Susquehanna University Press, 1988), 44–46.

[25] Rahner, *Foundations of Christian Faith*, 20.

[26] Ibid.

[27] For Rahner's classic exposition of this *Vorgriff*, see his *Spirit in the World*, trans. William Dych (New York: Herder and Herder, 1968).

different religions are diverse expressions or objectifications. Rahner, *pace* Lindbeck, is no experiential-expressive theorist of religion. Rather, this transcendental experience is embedded in each and every concrete particular experience of knowledge and volition as its condition of possibility. Second, though it is conscious (insofar as it is an act of the intellect and will), it is an unthematic and implicit knowledge and volition of being itself. Nevertheless, by its nature, it tends toward linguistic objectification. Third, this *Vorgriff* is essentially a dynamic drive of the intellect and will or *excessus* or intentionality toward being itself, which remains forever an asymptotic goal; it reaches out and anticipates but never grasps being as such as its object.

What is being itself, which the human spirit anticipates but never grasps? Rahner identifies it with God. For him the word *God* is used to refer to "the 'ineffable one,' the 'nameless one' who does not enter into the world we can name as a part of it. It means the 'silent one' who is always there, and yet can always be overlooked, unheard, and, because it expresses the whole in its unity and totality, can be passed over as meaningless."[28] Human beings are transcendentally oriented toward this God, and this basic and original orientation constitutes their permanent existential as spiritual subjects.

Since the goal of this human self-transcendence in knowledge remains forever unreachable, indefinable, and ineffable, the appropriate "name" for this reality, Rahner suggests, is "Mystery." The word "mystery" has the advantage over other names of God such as "absolute being," "being in an absolute sense," "ground of being," "ultimate cause," or even "God" insofar as these names run the risk of implying that God is one being, albeit the greatest, in the chain of other beings that can be categorically apprehended. Of course, the infinite horizon, which is the goal of transcendence and which is, as it were, the light by which we know other beings, cannot itself be given a name. For this name would situate the goal among the realities that are known within the horizon of this goal. The appellation Mystery is intended to underscore that the goal of transcendence is infinite, nameless, indefinable, and ineffable.

Moreover, because this Mystery is the term of transcendence not only of human knowledge but also of human freedom, will, and love, it is to be called Holy Mystery: "If transcendence moves in freedom and in love towards a term which itself opens this transcendence, then we can say that that which is nameless and which is not at our disposal and at whose complete disposal we exist, that this very thing is present in loving freedom, and this is what we mean when we say 'holy mystery.'"[29]

In the light of Rahner's reflections on God as Holy Mystery, it may be said that the different names by which various religions call upon God, though they are not merely diverse expressions of an alleged common core religious experience, are equivalent. This equivalence does not reside in a common root experience of the divine. The Jewish experience and conceptual articulation of God as Yahweh is not identical, culturally, philosophically, and theologically, with the

---

[28] Rahner, *Foundations of Christian Faith*, 46.
[29] Ibid., 65–66.

Christian experience and conceptualization of God as the Father of Jesus Christ, nor with the Muslim experience and conceptualization of God as Allah, and much less with the Hindu experience and understanding of God as Brahman or Vishnu. The list can go on indefinitely. Rather, in each of these categorically different religious experiences, which are expressed in different philosophical and theological concepts, there is embedded as their intrinsic condition of possibility the human person's self-transcendence in knowledge and love toward its source and term, that is, Holy Mystery. The equivalence of the divine names lies in the fact that they point to the source and term of human self-transcendence.

Various divine names are not synonyms designating the same divine being; rather, they affirm different things about divinity. Yet they are not totally incommensurable with one another, not because they are symbolizations of a common religious experience (a cultural-linguistic impossibility), but because of the human spirit's *Vorgriff* toward Holy Mystery as such. This transcendental experience, to reiterate, is not an experience apart from other experiences but is given in and through them, implicitly and unthematically, as the condition that makes them possible. It is the thread that links them together.

This transcendental experience, however, tends toward explicit symbolizations and takes the form of rituals, prayer, legal and ethical prescriptions, institutions, stories, doctrines, artistic works, and so forth. With regard to linguistic expressions, with which we are concerned here, we must recall the important distinction we drew earlier in this chapter drawn between first-order language and second-order language. First-order language (or *religious* language), used mainly in liturgical contexts, is vivid, concrete, emotional, often metaphorical; its function is to invite, persuade, prescribe, inspire, accuse, invoke, praise, adore. Second-order language (*theological* language) is abstract, rigorous, precise; its function is to describe, explain, and justify in a critical and systematic fashion what has been accepted in faith as normative and true. Of course, there are many words that cross the border between the two languages. Nevertheless, it is apparent that in liturgical contexts God is often invoked as the "Rock of refuge" rather than "ipsum esse subsistens," and vice versa, in theology, God is described as "Absolute Being" rather than "Shepherd of the flock."

What is important for our discussion of God-equivalents is that these two languages have different purposes. If there are God-equivalents in various religions, I suggest that in religious language they manifest themselves in the functions they perform for the community of believers, whereas in theological language they appear in the way they authoritatively regulate the religious community's discourse, attitude, and action. To use Wittgenstein's metaphor of game, religious language is like the movement of players; it performs in such a way that the game (that is, worship) is successfully carried out. Theological language is like the rules of the game; it ensures that the game is played fairly and correctly. Or to vary the metaphor, religion is like an idiom in which religious language functions like spoken words and texts to affirm what is true, to move readers to accept and live it, whereas theological language is like the grammar (morphology, syntax, semantics) ensuring that the words are correctly used and texts adequately written. Theological language is used in the context of a search for understanding the faith, principally by describing, explaining, and justifying it, whereas religious language, while not excluding understanding, aims at forming and transforming the community of believers.

Of course, divine names are used in both languages of different religions, and the quest for God-equivalents must take the distinctive uses of each language into account. In religious language the various names for divinity are equivalent to one another in the functions they perform. Suppose that one attends a Jewish Passover, a Christian Eucharist, a Muslim Dhu-al-Hijja, a Hindu *bhakti* ritual, a Shinto ceremony at a shrine, a sacrifice in an African religion, where the names of God or gods are invoked, what are these names intended to bring about? Are these functions identical or at least analogous? A partial list of the functions of these divine names includes the following: to call forth feelings of adoration, worship, praise, humility, or gratitude on the part of the believers; to remind them of the mighty acts that God has performed on their behalf; to urge them to commit themselves in faithful love to their God; to prescribe an appropriate behavior to inspire certain kinds of action or reinforce certain dispositions; to accuse failing believers of their sins and provoke them to repentance. Of course, not all divine names perform all these functions (and others unmentioned), nor do they perform them equally, but in their religious context divine names are equivalent to one another not so much in what they affirm of divinity (which may be extremely different) but in the effects they have on the worshipers.[30]

Whereas in religious language divine names are mutually equivalent in their functions, in theological language they are so in the way they regulate or authorize certain ways of speaking and acting. I agree with George Lindbeck that theological language does not make truth-claims. Ontological truth-claims are made in religious language; for example, the statement "God is a loving father" claims to correspond to objective reality. Theological language *assumes* the truth of this assertion and goes on to describe, explain, analyze, or defend it in a critical way and regulate which speech and behavior would be inconsistent or consistent with it. As Lindbeck puts it, "Just as grammar by itself affirms nothing either true or false regarding the world in which language is used, but only about language, so theology and doctrine, to the extent that they are second-order activities, assert nothing either true or false about God and his relation to creatures, but only speak about such assertions."[31]

---

[30] Two excellent collections of essays on religious and theological language may be mentioned: Robert P. Scharlemann, ed., *Naming God* (New York: Paragon House Publishers, 1985); and Robert P. Scharlemann and Gilbert E. M. Ogutu, eds., *God in Language* (New York: Paragon House Publishers, 1987). Very helpful studies on religious language include Peter Donovan, *Religious Language* (New York: Hawthorn Books, 1976); John Macquarrie, *God-Talk* (New York: Harper & Row, 1967), James I. Campbell, *The Language of Religion* (New York: The Bruce Publishing Co., 1971); Thomas Fawcett, *The Symbolic Language of Religion* (Minneapolis: Augsburg, 1971); Ian Ramsey, *Religious Language* (London: SCM Press, 1957).

[31] Lindbeck, *The Nature of Doctrine*, 69.

Divine names in theological language, I suggest, work in the same fashion. For example, the Christian names for divinity as "the Father Almighty, Creator of heaven and earth" or "the Father of our Lord Jesus Christ" or "Father, Son, and Spirit" serve as a grammar regulating which speech about the Christian God is consistent with Christian faith. For instance, a discourse on God that denies an ontological distinction between divinity and the world, or that affirms several equal gods, or that negates the plurality of "persons" in the one God would not be considered acceptable to Christian faith. Similarly, any behavior that accepts and promotes racism, sexism, or a caste system, for instance, would not be deemed compatible with the Christian naming of deity. The same should be said about the Jewish, Hindu, Muslim, Shintoist, Taoist, Zoroastrian, Yoruba, Nuer, etc., names for deity, of course with variations appropriate to their cultural contexts. The equivalence among these names resides in the manner in which they authorize or prescribe speech and conduct as harmonious with or opposed to their respective faith-contexts. This does not deny that there may be some (I suspect very few) profound conceptual similarities among various divine names.

This apparently negative position with regard to God-equivalents may prove to be an advantage in interreligious dialogue. Partners in dialogue need not come together with a prior conviction that they have a common concrete religious experience of which their religions are simply culturally different expressions and thus be forced to make an odious comparison to see which of them is the better expression. They can simply regard their religions and their conceptualizations as different languages with different grammars, proceed to examine how their religious language functions on behalf of their adherents, and determine how this theological language regulates their speech, attitudes, and behaviors. From the discussion it may emerge that despite profound differences in their liturgies and theologies, divine names in different religions have similar functions and grammatical rules.

In conclusion, it is important to remind oneself in a discussion on God-equivalents that all human language about God is nothing more than stammering, necessary though it is, about Holy Mystery. Holy Mystery is not so much a divine name as a reminder to us that the reality toward which our self-transcendence reaches out but never grasps is the infinite, the ineffable, the indefinable, the "Neti, neti," of which deity we know what he/she/it is not, as Saint Thomas says, rather than what it/she/he is.

7

Talking of God in Many
and Diverse Cultures and Religions

A GOD FOR ASIA

Imagine that you are going to Asia as a Christian missionary for the first time. Compared with missionaries in the sixteenth or seventeenth century, say, Francis Xavier in Japan, Matteo Ricci in China, Roberto de Nobili in India, and Alexandre de Rhodes in Vietnam, you have a far better chance of arriving there in one piece. Your trip will not take two or three years, the average time it took then to sail from Lisbon, Portugal, to Goa, India, or to Macao, China, depending on the weather, the condition of the sea, and the availability of ships. Unlike your forebears, you will not run the risk of being turned into pabulum for God's aquatic creatures or dying of any number of diseases on the way. The worst that may happen to you now is an overdose of movies, jet lag, and indigestion from airline food.

THE COMPLEX AND PLURALISTIC WORLD OF ASIA

The Asia you are about to enter is vastly different from that of the sixteenth or seventeenth century, when waves of Catholic missionaries, mostly Portuguese and Spanish, supported by the military and economic might of their countries, went in search of souls to save. It has grown far more complex, more diverse, and its peoples more numerous. Fortunately, you are much better informed than your predecessors about the complexity and variety of peoples and countries you plan to evangelize, together with their myriad languages, cultures, customs, and cuisines. You may even have close friends who hail from Asia with whom you have occasionally sampled Mongolian barbecue beef, Chinese wonton and sweet and sour pork, Vietnamese *pho* and spring rolls, Indian tandoori chicken, Japanese sashimi and sushi, Filipino *escabeche*, Korean *kim chee*, and Thai *som tum*. You may have participated in Chinese New Year or Vietnamese Tet celebrations; witnessed rituals of ancestor veneration at Asian funerals and weddings; and even visited Buddhist pagodas, Muslim mosques, and Confucian temples. You or one of your relatives might even be married to an Asian.

Everything in Asia today tends to fascinate and frustrate the visitor with its sheer size and dizzying variety.[1] Asia is the earth's largest continent and is home to nearly two-thirds of the world's population, with China and India accounting for almost half of the total population of the globe. Economically, the Asian continent is characterized by extremes. Some countries, such as Japan, Singapore, Taiwan, and South Korea, have technology and industry rivaling those of the most advanced countries in the West; others, such as Vietnam, Cambodia, Laos, North Korea, Bangladesh, Afghanistan, and several of the countries in Central Asia that have recently regained their independence, suffer from abject and widespread poverty. Among the Asian poor, women fare the worst: in Asia, female illiteracy is much higher than that of males, and female babies are more likely to be aborted than male ones. On the other hand, Asia is often depicted as the mysterious and fabulous Orient, abounding in sensual delights and bodily pleasures of every kind. Leaf through a glossy travel brochure and your imagination will transport you to exotic and erotic paradises such as those in Thailand, Hong Kong, and Indonesia, where the tourist industry has wrought devastation on the Asian cultural and moral landscape, especially with a brisk business in prostitution of women and children.

Politically, Asia displays a confusing array of regimes, from democracy to dictatorship, from separation of church and state to theocracy, from laissez-faire capitalism to orthodox communism. Culturally, the variety is no less breathtaking. An intricate mosaic of vastly different languages, races, ethnic groups, and cultures, Asia is far more heterogeneous than any other continent of the world. Indeed, it is widely questioned whether the terms *Asia* and *Asian* denote any commonality at all among the countries of the Near and Middle East, Central Asia, the Indian subcontinent, and the Far East!

Most significant, in view of Christian mission, is the striking fact that Asia is the cradle of the world's major religions—Hinduism, Judaism, Christianity, and Islam. Asia is also the birthplace of many other religious traditions, such as Zoroastrianism, Buddhism, Jainism, Sikhism, Confucianism, Taoism, and Shintoism, not to mention the many tribal or indigenous religions with their own beliefs and rituals. All of these religions and religious traditions have not disappeared, as Christian missionaries predicted. On the contrary, many of them have recently experienced a strong revival and have begun missionary work in the West.

With regard to Christianity in particular, it is extremely important to remember that Jesus was born in Asia and that Christianity had its roots in Asia, notwithstanding its later history and development in the West.[2] Today, in some countries,

---

[1] For a brief description of the Asian context, see Pope John Paul II's apostolic exhortation *Ecclesia in Asia* (*EA*), which was promulgated November 6, 1999, following the Special Assembly for Asia of the Synod of Bishops (April 19–May 14, 1998). For a study of the Asian Synod and the English text of *Ecclesia in Asia*, see Peter C. Phan, ed., *The Asian Synod: Texts and Commentaries* (Maryknoll, N.Y.: Orbis Books, 2000).

[2] *Ecclesia in Asia* stresses this fact: "We thank God for choosing Asia as the earthly dwelling of his incarnate Son, the Savior of the world" (no. 50).

such as the Philippines, Christianity is the dominant religion; in others, such as South Korea and Vietnam, Christians form a significant minority; in still others, such as North Korea, Vietnam, and China, the church is carefully controlled by the government; finally, in many Islamic states the church is discriminated against or forbidden altogether.[3] Even if Christianity currently constitutes only 3 percent of the Asian population, its Asian roots will facilitate its reentry into Asia, provided that it self-consciously retrieves its Asian cultural and religious heritage.

APPROACHING ASIA RELIGIOUSLY

How should Christians step into this multilingual, multiracial, multi-ethnic, multicultural, and multi-religious world of Asia and speak of God to the teeming masses of Asians? Clearly, the first requisite of God-talk in Asia is that it must be pluralistic. The God of Asia is not monochromatic, nor even polychromatic, if by color is meant only race, even if race is an important individual and social identity marker, in Asia as well as elsewhere. Asia is characterized by plurality and diversity not only in race but also, as we have seen, in language, ethnicity, politics, economics, culture, and religion. Consequently, any image of God that is not able, or willing, on the grounds of orthodoxy and fidelity to tradition, to engage these diversities seriously and to be enriched by them, or claims that it is the only possible or the best way of representing the divine, is doomed to incomprehensibility and irrelevance from the start.

Moreover, in our God-talk it is extremely important to recall that when Christianity entered Asia, it did not step into a religious void where God was dead or absent, whether in the first century, when, according to tradition, the apostle Thomas went to India; or in the third century, when Gregory the Illuminator succeeded in making Christianity the official religion of Armenia; or in the fifth century, when Christian missionaries penetrated the Arab kingdoms; or in the seventh century, when the first Christian church was built in China by Nestorian Christians; or in the thirteenth century, when the good news was preached to the Mongolians and the Turks; or in the sixteenth century, when waves of Jesuits, Dominicans, Franciscans, Augustinians, and others swept into various regions of Asia; or in the nineteenth century, when various Protestant denominations joined Catholic missionaries in converting Asian heathens. The Asian bishops at the Asian Synod drew attention to "the multiple and diversified action of the Holy Spirit who continually sows the seeds of truth among all peoples, their religions, cultures and philosophies. This means that these religions, cultures and philosophies are capable of helping people, individually and collectively, to work against evil and to serve life and everything that is good" (*EA*, no. 15). Hence, all God-talk to Asians must begin with an explicit and grateful acknowledgment of the presence of God's Spirit, who has been accompanying, inspiring,

---

[3] For a helpful account of the Catholic church in Asia, see Tom Fox, *Pentecost in Asia* (Maryknoll, N.Y.: Orbis Books, 2000).

comforting, liberating, transforming, sanctifying, and saving the peoples of Asia for hundreds if not thousands of years before Christianity appeared on the scene.

The attitude that behooves Christians when speaking of God to Asians must therefore be one of deepest respect and humility. Indeed, the first act of our Christian God-talk in Asia is, paradoxically, not to talk but to be silent, not to preach but to listen, not to teach but to learn. This behavior is not merely a polite thing to do, part of the social etiquette that a guest must observe in the host's home. Rather, it is steeped in the conviction that Asian cultures and religions, and the Asian peoples themselves, especially the poorest among them and even those whom Christians label heathens, have doctrines and practices that in certain respects are no less true and noble than, or are even superior to, those of Christianity. One need not be an enthusiast about Asia to grant some truth to what Pope John Paul II says about Asians:

> The people of Asia take pride in their religious and cultural values, such as love of silence and contemplation, simplicity, harmony, detachment, non-violence, the spirit of hard work, discipline, frugal living, the thirst for learning and philosophical enquiry. They hold dear the values of respect for life, compassion for all beings, closeness to nature, filial piety towards parents, elders and ancestors, and a highly developed sense of community. In particular, they hold the family to be a vital source of strength, a closely knit community with a powerful sense of solidarity. Asian peoples are known for their spirit of religious tolerance and peaceful co-existence (*EA*, no. 6).

This positive appreciation of Asian cultural, moral, and religious values must also shape the very content of our God-talk. Christians cannot effectively speak to Asians about God unless they first let themselves be taught about God by Asians. Indeed, how can we Christians speak of God's revelation in our Bible without meditating on the sacred scriptures of Asian religions, which, incidentally, are vastly more extensive than ours? How dare we deny a priori their inspired character? On what basis can we say that they are mere human invention and not also the creation of the Logos and the Holy Spirit? Why should we not use them to enlighten our minds and nourish our hearts, inside and outside our liturgical celebrations, not as substitutes for but as complements to our Bible?

When discoursing on the Christian God as Trinity, can we do so without learning from the Hindu faith in the *trimūrti* (the triformic god), that is, Brahmā as creator, Shiva as destroyer, and Vishnu as sustainer? When we represent God as father, will our predominantly if not exclusively masculine language not be challenged and enriched by the goddess tradition of the great Hindu epics such as the *Mahābhārata* and the *Rāmāyana* and of Hindu medieval theology (for example, the goddesses Durgā, Kālī, Rādhā, and Mahādevī)? When theologizing on the incarnation of the Logos in Jesus, do we not derive helpful insights from the Hindu belief in the descent of the gods into the world in their *avatars* as a free and gracious choice and as a playful act of divine self-enjoyment *(līlā)*, or the Buddhist notion of *śunyatā* (emptiness)? When speaking of the Spirit of

God as the divine breath and energy permeating the cosmos, do we not hear echoes in the Taoist view of *ch'i* as the primordial energy, the life force, the cosmic spirit that pervades and enlivens all things? And if we meditate on the God of the mystics who is beyond all concept and speech, should we not recall Lao Tzu's famous lines: "Tao can be talked about, but not the Eternal Tao. Names can be named, but not the Eternal Name. As the origin of heaven-and-earth, it is nameless. As 'the Mother' of all things, it is nameable"?[4]

When we proclaim God's *agape* (love) for us, will our message not be immeasurably enriched by the Buddhist notion of *karunā* (compassion), which is not a mere sense of pity, sentimental sympathy, or vicarious agony over the sufferings of others, but rather a compassion devoid of sorrow that leads to positive action on behalf of our fellow sufferers? And when explaining God's rule and providence over the world through God's will, can we neglect the Confucian notion of the Mandate of Heaven *(tian ming)*, in accord with which we must lead our private and public lives? When introducing Jesus and his ministry to Asians, must we not, as the Asian bishops insisted at the Asian Synod, make use of images that make sense to Asians, such as the Enlightened One (=the Buddha) and Spiritual Guide (=the guru) (*EA*, no. 20)?

In our exposition of God's commandments and the norms of Christian life, can we responsibly ignore the Buddha's teaching on the Eightfold Path and the Buddhist five precepts, or Confucius's teaching on the five virtues governing all our human relationships, that is, humaneness *(ren)*, righteousness *(i)*, proper ritual action *(li)*, wisdom in thought *(chih)*, and loyalty *(hsin)*, or the five pillars (*'ibādāt*) of Islam? When speaking of God's nonviolent resistance to evil on the cross, should we not relate it to the Hindu, Buddhist, and Jaina practice of *ahimsā* (non-injury), which the West learned from Mahātma Gandhi? In exhorting filial love of God and a life of intense prayer and faithful devotion to God, can we leave aside the *bhakti-mārga* (the path of devotion) of Hinduism, or the emphasis on faith in the Buddha and the recitation of his name in Pure Land Buddhism, or Guru Nānak's injunction to "worship the name of the Lord" in Sikhism? In urging obedience to God's holy will, should we not recall what Muhammad teaches about the duty of total and absolute surrender to the one God ("There is no god but God")? When Christians take pride in their monastic traditions, should they not be humbled by the even more ancient and rigorous practices of monastic life in the Buddhist *sangha* (community), the ascetic ideal of the *arhant* in Theravada Buddhism, the self-sacrifice and compassion of the bodhisattva in Mahayana Buddhism, and the meditation practices of Zen Buddhism?

With these questions I do not intend at all to suggest that Christian doctrines about God, Christ, the Spirit, and the moral life are similar to, let alone identical with, the doctrines and practices taught by Asian religions. Nor do I subscribe to the theology of religion, popularly known as pluralism and often associated with John Hick and Paul Knitter, according to which various religions are simply different ways, in principle equally valid, leading to the Real. Nor do I believe that there exists a prior core religious experience common to all religions that is

---

[4] Lao Tzu, *Tao Te Ching*, trans. John C. H. Wu (Boston: Shambhala, 1989), 3.

subsequently expressed in different categories. Anyone familiar with the teachings and practices of Asian religions will readily acknowledge that there are genuine and at times irreconcilable differences between them and those of Christianity and that each of these religions has its own goals and aims. Thus it is possible to argue that a particular religion is better than another, or at least that certain doctrines and practices of a particular religion are false, or that they are worse or better than those of another. But it is precisely *because* of these real differences that Asian religions can teach Christians something that they do not know or practice, or at least do not know or practice as well as non-Christians, just as in certain aspects Christianity can correct and enrich Asian religions.

TALKING OF GOD IN MULTICULTURAL AND MULTI-RELIGIOUS ASIA

In the remaining pages of this chapter I explore how we Christians can talk about God in the context of the many cultures and religions of Asia. My purpose here is not to do what has been referred to as comparative theology, a young discipline that attempts, by means of a close and critical analysis of a text or practice of a non-Christian religion, to obtain a better understanding of a Christian doctrine or practice. Rather, I indicate in general terms how the social, political, economic, cultural, and religious contexts of Asia require that certain themes or aspects of the Christian doctrine of God be given special, albeit not exclusive, emphasis rather than others.

The God That Takes the Side of the Poor

God-talk by the Asian bishops and theologians has been heavily influenced by liberation theology. Liberation theology, with its emphasis on the necessity of the option for the poor, did not, of course, originate in Asia. However, its promotion of justice and human development through the transformation of the socio-political and economic structures, and in particular its conception of the God of Jesus as one who takes the side of the poor have struck a sympathetic chord with Asian Christians, not least because Latin America and Asia share a common legacy of colonialism and economic exploitation by European powers. Repeatedly the Federation of the Asian Bishops' Conferences (FABC), in its plenary assemblies as well as through its various standing offices, has highlighted the urgent need for the church of Asia to make action on behalf of justice and participation in the transformation of the socio-political and economic life one of the top three priorities of the church's mission, the other two being inculturation and interreligious dialogue.[5]

---

[5] My reflections are based on the documents of the FABC and of its various offices. The FABC was founded in 1970, on the occasion of Pope Paul VI's visit to Manila, Philippines. Its statutes, approved by the Holy See *ad experimentum* in 1972, were amended several times and were also approved again each time by the Holy See. For the documents of the FABC and its various institutes, see Gaudencio Rosales and C. G. Arévalo, eds., *For All the Peoples of Asia: Federation of Asian Bishops' Conferences*, vol. 1, *Documents from 1970 to 1991* (Maryknoll, N.Y.: Orbis Books; Quezon City,

A careful review of the FABC's official statements as well as of the various documents issued by the FABC's standing offices shows a significant fact, namely, that there has been little interest on the FABC's part in a purely philosophical or even theological discourse on God, in what has been referred to as the immanent Trinity. That is, instead of discoursing on who God is in God's inner life and intra-trinitarian, eternal relations, as is often done in neo-Scholastic treatises on the triune God, the FABC's overwhelming focus has been on God's activities in the world and God's relationship to us in history, that is, in what God the Father has done for us and the world in his Son Jesus by the power of the Holy Spirit, or in what has been termed the economic Trinity. This lack of interest in metaphysical speculation on God and in the immanent Trinity may be a function of the Asian bent toward the practical and the mystical, but it is certainly also part of the FABC's deliberate methodological decision regarding how best to present God to Asians. The most effective way to explain *who* God *is* is to show *where* God is *present*. God's essence is revealed in God's actions.

For the FABC, God is present and active most clearly in the Asian poor.[6] With humility and courage the Asian bishops have made the preferential option for the poor the fundamental direction of the church of Asia. At the 1970 historic meeting in Manila, they declared:

> It is our resolve, first of all, to be more truly "the Church of the poor." If we are to place ourselves at the side of the multitudes in our continent, we must in our way of life share something of their poverty. The Church cannot set up islands of affluence in a sea of want and misery; our own personal lives must give witness to evangelical simplicity, and no man, no matter how lowly or poor, should find it hard to come to us and find in us their [*sic*] brothers.[7]

In explaining the causes of massive poverty in Asia, the bishops went beyond the *empirical* explanation (for example, poverty as the result of vice) and the *functional* explanation (poverty as the result of the economic cycle of boom and bust) to the *dialectical* explanation (poverty as a collective and conflictive phenomenon, the result of exploitation and oppression). At the first plenary assembly in 1974, the bishops declared of the Asian poor: "Poor, in that they are

---

Manila: Claretian Publications, 1992); Franz-Josef Eilers, ed., *For All the Peoples of Asia: Federation of Asian Bishops' Conferences*, vol. 2, *Documents from 1992 to 1996* (Quezon City, Manila: Claretian Publications, 1997); and Franz-Josef Eilers, ed., *For All the Peoples of Asia: Federation of Asian Bishops' Conferences*, vol. 3, *Documents from 1997 to 2002* (Quezon City, Manila: Claretian Publications, 2002). For a brief history of the FABC and a summary of its theological orientations, see Edmund Chia, *Thirty Years of FABC: History, Foundation, Context and Theology*, FABC papers, no. 106 (Hong Kong: FABC, 2003).

[6] For an analysis of the FABC's social teaching, see Peter C. Phan, *Christianity with an Asian Face: Asian American Theology in the Making* (Maryknoll, N.Y.: Orbis Books, 2003), 184–201.

[7] *For All the Peoples of Asia* 1:5 (no. 19).

deprived of access to material goods and resources. . . . Deprived, because they live under oppression, that is, under social, economic, and political structures which have injustice built in them."[8] Referring specifically to the Asian situation, the bishops criticized both classical capitalism and communism as productive of injustice. Of the destructive effects of capitalism on Asia, they said:

> We bishops and our experts came to see the causes of this distressing situation. Because of colonialism and feudalism and the introduction of Western classical capitalism, the traditional texture of Asian society with its inbuilt balances has been disrupted. Often the economies of these countries are not geared primarily to satisfying the requirements of the nation but rather to responding to external markets, and within the nation, not to the basic needs of people (food, housing, education, jobs) but to the demands of a consuming society. The principal beneficiaries of this system are the foreign markets and investors and the local elites. The victims are the poor who are the majority of the people.[9]

On the other hand, while recognizing some positive effects of communism, the Bishops' Institute for Social Action said: "Communism plays a very important role in Asia by the very fact that some 46% of all Asians live in communist states. . . . We now criticize communism because, while professedly promoting liberation, it has deprived man of his just human rights."[10]

At the Asian Synod the Asian bishops reaffirmed the determination of the church of Asia to be the "church of the poor": "The Church in Asia then, with its multitude of poor and oppressed people, is called to live a communion of life which shows itself particularly in loving service to the poor and defenseless" (*EA*, no. 32). Among the poor and defenseless the bishops highlighted victims of human rights abuses, migrants and overseas workers, indigenous and tribal peoples, women and children, refugees and asylum seekers (see *EA*, nos. 33–34). The areas to which the church's action in behalf of human development must be dedicated include the defense of human life, health care, education, and peacemaking. With regard to globalization, the bishops called for a "globalization without marginalization," urging careful attention to the cultural and moral aspects of globalization. They also encouraged the reduction and even the forgiving of the foreign debts that many Asian countries are incurring (see *EA*, nos. 35–40). Finally, attention was drawn to the blatant destruction of the environment by businesses in their unbridled desire for profit (see *EA*, no. 41).

A God-talk that takes into account Asia's socio-political and economic situation cannot but place in its forefront the God of the Hebrew prophets, who takes the side of "the widow, the stranger and the orphan (Ex 22:21–22; Dt 10:18; 27:19)," together with the prophets' "cry for justice, for the right ordering of human society, without which there can be no true worship of God (cf. Is

---

[8] Ibid., 1:15 (no. 19).
[9] Ibid., 1:212 (nos. 4 and 5).
[10] Ibid., 1:213 (no. 13).

1:10–17; Am 5:21–24)" (*EA,* no. 41). Such God-talk cannot but place at its center Jesus' message about the reign of God, in which the poor, the afflicted, the meek, those who hunger for justice, the merciful, the pure of heart, the peace-makers, and the persecuted are blessed by God. In Asia, talking about God without a deep and effective commitment to remove the sources of injustice, or of "the culture of death" for the poor, is nothing more than a noisy gong and a clanging cymbal, or worse, a balm for a guilty conscience and a theological prop for an exploitative social order. Indeed, in Asia God-talk is indissolubly linked with the proclamation of God's reign.[11] As John Paul II says, the Asian bishops' appeal for human development and for justice in human affairs in God-talk is both old and new: "It is old because it rises from the depths of our Christian tradition, which looks to that profound harmony which the Creator intends; it is new because it speaks to the immediate situation of countless people in Asia today" (*EA,* no. 41).

The God of Universal Harmony

John Paul II's statement quoted above hints at the second characteristic to be emphasized when speaking about God in Asia: God is the God of universal and cosmic harmony. Perhaps because of the immense diversity of Asia's cultural and religious heritages and the possibility of conflict and division generated by such diversity, the search for harmony, "that vibrant happiness or well-being which the parts of a dynamic totality attain by interacting with other pulsating and maybe conflicting parts,"[12] has been the hallmark of Asians. Harmony, it has been said, constitutes "the intellectual and affective, religious and artistic, personal and social soul of both persons and institutions in Asia."[13]

Given the common danger of misunderstanding harmony to mean papering over potentially conflictive differences, Asian theologians have repeatedly pointed out that harmony is not "an absence of strife" but rather the result of "acceptance of diversity and richness." Nor is it merely a pragmatic strategy for common living amid differences. Rather, it is "an Asian approach to reality, an Asian understanding of reality that is profoundly organic, i.e., a world-view wherein the whole, the unity, is the sum-total of the web of relations, and inter-action of the various parts with each other, in a word, *harmony,* a word that resonates with all Asian cultures."[14] Fundamentally, harmony is an Asian *spiri-tuality,* a way of relating to the Ultimate and the Transcendent, in which all the four dimensions of human existence are involved with one another: the individual person, the person's relationships with his or her fellow human beings,

---

[11] On how to speak of the kingdom of God in Asia, see Phan, *Christianity with an Asian Face,* 75–97.

[12] *For All the Peoples of Asia,* 2:232. Given the centrality of harmony in Asian thought, the FABC's Theological Advisory Commission has produced a lengthy document on it entitled *Asian Christian Perspectives on Harmony* (see *For All the Peoples of Asia* 2:229–98).

[13] *For All the Peoples of Asia,* 2:232.

[14] Ibid., 2:276 (no. 3.4).

the material universe, and God. God-talk in Asia, then, cannot be done effectively apart from this quest for universal and cosmic harmony.

This search for universal harmony is present in the teachings of various Asian religions. Hinduism is marked by a quest for a harmonious integration of the whole and the parts at all levels: individual, social, and cosmic. The cosmos is believed to be sustained by a harmonious order, society is held together by the order of *dharma* (law), and the individual achieves harmony by observing the cosmic order and society's moral and religious code. In Buddhism, harmony in the individual, which leads to liberation from suffering, is achieved by following the Eightfold Path which is centered on three aspects of life: morality *(sīla)*, cultivation of the mind *(samādhi)*, and wisdom *(prajñā)*. In Confucianism, harmony must be first realized in the individual by observing five relationships properly: between ruler and subject, between husband and wife, between parent and child, between elder sibling and younger sibling, and between friend and friend. Each of these five relationships implies a set of duties and obligations that must be fulfilled in the manner proper to one's station in life. Once harmony is realized in oneself, then it should be extended to the family, the state, and the world. According to Confucius, one cannot pacify the world without governing one's nation well, one cannot govern one's nation well without ordering one's family rightly, and one cannot order one's family rightly without achieving mastery over oneself.

This universal harmony is also cosmic. That is, because the human person is a microcosm reflecting the macrocosm, he or she must be in harmony with nature and the cosmos. This cosmic harmony is particularly emphasized in Taoism, with its teaching on noncontrivance or spontaneity *(tzu-jan)* and on the necessity of keeping in touch with the primitive, simple, undifferentiated source of creativity (nature as the "uncarved block").

Finally, harmony with oneself, harmony with one's fellow human beings, and harmony with the cosmos all are rooted in and sustained by harmony with God. Harmony with God is achieved by submitting oneself to and following in all things God's holy will. More than any other Asian religions, Islam stresses the duty of surrendering to God's will in mind, heart, and action.

Because of this quest for harmony, the Christian message that in Christ God "is reconciling the world to himself" and that the church must carry out a "ministry of reconciliation" (2 Cor 5:18–19) will find a sympathetic hearing among Asians. The Christian God is not only the God of justice but, precisely because of the restoration of the right order in society, also the God of harmony, communion, and reconciliation. In our God-talk to Asians, we must highlight the Christian teaching that in the beginning God created heaven and earth in full harmony and that originally there was harmony between man and woman and between humanity and the rest of the world. This universal harmony was disrupted by sin, and ever since the fall of humanity, God has been restoring harmony between God and humanity through the covenant with Israel, and ultimately through and in Christ. Christ's preaching of the reign of God and especially his death on the cross have reconciled to God the whole of humanity, even those who do not have faith in Christ, the majority of whom are Asian.

This vision of God as reconciler and restorer of universal and cosmic harmony has been explicitly adopted by the FABC as the church's guiding theology, one particularly suited to Asia's current situation of racial, ethnic, communal, and religious violence. It calls for an elaboration of a spirituality of harmony based on "cosmic Christology of harmony," a theology of the church as the "sacrament of unity," and an active commitment to harmony. Such a theology of God as restorer of harmony, interestingly enough, cannot be done, according to the FABC's Theological Advisory Commission, simply "by reading Christian revelation and applying its principles to the conflictual situation in Asia." Rather, "it has to be a reading and reflection of the realities themselves, along with other religious and cultural revelations, as well as of the messages continually emerging from the conflicts themselves." In other words, a theology of the God of universal and cosmic harmony can only be a "contextual theology" done in a spirit of "deep solidarity with the context and of an open appreciation of the rich religious and cultural traditions of Asia."[15]

The All-Inclusive God

The God of universal harmony, in the Asian context, can only be the All-Inclusive God, that is, the God who embraces all, irrespective of their religious belonging. As Aloysius Pieris, a Sri Lankan Jesuit theologian, has repeatedly argued, Asia is characterized by a double feature: degrading poverty and pervasive religiousness. Asian Christianity, according to Pieris, must undergo a double baptism: at the Jordan of Asian religions and on the Calvary of Asian poverty.[16]

Christian God-talk must be washed in this double baptism. As we have seen above, the God who is meaningful to Asians is the God who takes the side of the poor, and consequently, the church must be baptized on the Calvary of Asian poverty. In addition, God-talk that speaks of God as the God of universal harmony must bring about communion between Christianity and the diverse Asian religions without homogenizing their distinctive doctrines and practices. In other words, the church must be baptized at the Jordan of Asian religiousness.

How can this baptism be received? Through a sincere and humble dialogue among all religions. This dialogue takes a fourfold form: a dialogue of life, whereby communities of diverse faiths live harmoniously together; a dialogue of action, in which people of different faiths collaborate with one another on projects of human development; a dialogue of theological exchange, in which believers attempt to understand better one another's beliefs and practices; and a dialogue of religious sharing, which is the most difficult, in which believers, while remaining firmly rooted in their own traditions, share religious practices

---

[15]   Ibid., 2:292 (no. 5.2).
[16]   See Aloysius Pieris, *An Asian Theology of Liberation* (Maryknoll, N.Y.: Orbis Books, 1988), 62–63.

with the followers of another religion in order to enrich them and to be enriched spiritually by them.[17]

This fourfold dialogue, which the FABC has made one of the church's top priorities, is not geared toward converting other believers to Christianity, of course. Nevertheless, it is not an optional activity of the church's ministry to Asians; rather, it is an intrinsic part of Christian mission. As John Paul II affirms, "Interreligious dialogue is more than a way of fostering mutual knowledge and enrichment; it is part of the Church's evangelizing mission, an expression of the mission *ad gentes*. Christians bring to interreligious dialogue the firm belief that the fullness of salvation comes from Christ alone and that the Church community to which they belong is the *ordinary means* of salvation" (*EA*, no. 31). The most challenging question here is *how* to proclaim to Asians this truth about Jesus as the unique and universal savior and the church as the ordinary means of salvation and at the same time recognize explicitly and joyfully that, as John Paul II himself said in *Redemptoris missio*, "the Spirit's presence and activity affect not only the individuals but also society and history, peoples, cultures and religions" (*RM*, no. 28).

After Vatican II, doubt may no longer be raised about the possibility of salvation of non-Christians and even of nonbelievers. But as to the salvific value of the non-Christian religions themselves, there is a serious debate in contemporary theology of religion, and various positions have been classified under the convenient, albeit not entirely helpful, categories of exclusivism, inclusivism, and pluralism.[18] Without denigrating the role of Christ as savior and that of the church as sacrament of salvation, the FABC at its first Plenary assembly in Taipei in 1978 asked rhetorically: "How then [could] we not acknowledge that God has drawn our peoples to himself through them [non-Christian religions]?"[19] The Indian bishops elaborated on this salvific value of non-Christian religions more fully:

> In light of the universal salvific will and design of God, so emphatically affirmed in the New Testament witness, the Indian Christological approach seeks to avoid negative and exclusivistic expressions. Christ is the sacrament, the definitive symbol of God's salvation for all humanity. This is what the salvific uniqueness and universality of Christ means in the Indian

---

[17] See *For All the Peoples of Asia*, 2:169 (nos. 7–10). The FABC derives this notion of fourfold dialogue from the document *Dialogue and Proclamation* of the Pontifical Council for Inter-religious Dialogue and the Congregation for the Evangelization of Peoples. The English text of *Dialogue and Proclamation* is available in William Burrows, ed., *Redemption and Dialogue: Reading* Redemptoris Missio *and* Dialogue and Proclamation (Maryknoll, N.Y.: Orbis Books, 1993), 3–55.

[18] For a helpful presentation of contemporary theologies of religions, see Paul Knitter, *Introducing Theologies of Religions* (Maryknoll, N.Y.: Orbis Books, 2002); see also Jacques Dupuis, *Toward a Christian Theology of Religious Pluralism* (Maryknoll, N.Y.: Orbis Books, 1977); and idem, *Christianity and the Religions: From Confrontation to Dialogue* (Maryknoll, N.Y.: Orbis Books, 2002).

[19] Dupuis, *Toward a Christian Theology of Religious Pluralism*, 220.

context. That, however, does not mean there cannot be other symbols, valid in their own ways, which the Christian sees as related to the definitive symbol, Jesus Christ. The implication of all this is that for hundreds of millions of our fellow human beings, salvation is seen as being channeled to them not in spite of but through and in their various socio-cultural and religious traditions. We cannot, then, deny a priori a salvific role for these non-Christian religions.[20]

It is clear that God-talk that is meaningful in the multi-religious context of Asia must follow the theology of religion sketched out by the Indian bishops in the quotation given above.[21] In Asia to be religious is to be interreligious, and so the Christian God in Asia is not only multicolored but multi-religious as well.

Like Joseph's "amazing technicolor dreamcoat," the Christian faith is a many-splendored thing, and its God can never be monochromatic. Like light that refracts and produces color, God, who is Light (1 Jn 1:5), shines in all God's splendor and beauty in all parts of creation. In Asia, where diversity and pluralism abound, God appears in many forms, not least as the One in whom the poor find liberation, as the Reconciler in whom all races and cultures are brought into harmony, and as the All-Inclusive One to whom all religions lead.

---

[20] Phan, *The Asian Synod*, 22.
[21] For a summary of this "pluralistic inclusivism" in the theology of religion, see Chapter 4 herein.

8

Transformation and Liberation by Enlightenment

JESUS AS THE ENLIGHTENER AND AS THE ENLIGHTENED ONE

One of the most significant statements made by the Asian bishops at the Special Assembly of the Synod of Bishops of Asia (April 19–May 14, 1998), convoked by Pope John Paul II to prepare Christianity for its third millennium, was that many diverse ways must be used to speak about Christ to the Asian peoples if the message of the gospel is to make sense to them. For the Asian bishops, Jesus ultimately should be presented as fully divine and fully human, but, they insisted, different images should be pressed into service to make Jesus recognizable to Asians. After all, Jesus, they reminded their fellow Christians, was born in Asia. They suggested these images for Jesus: "the Teacher of Wisdom, the Healer, the Liberator, the Spiritual Guide, the Enlightened One, the Compassionate Friend of the Poor, the Good Samaritan, the Good Shepherd, the Obedient One."[1]

Among these images several have a distinctly biblical flavor, such as "the Compassionate Friend of the Poor," "the Good Samaritan, "the Good Shepherd," and "the Obedient One." Others are more generic, albeit solidly based on the Bible, such as "the Teacher of Wisdom," "the Healer," and "the Liberator." The remaining two, namely,"the Spiritual Guide" and "the Enlightened One," may appear rather alien to Western Christians, but to Asian ears they sound quite familiar, especially if they are translated into their equivalents in Asian religious traditions, the former as "the Guru" and the latter as "the Buddha." In this essay I dwell only on the image of Jesus as the Enlightened One or the Buddha and its correlative, that is, Jesus as the Light or the Enlightener. I will be brief in my reflection on Jesus as the Light that enlightens the world because this image is better known, at least among Christians, and

---

[1] This proposal was listed sixth in a list of fifty-nine proposals. It was incorporated in John Paul II's apostolic exhortation *Ecclesia in Asia*, promulgated after the synod on November 6, 1999, no. 20. For the English text of this exhortation, see Peter C. Phan, ed., *The Asian Synod: Texts and Commentaries* (Maryknoll, N.Y.: Orbis Books, 2002), 286–340.

devote the greater part of the chapter to the less conventional image of Jesus as the Enlightened One.

JESUS AS THE LIGHT OR THE ENLIGHTENER OF THE WORLD

One of the frequent symbols with which the New Testament describes Jesus' work of redemption and transformation is that of light dispelling darkness. The theme of light, which is a universal sacred symbol, is the thread that links the Hebrew and Christian scriptures and runs through the whole of biblical revelation, from beginning to end. In the beginning, God's first creative act was to bring forth light and separate it from darkness (Gn 1:3); at the end of history the New Jerusalem will need no sun or moon to shine on it because "the glory of God is its light" (Rv 21:23). God himself "is light and in him there is no darkness at all" (1 Jn 1:5).

Though God is pure and absolute light, throughout human history light and darkness have been locked in mortal combat, and the final destiny of humanity will be either life or death depending on whether it sides with darkness or light. In the Hebrew-Christian revelation this struggle between light and darkness is not conceived as metaphysical, as in Manichean dualism, but as intellectual and moral. In other words, light stands for knowledge, life, and salvation, and darkness for ignorance, death, and sin. The enlightenment that is God's gift of light brings about not merely an illumination of the intellect but a total liberation and transformation of the human person.

The Christian good news is that humans are not left to their own devices in this titanic struggle. As the Word or Wisdom of God, Jesus is proclaimed to be the perfect revealer enlightening the darkened minds of all human beings and giving them the true knowledge of the living God. As the mediator between God and humanity, Jesus, especially through his death and resurrection, reconciles humans with God, effects the forgiveness of their sins, and leads them to a new life of friendship with God, communion with their fellow human beings, and harmony with the cosmos.

The saving light that Jesus brings is associated with truth and life. Light, truth, life are synonymous ways of describing the one and same reality that is Jesus. To Thomas, who asked how he and other disciples could go to where Jesus was going, Jesus replied: "I am the way, the truth, and the life. No one comes to the Father except through me" (Jn 14:6). Because Jesus is the way, the enlightenment he accomplishes is never a mere dispelling of intellectual error and ignorance (truth) but always includes a total transformation and liberation of the person from oppression, death, and sin (life).

As the enlightener of humanity, Jesus is professed to be the light itself, not just a prism refracting the light that shines on humanity. At his birth the earth was bathed in heavenly light (Lk 2:9). Zechariah, the father of John the Baptist, prophesied that Jesus would be like "the dawn from on high [that] will break upon us, to give light to those who sit in darkness and in the shadow of death" (Lk 1:78–79). At the commencement of his ministry, Jesus is said to fulfill the prophet Isaiah's promise (9:1) that "the people who sat in darkness have seen a great light, and for those who sat in the region of death light has dawned" (Mt 4:15–16). Jesus understood that his mission was to proclaim the "recovery of sight to the blind" (Lk 4:18) and the synoptic Gospels report that during his ministry Jesus miraculously restored sight to the blind, an obvious symbol of his power of spiritual enlightenment.

More than any other New Testament writing, the Fourth Gospel emphasizes that Jesus is the light itself. At the outset it proclaims that in Jesus, the Word of God made flesh, life has come and that "the life was the light of all people" and "the light shines in the darkness and the darkness did not overcome it" (1:4–5). Jesus is "the true light, which enlightens everyone" (1:9). In the Johannine account of the healing of the man born blind, before curing him Jesus stated, "As long as I am in the world, I am the light of the world" (9:5). And after the healing, in light of the blind man's faith and the Pharisees' unbelief, he said, "I came into this world for judgment so that those who do not see may see, and those who see may become blind" (9:39). Again and again Jesus proclaimed himself to be the light enlightening the world: "I am the light of the world. Whoever follows me will never walk in darkness but will have the light of life" (8:12). Jesus urged his disciples to walk while they had him as the light: "The light is with you for a little while longer. Walk while you have the light, so that the darkness may not overtake you. If you walk in the darkness, you do not know where you are going. While you have the light, believe in the light, so that you may become children of the light" (12:35–36). Again: "I have come as light into the world, so that everyone who believes in me should not remain in the darkness" (Jn 12:46).

Though being the light itself, Jesus' light was not always resplendent throughout his earthly ministry because of his human condition, which hid it. On one occasion, however, at the transfiguration, his full identity was revealed, and "his face shone like the sun, and his clothes became dazzling white" (Mt 17:2). As in the theophanies recorded in the Jewish scriptures, the light at the transfiguration is the symbol of divinity, and in Jesus, who is the light, something of God, who "dwells in unapproachable light" (1 Tm 6:16), is made known.

JESUS THE ENLIGHTENED ONE OR THE BUDDHA

If Jesus is the light enlightening the world, how can the Asian bishops refer to him as the Enlightened One? Can light itself be enlightened, and if so, how and by what or by whom? Did Jesus ever have a profound and sweeping experience, comparable to that of Siddhārtha Gautama, as a result of which he gained new insight into reality and formulated a new body of teachings, analogous to the Buddha's "Middle Way" with its Eightfold Path? Though the image of Jesus as the Enlightened One evokes the Buddha, my intention here is not to compare and contrast Siddhārtha Gautama's experience of enlightenment under the Bō tree with a similar event, should there have been one, in the life of Jesus. Nor do I intend to investigate the similarities and dissimilarities between the account of Jesus' life in the Gospels and that of the Buddha in Aśvaghosa's *Buddhacarita*, or between the Buddha's teaching in the *dhammapada* and that of Jesus in the Sermon on the Mount, or between the *dharma* and the kingdom of God.[2]

Rather than focusing on the *inter*religious dialogue between Christianity and Buddhism on enlightenment, I would like to carry out an *intra*-religious study of the Christian basis and justification for naming Jesus the Enlightened One. At first sight there seems to be formidable theological objections against this new christological title. Being enlightened logically presupposes a previous stage of ignorance, delusion, mental error, and even sin, and normally implies as its condition of possibility a process of intense mental concentration as a controlled psychic exercise. The process may consist of increasingly refined and rigorous stages of mental concentration leading to the discovery of truth (for example, Patañjali's Yoga's eight steps, the highest of which is *samādhi;* or the Buddha's Eightfold Path, that is, the perfect "one-pointedness" of mind; or Tendai's fifty-two stages on the road to perfect enlightenment) or a sudden experience of awakening to one's true nature, as in Chinese and Japanese Zen *(satori).* The source of the enlightenment may be external, such as the teaching of a guru, or internal, by one's own inner light.

Enlightenment thus understood seems to go counter to certain traditional christological assertions. For instance, with regard to Jesus' human knowledge, since Jesus was totally and perfectly united with God in grace, classical theologians attribute to him not only experimental knowledge *(scientia experientiae),* that is, knowledge gained through normal empirical channels, but also infused knowledge *(scientia infusa),* that is, knowledge not derived from sensory experience but similar to that of the angels, and beatific knowledge *(scientia visionis),* that is, the face-to-face, direct, and immediate contemplation of God that is given to the blessed in heaven. The latter two types of knowledge, especially the beatific one, would exclude the possibility of a passage from ignorance, delusion, and mental error to knowledge, clarity of mind, and insight produced in enlightenment. This impossibility is even more obvious if one takes into account Jesus' all-knowing intellect, which he possessed by virtue of his divine nature. Also excluded a priori is the possibility of speaking of conversion in the case of Jesus, because he is professed to be not only free from all sin (sinlessness *de facto*) but also incapable of sinning (sinlessness *de iure*).

In light of all these traditional doctrines about Jesus, which seem to exclude any possibility of Jesus being enlightened, it is therefore intriguing that the Asian bishops suggested that the image of the Enlightened One may be an appropriate way of representing Jesus to the peoples of Asia. No doubt the background of the bishops' proposal is the story of Siddhārtha Gautama's enlightenment under the Bō tree, and their intention was to establish a dialogue between Christianity and Buddhism. To make this dialogue effective, however,

---

[2] This comparative work has been carried out effectively in many writings. Representative books include John P. Keenan, *The Meaning of Christ: A Mahāyāna Theology* (Maryknoll, N.Y.: Orbis Books, 1989); Leo D. Lefebure, *The Buddha and the Christ: Explorations in Buddhist and Christian Dialogue* (Maryknoll, N.Y.: Orbis Books, 1993).

it is necessary to show how the image of Jesus as the Enlightened One is consistent with that of him as the light that enlightens the world. Can it be argued that Jesus is the light that enlightens all and thus transforms and liberates all precisely *because* and *to the extent that* he himself is enlightened, so that enlightening and being enlightened grow in direct and not inverse proportion? Is this paradox affirmed in the New Testament and in the Christian tradition?

How Did Jesus Know?

The Christian faith professes that Jesus is fully divine and fully human, or to use the language of the Council of Chalcedon (451), he is "at once complete in divinity and complete in humanity, truly God and truly man . . . recognized in two natures [*physeis*], without confusion, without change, without division, without separation . . . coming together to form one person [*prosōpon*] and subsistence [*hypostasis*] . . . one and the same Son and only-begotten God the Word." How Jesus is divine has been expressed in different ways in the New Testament: God "appeared" in him (Ti 3:4); "emptied himself" in him (Phil 2:7); "was made flesh" in him (Jn 1:14); and "was present" in him (2 Cor 5:19). Of these four models (theophany, hiddenness, incarnation, and presence), that of incarnation gradually assumed predominance as the belief in the divinity of Jesus became more explicit among his followers. On the other hand, that Jesus was fully human, and more specifically, a Jewish male, living a fully human life, was taken for granted by his disciples.

In the Christian tradition since the fourth century, however, after Jesus' divinity was denied, especially by Arius, there was a tendency to emphasize the divinity of Jesus at the expense of his humanity. Even when his humanity was affirmed, it was said (for example, by monophysitism) to merge with his divinity in such a way that only one nature, that is, the divine, remained. It is within this context of crypto-monophysitism that the theory that Jesus possessed the infused and beatific knowledge since the moment of his conception eventually arose.

Several contemporary theologians, including Karl Rahner (1904–84), no longer attribute infused knowledge to the historical Jesus. All the knowledge Jesus ever gained originated in his sensory experiences. As to Jesus' alleged beatific vision, that is, his direct knowledge of God his Father and of his own divine identity, it is interpreted to be a pre-reflective, implicit, unthematic self-consciousness rather than a face-to-face vision of the divine essence. Such an explicit, thematized, direct beatific vision would exclude, in these theologians' view, genuine experiences of fear and suffering.

It is pointed out that one essential characteristic of human knowing is that it is limited and gradual. Jesus' self-consciousness and hence his awareness of his identity and of his relationship to God would be subjected to the same epistemological processes. Indeed, it is reported that after his return from the Temple at the age of twelve, the boy Jesus "increased in wisdom and in years, and in divine and human favor" (Lk 2:52). Such a growth would not be possible without some kind of inner enlightenment.

Furthermore, even if it is granted that Jesus did possess a highly special awareness of God. whom he addressed as Abba (Father dear), still there was sufficient evidence that such an awareness was not perfect from the outset but admitted gradual growth in intensity and clarity. Conducive to such growth was, no doubt, Jesus' practice of constant prayer during his ministry and especially during his agony in the garden and on the cross. In the garden he prayed that his Father spare him suffering and death, but that not his will but the Father's will be done (Lk 22:41). Clearly, Jesus needed to be enlightened as to his Father's will. On the cross Jesus cried out in despair: "My God, my God, why have you forsaken me?" (Mk 15:34). He must have received some divine assurance in the depths of his soul in order to be able to utter in total confidence before breathing his last, "Father, into your hands I commend my spirit" (Lk 23:46).

Last, it is also noted that at least on one occasion Jesus frankly admitted his ignorance in the matter of the timing of an important event: "But about that day or hour no one knows, neither the angels in heaven, nor the Son, but only the Father" (Mk 13:32). This is one of the few sayings of Jesus of which the authenticity is not in doubt, since his disciples would certainly not put on Jesus' lips a statement that would belittle his prophetic knowledge. It then follows that Jesus as the Son would need an enlightenment from the Father to know the date of either the impending destruction of Jerusalem or of the end of the world or both.

Was Jesus Enlightened about His Self-Identity and Mission?

Being enlightened brings about modification of old views and achievement of new insights. Did Jesus come to deeper self-awareness or change his understanding of his mission and ministry as a result of historical circumstances (enlightenment by external sources) or by internal sources (such as prayer)? Given the nature of the Gospels as confessional writings, it is hazardous and even impossible to reconstruct an exact biography, let alone a detailed account of the psychological and spiritual development of Jesus. Nevertheless, in contemporary New Testament scholarship, especially in the various "quests for the historical Jesus," there is a recognition that despite the fact the Gospels are not biographies, there is a core of facts whose historicity is beyond reasonable doubt.

One of the oft-discussed questions about Jesus' self-understanding is whether he shifted the focus of his mission as a result of unexpected circumstances and a new perception of God's will for him. There is no doubt that Jesus was baptized by John the Baptist, as reported by all three of the synoptic Gospels and as mentioned briefly by the Fourth Gospel. Jesus' willingness to receive baptism from John was a sign of his acceptance of the will of God, since in so doing he acknowledged John as a prophet and his baptizing ministry as coming "from heaven" (Mk 11:30). After Jesus' baptism there followed a theophanic scene composed of three acts: the opening of the heavens, the descent of the Holy Spirit, and the declaration from heaven that Jesus was the beloved Son in whom God was well pleased. Whether the theophany was an objective, public event of vision and audition available to all the spectators at the River Jordan or a purely interior experience of Jesus, it was, especially with the divine utterance, undeniably a moment of illumination for Jesus about his identity (the Son) and his mission (the Servant of God). This self-identity and mission were later further clarified and confirmed during the threefold temptation to which Jesus was subjected. The temptations involving food, power, and the proper object of worship, which recall the temptations of ancient Israel in the desert, focus on the meaning of Jesus being the Son of God and of his mission as the Servant of God. Through these temptations Jesus surely came to a better understanding, by means of the scriptural texts he cited, of the false and ultimately idolatrous ways to carry out his mission and of what trusting in God, not putting God to the test, and worshiping God alone meant.

Throughout his public ministry Jesus seems to have changed his mind about his mission as a result of his encounters with others. At the wedding at Cana, Jesus changed the timing of his mission by anticipating his "hour"—the revelation of his "glory"—because of his mother's entreaty by turning water into wine (Jn 2:1–11). Again, Jesus' mind was changed when the Canaanite woman's faith moved him to reverse his initial refusal. She had loudly begged him to cast the demon out of her daughter, but Jesus curtly told her that he was "sent only to the lost sheep of the house of Israel" and that it was not "fair to take the children's food and throw it to the dogs." But the woman replied, "Yes, Lord, yet even the dogs eat the crumbs that fall from their master's table." Then Jesus replied: "Woman, great is your faith! Let it be done for you as you wish" (Mt 15:28). Once he was "amazed" by the faith of a Roman centurion of Capernaum, the like of which he said he had not found in anyone in Israel (Mt 8:10).

As to the nature and scope of his mission itself, Jesus seems have undergone an important shift in understanding. According to a reconstruction of the chronology of Jesus' public ministry, it appears that after a spectacularly successful beginning in Galilee, Jesus was rejected by the populace, who perhaps were expecting a different kind of messiah. He made a final effort to gather them to his cause by sending out his disciples on a mission. But when even this mission failed, he realized he was called to be a victim whose death and vindication would usher in the kingdom of God. He then concentrated on the formation of his core group, the Twelve, and went up to Jerusalem for his final Passover and fatal confrontation with the religious authorities.

There seems to have been on Jesus' part a shift from the understanding of his mission as *proclaimer* of the coming of God's reign to being a *victim* for the kingdom of God though his death. Even if one does not agree with the details of the historical reconstruction, especially in identifying a pivotal event in Jesus' ministry as the watershed moment (for example, the cleansing of the Temple), still there is little doubt that Jesus' awareness of a link between the kingdom of God and the possibility of a violent death was not present at the beginning of his ministry and that this awareness deepened and intensified as the opposition of the religious establishment against him grew fiercer. From the murders of past prophets and of John the Baptist, his cousin, from his enemies' accusations that he worked miracles by demonic power and that he was a blasphemer and a false prophet, from the reactions of religious leaders to his triumphant entry into Jerusalem and to his cleansing of the Temple, from the perception of political authorities that his preaching was a threat to the Roman Empire, all these external factors and others could not fail to enlighten Jesus as to the inevitability of his violent death. Jesus did not intentionally court a violent death as a *means* to bring about the kingdom of God, but he willingly and consciously embraced it in obedience to his Father as the inevitable *result* of his preaching and acting in the name of God's reign. There was then very likely a gradual enlightenment in Jesus' consciousness as to the shape of his vocation and destiny: from being a proclaimer of God's final salvation to suffering as the victim whose death and vindication would realize the salvation he had proclaimed.

Was Jesus a Man of Faith?

Enlightenment produces knowledge, and this knowledge in religious matters is called faith. If Jesus was enlightened gradually with regard to his self-identity and mission, can it be said that he had faith? It is an irony that though Jesus spoke so eloquently about the necessity and the power of faith (Mk 9:23; 11:23) and praised people who had faith (as we have seen above) in a way that seemed to be from personal experiences, classical theology denied that he had faith, since faith implies lack of total knowledge, which was thought to be incompatible with Jesus' infused knowledge and beatific vision. Even the celebrated text in Hebrews 12:2, which urges Christians to look to "Jesus as the pioneer and perfecter of faith," is rendered in almost all translations with the possessive adjective "our" added to faith (though the Greek text does not have such a possessive adjective). In this way Jesus is made into the *object* of our faith and not the *model* of faith. Accordingly, Christians believe *in* him and not *like* him.

Such a view, however, suffers from a myopic understanding of faith exclusively as an intellectual assent to revealed truths. But even within this narrow conception of faith, it is still possible to argue that Jesus in his human intellect had to receive and assent to the truths that his Jewish faith taught him about God and God's activities in the world. Furthermore, as we have shown above, Jesus received the revelation that he is God's beloved Son (in Mark and Luke, in contrast to Matthew, the heavenly voice was addressed to Jesus: "You are my Son, my Beloved").

Furthermore, faith is much more than intellectual assent to revealed truths imperfectly understood. Above all, it is obedience to God's will and trust in God's love. In this respect Jesus, as Hebrews tells us, "although he was a Son . . . learned obedience through what he suffered" (5:8). As "pioneer" of our salvation, Jesus was made "perfect through sufferings" (2:10). As Philippians affirms, Jesus "became obedient to the point of death—even death on the cross" (2:8). Gerard O'Collins puts it well when he observes that an earthly Jesus who lived by the light of some unique knowledge and did not walk in the relative obscurity of faith would be very remote from the conditions of human and Christian life as we experience them.[3]

---

[3] Gerard O'Collins, *Interpreting Jesus* (New York: Paulist Press, 1983), 193.

LIGHT FROM LIGHT: ENLIGHTENER BECAUSE ENLIGHTENED

It would seem then that the Asian bishops' proposal to present Jesus as "the Enlightened One" or, if you will, as the "Buddha," has a strong biblical basis. But their point can be made even stronger by saying that Jesus is the enlightener of the world precisely *because* and *to the extent that* he himself is enlightened. Surely he is light, but, to use the language of the Nicene-Constantinopolitan creed, he is not simply light but "light from light" *(phōs ek phōtos)*. It is only because he originates as light from the Light that he can enlighten and reveal the Light perfectly and in this way liberate humans from darkness and bring them into the kingdom of light.

Perhaps no Gospel has spoken more extensively about the derived character of Jesus' light than the Fourth Gospel. Whereas Jesus in Matthew once said that "all things have been handed over to me by my Father" (11:27), in the Johannine Gospel he stated again and again that whatever he was and did, he received from God his Father, "Very truly, I tell you, the Son can do nothing on his own, but only what he sees the Father doing; for whatever the Father does, the Son does likewise" (5:19). Again: "I can do nothing on my own. As I hear, I judge; and my judgment is just, because I seek to do not my own will but the will of him who sent me" (5:30). Even more explicitly Jesus affirms that his teaching is a received teaching, that is, his enlightenment is itself enlightened: "My teaching is not mine but his who sent me" (7:16). Again, even more sharply, "I do nothing on my own, but I speak these things as the Father instructed me" (8:29).

It is no accident that in the Fourth Gospel the themes of Word, Wisdom, Revealer, Light, Life, Truth, Way, and Son come together as different ways to describe Jesus as the Enlightener of the world: "I am the light of the world. Whoever follows me will never walk in darkness but will have the light of life" (8:12). The later christological doctrine would elaborate in ontological terms the relationship between the "Father" and the "Son" and affirm the divinity of Jesus by saying that he is "one in substance with the Father" *(homoousion tō patri)*. But because Jesus' divinity is a "derived" divinity, a gift eternally poured out in love on him by his Father (and one may add, through the power of the Holy Spirit), so that he is "true God from true God" *(theon alēthinon ek theou alēthinou)*, it is equally important to remember that before (if such a term can be used of the Eternal Word and Wisdom) the Son can as Light enlighten the world, he is enlightened by his Father. The Enlightener is the Enlightened and vice versa. The Buddha is the Pathfinder and vice versa.

9

Jesus as the Universal Savior

GOD'S ETERNAL COVENANT WITH THE JEWISH PEOPLE

In recent years not a few Christian theologians, recalling Paul's teaching that God's covenant with Israel remains eternal (Rom 11:29), have affirmed that God's redemptive power is still at work in and through Judaism.[1] This recognition that Judaism continues to function as a way of salvation, at least for Jews, poses serious challenges to Roman Catholics because it seems, at first sight, to contradict their church's longstanding double teaching that Jesus is the unique, universal, and absolute savior and that outside the church there is no salvation. Hence, the affirmation of the continuing validity of God's covenant with Israel calls for a reexamination of these two traditional teachings, especially the former.[2] This chapter seeks to outline, from the Roman Catholic

---

[1] See, for instance, the following representative works: Norbert Lohfink, *The Covenant Never Revoked: Biblical Reflections on Christian-Jewish Dialogue* (Mahwah, N.J.: Paulist Press, 1991); and John T. Pawlikowski, *Jesus and the Theology of Israel* (Wilmington, Del.: Michael Glazier, 1989). An important document of the Vatican Commission for Religious Relations with Jews entitled *Notes on the Correct Way to Present the Jews and Judaism in Preaching and Catechesis in the Roman Catholic Church* (June 24, 1985) reiterates a statement made by John Paul II in his speech to the Jewish community of West Germany at Mainz on November 17, 1980: "the people of God of the Old Covenant, which has never been revoked" (no. 3). The permanence of the Jewish covenant is also affirmed by the *Catechism of the Catholic Church* (1992), no. 839. A recent and significant document of the Pontifical Biblical Commission, *The Jewish People and Their Sacred Scriptures in the Christian Bible* (May 24, 2001), makes a nuanced affirmation of the continuing validity of the Jewish covenant (Part II, no. 42): "Israel continues to be in a covenant relationship with God, because the covenant-promise is definitive and cannot be abolished. But the early Christians were also conscious of living in a new phase of that plan announced by the prophets and inaugurated by the blood of Jesus, 'blood of the covenant,' because it was shed out of love (cf. Rv 1:5b-6)." The English text of this document is available online.

[2] The Christian Scholars Group on Christian-Jewish Relations issued on September 1, 2002, a statement entitled *A Sacred Obligation: Rethinking Christian Faith in Relation to Judaism and the Jewish People,* which affirmed that "affirming God's enduring covenant with the Jewish people has consequences for Christian understanding of salvation." Elaborating this affirmation, the group goes on to say: "Christians meet God's saving power in the person of Jesus Christ and believe that this power is available to all

perspective, a theology of religions and of the role of Christ as savior that remains both harmonious with the Christian faith in Jesus as the savior of the whole humankind and receptive to the acknowledgment of Judaism as a still-valid way of salvation.

THE SECOND VATICAN COUNCIL (1962–1965) AND WORLD RELIGIONS

Any reinterpretation of the doctrine of the universality and uniqueness of Jesus as savior within Roman Catholic theology must take into account the teaching of the Second Vatican Council on the possibility of salvation for non-Christians and on the existence of "elements of truth and grace" within non-Christian religions. With regard to the salvation of non-Christians, Vatican II, reversing the church's centuries-old condemnation of non-Christians to hell,[3] affirms that "those who have not yet received the Gospel are related to the People of God in various ways" (*LG*, no. 16).[4] Among these people the council explicitly mentions five groups: Jews; Muslims; those seeking the unknown God in shadows and images through their religions; those who do not practice any specific religion but sincerely seek God; and those who, without any fault on their part, have not yet arrived at an explicit knowledge of God (for example, atheists). All these people, the council says, "may achieve eternal salvation," though of course not without the grace of Christ (*LG*, no. 16).[5]

---

people in him. Christians have therefore taught for centuries that salvation is available only through Jesus Christ. With their recent realization that God's covenant with the Jewish people is eternal, Christians can now recognize in the Jewish tradition the redemptive power of God at work. If Jews, who do not share our faith in Christ, are in a saving covenant with God, then Christians need new ways of understanding the universal significance of Christ." I myself am one of the signatories of the statement and in this chapter attempt to offer a new way of understanding the universal significance of Christ in the light of God's eternal covenant with the Jewish people. The full statement is available online.

[3] See, for instance, the Council of Florence's decree to the Jacobites (1442): "[The Holy Roman Church] . . . firmly believes, professes and preaches that 'no one remaining outside the Catholic Church, not only pagans,' but also Jews, heretics and schismatics, can become partakers of eternal life; but they will go to the 'eternal fire prepared for the devil and his angels' (Matthew 25: 41), unless before the end of their life they are joined to it." The English translation is taken from Joseph Neuner and Jacques Dupuis, eds., *The Christian Faith in the Doctrinal Documents of the Catholic Church* (New York: Alba House, 2001) . For an excellent analysis of the Roman Catholic teaching on "outside the church there is no salvation," see Francis A. Sullivan, *Salvation outside the Church? Tracing the History of the Catholic Response* (New York: Paulist Press, 1992).

[4] English translations of Vatican II's documents are taken from Austin Flannery, ed., *Vatican II: Constitutions, Decrees, Declarations* (Collegeville, Minn.: Liturgical Press, 1996).

[5] In its *Pastoral Constitution on the Church in the Modern World,* Vatican II explains how this possibility of salvation for non-Christians is realized: "For since Christ died for everyone, since all are in fact called to one and the same destiny, which is divine, we must hold that the holy Spirit offers to all the possibility of being made partners, in a way known to God, in the paschal mystery" (*LG*, no. 22).

With regard to non-Christian religions, Vatican II acknowledges that the "rites and customs of peoples," including therefore their religions, should be "saved from destruction" and "purified and raised up, and perfected for the glory of God" (*LG*, no. 17). In its *Decree on the Church's Missionary Activity* the council affirms that these religious elements "may lead one to the true God and be a preparation for the gospel" (*AG*, no. 3). These "elements of truth and grace" are the "secret presence of God" and "the seeds of the word" (*AG*, nos. 9, 11). In its *Declaration on the Relation of the Church to Non-Christian Religions* Vatican II mentions the primitive religions, Hinduism, Buddhism, Islam, and Judaism. Of these religions the council affirms: "The Catholic Church rejects nothing of what is true and holy in these religions. It has a high regard for the manner of life and conduct, the precepts and doctrines which, although differing in many ways from its own teaching, nevertheless often reflect a ray of that truth which enlightens all men" (*NA*, no. 2).

With regard to Judaism, in particular, the council acknowledges the "spiritual ties which link the people of the new covenant to the stock of Abraham" and said that "the church of Christ acknowledges that in God's plan of salvation the beginnings of its faith and election are to be found in the patriarchs, Moses and the prophets." It recalls Paul's teaching that "the Jews remain very dear to God, for the sake of the patriarchs, since God does not take back the gifts he bestowed or the choice he made" (*NA,* no. 4).[6]

It is of great importance to note that even though in *Nostra aetate* Vatican II treats Judaism alongside other religions, the Catholic church repeatedly affirms the unique and privileged position of Israel in God's plan of salvation and its special relationship to Christianity. Indeed, the Catholic church does not regard Judaism as just one of the non-Christian religions with which it enters into interreligious dialogue.[7] Rather, it affirms explicitly and unambiguously the reality of divine revelation and grace—and not merely "elements of truth and grace" or "secret presence of God" or "seeds of the word"—in Judaism as well as the continuing validity of God's covenant with Israel.

In spite of its positive evaluation of non-Christian religions in general and of Judaism in particular, Vatican II self-consciously refrains from affirming that these religions as such function as ways of salvation in a manner analogous, let alone parallel, to Christianity. In the last three decades, however, extensive reflections have been done on the relationship between Christianity, and

---

[6] The council goes on to say: "Even though the Jewish authorities and those who followed their lead pressed for the death of Christ (see Jn 19:6), neither all Jews indiscriminately at that time, nor Jews today, can be charged with the crimes committed during his passion. It is true that the church is the new people of God, yet the Jews should not be spoken of as rejected or accursed as if this followed from holy Scripture." The council "deplores all hatreds, persecutions, displays of anti-semitism leveled at any time or from any source against the Jews" (no. 4).

[7] In fact, the Catholic church's relations with Jews are not placed within the province of the Pontifical Council for Interreligious Dialogue but within that of the Pontifical Council for Promoting Christian Unity under the Commission for Religious Relations with the Jews.

by implication, Jesus Christ, on the one hand, and non-Christian religions, and especially Judaism, on the other. A new theology of religions has reassessed the role of Christ as the unique and universal savior and the function of non-Christian religions themselves within God's plan of salvation.

JESUS AS THE UNIVERSAL, UNIQUE, AND ABSOLUTE SAVIOR

Paul F. Knitter has helpfully categorized contemporary theologies of religions into four basic models: "replacement," "fulfillment," "mutuality," and "acceptance."[8] Needless to say, each of these four models views the role of Christ as savior and the three adjectives characterizing it (universal, unique, and absolute) very differently. The first model takes literally the New Testament affirmations that Jesus is the only and exclusive revealer, mediator, and savior of humankind (Jn 14:6; Acts 4:12; 1 Cor 3:11; 1 Tm 2:5; 1 Jn 5:12) and that an explicit faith in Jesus is absolutely necessary for salvation (Jn 3:36). The fourth model also professes that Jesus is the unique, universal, and absolute savior, as traditionally confessed by the Christian faith, but leaves the possibility of other "saving figures" and "ways of salvation" neither affirmed nor denied; about the latter it simply pleads ignorance. The third model takes the New Testament passages cited above and the three adjectives describing Jesus the savior not as literal, rational prose but as poetry affirming Jesus' specialness but not exclusivity. In other words, Jesus is *totus Deus*, that is, wholly God, insofar as he fully responded to God's love in the Spirit, but not *totum Dei*, that is the whole of God, understood in the metaphysical sense.

Before attempting a theology of Jesus as savior that is consonant with the Roman Catholic tradition and at the same time recognizes that the redemptive power of God is at work in the Jewish tradition, it is necessary to recall, albeit briefly, the teaching of *Dominus Iesus* of the Congregation for the Doctrine of the Faith (August 6, 2000) on Jesus as savior.[9] Concerned that religious pluralism may lead to relativism, the declaration reaffirms certain Christian doctrines, which it alleges have been denied by pluralists, such as the "fullness and definitiveness of the revelation of Jesus Christ," the unity between the saving work of the incarnate Word and that of the Holy Spirit, the "unicity and universality of the salvific mystery of Jesus Christ," the "unicity and unity of the church," and the unity between the reign of God and the church.[10] Of interest to our theme are

---

[8] See Paul F. Knitter, *Introducing Theologies of Religions* (Maryknoll, N.Y.: Orbis Books, 2002).

[9] For the English text of the declaration and a critical evaluation of it, see Stephen J. Pope and Charles Hefling, ed., *Sic et Non: Encountering* Dominus Iesus (Maryknoll, N.Y.: Orbis Books, 2002). The subtitle of *Dominus Iesus* is *On the Unicity and Salvific Universality of Jesus Christ and the Church*.

[10] The expressions in quotation marks are headings of the various sections of the declaration. The word *unicity*, which is the awkward transliteration of the Latin *unicitas*, connotes numerical and not merely qualitative uniqueness; that is, *DI* intends to affirm that Jesus, and no one else, is the only savior.

the declaration's statements on Jesus as the unique and universal savior and on the relation between Christianity and other religions.

With regard to Jesus as revealer, *DI* affirms that "in the mystery of Jesus Christ, the Incarnate Son of God . . . the full revelation of divine truth is given" (no. 5) and rejects the "theory of the limited, incomplete, or imperfect character of the revelation of Jesus Christ, which would be complementary to that found in other religions" (no. 6). Concerning Jesus as savior, *DI* states that "Jesus Christ has a significance and value for the human race and its history, which are unique and singular, proper to him alone, exclusive, universal, and absolute" (no. 15). As to the relationship between Christianity and other religions, *DI* condemns the view that the church is "*one way* of salvation alongside those constituted by the other religions, seen as complementary to the Church or substantially equivalent to her, even if these are said to be converting with the Church toward the eschatological kingdom of God" (no. 21). Hence, it says that even though "the followers of other religions can receive divine grace, it is also certain that *objectively speaking* they are in a gravely deficient situation in comparison with those who, in the Church, have the fullness of the means of salvation" (no. 22).

CHRIST AND CHRISTIANITY IN VIEW
OF THE CONTINUING VALIDITY OF THE JEWISH COVENANT

In the wake of the unexpected storm of protest against *DI* by many Christian as well as non-Christian theologians, some Vatican officials pointed out that Judaism was not targeted by the declaration's negative judgment on non-Christian religions (even though Judaism was not explicitly exempted by the declaration). While it is true that the Catholic church has always recognized the special status of Judaism and its historical and theological connections with Christianity, nevertheless, the claim that "Jews, who do not share our faith in Christ, are in a saving covenant with God," if anything, exacerbates the problems posed by religious pluralism, since it is claimed that at least one non-Christian religion, namely Judaism, is a way of salvation ("a saving covenant with God") apart, at least *prima facie,* from Christ and Christianity.

The challenge for Roman Catholic theologians, then, is to articulate a coherent and credible Christology and soteriology (theology of salvation) that honors the Christian belief in Jesus as the savior of all humankind and at the same time includes the affirmation that Judaism is and remains eternally a "saving covenant with God." In other words, what is needed is what has been called a non- or post-supersessionist Christology, or more generally, an inclusivist-pluralist Christology. It is to be noted here that the intent of this kind of Christology is not so much to elaborate a Christian theology of Judaism as such (which may or may not be interested in having its faith validated by Christians) as to reflect on how Christians should understand *themselves* in reference to Judaism and, by extension, to other religions.

Elements of a Post-supersessionist Christology

First and most fundamental element of a post-supersessionist Christology is an unambiguous and explicit rejection of the idea that since Christ is the "fulfillment," "fullness," and "definitiveness" of divine revelation, God's self-gift to and covenant with Israel have been abolished, either because of Israel's guilt in rejecting and killing Jesus (as implied in the charge of faithlessness and deicide against the Jews) or because of the intrinsic superiority of Jesus' ministry and of Christianity (the "new" covenant supplanting the "old" covenant). Rather, the two covenanted peoples of God, Israel and the church, are allowed by God to exist side by side in order to instruct and encourage each other "to do justly, and to love mercy, and to walk humbly" with their common God (Mic 6:8).

Second, there should be a retrieval of the ancient notion of multiple covenants. As Saint Irenaeus, the second-century bishop of Lyons, put it, God has made several covenants: under Adam, under Noah, under the Law, and under the gospel.[11] Hence, God is covenanted not only with Israel (under the Law) and Christians (under the gospel) but also with humanity as a whole (under Adam) and even with the entire universe (under Noah). The first three covenants (including God's covenant with Israel) have not been abolished or invalidated, nor have they been absorbed or dissolved into the fourth. Even though the first three have been, to use Irenaeus's expression, "recapitulated" in the fourth, that is, brought under Christ as their head, they have not lost their proper identity and integrity. On the contrary, precisely because they have been "recapitulated" in Christ, they have achieved and maintain their full identity and integrity, even today. Therefore, any talk about God's "new" covenant in Jesus must keep in mind the continuing significance and validity of these other covenants.

Third, the most challenging task of a post-supersessionist Christology consists in providing an explanation for how it is theologically possible to both recognize the continuing validity of God's covenant with Israel and maintain faith in Jesus as the person in whom God has acted to save humanity. There are two dimensions in this explanation, one concerning the activities of the Logos (Word) of God in Jesus (christological) and the other concerning the activities of the Holy Spirit (pneumatological).[12] According to the Christian faith, the divine Logos, the Son of God the Father, took flesh (or is incarnated) as a Jew, that is, in Jesus of Nazareth, and is therefore personally identified with him.[13] However, the Logos was not, and could not be, exhaustively embodied in Jesus of Nazareth, since Jesus was spatially and temporally limited and hence could not exhaustively express the divine, infinite saving power in his human words and deeds. This is part of what is meant by saying that the Logos "emptied

---

[11] See Irenaeus, *Against Heresies*, III, 11, 8.

[12] For a fuller development of the following points, see Chapter 4 herein.

[13] In technical language, the "person" of Jesus (the Greek terms are *hypostasis* or *prosōpon*), as the Council of Chalcedon (451) affirms, is the Logos himself, whereas his "natures" (in Greek, *ousia* or *physis*) are both divinity and humanity. In other words, *who* Jesus is, is the Logos; and *what* Jesus is, is human and divine.

himself" in the man Jesus and was subjected to human limitations (though not to sin). There is therefore a "distinction-in-identity" or "identity-in-distinction" between the eternal, "unincarnate" Logos and the Jew Jesus in whom the Logos became flesh in time and with whom he is personally identified. Hence, the activities of the Logos, though inseparable from those of Jesus, are also distinct from and go beyond Jesus' activities, before, during, and after the incarnation.

Fourth, the Holy Spirit, though intimately united with the Logos, is distinct from him and operates in a saving manner outside and beyond him, before, during, and after Jesus' ministry. The Holy Spirit "blows where it wills" (Jn 3:8). To use Irenaeus's colorful metaphor, the Logos and the Holy Spirit are the two "hands" of God the Father with which God acts in the world. Of course these two "hands" of God do not act independently of—much less in opposition to—each other; nonetheless, they operate distinctly and diversely from each other—though always in conjunction with each other. Thus, God's saving presence through Word and Spirit is not limited to the Christian covenant but was active and continues to be active in the history of Israel and, one might add, is extended to the whole human history, especially in the sacred books, rituals, moral teachings, and spiritual practices of all religions.

In this way, what the Holy Spirit says and does is truly different from, though not contradictory to, what the Logos says and does, and what the Logos and the Spirit do and say in Israel and in non-Christian religions may be truly different from, though not contradictory to, what Jesus and the Spirit do in Christianity. Needless to say, these activities of the Logos and the Spirit do not mean that the human responses that constitute part of Judaism and other non-Christian religions as religious institutions are always free from sin and error, but, of course the same thing must be said of Christians as well.

Fifth, religious pluralism, then, is not just a matter of fact but also a matter of principle. That is to say, Judaism and other non-Christian religions should be seen as part of the plan of divine providence and endowed with a particular role in the history of salvation. They are not merely a "preparation" for, "stepping stones" toward, or "seeds" of Christianity and destined to be "fulfilled" by it. Rather, they have their own autonomy and their proper role as ways of salvation, at least for their adherents.

Sixth, in light of what has been said above, one may question the usefulness of words such as *unique, absolute,* and even *universal* to describe the role of Jesus as savior today. They might have served the purpose of affirming the reality of God's definitive offer of salvation in Jesus for the whole humanity. But words are unavoidably embedded in socio-political and cultural contexts, and the contexts in which these words were used were, in many parts of the world, often tainted by colonialist imperialism, economic exploitation, political domination, and religious marginalization. No matter how they are theologically qualified—and they may die the death of a thousand qualifications!—words such as *uniqueness, absoluteness,* and *universality* connote in the ears of non-Christians, especially those who have been victims of violence and exploitation at the hands of Christians, arrogance, exclusiveness, and self-absorption. More important, they are not the most effective means to convey

Christ's message of humble service and compassionate love, especially to victims of political, economic, and religious persecution. In particular, in the post-Holocaust era, these expressions, I suggest, have outlived their usefulness and should be jettisoned and replaced by other, theologically more adequate equivalents.

Christ's uniqueness, absoluteness, and universality are not exclusive, eliminative, and abrogative but, to use Jacques Dupuis's expressions, constitutive" and "relational."[14] That is to say, because the Christ-event, according to the Christian faith, belongs to and is the definitive realization of God's plan of salvation, Christ is "constitutive" of salvation in a very special manner. In him God has brought about salvation for all humanity in a most effective and powerful manner.

Moreover, because non-Christian religions and in particular Judaism are themselves part of God's plan of salvation of which the Christ-event is the definitive point, Christ is related to these religions, especially Judaism, and vice versa. There is therefore a reciprocal relationship between Jesus and non-Christian religions, in particular Judaism. Hence, the Christ-event is not only constitutive but also relational. Autonomy and relatedness are not mutually contradictory but grow in direct proportion to each other. Furthermore, because non-Christian religions possess an autonomous function in the history of salvation, different from that of Christianity, they cannot be reduced to Christianity in terms of preparation and fulfillment.

Seventh, there is then a reciprocal relationship between Christianity and Judaism and the other religions. Not only are the non-Christian religions complemented by Christianity, but Christianity also is complemented by other religions. In other words, the process of complementarity, enrichment, and even correction is two-way or reciprocal. This reciprocity in no way endangers the Christian confession that the church has received from Christ the fullness of revelation, since it is one thing to receive the definitive gift of God's self-revelation in Jesus and quite another to *understand* it fully and to *live* it completely. Indeed, it is only in a sincere and humble dialogue with other religions that Christianity can come to a fuller realization of its own identity and mission and a better understanding of the constitutive revelation that it has received from Christ. By the same token, Judaism and other religions can achieve their full potential only in dialogue with one another and with Christianity.

Eighth, though Jesus Christ is confessed by Christians to be the fullness of revelation and the definitive savior, there is also a reciprocal relationship between him and other "saving figures," since Jesus' uniqueness—should this word still be used—or more appropriately, definitiveness, is not absolute but relational. In this sense Jesus' revelation and salvation are also complemented by God's self-revelation and redemption manifested in other saving figures. In this context it is useful to recall that Jesus did not and could not reveal everything to

---

[14] See Jacquis Dupuis, *Toward a Christian Theology of Religious Pluralism* (Maryknoll, N.Y.: Orbis Books, 1998), 283.

his disciples and that it is the Holy Spirit who will lead them to "the complete truth" (Jn 16:12–13). It is quite possible that the Holy Spirit will lead the church to the complete truth by means of a dialogue with other religions in which the Spirit is actively present.

Ninth, one of the fundamental truths of the Christian faith is the so-called Second Coming of Christ. Christians are still waiting in hope for the coming of Christ as the glorious Messiah and Lord to judge the living and the dead. The Pontifical Biblical Commission's important document *The Jewish People and Their Sacred Scriptures in the Christian Bible* asserts that when the Jewish messiah appears, he will have some of the traits of Christ and that Christians will recognize the traits of Jesus in him.[15] If this is true, then it is recognized that there are two ways of understanding the saving action of God in human history. One is through the christological symbols of the Jesus of the Christian faith; the other is through the religious symbols of Judaism, among which is the Jewish messiah. These two ways are distinct but do not contradict or eliminate each other. On the other hand, there will be, at least at the end of time, some significant overlapping between the Christian Jesus and the Jewish messiah. How they will ultimately converge at the end of time is a matter of faith and hope. Meanwhile, Christians and Jews must join their actions and hearts, in mutual forgiveness and love, so that the ultimate unity they hope and pray for may be realized as much as possible even here and now.

This brings us to the tenth and last but not least aspect of Christian-Jewish relations. Dialogue between Christianity and Judaism (as well as with other religions) cannot be carried out simply as an exchange of theological views, though this academic conversation has its own importance. Rather, this theological dialogue must be complemented by three other forms of dialogue, as the Pontifical Council for Inter-religious Dialogue and the Congregation for the Evangelization of Peoples have said:

a. The *dialogue of life,* where people strive to live in an open and neighborly spirit, sharing their joys and sorrows, their human problems and preoccupations. b. The *dialogue of action,* in which Christians and others collaborate for the integral development and liberation of people. c. The *dialogue of theological exchange,* where specialists seek to deepen their understanding of their respective religious heritages, and to appreciate each other's spiritual values. d. The *dialogue of religious experience,* where persons, rooted in their own religious traditions, share their spiritual riches,

---

[15] Pontifical Biblical Commission, *The Jewish People and Their Sacred Scriptures in the Christian Bible,* Part I, no. 21: "What has already been accomplished in Christ must yet be accomplished in us and in the world. The definitive fulfillment will be at the end with the resurrection of the dead, a new heaven and a new earth. Jewish messianic expectation is not in vain. It can become for us Christians a powerful stimulant to keep alive the eschatological dimension of our faith. Like them, we too live in expectation. The difference is that for us the One who is to come will have the traits of the Jesus who has already come and is already present and active among us."

for instance, with regard to prayer and contemplation, faith and ways of searching for God or the Absolute (*DP*, no. 42).[16]

It is only out of this humble and loving practice of the fourfold dialogue that an adequate theology of Jesus Christ as God's constitutive and relational saving action in human history and of God's eternal covenant with the Jewish people can be elaborated.

---

[16] The English text of *DP* is available in William Burrows, ed., *Redemption and Dialogue: Reading* Redemptoris Missio *and* Dialogue and Proclamation (Maryknoll, N.Y.: Orbis Books, 1993), 3–55.

10

Jews and Judaism in Light of the *Catechism of the Catholic Church*

ON THE WAY TO RECONCILIATION

Promulgated by Pope John Paul II on October 11, 1992, the *Catechism of the Catholic Church* became a best seller in many countries.[1] Six years in the making, the eight-hundred-page work received both enthusiastic encomium and harsh criticism.[2] However its merits are judged, the *Catechism*, if used as intended, will likely shape the Roman Catholic tradition for a long time to come. It stands to reason, then, that part of the effort to eradicate anti-Semitism from Roman Catholic theology and preaching must include an examination of the *Catechism*'s presentation of Jews and Judaism.

THE *CATECHISM* ON JEWS AND JUDAISM

The first thing to note is that, whereas Vatican II's *Nostra aetate* presents Judaism in the context of non-Christian religions, the *Catechism* intentionally avoids such an approach.[3] Instead, it adopts the scheme of Vatican II's *Lumen gentium*, which speaks of the various ways in which different people are related

---

[1] The original language of the text is French, published as *Catéchisme de l'Eglise Catholique* (Paris: Mame—Libreria Editrice Vaticana, 1992). Henceforth it will be referred to as the *Catechism*. Its *editio typica*, however, is in Latin. The English translation was published in June 1994. Because of the exclusive language of the official English version, I will provide my own English translation based on the French original.

[2] For a short history of the composition of the *Catechism*, see Joseph Ratzinger, "Progress Report on the Universal Catechism," *The Living Light* 27/1 (1991), 131–38; and William J. Levada, "The Catechism for the Universal Church," *The Living Light* 26/3 (1990), 199–209. For a bibliography on the project of composing a universal catechism and on its draft, see Thomas J. Reese, "Bibliographical Survey on the Catechism for the Universal Church," *The Living Light* 27/3 (1991), 151–57. For a critical but balanced introduction to the *Catechism*, see Berard Marthaler, ed., *Introducing the* Catechism of the Catholic Church: *Traditional Themes and Contemporary Issues* (New York: Paulist Press, 1994).

[3] *NA* briefly describes, with increasing length, Hinduism, Buddhism, Islam, and Judaism.

to the church in their search for God (*LG*, no. 16).[4] Jews are placed in the category of "those who have not yet received the Gospel" and are said to be "related to the People of God in various ways" (*Catechism*, no. 839).

Judaism and Divine Revelation

In comparison with Vatican II, however, the *Catechism* makes two new points. First, in contemporary Catholic theology there is a debate on whether non-Christian religions are merely the fruit of the human search for God or have already participated in divine revelation. The *Catechism* declines to settle this issue on the grounds that the Magisterium has not made a sufficiently clear pronouncement on the matter.[5] However, it recognizes the special position of Judaism vis-à-vis other non-Christian religions: "The Jewish faith, unlike other non-Christian religions, is already a response to God's revelation in the Old Testament" (no. 839). In an earlier chapter on God's coming to meet humanity and the various stages of God's self-revelation, the *Catechism* speaks of God's self-communication to the first parents, to Noah, and to Abraham: "The people descended from Abraham would be the trustees of the promise made to the patriarchs, the chosen people, called to prepare for that day when God would gather all his children into the unity of the church" (no. 60). Clearly, then, whatever opinion one holds about the revelatory character of other religions, doubt cannot be entertained that God's self-revelation has taken place in Judaism. Christian theologians must be mindful of this unique position of Judaism as a revealed religion.

Second, the *Catechism* explicitly raises the issue of the Messiah and points out the difference in the expectation of the Messiah among Christians and Jews:

> And when one considers the future, God's people of the old covenant and the new people of God tend toward similar goals: expectation of the coming (or the return) of the Messiah. But one awaits the return of the Messiah who died and rose from the dead and is recognized as Lord and Son of God; the other awaits the coming of a messiah whose features remain hidden till the end of time; and the latter waiting is accompanied by the drama of not knowing or of misunderstanding Christ Jesus (no. 840).

This common, though different, expectation of the messiah constitutes an important ground for doctrinal dialogue and practical collaboration between adherents of these two religions.

Mention of the messiah brings us to consider how the *Catechism* regards the relationship between what it calls the "Old Testament" and the "New Testament"

---

[4] Choosing the words carefully, the document speaks of Roman Catholics as "fully incorporated" into the church, non-Catholic Christians as "joined" to the church, and non-Christians as "related" to the church.

[5] See Joseph Ratzinger, "Progress Report on the Universal Catechism," *The Living Light* 27/3 (1991), 136.

and the connected question of how to interpret the Old Testament.[6] The First Testament, the *Catechism* declares, "is an indispensable part of Sacred Scripture. Its books are divinely inspired and retain a permanent value, for the Old Testament has never been revoked" (no. 121). With regard to the interpretation of the scriptures, the *Catechism* stresses the importance of discerning the "literal meaning" of a text conveyed by the human authors in their words (nos. 109–16). But it also recognizes the necessity of going beyond the literal sense of the Bible to discover its "spiritual sense," dividing the latter, according to an ancient usage, into allegorical, moral, and analogical senses (nos. 116–18).

More specifically, in interpreting the First Testament the *Catechism* affirms the legitimacy of the typological approach prevalent before the advent of the historical-critical method. Typology, it argues, is justified by the unity between the two testaments, provided that the continuing efficacy and validity of the First Testament is maintained: "Christians therefore read the Old Testament in the light of Christ crucified and risen. Such typological reading discloses the inexhaustible content of the Old Testament; but it must not make us forget that the Old Testament retains its own intrinsic value as revelation reaffirmed by our Lord himself. Besides, the New Testament has to be read in the light of the Old" (no. 129).

This typological approach or the promise-fulfillment scheme also governs the *Catechism*'s understanding of the church's liturgical worship: "In the sacramental economy the Holy Spirit fulfills what was prefigured in the old covenant" (no. 1093). Fulfillment, however, does not imply abolition; on the contrary, the *Catechism* says, the church's liturgy has retained elements of the worship of the old covenant as "integral and irreplaceable" (no. 1093), adopting them as its own. Such elements include reading the First Testament, praying the Psalms, and recalling the saving events and significant realities of the Jewish history. The *Catechism* urges that catechesis unveil "what lay hidden under the letter of the Old Testament: the mystery of Christ" (no. 1094). This catechesis is called typological because "it reveals the newness of Christ on the basis of the 'figures' (types) that announce the deeds, words, and symbols of the first covenant" (no. 1094). Catechesis, should not, however, look only toward the past.

---

[6] For an informative and balanced study of the teaching of the *Catechism* on biblical hermeneutics, see Joseph Jensen, "Beyond the Literal Sense: The Interpretation of Scripture in the Catechism of the Catholic Church," *The Living Light* 29/4 (1993), 50–60. With regard to the term *Old Testament* Jensen argues persuasively that what is referred to as the "Old Testament" in the Christian scriptures is not identical with the Hebrew scriptures in terms of its contents and the order in which its books are arranged. He also agrees with Lawrence Boadt that alternative terms such as *The First Testament* and *The Prime Testament* run the risk of reading of the Bible in a disjunctive way rather than from the final viewpoint of the New Testament. He is careful to point out, however, that the use of the term *Old Testament* should not suggest that God's covenant with Israel is no longer valid or has been superceded. Even with this caveat, it is often the case that among average Christians the term *Old Testament,* given the long history of the Christian "teaching of contempt" against Jews, conveys obsoleteness and supersession. For this reason I use *First Testament* and *Second Testament* when speaking for myself and *Old Testament* and *New Testament* when quoting the *Catechism.*

Interestingly, the *Catechism* affirms that "a better knowledge of the Jewish people's faith and religious life *as professed and lived even now* can help our better understanding of certain aspects of Christian liturgy" (no. 1096, emphasis added).[7]

The typological approach is also operative in the *Catechism*'s understanding of the relationship between what it calls "the Old Law" and "the New Law or the Law of the Gospel." It acknowledges that God has revealed his law to Israel and that the "Law of Moses," summed up in the Ten Commandments, is "holy, spiritual, and good." Nevertheless, it is "still imperfect": "Like a tutor it shows what must be done, but does not of itself give the strength, the grace of the Spirit, to fulfill it. Because of sin, which it cannot remove, it remains a law of bondage" (no. 1963). Again typology predominates: "The Old Law is a preparation for the gospel. . . . It prophesies and presages the work of liberation from sin that will be fulfilled in Christ; it provides the New Testament with images, types, and symbols for expressing the life according to the Spirit" (no. 1964). Concerning the sabbath, for example, which is said to be "at the heart of Israel's law" (no. 348), the *Catechism* declares that for Christians the ceremonial observance of Sunday, which is "the eighth day" (no. 349), "replaces that of the sabbath" (no. 2175).

In sum, in its exposition of the relationship between Judaism and the church the *Catechism*'s basic metaphor is that of promise-fulfillment, preparation-consummation, foretelling-realization: "The remote preparation for this gathering together of the people of God begins when God calls Abraham and promises that he will become the father of a great people. Its immediate preparation begins with Israel's election as the people of God. By this election, Israel is to be the sign of the future gathering of all nations. But the prophets also accuse Israel of breaking the covenant and behaving like a prostitute. They announce a new and eternal covenant. Christ instituted this covenant" (no. 762).

Jesus and the Jews

One of the central themes in Jewish-Christian dialogue is the relationship of Jesus to the Law and to the Jews of his time, both in his public ministry and at his death. The *Catechism* speaks of Jesus as "the only one who could keep it [the Law] perfectly" (no. 578), as the one who "did not abolish the Law but fulfilled it by giving its ultimate interpretation in a divine way" (no. 581). Furthermore, according to the *Catechism*, Jesus had the deepest respect for the Temple, was willing to pay the Temple tax, and even "identified himself with the Temple by presenting himself as God's definitive dwelling place among humanity" (no. 586). Nevertheless, Jesus' attitude toward the Law and the Temple

---

[7] The italicized part seems to be a quotation from John Paul II's March 6, 1982, speech to the delegates of episcopal conferences and other experts meeting in Rome to study the relations between the church and Judaism, though reference to it is not given. Regrettably, the *Catechism* does not follow its own counsel when it expounds Christian worship and prayer.

scandalized the Pharisees and the Sadducees. Of the Pharisees the *Catechism* says: "This principle of integral observance of the Law not only in the letter but in spirit was dear to the Pharisees. By giving Israel this principle they had led many Jews of Jesus' time to an extreme religious zeal. This zeal, were it not to lapse into 'hypocritical' casuistry, could only prepare the people for the unprecedented intervention of God through the perfect fulfillment of the Law by the Righteous One in place of all sinners" (no. 579).[8]

According to the *Catechism*, Jesus asked the "religious authorities" of Jerusalem to believe in him; but such an act of faith demands "a mysterious death to self" (no. 591). It is understandable, then, the *Catechism* goes on to say, that they refused Jesus' demand and "judged that he deserved the death sentence as a blasphemer. The members of the Sanhedrin were thus acting at the same time out of 'ignorance' and the 'hardness' of their 'unbelief'" (no. 591).

With regard to Jesus' trial, the *Catechism* notes the division of opinion among "the Jewish authorities." But it makes it clear that "the Sanhedrin, having declared Jesus deserving of death as a blasphemer but having lost the right to put anyone to death, handed him over to the Romans, accusing him of political revolt. . . . The high priests also threatened Pilate politically so that he would condemn Jesus to death" (no. 596).

Judaism and Prayer

The last part of the *Catechism*, which deals with prayer, offers profound insights on prayer in Judaism. Viewing prayer as "a reciprocal call, a covenant drama" (no. 2567) between God and humanity, God searching for and responding to humans and humans responding to and searching for God, the *Catechism* describes Jewish prayer by locating it in the history of the Jewish people. With a deft touch and a sure sense of synthesis, it presents the various forms of Jewish prayer beginning with Abraham and ending with the psalter.

In Abraham's "attentiveness of the heart" to God's word, the *Catechism* sees the essence of prayer (no. 2570). The patriarch, in his obedience to God's command to sacrifice his only son, is seen as "the father of believers . . . conformed to the likeness of the Father, who will not spare his own Son but will deliver him up for all" (no. 2572). In Jacob's nightlong wrestling with a mysterious figure, it acknowledges the symbol of prayer as "a battle of faith and as the

---

[8] This text is quite ambiguous: on the one hand, the *Catechism* praises the Pharisees for their "principle of integral observance"; on the other hand, this principle is said to have led many Jews to "extreme religious zeal," which turned into "hypocritical casuistry" (reference is made to Mt 15:3–7 and Lk 11:39–54). In fact, the text did not explicitly say that the Pharisees' "extreme religious zeal" *de facto* turned into "hypocritical casuistry." Rather, it says circuitously that this zeal could have prepared people to welcome Jesus if it "did not wish to turn itself into a hypocritical casuistry." The French text reads: "Celui-ci [i.e., extreme religious zeal], s'il ne voulait pas se résoudre en une casuistique 'hypocrite', ne pouvait que préparer le Peuple à cette intervention de Dieu inouïe que sera l'exécution parfaite de la Loi par le seul Juste à la place de tous les pécheurs."

triumph of perseverance" (no. 2573). The prayer of Moses is "the most striking example of intercessory prayer" (no. 2574) and his experience of the burning bush is "one of the primordial images of prayer in the spiritual tradition of Jews and Christians alike" (no. 2575). David is proclaimed as "the first prophet of Jewish and Christian prayer" (no. 2579). The Temple is for the Jewish people "the place of their education in prayer: pilgrimages, feasts, and sacrifices, the evening offering, the incense, and the bread of the Presence ("shrewbread")— all these signs of the holiness and glory of God Most High and Most Near were appeals and ways of prayer" (no. 2581). However, because "ritualism often encouraged an excessively external worship" (no. 2581), the prophets, in particular Elijah, were commissioned by God to educate their people in "faith and conversion of heart" (no. 2581). Finally, the psalms, "the masterwork of prayer in the Old Testament, . . . both nourished and expressed the prayer of the People of God gathered during the great feasts at Jerusalem and each Sabbath in the synagogues. . . . Prayed by Christ and fulfilled in him, the psalms remain essential to the prayer of the church" (nos. 2585–86).

The final line of the last quotation reveals both the strength and weakness of the *Catechism*'s treatment of Jewish prayer. On the one hand, it recognizes Jewish prayer, especially the psalms, as an essential and permanent element of Christian prayer. On the other hand, following its typological approach, the *Catechism* sees it primarily as foreshadowing and announcing the prayers of Christ and the church. Every Jewish master of prayer from Abraham to Moses to David to Elijah is viewed principally as a type of Christ, whose practice of and teaching on prayer fulfilled all Jewish prayers.

Jesus as the Hope of Israel

It was pointed out above how the *Catechism* views Jews and Christians as having a similar goal, that is, the expectation of the coming or return of a messiah whose "features remain hidden till the end of time" for Jews, and how this expectation of the Jews is "accompanied by the drama of not knowing or of misunderstanding Jesus" (no. 840). In its exposition of the glorious return of Jesus, the *Catechism* repeats Paul's teaching on the "conversion" of all Israel as the condition for Jesus' parousia, without however explaining how it will come about:

> The glorious Messiah's coming is suspended at every moment of history until his recognition by "all Israel," for "a hardening has come upon part of Israel" in their "unbelief" toward Jesus. . . . The "full inclusion" of the Jews in the Messiah's salvation, in the wake of "the full number of the Gentiles" will enable the People of God to achieve "the measure of the stature of the fullness of Christ," in which "God may be all in all" (no. 674).

Because the *Catechism* does not proffer any exegesis of Romans 9—11, it is not clear what it means by "the 'full inclusion' of the Jews in the Messiah's salvation." It may leave the impression that all Jews will somehow join the church and become Christians, which is far from what Paul had in mind.[9]

THE *CATECHISM* IN LIGHT OF EARLIER CHURCH DOCUMENTS

Commentators on the *Catechism* have noted the extraordinarily large number of quotations from a variety of sources that are often strung together in its text. It is all the more surprising, then, that in discussing Judaism and its relationship to Christianity the *Catechism* failed to make use of earlier ground-breaking church documents, except for an abbreviated citation from *NA*.[10] It is also regrettable that in its condemnation of discrimination it does not cite the only text of Vatican II that explicitly rejects anti-Semitism: "The church repudiates all persecutions against any human being. Moreover, mindful of its common patrimony with the Jews, and motivated by the gospel's spiritual love and by no political considerations, it deplores the hatred, persecutions, and displays of anti-Semitism directed against the Jews at any time and from any source" (*NA*, no. 4).[11]

Among Roman documents on the relationship between Judaism and Christianity with which the *Catechism* should be compared and contrasted, two obtain pride of place: *Guidelines and Suggestions for Implementing the Conciliar Declaration* Nostra aetate *(4)* (December 1, 1974) and *Notes on the Correct Way to Present the Jews and Judaism in Preaching and Catechesis in the Roman Catholic Church* (June 24, 1985), both issued by the Vatican Commission for Religious Relations with the Jews.[12]

---

[9] For a helpful interpretation of Romans 9—11, see Sidney G. Hall, III, *Christian Anti-Semitism and Paul's Theology* (Minneapolis: Fortress Press, 1993), 113–27. Hall argues that Paul did not demand of the Jews that they "accept Christ" and thus become Christians but that they accept "the gospel of Christ," namely, the inclusive claim that Gentiles are beloved children of Abraham outside the Law.

[10] The citation is taken from paragraph 4: "Neither all Jews indiscriminately at that time, nor Jews today, can be charged with the crimes committed during his Passion. . . . The Jews should not be spoken of as rejected or accursed as if this followed from holy Scripture." It is somewhat strange that in a book purported to be the standard for catechetical instruction and preaching, the rest of the paragraph is omitted: "All should take pains, then, lest in catechetical instruction and in the preaching of God's Word they teach anything out of harmony with the truth of the gospel and the spirit of Christ."

[11] The *Catechism* deals with discrimination in nos. 1934–38. In condemning discrimination it cites *GS*, no. 29: "Every form of social or cultural discrimination in fundamental personal rights on the grounds of sex, race, color, social conditions, language, or religion, must be curbed and eradicated as incompatible with God's design."

[12] The English texts are available in Eugene Fisher and Leon Klenicki, eds., *In Our Time: The Flowering of Jewish-Catholic Dialogue* (New York: Paulist Press, 1990), 29–50. The first document will be referred to as *Guidelines*, the second as *Notes*. The pages refer to those of this book. Fisher provides an introduction to these two documents, Klenicki a critical evaluation of them. Another document, entitled *Within Context: Guidelines for the Catechetical Presentation of Jews and Judaism in the New Testament* (1986), is of great importance for our theme. It is not issued by the Vatican but was prepared in collaboration by the Secretariat for Catholic-Jewish Relations of the

A comparison between the *Catechism,* on the one hand, and *Guidelines* and *Notes,* on the other, shows that the former represents an unfortunate step backward in the understanding of the relationship between Judaism and Christianity. I will highlight some areas in which this regression occurs.

First, we have seen how in the area of hermeneutics the *Catechism*'s approach is predominantly typological.[13] Despite its caveat that the First Testament books "retain a permanent value, for the Old Covenant has never been revoked" (no. 121) and that the literal sense, discovered by means of the historical-critical method, is primary, the *Catechism* has made little effort to understand the original meaning of the First Testament texts. It does not seem to be aware of the fact that "typology . . . makes many people uneasy and is perhaps the sign of a problem unresolved" and that "there is a Christian reading of the Old Testament which does not necessarily coincide with the Jewish reading."[14] *Notes* has pointed out the need for balancing "a number of pairs of ideas which express the relation between the two economies of the Old and New Testaments: Promise and Fulfillment, Continuity and Newness, Singularity and Universality, Uniqueness and Exemplary Nature."[15] Unfortunately, it cannot be said that this balance is achieved in the *Catechism*; in fact, supersessionist overtones can be heard in its Christology and ecclesiology. To silence these voices the *Catechism* would do well to incorporate into its exposition of the hermeneutics of the New Testament such paragraphs as the following:

> It is essential to remember that the gospels represent theological reflections on the life and teaching of Jesus which, while historically based, were not intended by their authors to be eyewitness accounts. . . . Using methods familiar to us from contemporary Jewish apocalyptic and Essene writings (e.g., the Dead Sea Scrolls), as well as early rabbinic literature, the New Testament authors sought to explain their experience of Jesus in terms of their Jewish heritage, especially by using passages from the

---

National Conference of Catholic Bishops, the Education Department of the United States Catholic Conference, and Interfaith Affairs Department of the Anti-Defamation League of B'nai B'rith. The text is also available in Fisher and Klenicki, *In Our Time,* 59–74.

[13] The following works on the relationship between the First and Second Testaments deserve notice: Clark M. Williamson, *Has God Rejected His People?* (Nashville, Tenn.: Abingdon Press, 1982); idem, *Interpreting Difficult Texts: Anti-Judaism and Christian Preaching* (Philadelphia: Trinity Press International, 1989); Helga Croner, Leon Klenicki, and Lawrence Boadt, eds., *Biblical Studies: Meeting Ground of Jews and Christians* (New York: Paulist Press, 1980); *God's Mercy Endures Forever: Guidelines on the Presentation of Jews and Judaism in Catholic Preaching* (Washington, D.C.: NCCB, 1988).

[14] *Notes,* 42.

[15] *Notes,* 40. The document goes on to urge the catechist to show that "promise and fulfillment throw light on each other; newness lies in a metamorphosis of what was there before; the singularity of the people of the Old Testament is not exclusive and is open, in the divine vision, to a universal extension; the uniqueness of the Jewish people is meant to have the force of an example" (ibid).

Hebrew Scriptures. When reading the prophets (e.g., Isaiah 7:14, 52–53; Hosea 11:1; Micah 5:1), the Evangelists interpreted Jewish hopes for the deliverance as foretelling Jesus' coming. Such post-Resurrection insights do not replace the original intentions of the prophets. Nor does Christian affirmation of the validity of the Evangelists' insight preclude the validity of post-New Testament and present Jewish insight into the meaning of prophetic texts.[16]

Second, the *Catechism*'s Christology, besides being markedly supersessionist, is also strangely muted on the Jewishness of Jesus, a point strongly emphasized by contemporary Christology.[17] Because of its one-sided descending Christology, it is unable to make it clear that

> Jesus was and always remained a Jew, his ministry was deliberately limited "to the lost sheep of Israel" (Mt 15:24). Jesus is fully a man of his time, and of his environment—the Jewish Palestinian one of the first century, the anxieties and hopes of which he shared.[18]

The *Catechism*'s description of Jesus' contemporaries leaves something to be desired as well. Its characterization of the Pharisees borders on caricature with its oblique reference to their "hypocritical casuistry" (no. 579).[19] True, the *Catechism*

---

[16] *Within Context*, 62. In introducing *Notes*, Bishop Jorge Mejia writes: "It is not always an easy matter to present the relations between both Testaments in a way that fully respects the validity of the Old Testament and shows its permanent usefulness for the Church. . . . In no way is 'typological' usage a devaluation of the validity proper to the Old Testament. Rather to the contrary . . . the importance of the Old Testament for Judaism is underlined. So, too, is the importance of Jews and Christians hearing the Old Testament together, so that together, in the path opened by the prophetic tradition, we may become more deeply engaged as fellow partisans for humanity today. . . . It should be noted that the limits of 'typological' usage are acknowledged, and other possible ways of reading the Old Testament in relation to the New are not excluded" (54). It is unfortunate that the limits of typology and the possibility of alternative interpretations are not explicitly acknowledged by the *Catechism*.

[17] On the Jewishness of Jesus, *Within Context* declares: "Jesus was born, lived and died a Jew of his times. He, his family and all his original disciples followed the laws, traditions and customs of his people. The key concepts of Jesus' teaching, therefore, cannot be understood apart from the Jewish heritage" (59). The literature on Jesus and Judaism has grown by leaps and bounds. The following works are representative: E. P. Sanders, *Jesus and Judaism* (Philadelphia: Fortress Press, 1985); Gerard Sloyan, *Is Christ the End of the Law?* (Philadelphia: Westminster, 1978); Harvey Falk, *Jesus the Pharisee* (New York: Paulist Press, 1985); Bernard J. Lee, *The Galilean Jewishness of Jesus* (New York: Paulist Press, 1988); Leonard Swidler, *Yeshua: A Model for Moderns* (Kansas City: Sheed & Ward, 1988); James H. Charlesworth, *Jesus within Judaism* (New York: Doubleday, 1988); and Michael Hilton and Gordian Marshall, *The Gospels and Rabbinic Judaism: A Study Guide* (New York: KTAV and ADL, 1988).

[18] *Notes*, 44.

[19] For literature on the Pharisees, see Ellis Rivkin, *The Hidden Revolution: The Pharisees' Search for the Kingdom of God Within* (Nashville, Tenn.: Abingdon Press, 1978).

does say that Jesus' relations with the Pharisees were not exclusively polemical; many were his friends, and many of their teachings and practices were shared by Jesus (see no. 575). Nevertheless, it seems to take the Gospels' account of the polemics between Jesus and the Pharisees at face value. There is no explicit acknowledgment that "some references hostile or less favorable to the Jews have their historical context in conflicts between the nascent Church and the Jewish community" and that "certain controversies reflect Christian Jewish relations long after the time of Jesus."[20] Though the *Catechism* declines to judge the conscience of the participants in Jesus' trial, it comes perilously close to accusing the members of the Sanhedrin of bad faith when it affirms that they were acting out of not only ignorance but also the hardness of their unbelief (see no. 591). To accept Jesus' claim regarding his identity and mission, the *Catechism* argues, requires "a mysterious death to self" (no. 591), a painful process the members of the Sanhedrin were allegedly unwilling to undergo.

Third, in its account of Jesus' trial, the *Catechism* rightly rejects the deicide charge and insists that "the church does not hesitate to impute to Christians the gravest responsibility for the torments inflicted upon Jesus" (no. 598).[21] Nevertheless, it seems to take the Gospels' narratives of Jesus' passion as entirely eyewitness accounts of historical events and tends to gloss over the fact that the passion narratives are "post-Resurrection reflections from different perspectives on the meaning of Jesus' death and resurrection."[22] And even though the *Catechism* warns that we should not impute collective responsibility on the "Jews in Jerusalem as a whole" (no. 597) for Jesus' trial and death, unfortunately it continues to speak of "the Jewish authorities" in general in connection with Jesus' passion, as if it were possible to identify with certainty who the "Jewish authorities" actually were. It has been remarked by biblical scholars, for instance, that the Pharisees are not depicted in the passion narratives as playing a significant role in Jesus' death. In general, had a paragraph such as the following been added in the *Catechism*, a more accurate understanding of the passion story would have been facilitated:

> Neither John nor Luke record a formal Sanhedrin "trial" of Jesus, making such a scene historically uncertain. Likewise there is a tendency from the earlier gospels (especially Mark) to the later (Matthew and John) to place more and more of the onus on "the Jews" and less on Pilate, who alone had the authority to order a crucifixion (Jn 18:31), a notion emphasized in

---

[20] *Notes*, 46.

[21] For studies on Jesus' trial, see Hairn Cohen, *The Trial and Death of Jesus* (New York-KTAV, 1977); Donald Juel, *Messiah and Temple* (Missoula, Mont.: Scholars Press, 1977); S. G. F. Brandon, *The Trial of Jesus of Nazareth* (New York: Stein and Day, 1979); Gerard Sloyan, *Jesus on Trial* (Philadelphia: Fortress Press, 1973); John T. Townsend, *A Liturgical Interpretation of Our Lord's Passion in Narrative Form* (New York: National Conference of Christians and Jews, 1985).

[22] *Within Context*, 67.

Matthew's "hand-washing" scene (Mt 27:24). The use of the general term, "the Jews" in the Passion narrative of the Gospel of John can lead to a sense of collective guilt if not carefully explained.[23]

It is obvious that if the *Catechism*'s uncritical retelling of the passion narratives is transmitted in catechesis and preaching without a careful attempt at contextualizing passages describing the conflicts between Jesus and various Jewish groups, it will lead to a misunderstanding of the nature of the Gospels' account of Jesus' trial and death and even to anti-Jewish hostility, as history has shown all too well. In this context the danger of anti-Semitism present in passion plays, still popular in many Catholic countries, should be duly noted.[24]

Finally, the *Catechism*'s treatment of what it calls "the Old Law" (no. 1962) is one-sidedly supersessionist and requires extensive amendment. Its repeated description of "the Old Law" as "the first stage of revealed Law" (nos. 1962 and 1980) and as "a preparation for the gospel" (nos. 1964 and 1982) undermines the perennial validity of the Torah as God's will for the Jewish people, despite heroic protestations to the contrary. Above all, the *Catechism*'s sharp contrast between "the Old Law," "a law of bondage" that "shows what must be done but does not of itself give the strength, the grace of the Spirit, to fulfill it" (no. 1963), on the one hand, and "the New Law or the Law of the Gospel" that is "the perfection here on earth of the divine law, natural and revealed . . . the interior law of charity" (no. 1965) and "the grace of the Holy Spirit" (no. 1966), on the other hand perpetuates the deleterious "Law *vs.* Gospel" motif of Reformation theology.

In contrast to this view, one must unambiguously speak of the Torah "as the revealed will of God, the response God expects of the people whom He has saved and with whom He has entered into an eternal, unbreakable covenant."[25] With regard to Paul's attitude to the Torah in particular, it must be remembered that "he never suggested that the Law (Torah) had ceased to be God's will for the Jewish people." Regarding the Jews and the Torah, Paul states that "even after the founding of the Church, the relationship is enduring and valid, for 'God's gifts and call are irrevocable.'"[26]

---

[23] Ibid., 68.

[24] See Saul S. Friedman, *The Oberammergau Passion Play* (Carbondale, Ill.: Southern Illinois University Press, 1984); and *Criteria for the Evaluation of Dramatization of the Passion* (Washington, D.C.: NCCB, 1988), a document issued by the Bishops' Committee for Ecumenical and Interreligious Affairs.

[25] *Within Context*, 66. The text goes on to say that "Jesus accepted and observed the Law (cf. Gal. 4:4; Lk 2:21–24), extolled respect for it, and invited obedience to it (Mt. 5:17–20). Therefore, it can never be valid to place Jesus' teaching (gospel) in fundamental opposition to the Torah. The dynamic reality that is Jewish Law should never be depicted as 'fossilized' or reduced to 'legalism'" (66). *Guidelines*, 34, also states: "The Old Testament and the Jewish tradition founded upon it must not be set against the New Testament in such a way that the former seems to constitute a religion of only justice, fear and legalism, with no appeal to the love of God and neighbor (cf. Dt 6:5; Lv19:18; Mt 22:34–40)."

[26] *Within Context*, 66.

GOING BEYOND THE *CATECHISM* IN PREACHING AND CATECHESIS

The *Catechism* has deliberately left the task of adaptation of doctrinal presentations and catechetical methods required by particular circumstances and needs to national and local catechisms and to those responsible for the teaching of the faith. In addition to those areas (for example, covenant and election, the scriptures, Torah and Law, Christology, and messiahship) in which its teachings, in my judgment, call for emendation and expansion, as suggested above, there are important themes in Jewish-Christian dialogue that the *Catechism* has left unmentioned but must be brought to attention in catechesis and preaching in order to do full justice to the complex relationship between Judaism and Christianity. Limited space allows me to offer no more than hints on only the four most important of these.

First, catechesis and preaching must draw attention to the history of the Holocaust/Shoah and the deep-seated anti-Semitism in the Christian Church's theology and practice that was partially responsible for Hitler's attempted "final solution of the Jewish question."[27] Furthermore, preachers and catechists must be aware of the implications of the Shoah for the Christian discourse on God and Christ.[28]

A second explosive yet unavoidable issue in preaching and religious education is the question of the state of Israel. No doubt the foundation of the state of Israel is the single most important event in the Jewish history since the destruction of Jerusalem and the Second Temple by the Romans in 70 C.E. As Hans Küng points out, "The present-day state of Israel is a political entity, but by virtue of its whole tradition it also has a religious dimension."[29] Because of this

---

[27] The literature on the Holocaust is immense. From the Christian perspective, see David A. Rausch, *A Legacy of Hatred: Why Christians Must Not Forget the Holocaust* (Chicago: Moody, 1984). Michael McGarry has given a helpful account of the Holocaust in "The Holocaust: Tragedy of Christian History," in *Introduction to Jewish-Christian Relations*, ed. Michael Shermis and Arthur E. Zannoni, 63–86 (New York: Paulist Press, 1991). Another very helpful presentation can be found in Hans Küng, *Judaism: Between Yesterday and Tomorrow*, trans. John Bowden (New York: Crossroad, 1992), 219–81. For an evaluation of this monumental work, see Peter C. Phan's review in *Dialogue & Alliance* 6/ 4 (1992–93), 144–47.

[28] For a survey on God-talk after Auschwitz, see Küng, *Judaism*, 564–609; John T. Pawlikowski, *The Challenge of the Holocaust for Christian Theology* (New York: ADL, 1980); Elizabeth Schüssler Fiorenza and David Tracy, eds., *The Holocaust as Interruption: A Question for Christian Theology* (Edinburgh: T & T Clark, 1984); Clark M. Williamson, *A Guest in the House of Israel: Post-Holocaust Church Theology* (Louisville, Ky.: Westminster/John Knox, 1993). For post-Holocaust Christology, see Michael B. McGarry, *Christology after Auschwitz* (New York: Paulist Press, 1977); and John T. Pawlikowski, *Christ in the Light of the Christian Jewish Dialogue* (New York: Paulist Press, 1982); idem, *Jesus and the Theology of Israel* (Wilmington, Del.: Michael Glazier, 1989); idem, "Christian Theological Concerns after Auschwitz," in *Visions of the Other: Jewish and Christian Theologians Assess the Dialogue*, ed. Eugene J. Fisher, 28–51 (New York: Paulist Press, 1994).

[29] Küng, *Judaism,* 522.

religious dimension and the church's responsibility for justice and peace, catechesis and preaching cannot skirt the issue of the state of Israel and all its attendant political problems (such as the rights of the Palestinians).[30]

Third, because the foundation of the state of Israel as well as the continuing existence of Judaism as a world religion has shattered the supersessionist or displacement theology inherent in the Christian teaching of contempt against Jews and Judaism, it is necessary that catechesis and preaching approach Judaism not as the "old covenant" to which Christians claim to have succeeded as the "New Israel" or the "new people of God." Rather, if Judaism is to be understood at all, it must be studied as a living religion with which Christians have to enter into dialogue and from which they must learn in order to understand their own beliefs and practices. This task is incumbent upon catechists and preachers whether they expound scripture or worship or morality or spirituality. Areas to be covered include biblical hermeneutics and Jewish religious traditions (for example, doctrine of God, ethics, mission, prayer and liturgy, the relationship between Torah and gospel). In particular, catechetical preparation should explain how Christian sacraments, especially the Eucharist, are rooted in the Jewish tradition and how the church's liturgical cycle of feasts parallels that of the synagogue and draws its origins and continuing sustenance from it.[31]

Fourth, intimately connected with the issue of Judaism as a revealed living religion is the question of Christian mission to the Jews. Preaching and catechesis must squarely face the problem of whether Christians are called to carry out their mission to the Jews. The *Catechism* deals with mission in detail (nos. 849–56) but does not have anything specific to say about mission to the Jews. It is universally agreed today that all forms of proselytism must be rejected in the pejorative sense of the term, that is, the attempt to win converts by means of

---

[30] For a helpful discussion of this issue, see ibid., 519–83; and Robert Andrew Everett, "The Land: Israel and the Middle East in Jewish-Christian Dialogue," in Shermis and Zannoni, *An Introduction to Jewish-Christian Dialogue*, 87–117. For the theme of land in Jewish faith, see Walter Brueggemann, *The Land: Place as Gift, Promise, and Challenge in Biblical Faith* (Philadelphia: Fortress Press, 1977); W. D. Davies, *The Territorial Dimension of Judaism* (Berkeley and Los Angeles: University of California, 1982); and Anthony Kenny, *Catholics, Jews, and the State of Israel* (New York: Paulist Press, 1993).

[31] On these issues, see *Within Context*, 62–72. Works that are useful in promoting an understanding of the connections between various aspects of Judaism and Christianity include Asher Finkel and Lawrence Frizzell, eds., *Standing before God: Studies on Prayer in Scripture and Tradition* (New York: KTAV, 1981); J. Petuchowski and M. Brocke, eds., *The Lord's Prayer and Jewish Liturgy* (New York: The Seabury Press, 1978); Leon Klenicki and Gabe Huck, eds., *Spirituality and Prayer: Jewish and Christian Understandings* (New York: Paulist Press, 1983), Stuart E. Rosenberg, *Christians and Jews: The Eternal Bond* (New York: Frederick Ungar, 1985); and Gillian Feeley-Harnick, *The Lord's Table: Eucharist and Passover in Early Christianity* (Philadelphia: University of Pennsylvania Press, 1981). Very helpful works on how to present Jews and Christians in preaching are Clark M. Williamson and Allen J. Allen, *Interpreting Difficult Texts: Anti-Judaism and Christian Preaching* (Philadelphia: Trinity Press International; London: SCM Press, 1989); Clark M. Williamson, *When Jews and Christians Meet* (St. Louis: CBP Press, 1989); NCCB, *God's Mercy Endures Forever*.

cajolery, pressure or intimidation, or other improper methods. But is it not possible to acknowledge further that Jews are already in a covenantal relationship with God and therefore that Christians are not called to convert Jews to their faith?[32] Rather, the mission of both Jews and Christians is to be understood as dialogue, mutual witness, and service to the world.[33]

It remains to be seen whether the *Catechism*, like its predecessor, the *Roman Catechism*, will set the standard for future preaching and catechesis in the church. While its virtues are many, so are its inadequacies, especially in matters regarding the relationship between Judaism and Christianity. Its teachings on this theme can and must be corrected and complemented by recent developments in theology. More important, these church pronouncements and theological developments, if they are to bear fruit, must be incorporated into catechesis and worship. Otherwise, they will serve naught, or as Williamson strikingly puts it:

> Unless education, preaching, and worship in local congregations are appropriate to the good news of Gods all-inclusive love and God's command that justice be done to all those whom God loves, none of the church's fine theological pronouncements on relations between Christian and Jews will, in the end, be worth a fig.[34]

---

[32] Christians who affirm the necessity of mission to the Jews often appeal to Matthew 28:19: "Make disciples of all the nations [*ethné*]." However, biblical scholars question this interpretation and suggest that *ethné* should be read in the Jewish context as referring to the *goyim* and therefore that the missionary mandate is not to be taken as applied to the Jews (see Daniel Harrington and Douglas Hare, "Make Disciples of All the Gentiles," *Catholic Biblical Quarterly* 37 [1975], 359–69).

[33] On the church's mission to the Jews, there has been in the last decade a clear shift away from the missionary approach to the Jews and toward a dialogical relationship between the church and the Jewish people. See Allan Brockway, Paul van Buren, Rolf Rendtorff, and Simon Schoon, eds., *The Theology of the Churches and the Jewish People: Statements by the Council of Churches and Its Member Churches* (Geneva: WCC Publications, 1988), 173–76; see also Helga Croner and Leon Klenicki, eds., *Issues in the Jewish-Christian Dialogue: Jewish Perspectives on Covenant, Mission and Witness* (New York: Paulist Press, 1979); Martin Cohen and Helga Croner, eds., *Christian Mission— Jewish Mission* (New York: Paulist Press, 1982); Helga Croner, ed., *More Stepping Stones to Jewish-Christian Relations: An Unabridged Collection of Christian Documents 1975–1983* (New York: Paulist Press, 1985).

[34] Williamson, *A Guest in the House of Israel*, 47.

11

The Holocaust

REFLECTIONS FROM THE PERSPECTIVE
OF ASIAN LIBERATION THEOLOGY

The trauma caused by the systematic slaughter of six million Jews by the Nazis from 1933 to 1945 was indelibly branded on the Jewish collective psyche. During the half century that separates us from the Holocaust (Shoah or Churban), a veritable avalanche of writings by both Jewish and Christian thinkers has explored its implications for their faith and practice. As Franklin Littell has argued, the Holocaust is as much a central event in Christian history as it is in Jewish history.[1]

Within the sphere of Christian theology, liberation theology, which has by now moved beyond its original Latin American context and its Catholic home

---

[1] See Franklin Littell, "Christendom, Holocaust and Israel," *Journal of Ecumenical Studies* 10 (Summer 1973), 483–97; and idem, *The Crucifixion of the Jews* (New York: Harper & Row, 1975). For helpful bibliographies on the Holocaust, see the massive work of Steven T. Katz, *The Holocaust in Historical Context,* vol. 1, *The Holocaust and Mass Death before the Modern Age* (New York: Oxford University Press, 1994), 583–677; vol. 2, *The Holocaust and Mass Death in the Modern Age,* and vol. 3, *The Uniqueness of the Holocaust,* have been announced but have not yet appeared. Bibliography on the Jewish-Christian dialogue can be found in the following works: A. Roy Eckardt, "Recent Literature on Christian-Jewish Relations," *The Journal of the Academy of Religion* 49/1 (1981), 99–111; Eugene J. Fisher, *Faith without Prejudice: Rebuilding Christian Attitudes Toward Judaism,* rev. and exp. ed. (New York: Crossroad, 1993), 195–205; Eugene Fisher, ed., *Visions of the Other: Jewish and Christian Theologians Assess the Dialogue* (New York: Paulist Press, 1994), 90–98; Eugene J. Fisher and Leon Klenicki, eds., *In Our Time: The Flowering of Jewish-Catholic Dialogue* (New York: Paulist Press, 1990), 107–61; James H. Charlesworth, ed., *Jews and Christians: Exploring the Past, Present, and Future* (New York: Crossroad, 1990), 242–48; Norman A. Beck, *Mature Christianity in the Twenty-first Century: The Recognition and Repudiation of the Anti-Jewish Polemic in the New Testament,* rev. and exp. ed. (New York: Crossroad, 1994), 346–52; James F. Moore, *Christian Theology after the Shoah* (Lanham, Md.: University Press of America, 1993), 177–82; Peter van der Osten-Sacken, *Christian-Jewish Dialogue: Theological Foundations,* trans. Margaret Kohl (Philadelphia: Fortress Press, 1986), 203–7; Michael E. Lodahl, *Shekhina/Spirit: Divine Presence in Jewish and Christian Religion* (New York: Paulist Press, 1992), 223–31; Clark M. Williamson, *A Guest in the House of Israel: Post-Holocaust Church Theology* (Louisville, Ky.: Westminster/John Knox Press, 1993), 317–35.

to grow deep roots in other continents and in different ecclesial soils, can no doubt be regarded as the most influential and challenging development in modern theology.[2] Yet, curiously enough, Johann Baptist Metz's dictum that no future theological construction be unaffected by Auschwitz,[3] seems to have had no effect on liberation theology, although Metz's anti-bourgeois political theology has otherwise exerted a significant influence on liberation theology. No Latin American Christian liberation theologian has so far dealt extensively with the Holocaust as a theological theme, much less consciously shaped his or her theology in the light of the Holocaust itself.[4] This observation is no less true of Asian liberation theologians. By contrast, some Jewish theologians such as Dan

---

[2] The writings of Latin American liberation theologians are already well known and need not be cited here. It is sufficient to mention the names of Gustavo Gutiérrez, Juan Luis Segundo, Leonardo Boff, Clodovis Boff, and Jon Sobrino. Works that present liberation theology from the global perspective include Curt Cadorette et al., eds., *Liberation Theology* (Maryknoll, N.Y.: Orbis Books, 1992); Alfred T. Hennelly, *Liberation Theologies: The Global Pursuit of Justice* (Mystic, Conn.:Twenty-Third Publications, 1995); and Priscilla Pope-Levison and John R. Levison, *Jesus in Global Contexts* (Louisville, Ky.: Westminster/John Knox, 1992).

[3] Metz's full statement reads as follows: "What Christian theologians can *do* for the murdered of Auschwitz and thereby for a true Christian-Jewish ecumenism is, in every case, this: Never again to do theology in such a way that its construction remains unaffected, or could remain unaffected, by Auschwitz. In this sense, I make available to my students an apparently very simple but, in fact, extremely demanding criterion for evaluating the theological scene: Ask yourselves if the theology you are learning is such that it could remain unchanged before and after Auschwitz. If this is the case, be on your guard!" See *The Emergent Church*, trans. Peter Mann (New York: Crossroad, 1981), 28.

[4] It is significant that even in a book such as *On Job: God-Talk and the Suffering of the Innocent* (Maryknoll, N.Y.: Orbis Books, 1987), which deals with the possibility of believing in and speaking about God in the face of massive innocent suffering, Gustavo Gutiérrez does not discuss the Holocaust at all. Perhaps Gutiérrez may be excused by his intention to focus on "what it means to talk of God in the context of Latin America, and more concretely in the context of the suffering of the poor—which is to say, the vast majority of the population" (xviii). In the conclusion of his book Gutiérrez maintains that in Latin America the question is not precisely "How are we to do theology after Auschwitz?" but rather "How are we doing theology *while Ayacucho lasts?*" since cruel murder on a massive scale is *still* going on (102). A book edited by Otto Maduro, *Judaism, Christianity and Liberation: An Agenda for Dialogue* (Maryknoll, N.Y.: Orbis Books, 1991) contains two essays by two Christian Latin American theologians, one by Pablo Richard entitled "Jewish and Christian Liberation Theology" (33–39), the other by Julio de Santa Ana entitled "The Holocaust and Liberation" (40–52). This volume deals with various aspects of the Jewish-Christian dialogue from the perspective of liberation theology. Even though Latin American liberation theologians have not written extensively on Judaism, their writings, especially their understandings of Jesus and his Jewish context, have been subjected to a stringent critique from the vantage point of contemporary Jewish-Christian dialogue. See Leon Klenicki, "The Theology of Liberation: A Latin American Jewish Exploration," *American Jewish Archives* 35 (April 1983), 27–39; and John T. Pawlikowski, *Christ in the Light of the Christian-Jewish Dialogue* (New York: Paulist Press, 1982), 59–73. Pawlikowski examines Gustavo Gutiérrez, José Miguez Bonino, Jon Sobrino, and Leonardo Boff. Outstanding among feminist Christian theologians who have written extensively on liberation theology and Judaism is Rosemary Radford Ruether. See her book, written together with her husband, Herman J. Ruether, *The Wrath of Jonah: Religion and Nationalism in the Israel-Palestinian Conflict* (San Francisco: Harper & Row, 1989).

Cohn-Sherbok and Marc Ellis have attempted to bring insights of liberation theology to bear on their understanding of Judaism and the state of Israel.[5]

In this chapter an attempt will be made first to unmask vestiges of anti-Judaism in some representative writings by Asian theologians; their anti-Judaism is all the more pernicious as it is mostly unconscious.[6] Second, resources of Asian liberation theology are harnessed to address some of the issues raised by the Holocaust and Holocaust theology.[7] Finally, some suggestions are made for furthering the conversation between Asian liberation theology and contemporary Christian theology of Judaism.

JEWS AND JUDAISM
IN ASIAN THEOLOGY

Historical records show that Jews were present in East Asia when Christians moved out of the borders of the Roman empire, from West Asia into East Asia.[8] If the *Acts of Thomas* can be trusted, the first convert of Saint Thomas, the Apostle to India, was a little Jewish flute girl at the court of the Indian king Gundaphar.[9] In Asia, as elsewhere, the Jewish communities of the Second Diaspora were often the first focus of Christian evangelization. According to *The Doctrine of Addai*, written between 390 and 430, the missionary Addai, reputedly Saint Thomas's disciple, when he first came to Edessa, the capital of the tiny kingdom of Oshroene, sought out the Jewish community, lodging with "Tobias, the son of Tobias." According to the same document, one of the four

---

[5] See Dan Cohn-Sherbok, *On Earth as It Is in Heaven: Jews, Christians, and Liberation Theology* (Maryknoll, N.Y.: Orbis Books, 1987); Marc Ellis, *Toward a Jewish Theology of Liberation* (Maryknoll, N.Y.: Orbis Books, 1987); idem, *Beyond Innocence and Redemption: Confronting the Holocaust and Israeli Power* (San Francisco: Harper & Row, 1990). For evaluations of Jewish liberation theology, see the following essays in Maduro, *Judaism, Christianity and Liberation:* Judd Kruger Levingston, "Liberation Theology and Judaism" (1–19); Michael Lerner "Breaking the Chains of Necessity: An Approach to Jewish Liberation Theology" (55–64); Rosemary Radford Ruether, "False Messianism and Prophetic Consciousness: Toward a Liberation Theology of Jewish-Christian Solidarity" (83–95); Richard L. Rubenstein, "Jews, Israel, and Liberation" (96–109); and Norman Solomon, "Economics and Liberation: Can the Theology of Liberation Decide Economic Questions?" (122–39).

[6] I use *anti-Judaism* rather than *anti-Semitism* because this hostility against Jews and Judaism was based primarily on theological motives rather than on racial ideologies and/or economic stereotyping.

[7] By "Asian theology" I refer to the theology done by Indian, Japanese, Korean, Sri Lankan, and Taiwanese theologians with whose writings I am familiar.

[8] For a history of Asian Christianity from the beginnings to 1500, see the monumental work of Samuel Hugh Moffett, *A History of Christianity in Asia*, vol. 1 (Maryknoll, N.Y.: Orbis Books, 1998). I am indebted to Moffett for information on the early history of Christianity in Asia and bibliographies related to it.

[9] The two modern translations of the *Acts of Thomas* are, from the surviving Syriac text, A. F. J. Klijn, *The Acts of Thomas: Introduction, Text and Commentary* (Leiden: Brill, 1962); and from a Greek text, G. Bornkamm, "The Acts of Thomas," in E. Hennecke, *New Testament Apocrypha*, vol. 2, ed. W. Schneemelcher, English edition by R. M. Wilson (London: Lutterworth, 1965).

groups of people who accepted Addai's teaching—the others being the nobility and members of the royal family of Oshroene, pagan religious leaders, and the common people—were Jews "skilled in the law and prophets, who traded in silk."[10]

When Matteo Ricci arrived in China, he found a colony of Jews in Kaifeng but no Christians.[11] In 1595 he found pockets of Christians ("five or six families") in Nanjing and elsewhere in central China who seemed to have lost all their earlier beliefs, making their churches into temples and in many cases even converting to Islam. The only traces of the Christian faith among them were their rudimentary knowledge of the psalter and the sign of the cross that they made over their foods.[12] In 1602 Ricci was informed that in the northwestern regions of China, in the old kingdom of Xixia, there were "certain white men with flowing beards who had churches with bell towers, ate pork, worshiped Mary and Isa (as they called Christ our Lord) and adored the Cross."[13]

In Beijing, in the summer of 1608, Ricci received a visit from a Chinese Jew by the name of Ai Tian, who had come to the capital to take the examinations for the doctoral degree. Assuming that Ricci was a Jew, Ai Tian told him that there were in his hometown ten or twelve families of Jews and a magnificent synagogue, which they had only recently renovated at the cost of ten thousand gold pieces, and that there was an even larger Jewish community in Hangzhou. Ricci was also told that in Kaifeng there were certain strangers whose ancestors came from abroad and who observed the religious custom of venerating a cross. About three years later Ricci despatched a Jesuit Chinese lay brother to Kaifeng to verify his visitor's report about the presumed Christians. The brother confirmed the accuracy of the Jewish informant but said that these Christians, perhaps for fear of persecution, were reluctant to admit to being Christian.[14]

From his conversations with Chinese scholars, Ricci discovered that the Chinese word *huihui* referred not only to Muslims but also to scattered communities of Jews ("the *huihui* who reject the sinews"—a reference to Jacob's wrestling with the angel) as well as to the descendants of the Nestorian Christians ("the *huihui* of the cross").[15] A great stone discovered in 1623 at Xian, the ancient T'ang dynasty's capital Chang'an, inscribed "A Monument Commemorating the

---

[10] *The Doctrine of Addai* exists in two manuscripts, an early fifth-century one, discovered by Cureton in 1848 and published in 1864, and the other, more complete, dated to the sixth century, from the Imperial Public Library of St. Petersburg, translated and edited by George Phillips as *The Doctrine of Addai the Apostle* (1876). See W. Cureton, *Ancient Syriac Documents Relative to the Earliest Establishment of Christianity in Edessa and the Neighboring Countries . . .* (London, 1864; reprint Amsterdam: Oriental Press, 1967).

[11] See *Opere storiche del P. Matteo Ricci*, vol. 2, ed. Pietro Tacchi Venturi (Macerata, 1913), 289–93.

[12] See *Fonti Ricciane*, ed. Pasquale M. D'Elia, vol. 2 (Rome, 1942–49), 320.

[13] See ibid., 141 n. 4.

[14] See ibid., 323.

[15] See Jonathan Spencer, *The Memory Palace of Matteo Ricci* (New York: Viking Penguin, 1984), 95.

Propagation of the Ta-ch'in [Syrian] Luminous Religion in China," speaks of the arrival of a Nestorian missionary in the Chinese capital in 635. The missionary's name was Alopen; he came carrying "the true Sutras" with him and was requested by King T'ai-tsung to translate the scripture into Chinese. With funds from the king's own treasury the first Christian church was built in China in 638.[16]

That the word *huihui* was used during the Ming dynasty to refer to Jews, Christians, and Muslims alike implies that in Chinese eyes these three Western religions with their belief in the one God were basically the same. It may also indicate that the relationships among the followers of these three related religions in China, in contrast to the long history of mutual hatred in Europe, had been amicable, so that the Chinese did not have any reason to regard them as possessing separate or rival identities. Indeed, when Emperor Wanli saw the full-length portraits of the Jesuits in Beijing, he looked at them for a moment and pronounced, "They are *huihui*."[17]

That relationships between Jews and Christians in China during Ricci's time were friendly is testified by the fact that when the lay brother was sent a second time to Kaifeng, this time to visit the head of the synagogue, with a letter from Ricci stating that he had at his house in Beijing all the books of the Old Testament as well as those of the New Testament, the rabbi gave the brother a very warm welcome. But he took exception to Ricci's affirmation that the Messiah had already come, saying that the Messiah would not come for another ten thousand years. Despite this difference of opinion, however, the head of the synagogue added that, given Ricci's reputation and learning, he would confer upon Ricci the dignity of high priest of the synagogue, if he would join the Jewish faith and abstain from eating pork.[18] Later, three other Jews, one of whom was the nephew of the first visitor, came from the same city to Beijing and were warmly received by the Jesuits. All three eventually decided to receive baptism after being convinced that the Messiah had come in Jesus.

It is significant that Ricci, despite the fact that he had had firsthand experiences of Christians' hostility toward Jews, first in his hometown Macerata, then in Rome and in Goa, refrained from polemic with the Jews.[19] In his famous "catechism," *The True Meaning of the Lord of Heaven*, Ricci does not make any disparaging remark about the Jews.[20]

---

[16] On the first Christian mission to China, see Moffett, *A History of Christianity in Asia*, 1:288–323.

[17] D'Elia, *Fonti Ricciane*, 2:130.

[18] See ibid., 324–25.

[19] For an account of Ricci's experiences of anti-Judaism, see Spencer, *The Memory Palace of Matteo Ricci*, 108–11.

[20] See Matteo Ricci, *The True Meaning of the Lord of Heaven*, trans. Douglas Lancashire and Peter Hu Kuo-chen (St. Louis: The Institute of Jesuit Sources, 1985). Indeed, in this work, Ricci does not mention the Jews at all, though he could have done so in the last chapter of his book, where he gives a brief account of God's plan of salvation, in particular of Mary and Jesus.

By contrast, anti-Judaism is pronounced in a later influential catechism. When Alexandre de Rhodes, the Jesuit missionary to Vietnam,[21] wrote his *Cathechismus pro iis, qui volunt suscipere Baptismum, in octo dies divisus*,[22] he transmitted to the East much of the centuries-long anti-Judaic heritage of Christian theology. Speaking of Jesus' performing of miracles, de Rhodes paints a very dark portrait of the scribes and Pharisees, highlighting their jealousy and hatred of Jesus:

> Among the Jews the Lord had many and very skillful enemies, because their works were evil. These were called *Scribae* and *Pharisaei*. . . . Many powerful people hated the light the Lord projected in the holiness of his life as well as in his admirable doctrine because they were charged with various sins. As a result, people venerated him and abandoned the *Pharisaei* to follow him. This increased the jealousy of the *Scribae* and *Pharisaei* who sought to destroy the Lord's reputation in front of people by means of calumnies under the guise of piety and religion.[23]

After relating Jesus' healing of the man born blind, de Rhodes comments on the pride and spiritual blindness of the Pharisees: "Those who in their pride rely on their own wisdom and refuse to accept the Word of God, will fall into many sins; they become blind and finally fall into the precipice of eternal death. Thus, the *Pharisaei*, impious and proud they were, refusing to accept the light of the Lord Jesus manifested by so many miracles, became blind and finally fell into the ruin of eternal damnation."[24] At the end of the sixth catechetical day, de Rhodes urges his catechumens to embrace the Christian faith by rejecting the "hard-heartedness of the Jews": "Let us detest the hard-heartedness of the Jews, let us adore the Lord, and let us embrace ardently in

---

[21] Alexandre de Rhodes (1593–1660) came to Cochinchina (Central Vietnam) in 1624, started his mission in Tonkin (North Vietnam) in 1627, and was expelled from there in 1630. He came back to Cochinchina in 1640 and worked there off and on until 1645. Again expelled from Cochinchina, he was sent to Rome to lobby for the establishment of a hierarchy in Vietnam. In 1654 he left for the mission in Persia and died there in 1660. Besides producing many important historical works on the beginnings of Christianity in Vietnam and a Vietnamese-Portuguese-Latin dictionary, de Rhodes wrote a catechism, the first book written in the Romanized script. For the life and work of Alexandre de Rhodes, see Peter C. Phan, *Mission and Catechesis: Alexandre de Rhodes and Inculturation in Seventeenth-Century Vietnam* (Maryknoll, N.Y.: Orbis Books, 1998).

[22] The catechism was published in Rome in 1651 under the auspices of the Congregation of the Propaganda Fide. For an extensive discussion of this catechism, see Phan, *Mission and Catechesis;* for an English translation of this work, see ibid., 211–315. The catechism has also been translated into Thai.

[23] Ibid., 278. De Rhodes's views of the Jews and the Pharisees are derived exclusively from the Gospel of John, upon which later Christian anti-Judaism depends heavily. For an excellent study of anti-Judaism in the Gospel of John, see R. Alan Culpepper, "The Gospel of John as a Threat to Jewish-Christian Relations," in *Overcoming Fear between Jews and Christians*, ed. James M. Charlesworth, 21–43 (New York: Crossroad, 1992).

[24] Phan, *Mission and Catechesis,* 280.

our minds his divine teaching in order to be enlightened now, and to obtain eternal life later."[25]

In his narrative of Jesus' passion, de Rhodes repeatedly refers to "the Jews" as accomplices in the killing of Jesus and affirms that the destruction of Jerusalem by the Romans was God's punishment for this crime: "Because this crime of the Jews was the most atrocious since the creation of the world, it should not pass without receiving even in this life its punishment."[26] As evidence of the severity of divine punishment, he cites Flavius Josephus's "incredible and horrible story of a [Jewish] hungry mother who was suckling her child; she killed it with her own hands, cooked it, and ate it."[27] De Rhodes repeats the common view among Christians that all the calamities that happened to the Jews during the siege and destruction of Jerusalem were "divine vengeance against the evil Jews," whereas those who had accepted the Christian faith could escape them.[28]

It goes without saying that de Rhodes's remarks about the Jews and the Pharisees, blameworthy as they are, do not necessarily reflect a conscious anti-Judaism on his part. Rather, they are inherent in Christianity's "teaching of contempt" against Jews, which he inherited in his theological studies in Rome. Nevertheless, they are no less lethal; they have seeped into not only catechesis in Asia but also into widespread popular devotions such as the Way of the Cross[29] and passion plays.[30]

---

[25] Ibid., 282.

[26] Ibid., 297.

[27] Ibid., 297.

[28] Ibid., 297–98. De Rhodes's implicit anti-Judaism is all the more poignant as he was a descendant of Jews. The de Rhodes family was from Catalayud, Spain. Probably the family left for Avignon toward the end of the fifteenth century, when the Spanish Inquisition was becoming very harsh against "converted" Jews. The family's original name was *Rueda*, written as *Rode* in Provençal. *Rode* or *rouelle* means "a small wheel," which Jews were required to wear on their clothes during the Middle Ages. The *de* was added to the name as an elegant way to hide the true ethnic origin of the family.

[29] De Rhodes introduced a paraliturgical devotion called *ngam dung* (standing meditation). To enable Christians to participate in the liturgy of the Holy Week, in particular the Tenebrae, and to obviate their ignorance of Latin, de Rhodes composed in Vietnamese the mysteries of the passion in fifteen *ngam* (meditations). Each of the meditations is declaimed, with the accompaniment of drum and gong, by one of the faithful, most often a man, who stands *(dung)* on a platform in the middle of the church. Behind the platform there is a crucifix and a fifteen-branch candelabrum. At the end of each meditation, a candle is extinguished, followed by the common recital of one Our Father, seven Hail Marys, and one Glory Be. This well-attended devotion, which resembles the classical theater *(cheo, tuong)*, with its dialogues between the assembly and the declaimer, and the use of drum and gong, is still celebrated in many parts of Vietnam on every Friday of Lent and each evening of the Holy Week. Unfortunately, in these meditations there is no lack of disparaging statements against Jews and Judaism.

[30] Passion plays are very popular in the Philippines and are also widespread in Vietnam. They were probably introduced to Vietnam by Portuguese and Spanish missionaries in the seventeenth century. In these dramatizations of the passion a lot of negative stock ideas about Jews and Judaism are given a vivid form. On the dangers of dramatizations of the passion, see the excellent document issued by the Bishops' Committee for Ecumenical and Interreligious Affairs, *Criteria for the Evaluation of Dramatization of the Passion* (Washington, D.C.: NCCB, 1988).

While such a negative view of Jews and Judaism, deplorable as it is, may be excusable in the seventeenth century due to the lack of historical knowledge of the Judaism of Jesus' times, one is surprised to see the persistence of such a view in some contemporary Asian theologians. Like their Latin American counterparts, some Asian theologians tend to set in sharp contrast the difference between Jesus and his message about the kingdom of God, on the one hand, and various groups of Jews on the other. For example, Aloysius Pieris, an influential Sri Lankan Jesuit theologian, explains Jesus' baptism in the Jordan at the hand of John the Baptizer as a "prophetic gesture" and contrasts it starkly with other spiritualities of his time:

> I observe that Jesus was faced with several streams of traditional religiousness when he answered this prophetic call. Not every kind of religion appealed to him. From his later reactions we gather that the narrow ideology of the Zealot movement did not attract him. Nor did the sectarian puritanism of the Essenes have any impact on him. As for the Pharisaic spirituality of self-righteousness, Jesus openly ridiculed it. His confrontations with the Sadducees—the chief priests and elders—indicate that he hardly approve their aristocratic "leisure class" spirituality. Rather, it was in the ancient (Deuteronomic) tradition of prophetic asceticism represented by the Baptizer that Jesus discovered an authentic spirituality and an appropriate point of departure for his own prophetic mission. In opting for this form of *liberative* religiousness to the exclusion of others, which appeared enslaving, he indulged in a species of "discernment," which we Christians in Asia, confronted with a variety of ideological and religious trends, are continually invited to make.[31]

While one may agree with Pieris's characterization of Jesus' spirituality as prophetic and liberative, one must object to his labeling the spirituality of the Zealots as "narrow ideology," that of the Essenes as "sectarian puritanism," that of the Pharisees as "self-righteousness," and that of the Sadducees as "aristocratic, 'leisure class' spirituality." Pieris is, of course, within his rights to contrast Jesus' spirituality with other ideal *types* of spirituality, but to attribute "narrow ideology," "sectarian puritanism," "self-righteousness," and "'leisure class'

---

[31] Aloysius Pieris, *An Asian Theology of Liberation* (Maryknoll, N.Y.: Orbis Books, 1988), 46. One of Pieris's theological leitmotifs is that Jesus underwent a double baptism: at the River Jordan (prophetic religiousness) and on the cross (material poverty). He argues that Asian churches, if they are to become churches *of* Asia and not only *in* Asia, must immerse themselves in this double baptism, living the religiousness of Asian religions and struggling for the liberation of the poor. For an interpretation of Pieris's Christology, see Peter C. Phan, "Jesus the Christ with an Asian Face," *Theological Studies* 57 (1996), 406–10. Other works by Pieris include *Love Meets Wisdom: A Christian Experience of Buddhism* (Maryknoll, N.Y.: Orbis Books, 1988) and *Fire and Water: Basic Issues in Asian Buddhism and Christianity* (Maryknoll, N.Y.: Orbis Books, 1996).

spirituality" to specific historical groups and to stigmatize these spiritualities as "enslaving," especially when these groups have been maligned throughout Christian history, is, besides being historically inaccurate, to perpetuate the worst caricatures of them.

Similarly, Choan-Seng Song, a prolific Presbyterian Taiwanese theologian, has repeatedly contrasted Jesus' behavior and attitude with those of "Jewish authorities."[32] Commenting on Job's theological struggle, Song argues that "it is a struggle to be liberated from the God of the traditional religion and become free for God in God's own self."[33] Again says Song: "Job's dialogue with his friends turns out to be not a dialogue at all. It becomes Job's struggle against the false God of religious traditions and theological orthodoxy. His real adversary is not his friends, but the false God they defend. To debunk that false God becomes his preoccupation. 'I am ready to argue with God,' says Job with determination—the God of my friends, the God of my religion, the God of my ancestors."[34] The God of traditional religions is, according to Song, "the God of retribution." It is true that Song's rejection of the God of retribution forms part of his critique of religion and religious traditions in general; still, in this context it is the Jewish religion that is directly targeted ("the God of my friends, the God of my religion, the God of my ancestors").[35]

---

[32] Choan-Seng Song (b. 1929) is currently president of the World Alliance of Reformed Churches and professor of theology and Asian cultures at the Pacific School of Religion, Berkeley, California, and regional professor of theology at the South East Asia Graduate School of Theology in Singapore and Hong Kong. His publications include *Third-Eye Theology: Theology in Formation in Asian Settings* (Maryknoll, N.Y.: Orbis Books, 1979; rev. ed. 1990); *The Compassionate God* (Maryknoll, N.Y.: Orbis Books, 1982); *Tell Us Our Names: Story Theology from an Asian Perspective* (Maryknoll, N.Y.: Orbis Books, 1984); *Theology from the Womb of Asia* (Maryknoll, N.Y.: Orbis Books, 1986); *Jesus, the Crucified People* (New York: Crossroad, 1990); *Jesus and the Reign of God* (Minneapolis: Fortress Press, 1993); and *Jesus in the Power of the Spirit* (Minneapolis: Fortress Press, 1994); *The Believing Heart: An Invitation to Story Theology* (Minneapolis: Fortress Press, 1999). On Song's theology, see Peter C. Phan, "Experience and Theology: An Asian Liberation Perspective," *Zeitschrift für Missionswissenschaft und Religionswissenschaft* 77 (1993), 114–18; on his Christology, see Phan, "Jesus the Christ with an Asian Face," 417–21.

[33] Song, *Jesus, the Crucified People*, 44.

[34] Ibid., 54.

[35] Elsewhere Song explicitly criticizes Judaism's notion of God as a "high-voltage God," that is, as a being remote from and dangerous to the common people, in contrast to the God of Jesus who is near and available to all, none excluded: "As the heir to the religion of the Old Testament, Judaism is a very high-voltage religion. The God of Judaism is carefully protected from unworthy men and women polluted with cares of this world. Persons in the street are unclean because the niceties of religious laws and rituals are just too remote from their daily lives. This God is even more remote from the pagans who have no pious blood, not even a drop of it, in their veins. They are thoroughly contaminated by sins and impiety. To all these persons the God of Judaism is a very dangerous God. They can only try to imagine what that God looks like from the outer court of the Temple. It is this high-voltage religion that Jesus dared to challenge. In the end Jesus was 'electrocuted' by that high-voltage religion" (Song, *The Compassionate God*, 110). It must be pointed out that Song applies the same critique to Christianity.

Furthermore, contrasting "the God of retribution" of Judaism and of religion in general with the "Abba" of Jesus, Song highlights the distance between them, especially on the cross. Commenting on Jesus' cry—"My God, my God, why have you abandoned me?"—Song argues against Jürgen Moltmann that Jesus' words do not refer to the separation between God the Father and God the Son in an alleged intra-trinitarian conflict.[36] Rather, in Song's understanding, they express the radical opposition between "the God of retribution," "the God portrayed in the story of the flood in the Hebrew Scriptures,"[37] "the God of legalism, the God of religious absolutism, the God of theological dogmatism,"[38] on the one hand, and Jesus' Abba, the God of "*karuna*" (compassion), on the other, the God to whom the cross of Jesus is itself "an act of shame, disgrace, and outrage committed by human beings, an act that offends and shocks the moral feelings of the human community and the heart of God, who loves Jesus and other human beings as Abba, as Parent."[39]

This same radical opposition between Jewish religious authorities and Jesus is carried by Song into his interpretation of Jesus' trial before the Sanhedrin. Using the categories of "official" and "popular" histories, the former being "stories told by the king, the ruler, the rich and the powerful . . . history taught in school, recited on official occasions, and preserved in the national archives and annals,"[40] and the latter being "stories remembered and circulated by the ruled, the powerless, and the poor . . . by word of mouth, passed on in handwritten copies, and preserved not in national archives and records, but in the memories of people,"[41] Song suggests that what was on trial at the Sanhedrin was "popular history," that is, the history of Jesus and his friends: "Tried with him is a host of the women and men with whom Jesus has been associated—prostitutes, tax-collectors, sinners, people who are poor, men, women, and children who are socially and religiously discriminated against."[42]

Over against this popular history stands the "official history" represented by the Sanhedrin and the Pharisee in Jesus' parable about the two men who went to the Temple to pray (Lk 18:10–14). The prayer of the Pharisee "does not radiate his own self-confidence only, however. It radiates the self-confidence of his proud

---

[36] See Song, *Jesus, the Crucified People*, 98: "The cross is *not*, as some theologians would have us think, Jesus-God tearing away from God, the Son-God going through the pain of separation from the Father-God. The cross is not such a 'theo'-logical thing. It is not 'the Second Person' of the Trinity forsaken by 'the First Person' of the Trinity. Nor is it 'the Second Person' of the Trinity left in the lurch by 'the Third Person' of the Trinity. Such 'trinitarian' language makes little sense of the cross on which Jesus died. Highly abstract theological such as this almost suggests a mutiny within God."

[37] Ibid., 75.

[38] Ibid., 122.

[39] Ibid., 82. It is clear that Song does not limit the concept of the God of retribution to Judaism alone but thinks that it is also endemic to Christian theological tradition, indeed to any organized religion. The God of retribution is "the God of an organized religion and a religious hierarchy" (98).

[40] Song, *Jesus and the Reign of God*, 190.

[41] Ibid., 190.

[42] Ibid., 197.

tradition, the religious hierarchy, and the whole complexity of rituals and teachings. In other words, the prayer is the epitome of the entire official history."[43]

Song concludes:

> What we see at the supreme council of priests and teachers is the confrontation of the popular history of Jesus and the official history of the religious authorities. Much was at stake, especially on the part of the official history. It had to maintain its officiality. It had to defend its legitimacy. It had to assert its power and authority. In contrast the popular history that Jesus carried with him to the trial had no officiality to maintain; its "popularity," its being of people, in itself made it more "official" than any other claim to officiality.[44]

In reading Song's interpretation of Jesus' trial and death one cannot help but be powerfully moved by his passion for justice and his solidarity with the poor and the oppressed. On the other hand, with the hindsight of the Holocaust, one cannot but reject the facile way in which Song associates "the God of retribution" with the religion of Job's ancestors in contrast to the Abba of compassion of Jesus, and the way in which he associates the oppressive "official history" with the Sanhedrin and Jewish religious authorities in contrast to the liberating "popular history" of Jesus and his marginalized people.

As with Pieris, Song is within his rights to contrast Jesus' understanding of God and behavior with other ideal *types* of understanding of God and behavior. But he runs the terrible risk of perpetuating the injustice, perpetrated throughout the history of Christianity, of stereotyping Judaism and different groups of Jews when he ascribes a legalistic concept of God to Judaism and an oppressive and hypocritical behavior to specific groups of Jews such as the Pharisees and the members of the Sanhedrin.[45]

ASIAN LIBERATION THEOLOGY AND HOLOCAUST THEOLOGY

Despite these vestiges of mostly unintentional anti-Judaism, Asian liberation theology offers rich resources to address some of the issues confronting Holocaust theology.[46] Stephen R. Haynes has provided a useful definition of

---

[43] Ibid.

[44] Ibid., 205.

[45] In general, Asian liberation theologians are not well acquainted with recent studies on the historical Jesus and on the Second Temple period in Judaism, in particular the Pharisees. This lack of proper knowledge is also present in many Latin American liberation theologians, as John Pawlikowski has correctly pointed out. Had they possessed this knowledge, liberation theologians would have avoided the approach of articulating the meaning of the Christ-experience in terms of Jewish rejection and would have constructed a Christology by incorporating Jewish cultural and religious values.

[46] As was mentioned above, the Holocaust has radically challenged both Jewish and Christian theologies. Holocaust theologians claim that the Holocaust represents the "end point," "interruption," "crisis," "break," "rupture," and "paradigm shift" in both theologies.

Holocaust theology as "any sustained theological reflection for which the slaughter of six million Jews functions as a criterion, whether the *Shoah* displaces or merely qualifies traditional theological criteria and norms such as Scripture, tradition, reason, and religious experience."[47] As mentioned above, to date no Asian liberation theologian has set out to develop his or her theology using the Shoah as its overarching criterion and norm. Nevertheless, a meaningful dialogue between Holocaust theology and Asian liberation theology is possible on the basis of what the latter has said about some of the issues that Holocaust theology considers pivotal. Among the many themes of Christian Holocaust theology, I concentrate here on four: the concept of God, covenant, Christology, and the ethics of power.[48]

The God of *Karuna*: The "Mute God"

While Orthodox Jewish theologians have generally tended to minimize the negative impact of the Holocaust on the Jewish belief in God,[49] most Jewish and

---

[47] Stephen R. Haynes, "Christian Holocaust Theology: A Critical Assessment," *Journal of the American Academy of Religion* 62/2 (1994), 554. In this essay Haynes offers an informed and balanced critique of Christian Holocaust theologians (e.g., A. Roy Eckardt, Alice L. Eckardt, Franklin Littell, Harry James Cargas, Paul Van Buren, and Robert Willis), especially their unconditional support for the state of Israel, to which they assign a profound theological significance, raising it to the status of a "theological datum." For Haynes's evaluation of Karl Barth, Jürgen Moltmann, and Paul Van Buren, see *Prospects for Post-Holocaust Theology* (Atlanta: Scholars Press, 1991).

[48] Stephen R. Haynes lists eleven topics for post-Holocaust theology in the 1990s: covenant, Jewish monotheism *vs.* Christian trinitarianism, messianism, the church-Israel relationship, the theological significance of the Holocaust, the status of Christian anti-Judaism, the place of scriptural and theological traditions in the church's revision of its understanding of Israel, the Jewish desire to be left alone, Christian Zionism, the identity of a Jew, and secular *vs.* theological conceptions of Israel (see *Prospects for Post-Holocaust Theology,* 277–84). On the other hand, John T. Pawlikowski sees the challenges of the Holocaust for Christian theology in three areas: the concept of God, Christology, and ethics (in particular the ethics of using power). See his "The Shoah: Continuing Theological Challenge for Christianity," in *Contemporary Christian Religious Responses to the Shoah,* ed. Steven L. Jacobs, 140–65 (Lanham, Md.: University Press of America, 1993); and "Christian Theological Concerns after the Holocaust," in *Visions of the Other: Jewish and Christian Theologians Assess the Dialogue,* ed. Eugene J. Fisher, 28–51 (New York: Paulist Press, 1994). For a very helpful work on how to rethink Christian faith in the light of Judaism, see Mary C. Boys, *Has God Only One Blessing? Judaism as a Source of Christian Self-Understanding* (New York: Paulist Press, 2000).

[49] David Hartman and especially Michael Goldberg refuse to take the Holocaust as the "master story" on which to interpret the history of Israel. Both regard the story of the Exodus and God's covenant with Israel at Sinai as the fundamental stories in which the meaning of Israel's survival is to be found and call for a renewed faithfulness to the covenant as a way to guarantee Jewish survival. See David Hartman, *A Living Covenant: The Innovative Spirit in Traditional Judaism* (New York: Macmillan, 1985); and Michael Goldberg, *Why Should Jews Survive? Looking Past the Holocaust toward a Future* (New York: Oxford University Press, 1995).

Christian Holocaust theologians maintain that the Holocaust has shattered the traditional belief in God, that is, a God who is both infinitely good and omnipotent. Richard Rubenstein claims that the Shoah destroyed any possibility of believing in a covenantal God of history and calls for a "paganism" in which human existence is lived within the confines of the material world, without any transcendence.[50] Emil Fackenheim is convinced that the image of God was destroyed during the Holocaust and urges a restoration of the divine image in which God's power is curtailed.[51] For Arthur Cohen the Holocaust as the *tremendum* erased the conventional image of God as an interventionist in human history; he attempts to fashion a new image of God in which human freedom and rationality are recognized.[52] Irving Greenberg believes the Shoah removes the image of God as a "commanding" being in a covenantal relationship; rather, the covenant is now to be understood as a purely voluntary act that highlights human responsibility.[53]

Catholic theologian John Pawlikowski applauded these thinkers' attempts at reconceiving the divine-human relationship after the Holocaust, especially their rejection of any simplistic belief in an interventionist God in history. But he finds them ultimately unsatisfactory because "they would appear to have left humanity too much to its own whims after the *Shoah*. They have not adequately explored whether God continues to play a significant role after the *Shoah* in the development of a moral ethos within humanity that can restrain radical evil. The role they have in fact assigned to God is not potent enough."[54]

With their reflections on the human-divine relationship, Asian liberation theologians can offer a significant contribution to the project of reconceptualizing God in a manner appropriate to our post-Holocaust time. As we have seen above, Choan-Seng Song rejects the "God of retribution" and argues for the "God of compassion." Describing the compassionate God as "the speaking God" (sometimes in anger), "the listening God," and "the remembering God," Song goes on to speak of God as "the mute God." Jesus' Abba-God, who spoke, listened, and

---

[50] See Richard Rubenstein, *After Auschwitz: Radical Theology and Contemporary Judaism* (New York: Bobbs-Merrill, 1966).

[51] See Emil Fackenheim, *The Jewish Return into History* (New York: Schocken Books, 1978). See also his *God's Presence in History: Jewish Affirmations and Philosophical Reflections* (New York: New York University Press, 1970) and *To Mend the World: Foundations of Future Jewish Thought* (New York: Schocken Books, 1982).

[52] See Arthur Cohen, *The Tremendum: A Theological Interpretation of the Holocaust* (New York: Crossroad, 1981).

[53] See Irving Greenberg, "The Voluntary Covenant," *Perspectives* 3 (New York: National Jewish Resource Center for Learning and Leadership, 1982); see also his magisterial essay "Cloud of Smoke, Pillar of Fire: Judaism, Christianity, and Modernity after the Holocaust," in *Auschwitz: Beginning of a New Era? Reflections on the Holocaust*, ed. Eva Fleischner, 7–55 (New York: Anti-Defamation League of B'nai B'rith, 1974).

[54] Pawlikowski, "The *Shoah*," 149. Pawlikowski goes on to develop his notion of a "compelling" God by which one can "recover a fresh sense of transcendence to accompany our heightened sense of human responsibility after the *Shoah*" (149). He further suggests that this notion of a "compelling" God can be obtained only though sacramental celebration and prayer.

remembered throughout Jesus' life, Song suggests, became the mute God when his Son died on the cross. More precisely, the God of Jesus was shocked into silence by grief: "The silence of Jesus' God must have been the silence of grief. God was grieved into silence. It must have been a deep grief. When grief is shallow, silence does not follow. . . . Shallow grief can make us talkative. . . . But deep grief renders us silent. It deprives us of the power of speech."[55] Was God silent during the Holocaust, not because God had abandoned God's covenanted people or was absent from them, but because God was shocked into silence by the horror of their sufferings?

But silence, Song points out, is not necessarily a sign of weakness; it can also be a "silence of protest." Just as Jesus' silence before the religious authorities and the Roman court was a silence of protest, God's silence at the cross was a silence of protest: "God did not respond to Jesus' cry, not because God had abandoned him, but because God's horror and grief must have turned into silent protest. 'Look!' God must have been filling the air with silent grief and protest saying, 'What have you human beings done to Jesus, "my beloved Son"?'"[56] Was God not protesting with horror and grief during the Holocaust: "Look! What have you human beings, Nazis and otherwise, done to Israel, my beloved and chosen people?"

Furthermore, God's silence is not just grief and protest. For Song, it is also "a silence of pity *(karuna)*":

> It is not just anger. It is not simply grief. It is not merely protest. It, above all, must be pity, *karuna*, the matrix, the womb, engaged in the creation of life and nourishment of it. In that silence of the womb, pity *(karuna)* struggles to empower the embryo of life for the day of fulfillment. That silence of God is like a womb enveloping Jesus on the cross, empowering him during the last moments of his life and nourishing him for the resurrection of a new life from the womb.[57]

Since the Holocaust, has God not been the God of *karuna* for the Jews, empowering and nourishing them, not merely for survival in a secular and militarily powerful state, but "*to serve as God's People upon whom the redemption of God's world and God's own name uniquely depends.*"[58]

Lastly, the God of compassion is not an omnipotent God. Song laments the fact that "the answer of traditional theology to this world of power is a powerful God. It invokes a powerful God and prays to an omnipotent God for intervention. Power must be counteracted with power."[59] Rather, the God of compassion is the God who has "the power to love others and to suffer with them."[60]

---

[55] Song, *Jesus, the Crucified People*, 115.

[56] Ibid., 116.

[57] Ibid., 119.

[58] Goldberg, *Why Should Jews Survive?* 168.

[59] Song, *Jesus in the Power of the Spirit*, 185.

[60] Song, *Theology from the Womb of Asia*, 165.

Song insists that "the cross of Jesus is the cross of God. The cross people have to bear is the cross of God too. The cross of Jesus and the cross of suffering women, men, and children are linked to God and disclose the heart of the suffering God."[61]

But Song is quick to point out that a suffering God alone is no help: " A God easily carried away by sentiments, offers no help in hell. That God would be too overwhelmed by the sight of pain and suffering to know what to do. ... A tearful God may invite our sympathy but not our trust and confidence."[62] What is needed is the God of powerful grace: "To have the will to live in hell and to see the eternal light of hope in the midst of perpetual darkness, we need God's grace, not weak grace, but strong grace, not sentimental grace, but no-nonsense grace, not fragile grace, but *powerful* grace. This is the grace with which God created heaven and earth."[63] But this powerful grace, Song argues, is not available to us until in faith we become active participants in its working in history, until in faith we get involved in the struggle against the power that oppresses us. Ultimately, for Song, the God of compassion who suffers with us invites and empowers us to take up our own responsibility in freedom to liberate ourselves from those who oppress us.

In our post-Shoah time, God can no longer be an omnipotent God, carrying out his will without the collaboration of his creatures, totally transcendent to human history, and stranger to the suffering of people in the world. In the eyes of Asian liberation theologians, God bears the crosses of all men, women, and children. However, God does not simply suffer with those who suffer. On the contrary, if the cross of Jesus is any indication, God protests against their suffering, wants to remove it, and will vindicate those who suffer against their oppressors. But God removes suffering and vindicates the oppressed not by intervening from outside of history, without the resources and collaboration of the suffering people; rather, with his powerful grace God calls forth and empowers those who suffer from oppression and injustice to take charge of their destiny and struggle for their liberation.

God's Covenant with All Nations and All Peoples

Intimately related to the question of God in post-Holocaust theology is the issue of election and covenant, and in connection with it, of the relationship

---

[61] Song, *Jesus, the Crucified People*, 122.

[62] Song, *Jesus in the Power of the Spirit*, 188.

[63] Ibid., 190. For Song's contrast between God's power and human dictatorship and totalitarianism, see his *Tell Us Our Names: Story Theology from an Asian Perspective*, 163–80. Song argues that the "power" of God leads to "people politics" (democracy) as opposed to "power politics" (autocratic rule). Moreover, Song also believes that "people politics" will lead to what he calls the "politics of the cross" of Jesus, but he immediately adds: "The powerless cross proves so powerful that throughout the centuries it has empowered countless persons to struggle for justice and freedom. In the name of the cross Christian give witness to the God of love and mercy in a world of hate and conflict" (180).

between Israel and the church. Part of the Christian "teaching of contempt" against Jews and Judaism is the supersessionist or displacement doctrine, according to which God's covenant with Israel has been abolished and replaced by God's new covenant with the church. In contemporary theology various typologies or models have been proposed to understand the nature of the relationship between Israel and the church, and different categories have been put forward to express it.[64] With regard to the covenant, questions have been raised as to how many covenants there are, and in Christian-Jewish dialogue it is now customary to classify various Christian theologies of the covenant into three types: single-covenant, double-covenant, and multi-covenant perspectives.[65] The single-covenant view conceives of Jews and Christians as basically partners of an ongoing, integrated covenantal tradition lived out by each not so much in different contents as in different modes. In this view Gentiles can be saved only through linkage with the Jewish covenant, something made possible in and through the Christ-event. The double-covenant view emphasizes the distinctiveness of each tradition but insists that both are ultimately crucial for the complete emergence of the kingdom of God. The multi-covenant perspective regards the Jewish and Christian covenants as two among an undetermined number of covenants that God makes with different religious traditions among which none can claim universality and normativity for others.

Asian liberation theologians have not directly dealt with the issue of the number of covenants, but their reflections on the relationship between God and Asian peoples throw a helpful light on it. Confronted with religious pluralism, which is the hallmark of Asia, Asian theologians have raised the question of how God is related to them. Leading the discussion, once again, is Choan-Seng Song. In an effort to fashion a "transpositional theology," that is, a theology that is distinctly Asian in character, he attacks the "ethno-religious centrism" of Jewish and Christian theologies. By centrism Song means the attitude of both Judaism and Christianity to take themselves exclusively as the center, norm, and goal of human history.[66] Such a view, in his judgment, leads to rigidity, homogeneity,

---

[64] For Bertold Klappert's eight models, see his *Israel und die Kirche: Erwägungen zur Israellehre Karl Barths* (Munich: Kaiser, 1980). Klappert speaks of "substitution," "integration," "typology," "illustration," "subsumation," "complementarity," "representation," and "participation" models. Klappert considers the first five as negative, and the last three as positive. Marcus Barth summarizes four models: Israel's replacement by the church; partial continuity between Israel and church, which is the former's remnant; schism in the one people of God, which brought out the "split people"; and complementarity between Israel and church. See his *The People of God* (Sheffield: JSOT Press, 1983).

[65] For further information on these types, see Chapter 9 herein.

[66] Song believes that centrism is best expressed by Arend van Leeuwen when he writes: "Israel and the land of Israel represent the whole earth, the whole of mankind. Israel herself is a new creation, and her land the token of a new earth which the Lord will create. For that reason the life of the whole earth hangs upon the promise that Israel is to return to her land. . . . The Lord reveals to Israel, his people, what his purpose is for the whole earth" (*Christianity in World History* [London: Edinburgh House, 1964], 104). Quoted in Song, *The Compassionate God*, 79.

and above all exclusivism that refuses to see God's presence and activity outside the boundaries of one's own community.

Rather than election and covenant which evoke privilege and particularism and create the us *vs.* them mentality, Song prefers the symbol of reign of God: "The reign of God, according to Jesus, is not an institution but people—people with dignity as human beings regardless of their backgrounds and entitled to freedom and justice, people affirming their full humanity and refusing to accept the conditions that belittle that humanity."[67] What unites Jews, Christians, and all other peoples is not a particular election by God but their common humanity and their shared struggle to defend it whenever and wherever it is threatened and oppressed. By shifting the emphasis from covenant to the reign of God, Song wants to avoid the theological exclusivism that has characterized certain types of theology of religion.[68]

This focus on the reign of God forces us, according to Song, to overcome our ethnocentric concept of God. Quoting "The People's Creed" written by a Christian from Zimbabwe with approval, Song says that God is "a color-blind God" who has created "technicolor people."[69] Overcoming religious "centrism" also allows us to recognize "the saving activity of God in the world of nations and peoples, in the community of people of other religions as well as in the community of Christians."[70]

This rejection of religious centrism is also espoused by some Asian feminist theologians such as Kwok Pui-lan and Chung Hyun Kyung. Aware that the Bible has been used in the colonial discourse to legitimate belief of the inferiority of Asian peoples and the deficiency of Asian cultures and suspicious of the Bible's patriarchal bias, Kwok Pui-lan believes that the concept of election and hence covenant leads to exclusion of the Other. Following Cain Hope Felder she affirms that "the explicit concept of Yahweh's preference for Israel over other nations and peoples developed into a religious ideology relatively late, that is, in the period of Deuteronomic history toward the end of the seventh century B.C.E."[71] Chung Hyun Kyung also sees a connection between the claim

---

[67] Song, *Jesus and the Reign of God*, 44. For a discussion of the symbol of the reign of God for Asians, see Peter C. Phan, "Kingdom of God: A Theological Symbol for Asians?" *Gregorianum* 79/2 (1998), 295–322.

[68] For a discussion of the three types of theology of religion, exclusivism, inclusivism, and pluralism, see Peter C. Phan, "Are There Other 'Saviors' for Other Peoples? A Discussion of the Problem of the Universal Significance and Uniqueness of Jesus the Christ," in *Christianity and the Wider Ecumenism*, ed. Peter C. Phan, 163–80 (New York: Paragon House, 1990).

[69] Song, *Jesus and the Reign of God*, 45. The text of "The People's Creed" is found in Canaan Banana, *The Gospel according to the Ghetto* (Geneva: World Council of Churches, 1974), 8.

[70] Song, *Jesus in the Power of the Spirit*, 226.

[71] See Kwok Pui-lan, *Discovering the Bible in the Non-Biblical World* (Maryknoll, N.Y.: Orbis Books, 1995), 89–90. Kwok Pui-lan is also aware that the concept of election and covenant has been used by Christians to oppress Jews. Furthermore, though urging against anti-Semitism in feminist interpretation, she regards the Hebrew scriptures simply as "one significant religious resource of humankind illuminating the human capacity to love, to struggle, to repent, and to cry in joy" (89).

to a special election by God and colonialism practiced by the West upon Asia. Rather than starting from and relying on the history of the covenant of God with Israel and Christianity, of which the Bible is the normative record, she urges that Asian women construct their theology on their own stories:

> The text of God's revelation was, is, and will be written in our bodies and our peoples' everyday struggle for survival and liberation. God did not come first to Asian women when Western missionaries brought the Bible to Asia. God has always been with us throughout our history, long before Jesus was born. The location of God's revelation is our life itself. Our life is our text, and the Bible and church tradition are the context which sometimes becomes the reference for our own ongoing search for God.[72]

Asian liberation theologians generally reject the Christian supersessionist doctrine with regard to God's covenant with Israel. By the same token, they also reject Christianity's claim to an exclusive and total possession of a new and perfect covenant with God. Rather, they insist on God's no less real presence in other religions with their own scriptures and rituals and in other peoples, especially in those who are poor and who suffer. Instead of focusing on a special election by and covenant with God, they regard our common humanity and our shared struggle for its liberation from all forms of oppression as the basis for constructing an understanding of our relationship with God and with each other. In this way Asian liberation theologians broaden the perspective of the discussion among Holocaust theologians of the issue of God's election and covenant.

Christ, the Marginal Person Par Excellence

For Holocaust theology Christology has become the *instantia crucis*. With rhetorical flourish Rosemary Radford Ruether declares that "anti-Judaism developed theologically in Christianity as the left hand of Christology. That is to say, anti-Judaism was the negative side of the Christian claim that Jesus was the Christ."[73] Naturally, then, post-Holocaust theologians have made special efforts to reformulate a Christology that is free from anti-Judaism.[74]

---

[72] Chung Hyun Kyung, *Struggle to Be the Sun Again: Introducing Asian Women's Theology* (Maryknoll, N.Y.: Orbis Books, 1990), 111. Chung also suggests that Asian women theologians "must move away from our imposed fear of losing Christian identity, in the opinion of the mainline theological circles, and instead risk that we might be transformed by the religious wisdom of our people" through the method of "*survival-liberation centered syncretism*" (113).

[73] Rosemary Radford Ruether, "Anti-Semitism and Christian Theology," in Fleischner, *Auschwitz*, 79. The responses of Walter Burghardt and Yosef Hayim Yerushalmi to Ruether's essay offer important corrections to Ruether's exaggerations (93–107).

[74] Those whose efforts are to be noted include Eugene B. Borowitz, *Contemporary Christologies: A Jewish Response* (New York: Paulist Press, 1980); Michael B. McGarry, *Christology after Auschwitz* (New York: Paulist Press, 1977); Pawlikowski, *Christ in the Light of the Christian-Jewish Dialogue*; idem, *Jesus and the Theology of Israel* (Wilmington, Del.: Michael Glazier, 1989).

Asian liberation theologians too have been busy shaping a Christology that would make sense to their situation. Aloysius Pieris develops a portrait of Christ as a poor monk, Choan-Seng Song an image of Christ as the crucified people, and Chung Hyun Kyung a picture of Jesus as a suffering and liberating woman.[75] Here I focus on the portrait of Jesus as a marginal person developed by Jung Young Lee.[76]

Drawing upon his experiences as an immigrant and the history of Chinese, Japanese, and Korean immigrants in the United States, Lee defines his and their experiences as being on the margin as opposed to being at the center. By "marginality" Lee means not only being "in-between," that is, the experience of the people-on-the-margin as described by those who dwell at the center. This classical understanding of marginality is one-sided because it is framed by the central group, and it emphasizes the negative effects of marginality, such as ambivalence, excessive self-consciousness, restlessness, lack of self-confidence, pessimism, and the like. It needs to be corrected and complemented by the self-understanding of the marginalized people themselves. Marginal people, according to Lee, see themselves primarily as being "in-both." As Asian Americans, Asian immigrants are both Asian and American. To stress "in-bothness" means first of all affirming one's racial, cultural, and religious origins. Being on the margin, however, prevents this affirmation of ethnic, cultural, and religious particularity from being excessive, since the margins are where different worlds touch each other and merge into each other.

Being "in-between" and "in-both" are not mutually exclusive; both have something true to say about being an immigrant. They need to be brought together in a holistic understanding of marginality. Lee suggests that being "in-between" and "in-both" are included in being "in-beyond." To be in-between and in-both the Asian and American worlds, the immigrant must be in-beyond them. And the symbol of being in-beyond is to be a "hyphenated" person.[77]

With this understanding of marginality Lee rereads the incarnation, birth, life, death, and resurrection as stories of divine marginalization and develops a

---

[75] For studies of Asian Christologies, see Peter C. Phan, "Jesus the Christ with an Asian Face," *Theological Studies* 57 (1996), 399–430; and R. S. Sugirtharajah, ed., *Asian Faces of Jesus* (Maryknoll, N.Y.: Orbis Books, 1993).

[76] Jung Young Lee (1935–96) was an American-Korean theologian. Besides a portrait of Jesus as a marginal person, Lee also uses the *yin-yang* metaphysics to show that Jesus is the perfect realization of change. Among his many works see *God Suffers for Us: A Systematic Inquiry into the Concept of Divine Passibility* (The Hague: Martinus Nijhoff, 1974); *The Theology of Change: A Christian Concept of God from an Eastern Perspective* (Maryknoll, N.Y.: Orbis Books, 1979); *Marginality: The Key to Multicultural Theology* (Minneapolis: Fortress Press, 1995); and *The Trinity in Asian Perspective* (Nashville, Tenn.: Abingdon, 1996). For a discussion of Lee's Christology, see Phan, "Jesus the Christ with an Asian Face," 410–17.

[77] Lee contends that metaphysically, the situation of the immigrant as being "in-between," "in-both," and "in-beyond" corresponds to the dipolar reality of *yin* and *yang*, and epistemologically, it corresponds with the inclusive position of both-and and neither-nor as opposed to that of either-or.

portrait of Jesus as a "new marginal person *par excellence.*"[78] To indicate this
fact, Lee places a hyphen between Jesus and Christ: "I use a hyphenated 'Jesus-
Christ' because Jesus is the Christ, while the Christ is also Jesus. In other words,
Jesus as the Christ is not enough. He is also the Christ as Jesus. Just as 'Asian-
American' means an Asian and an American. Whenever I say Jesus, I mean
Jesus-Christ; whenever I say Christ, I mean Christ-Jesus. They are inseparable,
two facets of one existence."[79] In particular, in his death and resurrection, according to Lee, Jesus becomes the new marginal person by embracing both total
negation and total affirmation; Jesus becomes a new "creative core." This new
creative core is the point of intersection between two worlds, between the center and the margin, and creates a new world, a new circle with Jesus as the new
core or center. But this new core is not another center of centrality; in fact, it
marginalizes the old centers of marginality and turns the margins into the new
creative core. The new core will not become another center of centrality, for it
remains at the margin of marginality. In this way the new creative core can
reconcile the center with the margin and vice versa. Jesus as the new creative
core is the perfect new marginal person, "because in him every marginal deter-
minant is nullified, and everyone can overcome his or her marginality. In the
creative core of Jesus-Christ, racism is overcome, sexism is no longer in practice, the poor become self-sufficient, the weak find strength."[80]

Is it not possible that in this Asian Christology, in which the claim of messianic fulfillment for Jesus is relativized, and yet in which Christ is granted the
status of a new creative core reconciling the margin with the center and the
center with margin, Christians, who have relegated Jews to the margin of their
circle, can bring Jews to their center? In this Asian Christology, is it not possible that Jews, who have long occupied the margin of a Christian society, can
be brought into a new center, not in order to relegate other groups, whether
Christian or Palestinian, to the margin of their newly founded state but to reconcile them with themselves in the new center?

Power or Release from *Han*?

Millennia of oppression leave indelible scars not only on the oppressed persons' bodies but on their souls as well. To overcome this state of helplessness
and to prevent it from ever recurring, the oppressed people, once liberated, establish all kinds of institutions to perpetuate the memory of their oppression.
Their stories of oppression and suffering can produce even a religion *sui generis.*
This is, according to Rabbi Michael Goldberg, what has happened to the Holocaust. There is now "the Holocaust cult": the Holocaust with its dogma of survival at any cost has replaced the Jewish faith in God and functions as "civil
Judaism"; it has a cult in the observance of Yom Hashoah; it erects shrines and

---

[78] Lee, *Marginality*, 71.
[79] Ibid., 78.
[80] Ibid., 98.

museums; and it has its own priesthood.[81] In particular, the Holocaust gave birth to the state of Israel, which in the eyes of some Jews and Holocaust theologians has acquired the status of an article of faith totally immune from any possible criticism.

Asia, too, has its own holocausts, in the long past as well as in recent years, from centuries of political oppression and colonialism to the "Rape of Nanjing" to the "Killing Fields." Oppressed Asian peoples, too, have perpetuated their histories of suffering to make sure that their descendants and others will not forget them and that oppression will not be repeated. Among Asian liberation theologians, Korean theologians have devoted much attention to the theme of the suffering and oppression of the *minjung*. By *minjung*, a Korean word that literally means the "popular mass," but which is left untranslated, is meant "the oppressed, exploited and suppressed politically, economically, socially, culturally, and intellectually, like women, ethnic groups, the poor, workers and farmers, including intellectuals themselves."[82]

According to *minjung* theologians, prolonged oppression and humiliation of the Korean *minjung* by foreign powers such as the Chinese and the Japanese and by their own dictators have produced in them a deep sense of *han*. *Han*, another Korean word that defies exact translation and is left untranslated literally means "anger," "grudge," or "sad resentment." It is defined by Hyun Young Hak as "a sense of unresolved resentment against injustice suffered, a sense of helplessness because of the overwhelming odds against, a feeling of total abandonment ('Why has Thou forsaken Me?'), a feeling of acute pain and sorrow in one's guts and bowels making the whole body writhe and wiggle, and an obstinate urge to take 'revenge' and to right the wrong all these constitute."[83] It is agreed by *minjung* theologians that Korean women constitute "the *minjung* of the *minjung*" and suffer from "the *han* of *han*."

---

[81] See Goldberg, *Why Should Jews Survive?* 41–59.

[82] Chung Hyun Kyung, "'Han-pu-ri': Doing Theology from Korean Women's Perspective," in *We Dare to Dream: Doing Theology as Asian Women*, ed. Virginia Fabella and Sun Ai Lee Park, 138–39 (Hong Kong: Asian Women's Resource Centre for Culture and Theology, 1989; Maryknoll, N.Y.: Orbis Books, 1990). Chung is quoting from David Kwang-sun Suh, mentioned below. For discussions of *minjung* theology, see Jung Young Lee, ed., *An Emerging Theology in World Perspective: Commentary on Korean Minjung Theology* (Mystic, Conn.: Twenty-Third Publications, 1988); David Kwang-sun Suh, *The Korean Minjung in Christ* (Hong Kong: Christian Conference of Asia, 1991); Commission on Theological Concerns of the Christian Conference of Asia, *Minjung Theology: People as the Subjects of History* (Maryknoll, N.Y.: Orbis Books, 1983); and Phan, "Experience and Theology," 118–20.

[83] Hyun Young Hak, "Minjung: The Suffering Servant and Hope," a lecture given at James Memorial Chapel, Union Theological Seminary, New York, April 13, 1982, p. 2, quoted in Chung Hyun Kyung, *Struggle to Be the Sun Again*, 42. Moon Hee-suk gives another description of *han* as "the anger and resentment of the minjung which has been turned inward and intensified as they become objects of injustice upon injustice." See his *A Korean Minjung Theology: An Old Testament Perspective* (Maryknoll, N.Y.: Orbis Books, 1985), 1–2. James Cone, a proponent of black theology, suggests that the equivalent of *han* is the blues in black experience in North America.

There are two ways to deal with *han*. One is passively to accept and internalize it as one's fate, which leads to resignation and despair. The other is to refuse it and work toward eliminating it. The process of resolving *han* is called *dan*, literally "cutting off." According to Kim Chi-ha, a Korean Catholic poet and activist, it takes place on both individual and collective levels. On the individual level it requires self-denial or renunciation of material wealth and comforts. This self-denial will cut off the *han* from our hearts. On the collective level *han* can work toward the transformation of the world by raising humans to a higher level of existence. This process, again according to Kim Chi-ha, is composed of four steps: realizing the presence of God in us and worshiping God, allowing this divine consciousness to grow in us, practicing what we believe about God, and struggling against injustice by transforming the world.[84]

Other more traditional and less militant ways to remove *han* include rituals, drama, mask dance, and shamanism. By means of these activities the participants achieve "critical transcendence" through which past *han* is resolved and liberation achieved.[85]

The Holocaust has produced in the Jews a kind of *han*. Instead of internalizing it as their divinely ordained fate, most Jews believe it is incumbent upon them to remove it by securing power and using it against those who threaten their survival. One of the results of this effort of empowerment, together with the Zionist movement, is the founding of the state of Israel. But as is well known, the battered child will often grow up into a child batterer, and the oppressed, once they have achieved power, will turn into oppressors if they are driven by fear and forsake moral norms. That the state of Israel has been guilty of abusing its power, especially in its treatment of Palestinians, is doubted by few. Even ardent Holocaust theologians have been critical of certain policies of the Israeli government vis-à-vis the Palestinians, especially during the *intifada*.[86] Furthermore, as Michael Goldberg has pointed out, the memory of the Holocaust has been used by some Jews as both a moral sword and shield—"a sword of moral criticism with which to prick the consciences of others and a shield to deflect the sting of that selfsame criticism from their own consciences."[87] The rabbi feels obligated to remind his fellow Jews that "even victims can still sin."[88] Marc Ellis, a Jewish liberation theologian, has called for the "deabsolutization"

---

[84] See Lee, ed., *An Emerging Theology in World Perspective*, 10–11. Besides Kim Chi-ha two other prominent proponents of *minjung* theology are Professor Suh Nam-dong and Professor Ahn Byung-mu.

[85] Korean feminist theologians highlight the role of women as priestesses in shamanistic rituals (*mudang*) as a way to liberate them from their manifold bondage. See Chung Hyun Kyung, "Opium or Seed for Revolution? Shamanism: Women-Centered Popular Religiosity," in *Theologies of the Third World: Convergences and Differences*, ed. Leonardo Boff and Virgilio Elizondo, 96–104 (Edinburgh: T. & T. Clark, 1988).

[86] See Irving Greenberg, "The Ethics of Jewish Power," in *Perspectives* (New York: National Jewish Resource Center for Learning and Leadership, 1988): 1–27. For other critics of Israeli policies, see Ellis, *Beyond Innocence and Redemption*, 56–94.

[87] Goldberg, *Why Should Jews Survive?* 126.

[88] Ibid., 128.

of the state of Israel and of the Holocaust in working out a resolution to the Israeli-Palestinian conflict and a new Jewish theology.[89]

John Pawlikowski has persuasively argued that one of the theological challenges of the Holocaust is the question of the ethics of power. He agrees with Jewish Holocaust theologians such as Emil Fackenheim and Irving Greenberg that after the Shoah the Jews cannot rely on divine intervention in human history to protect them, even if they consider themselves a covenanted people, but must assume responsibility through the use of power for their survival.[90] But he hastens to quote Romano Guardini, warning that we must "integrate power into life in such a way that man can employ power without forfeiting his humanity, or to surrender his humanity to power and perish."[91]

It is here that *minjung* theologians' reflections on the process of resolving *han* will prove helpful. For, besides the struggle to bring about justice and freedom for themselves and to become subjects of their own histories, the oppressed people, according to *minjung* theologians, must practice, not as an alternative to the social and political struggle but as a necessary complement to it, a spiritual discipline that will bind them in solidarity with other victims and thus prevent their exercise of power from becoming abusive and repressive. Such spirituality has been described as "concrete and total," "creative and flexible," "prophetic and historical," "community-oriented," "pro-life," "ecumenical, all embracing," and "cosmic, creation-centered."[92] Ultimately, such a spirituality will lead victims to recognize their role as potential victimizers and that fully to overcome injustice and suffering and to achieve freedom, they must make the painful journey from a self-absorbed obsession with their own suffering to altruistic actions to redress injustices on behalf of their fellow innocent sufferers, from self-righteous protestations of innocence to a humbling and humanizing encounter with the mysterious and free God, from an arrogant demand for satisfaction of their rights to a grateful recognition of God's gratuitous love.[93]

Michael Lerner, in developing an approach to Jewish liberation theology, insists on the same dynamics:

> The Torah screams out to the Jews a very different message: When you go into your land, do not re-create Egypt, *do not re-create a world of oppression.* You do not have to do so. Your own experience as people who were oppressed may create a psychological tendency to become oppressors, but it simultaneously has created another possibility: the possibility of

---

[89] See Ellis, *Toward a Jewish Theology of Liberation* and especially *Beyond Innocence and Redemption.*

[90] See Pawlikowski, "The *Shoah*," 161–63.

[91] Ibid., 164.

[92] See Chung Hyun Kyung, *Struggle to Be the Sun Again,* 91–96.

[93] This is the suggestion made by Gustavo Gutiérrez in *On Job.* Gutiérrez speaks of the "language of prophecy" and the "language of contemplation" required in dealing with the evil of innocent suffering. For a discussion of these two languages, see Peter C. Phan, "Overcoming Poverty and Oppression: Liberation Theology and the Problem of Evil," *Louvain Studies* 20 (1995), 3–20.

remembering your experience, and using that as a basis for identifying with the oppressed, and not re-creating that oppression for others in the present.[94]

Furthermore, should this process not finally lead Jews and Christians to asking for forgiveness and granting forgiveness, and ultimately to mutual reconciliation? As Stanley Hauerwas says:

> The reality of the Holocaust cannot be made to go away by continuing to weigh up guilt and responsibility. Such exercises, while not completely pointless, often come close to being obscene. Rather what we and the Jew must both do is to remember. But without forgiveness we Christians are tempted simply to forget, deny, or wallow in inaction; and Jews are tempted to lose their humanity in humiliation or vengeance. But if we are forgiven we have the chance to remember and to make this terrible event part of our common history so that we can together make a different human story for the future and look forward to the day when God's reign will come and we can embrace as brother and sister.[95]

HOLOCAUST THEOLOGY AND ASIAN LIBERATION THEOLOGY: THE CONTINUING DIALOGUE

In 1995, fifty years after atomic bombs were dropped on Hiroshima and Nagasaki, Japan remembered not only Japanese victims of the war but Jewish victims as well. A Holocaust museum dedicated to the memory of 1.5 million Jewish children murdered by the Nazis was opened in June of the same year in Fukuyama, a city near Hiroshima. Anne Frank's diary, translated into Japanese, was also exhibited in Hiroshima's Peace Park.

Less known is what has been called the Fugu Plan, Japan's top-secret plan to create an "Israel in Asia." Conceived by Japanese diplomats, industrialists, and military leaders, this scheme involved offering displaced European Jews a safe haven in Japan-controlled Manchuria. Its purpose was twofold: obtaining Jewish financial and technical resources in exchange for physical safety, and improving Japan's image with the United States and gaining the sympathy of America's influential Jewish population. The plan was called the Fugu Plan because, though advantageous to Japan, if mishandled, it would backfire like the blowfish, delicious but deadly if incorrectly cooked, called *fugu* in Japanese. Though this plan foundered with Japan's entry into the Tripartite Pact with Nazi Germany and Italy in 1940, it saved from the Holocaust thousands of Jews who were issued Japanese transit visas and given wartime refuge in Asia.[96]

---

[94] Lerner, "Breaking the Chains of Necessity," 57.

[95] Stanley Hauerwas, "Resurrection, the Holocaust, and Forgiveness: A Sermon for Eastertime," in *Removing Anti-Judaism from the Pulpit*, ed. Howard Clark Kee and Irwin J. Borowsky (New York: Continuum, 1996), 119–20.

[96] See Marvin Tokayer and Mary Swartz, *The Untold Story of the Japanese and the Jews during World War II* (New York: Paddington, 1979).

These two unlikely events symbolize the dialogue between Holocaust theology and Asian liberation theology. Conceived apart in different times and at different places but in the same womb, namely, the common faith in the God of Abraham, Isaac, and Jacob, they are brought together like long-lost twins in an unexpected reunion. As often happens between siblings, their relationships may not always be smooth, there may be misunderstanding and even rivalry, and sometimes ugly things are said, in this case by the younger against the elder.

Though dissimilar, these twin theologies have some identical genes. Both were born in the crucible of prolonged and bitter oppression and injustice. Because of their experience of innocent suffering, they are animated by a burning sense of justice. And in their struggle for liberation, both appeal to the Exodus, the founding event of both Judaism and Christianity, as the source of their empowerment. They put their faith and trust in a God who sides with the poor and the oppressed. To galvanize people of other faiths to the same struggle for freedom and justice, they also appeal to their common humanity and dignity.

But like twins they are not only blessed with similar strengths but are also susceptible to the same diseases. In insisting upon suffering and empowerment as well as on innocence and redemption,[97] both Holocaust theology and Asian liberation theology run the risk of romanticizing the people whose interests they serve, whether the state of Israel or the *minjung* or the women within the *minjung*, placing them beyond the realm of evil and turning them into new messiahs and idols. They run the risk of forgetting the real danger of yesterday's oppressed becoming tomorrow's oppressors. Furthermore, when the people they defend achieve independence and power, both theologies insist that they and their policies be judged according to the common standards of morality of the nations, opting for normalization rather than specialness, thereby losing their distinctive if not unique character as God's covenanted people, the Jews obscuring their prophetic legacy and the Asian Christians their Christian heritage vis-à-vis other religious communities.

Fortunately, these diseases are not fatal to these two theologies because they do possess, each within itself, antibodies to fight against them. However, their immunity will be much improved if in a continuing dialogue they share with each other their particular strengths and set up defenses against common dangers, just as the Japanese remembered not only the Japanese victims of the atomic bombs but also the Jewish victims of the Holocaust, and as the architects of the Fugu Plan, even out of self-interest, attempted to save European Jews from the Nazi death camps.

---

[97] According to Marc Ellis, these are the two themes of early Holocaust theology represented by Elie Wiesel and Emil Fackenheim. The third theme is specialness and normalization, which is embodied in the writings of Irving Greenberg (see Ellis, *Beyond Innocence and Redemption*, 2–6).

12

Holy War, Unholy Violence

PERSPECTIVES ON RELIGION AND PEACEBUILDING

Holy war, unholy violence, holy violence, unholy war, however the terms *war, violence, holy, unholy* are paired together, they capture the anger and despair, the fear and hope that grip the hearts not only of North Americans in the post–September 11 era but also of most people around the world.

Hold a globe in your hands and trace with your fingers the areas in which war and violence are now raging. Recite aloud the names of sundry continents and countries where hundreds of thousands of people are being murdered because of racial, ethnic, and religious differences or out of a naked lust for economic and political power. Listen to the heartrending wailing of the families of those whose bodies have just been blown to pieces by a terrorist's explosives or by the "shock and awe" fireworks of thousands of smart bombs. Watch houses and buildings and towers, creations of human love and ingenuity, collapse into clouds of dust and feel the terror of the occupants crushed and trapped beneath them. Peer into the desperate or vacant eyes of survivors of war brutalities in refugee camps and fathom their hopelessness. Plumb the sorrow of the families and friends of the dead soldiers, whose dreams and hopes have been snuffed out before their time. Observe children toting guns and arms with glee and gusto, as if they were toys, trapped in the perpetual vortex of killing and destruction. Think of hundreds of billions of dollars spent on devising ever more lethal weapons capable of obliterating humans but leaving their material surroundings intact, money that could be used to educate the minds, feed the hungry, and heal the sick the world over. Imagine the destructive impact of war on the human psyche, saturating it with desire for vengeance and hatred. Envision the long-lasting damages warfare inflicts on the environment, the earth disemboweled, the vegetation scorched, the air polluted, the water poisoned.

Then ponder in your hearts Jesus' blessing and promise in the Beatitudes: "Blessed are the peacemakers, for they will be called children of God" (Mt 5:9). Recall Jesus' unequivocal command: "Do not resist an evildoer. But if anyone strikes you on the right cheek, turn the other also; and if anyone wants to sue you and take your coat, give your cloak as well; and if anyone forces you to go one mile, go also the second mile" (Mt 5:39–41). And, "Love your enemies and

186

pray for those who persecute you, so that you may be children of your Father in heaven; for he makes his sun rise on the evil and on the good, and sends rains on the righteous and on the unrighteous" (Mt 5:44–45). And, "If you forgive others their trespasses, your heavenly Father will also forgive you; but if you do not forgive others, neither will your Father forgive your trespasses" (Mt 6: 14–15). Let these and many other similar sayings of Jesus sink into the depths of your soul and, above all, as you contemplate Jesus' own ministry, suffering, and death, ask yourselves: Are these words merely rhetorical and pious exhortations of an impractical and idealistic Jew of the first century of the Common Era that Christianity, let alone a political entity, can ill afford to accept as moral norms in the complexities of today's world, or are they the Lord Jesus' ever-truthful promise and ever-binding command that his followers must obey and practice in imitation of his very life and death so that God's reign may come?

But, it may be asked, how can American Christians take to heart these teachings of Jesus and put them into practice, living as they are in a nation that is the world's only superpower and that has launched, for the first time, a preemptive war against another country, on highly dubious pretexts; whose commander-in-chief, in a blasphemous twisting of Jesus' words, declared that who is not with us is against us; and whose cultural products, from movies to television shows to comic books, glorify violence and war? How can American Christians accept Jesus' command of peacemaking, loving enemies, and forgiving offenders when they are constantly warned by the various color codes of Homeland Security that they are under attack by nameless and faceless enemies? With regard to American Catholics in particular, how can they take up the task of international peacemaking and peacebuilding while the scandal of clergy sex abuse and its aftermaths have effectively discredited the moral authority of the American bishops, whose collective voice was not taken seriously by any politician in the days preceding the war against Iraq? More broadly still, how can all believers, irrespective of their religious allegiances, work together, each out of his or her own faith tradition, to transform, to use Pope John Paul II's memorable phrases, our "culture of death" into a "civilization of love," a civilization that rejects violence and hatred and war, reconciles victims with victimizers, and builds a society of justice and peace?

In attempting to find answers to these questions I do not intend to discuss whether pacifism or the just-war tradition is still valid in the context of the post–September 11 international order, though I will touch upon these two themes, albeit briefly, since they are germane to my topic. Much less do I want to initiate a never-ending discussion of the morality of America's ongoing war in Iraq. Rather, I intend first to investigate whether and how religion in general and Christianity in particular as a social organization have contributed to the rise of violence and war. Next, I will explore whether religions, in particular Christianity, even if burdened by their scandalous legacy of violence, have a necessary and pivotal role in building peace and reconciliation, especially today. Finally, I will highlight some of the contributions of Asian non-Christian religions to the process of peacemaking and reconciliation.

RELIGION, VIOLENCE, AND WAR

In the wake of recent sensational acts of religious violence, a spate of books has documented in detail the historical connections between religion and violence.[1] Though violence can and must be understood to include not only physical assault and torture but also psychological coercion, economic injustice, political repression, and infringement of human rights, to all of which various religions have contributed their share, in this chapter I limit my considerations to armed conflicts between sovereign states (international war) and between factions within a state (civil war). No doubt the causes for war are many, such as ideology, politics, race, economics, and religion, but it is a fact that in modern times religion, or at least appeal to religion, has played a predominant role in imperialism, nationalism, and militarism.

Believers and Violence

Current literature on religious violence has shown how religion has provided, in the past as well as now, the motivation, the justification, the organization, the language, the symbols, and the world view for innumerable acts of physical violence and wars. Mark Juergensmeyer has shown how religious violence is "performance violence"; that is, acts of religious violence are both "performative events," in that they make a symbolic statement, and "performative acts," insofar as they intend to change things, in the manner of liturgical and sacramental acts. Like these, they are performed in symbolic places, at dramatic times, and in the sight of a public audience.[2] More significantly, war and violence are justified by appealing to the widespread religious notion of cosmic war. Religious militants declare themselves to be called by God to wage, even unto total destruction, a final and decisive battle between good and evil, light and darkness, order and chaos. Assured of the inevitability of a total victory, they transform themselves into holy martyrs for the reign of God and demonize their ordinary enemies into cosmic foes. As Juergensmeyer puts it:

---

[1] See, for instance, Walter Wink, *The Powers That Be: Theology for a New Millennium* (New York: Doubleday, 1998); Joseph H. Ehrenkranz and D. Coppola, eds., *Religion and Violence, Religion and Peace: Essays from the Center for Christian-Jewish Understanding Conference in Auschwitz, Poland, May 1998* (Fairfield, Conn.: Sacred Heart University Press, 2000); John L. Esposito, *The Islamic Threat: Myth or Reality*, 3d ed. (New York: Oxford University Press, 1999); idem, *Unholy War: Terror in the Name of Islam* (New York: Oxford University Press, 2002); Leo D. Lefebure, *Revelation, the Religions, and Violence* (Maryknoll, N.Y.: Orbis Books, 2000); Mark Juergensmeyer, *Terror in the Mind of God: The Global Rise of Religious Violence* (Berkeley and Los Angeles: University of California Press, 2000); R. Scott Appleby, *The Ambivalence of the Sacred: Religion, Violence, and Reconciliation* (Lanham: Rowman & Littlefield Publishers, 2000); Marc Gopin, *Holy War, Holy Peace: How Religion Can Bring Peace to the Middle East* (New York: Oxford University Press, 2002); and Charles Kimball, *When Religion Becomes Evil* (New York: HarperCollins, 2002).

[2] Juergensmeyer, *Terror in the Mind of God*, 122–44.

Thus violent images have been given religious meaning and domesticized. These acts, although terribly real, have been sanitized by becoming symbols; they have been stripped of their horror by being invested with religious meaning. They have been justified and thereby exonerated as part of a religious template that is even larger than myth and history. They are elements of a ritual scenario that makes it possible for the people involved to experience safely the drama of cosmic war.[3]

Perhaps it may be objected that it is more accurate and fair to say that it is the followers of particular religions who commit acts of violence and engage in war, often with self-serving claims of religious justification, rather than religion itself, which is a holy communal response to the sacred. Whether such an attempt to exculpate religion is valid or not will be examined shortly, but the point of the objection is well taken: religion does not exist in a vacuum, apart from the beliefs, rituals, ethics, and behaviors of flesh-and-blood believers. Historically, religion is deeply intertwined with ethnicity and nationhood, the other markers of personal and group identity, by turn reinforcing and being reinforced by them. Indeed, the combination of ethnicity, nationalism, and religion was the deadly mix fueling more than half of the world's civil wars from 1945 to 1960, three-quarters of them from 1960 to 1990, and an even greater proportion after the collapse of the Soviet Union in 1991.[4]

With this caveat about the abuse of religion to incite war and violence in mind, it is not difficult to show that adherents of *all* major religions, with no exception, have engaged in massive and systematic violence in the name of their faiths against other believers or nonbelievers and against their own fellow believers, often with the official sanction and encouragement of their hierarchy. As Charles Kimball has noted, "More wars have been waged, more people killed, and more evil perpetrated in the name of religion than by any other institutional force in history. The sad truth continues in our present day."[5]

In the current political situation, whenever conversation turns to holy war, Americans almost instinctively conjure up images of Osama bin Laden and Muslim fundamentalists and their jihad—often translated "holy war"—and the suicide bombers, or as they prefer to be called, "self-chosen martyrs," of the Middle East.[6] But it is also necessary to recall that violence and war are not the reserved domain of Muslims. A quick glance at contemporary world politics reveals that acts of violence and wars prosecuted by believers of all religions are justified by means of religious world views: Muslims and Christians in Nigeria and the Philippines; Serbian Orthodox, Croatian Catholics, and Bosnian Muslims in the former Yugoslavia; Hindus and Muslims, and Sikhs and Hindus

---

[3] Ibid., 160.

[4] See Appleby, *The Ambivalence of the Sacred*, 58.

[5] Kimball, *When Religion Becomes Evil*, 156.

[6] For a survey of recent violent activities by Muslims, see Juergensmeyer, *Terror in the Mind of God*, 60–83; Esposito, *The Islamic Threat*; and Esposito, *Unholy War*.

in India; Buddhists and Hindus in Sri Lanka; Protestants and Catholics in Northern Ireland.[7] In the United States acts of violence against abortion clinics and abortion doctors have been justified on Christian principles by Rev. Michael Bray and Rev. Paul Hill; against homosexuals by Eric Robert Rudolph; against the federal government by Timothy McVeigh and various militia movements whose aim is to make the United States a "Christian" nation.[8]

As far as Christians are concerned, they too, despite Jesus' teachings on non-violence, love, and forgiveness, have had a lion's share of violence and war as anti-Semitism, the Crusades, the Inquisition, the Thirty Years' War, and the Holocaust, to mention only a few notorious cases, amply demonstrate. Concerning the Crusades in particular, it is well to remember that they were officially called for and sponsored by popes and Christian princes as a holy war. Whereas soldiers prior to the Crusades had to do penance for killing, even in a just cause, in the Crusades the slaughter of Muslims, vilified by Pope Urban II in his impassioned sermon at Clermont, France, in 1095, as "an accursed race, utterly alienated from God,"[9] was considered a penitential act to which indulgences were attached. As a whole, a persuasive case can be made that the history of Christianity contains more violence and bloodshed and official sanction for them than that of most other religions.

The case for the complicity of believers, either as individuals or as groups, with violence and war is perhaps too easy to make. Anyone with a passable knowledge of the history of the major religions needs no lengthy argument to be persuaded of the responsibility of believers for war and violence. The more difficult and controversial question is whether religion as such, in its historical emergence and by its very nature, is intrinsically an institution of violence, apart from what religious believers may or may not have done. Among contemporary philosophers who have reflected long and hard on the connection between religion and violence is the French historian, literary critic, and anthropologist René Girard (b. 1923). His mimetic scapegoat theory offers original insights into how violence is endemic to culture and religion.[10]

---

[7] For helpful accounts of these conflicts, see Appleby, *The Ambivalence of the Sacred.*

[8] For accounts of these "soldiers for Christ," see Juergensmeyer, *Terror in the Mind of God,* 19–43.

[9] Pope Urban II, quoted in Roland H. Bainton, *Christian Attitudes toward War and Peace* (Nashville, Tenn.: Abingdon, 1969), 111.

[10] For a helpful introduction to Girard's thought, see James G. Williams, ed., *The Girard Reader* (New York: Crossroad, 1996), which also contains Girard's bibliography up to May 1996. Of special interest to our theme are Girard's *Violence and the Sacred,* trans. Patrick Gregory (Baltimore: Johns Hopkins University Press, 1977; French original, 1972) and *Things Hidden since the Foundation of the World: Research Undertaken in Collaboration with Jean-Michel Oughourlian and Guy Lefort,* trans. Stephen Bann and Michael Metteer (Stanford, Calif.: Stanford University Press, 1987; French original, 1978). For a short and lucid explanation of Girard's thought, see the Foreword by James G. Williams in René Girard, *I See Satan Fall Like Lightning,* trans. J. G. Williams (New York: Orbis Books, 2001), ix–xxiii.

René Girard and the Violence of Religion

According to Girard, violence is rooted in human desire or imitation, which he terms *mimesis* in order to emphasize its unconscious and conflictive aspects. Mimesis evokes desire, and desire constitutes mimesis. Because humans are finite and therefore lacking in being and things, they necessarily desire them, often unconsciously. Moreover, they do not desire these things directly but indirectly. That is, we learn what is desirable through what those whom we take as our models desire. The objects of our desire, things and being, are mediated to us by our models. We desire by imitating our models' desires. We desire what our models have or desire.

Hence, mimetic desire has a triangular structure: (1) the self or subject that desires, (2) the object that is desired, (3) and the mediator or model that mediates the object to the desiring subject. Mimetic desire makes human beings into "interdividuals"—Girard's only neologism; that is, in mimetic desire we are not the other or the model but at the same time we are constituted by the other or the model. Each individual is defined by a set of mimetic relationships.

Since the object desired by the subject is the same as that which is mediated by the model, and since mimesis is characterized by acquisition and appropriation, mimetic relationship inevitably leads to conflict and violence between the subject and his or her model, or between the various subjects trying to imitate their common model. Eventually mimetic desire produces a situation called scandal or stumbling block in which persons or groups of persons feel blocked from obtaining what they desire, either because they cannot displace their model and get what their model has, or because their mutual rivalry prevents them from obtaining the same thing they all desire. As Girard puts it, "Each becomes the imitator of his own imitator and the model of his own model. Each tries to push aside the obstacle that the other places in his path. Violence is generated by this process; or rather violence is the process itself when two or more partners try to prevent one another from appropriating the object they all desire through physical or other means."[11] Mimetic desire and rivalry, Girard acknowledges, was his first intellectual discovery.

Girard's second discovery consists in realizing how much light his mimetic-desire theory sheds on the emergence of culture and religion in general. It lies at the heart of his universal anthropology and is embodied in his concept of scapegoating. According to Girard, culture and religion emerge out of mimetic desire. By culture he means anything and everything constructed by humans to overcome chaos and random violence. To achieve this goal, culture creates and maintains the system of differences between us and them, between here and there, between this and that. This system is identified by Girard as the "scapegoat mechanism" or victimization. This system, often unconsciously produced, allows members of the society to converge upon a scapegoat or victim, represented by them, there, and that. The result of this victimization is what Girard

---

[11] Williams, *The Girard Reader*, 9.

terms "scapegoat as effect"; that is, "that strange process through which two or more people are reconciled at the expense of the third party who appears guilty or responsible for whatever ails, disturbs, or frightens the scapegoaters. They feel relieved of their tensions and they coalesce into a more harmonious group. They now have a single purpose, which is to prevent the scapegoat from harming them, by expelling and destroying him."[12]

Girard calls this identification and lynching of a victim by the community the "single victim mechanism." This mechanism is the work of Satan and *is* Satan. Satan is the "accuser," or more precisely, the community's power of accusing someone and turning him or her into a scapegoat to be eliminated in order to overcome the disorder (the "scandal") produced by mimetic desire and restore order to the community. The victim is demonized and is regarded as the devil in whom the power of Satan dwells.

Religion reinforces and is reinforced by this "single victim mechanism" through mythology and ritual. In mythology, Girard points out, there is real violence though it is often disguised. Despite their fantastic elements, myths speak of situations of real social crisis, disorder, and violence, and these situations are resolved by means of the community's violent act of killing the scapegoat. However, this violence is disguised by the fact that in these myths the community really believes in the guilt of the victim. The community transfers blame to the victim and is therefore exonerated.[13] In religious rituals, again according to Girard, the act of sacrifice is rooted in the single victim mechanism. Rituals reenact the community's ancient act of killing the animal or human scapegoat to gain relief from the conflict and violence caused by mimetic desire, or they "re-actualize" the community's act of expelling the victim from its midst after transferring its guilt to him or her (symbolized, for example, by the driving of the he-goat into the desert, as prescribed in Leviticus 19). Ritual sacrifices therefore participate in the victimization system of society. Just as human culture originates in the "founding murder," as narrated in myths such as the Babylonian story of Marduk's creation of the world by means of the body of Tiamat, whom he has slain, so religion with its ritual sacrifices is steeped in conflict and violence.

If Girard's universal anthropology with its threefold process of mimetic desire, violence, and scapegoating is correct—and there is much in it that commends itself, though it does not lack critics[14]—then violence is not merely an

---

[12] Ibid., 12.

[13] For Girard's analysis of violence in myths, see his *The Scapegoat*, trans. Yvonne Freccero (London: The Athlone Press, 1986).

[14] Critics have pointed out that Girard's theory of the founding murders and the origin of human culture and religion in mimetic desire and scapegoating is highly speculative and cannot be verified empirically. Furthermore, they have objected to his reduction of religion to the sole function of preventing violence. In addition, it has been noted that not all religious sacrifices imply bloodshed and violence, since there are in many religions bloodless sacrifices such as offerings of fruits, grains, foods from plants, milk and milk products, and alcoholic libations. Also, sacrifices need not always stem from victimization. As Girard himself has lately acknowledged, it may indicate a person's willingness to give himself or herself up to others or to God out of love and faithfulness to

aberration of misguided and overzealous fundamentalists and extremists, easy targets of exploitation by callous and unscrupulous politicians, but is endemic to religion itself and to human culture, of which religion is an essential component. Hence, the attempt to exculpate religion and blame violence on uninformed and misguided religious adepts not only fails to understand its intrinsic connection with violence but also perpetuates the process of concealing and disguising the origin of violence itself.

RELIGION
AND PEACEBUILDING

So far we have considered Girard's two discoveries, namely, mimetic desire and scapegoating, in showing how violence is endemic to religion. There is, however, a third discovery, one that is of great interest for our theme, which Girard sees as the linchpin of his "anthropology of the cross."[15] Girard holds that the Bible, and in particular the Gospels, unmask the victim mechanism that is operative in culture and religion and shows that unlike the scapegoating mob, the Christian God takes the side of the victim. By analyzing biblical narratives such as Cain and Abel, Joseph and his brothers, Job and his friends, the Servant of Yahweh songs, the prophets' condemnation of sacrifices, a number of psalms, and above all, the teaching, death, and resurrection of Jesus,[16] Girard argues that in the history of Israel and in Jesus, God appears as the innocent victim who suffers death as a scapegoat. In this way, far from demanding victims and sacrifices, the God of Jesus exposes and subverts the scapegoat mechanism as a fraud and a deception and responds to our mimetic rivalry and violent victimization with nonviolent love. That God is on the side of the victim is, for Girard, the center and the uniqueness of biblical revelation and religion, and it challenges Christians to be nonviolent.

Whether Girard's claim that nonviolence is unique to Hebrew-Christian religion is valid will be examined shortly. But there is no doubt whatsoever that Jesus enjoins nonviolence on his followers. Nor is there any doubt that Jesus and his God take the side of the victim, as liberation theologians of every stripe have been asserting with their notion of the preferential option for the poor. Before considering how religion and in particular Christianity, despite their legacies of violence, can contribute to peacemaking and peacebuilding, it will be helpful to determine the nature of the nonviolence that is commanded by Jesus.

---

the other. In sum, it is doubtful that scapegoating is as universal as Girard claims, even though his theory does illumine a wide range of elements of culture and religion, especially their connections with violence and war. For an insightful evaluation of Girard's theory of violence, scapegoating, and religion, see Lefebure, *Revelation, the Religions, and Violence*, 20–23.

[15] Williams, *The Girard Reader*, 294.

[16] See René Girard, *Job: The Victim of His People*, trans. Yvonne Freccero (London: The Athlone Press, 1987).

Jesus and Nonviolent Resistance

Jesus' nonviolence has sometimes been understood to mean non-resistance, violent or otherwise. His statements about not resisting evil, turning the other cheek, giving up the cloak, going the second mile are often cited in support of this interpretation. However, such an interpretation is obviously unfounded, since Jesus embodied in his own ministry and death a most radical resistance to evil of every kind. Jesus' nonviolence is not, as Walter Wink has convincingly shown, a rejection of non-resistance but of both passivity and violence. As Wink puts it, Jesus's is the "third way": "A way that is neither submission nor assault, flight or fight, a way that can secure your human dignity and begin to change the power equation, even now, before the revolution."[17]

In this context Wink offers an insightful interpretation of Jesus' sayings on nonviolent resistance, which have often been misunderstood. "Do not resist an evildoer" (Mt 5:39) does not mean remaining passive but rather not resisting an evildoer with violent means. The Greek word for "resist" is *antistenai* (literally, to stand [*stenai*] against [*anti*]), which is often used in the Greek version of the Hebrew Bible as a technical term for warfare, where the two opposing armies march toward each other until they "stand against" each other. "Turn the other cheek [that is, the left cheek]" (Mt 5:39) to someone striking you on the right cheek does not mean to allow the attacker to harm you further but is rather an act of defiance against the striker. This is so because someone can strike you on the right cheek only by using a backslap with his right hand, since it is forbidden to use the left hand except for unclean tasks. Thus, by offering the left cheek you prevent your striker from backslapping you further with his right hand. And if your opponent strikes your left cheek with his right fist, he makes himself your social equal, which of course he does not wish to do, since only equals fight with fists. "Give the cloak as well" (Mt 5:40) is not letting the creditor commit further injustice against the debtor but allowing oneself to be stripped naked and in this way exposing the cruelty and brutality of the social system by which the creditor has exploited the debtor in the first place. "Go also the second mile" (Mt 5:41) is not submitting oneself to further forced labor but inducing the soldier to commit an infraction of the military code that permitted the carrying of the pack for one mile only and thus exposing the culprit to severe penalties.[18]

Religious Peacemaking and Peacebuilding

Clearly, then, Jesus advocated resistance, but only by nonviolent means. But what must Christians do, theoretically and practically, in order to follow Jesus' nonviolent way? How can Christianity as an institution work for peacemaking and peacebuilding?

---

[17] Wink, *The Powers That Be*, 110.

[18] See ibid, 98–109; and Walter Wink, "Beyond Just War and Pacifism: Jesus' Nonviolent Way," *Review and Expositor* 89 (1992): 197–214.

On the theoretical level, the first task is to rethink the just-war doctrine. This is not the place to rehearse the long history of the development of this doctrine.[19] Suffice it to note that the various conditions that have been set for a just war can hardly, if ever, be realized, especially today, given the existence of nuclear weapons and the nature of stateless terrorism and "asymmetrical warfare."[20] Drew Christiansen has pointed out that in the post–Vatican II era the Catholic church has moved toward to a hybrid doctrine of just war and nonviolence according to which the constant commitment must be "to strive for justice through nonviolent means," while acknowledging that "when sustained attempts at nonviolent action fail to protect the innocent against fundamental injustice, then legitimate political authorities are permitted as a last resort to employ limited force to rescue the innocent and establish peace."[21] Christiansen also notes how recent popes, in particular John Paul II, and various officials of the Vatican have expressed serious doubt about the usefulness as well as the applicability of the just-war doctrine in our present condition.[22]

---

[19] For a lucid summary, see Kenneth R. Himes, "Pacifism and the Just War Tradition in Roman Catholic Social Teaching," in *One Hundred Years of Catholic Social Thought: Celebration and Challenge*, ed. John A. Coleman, 329–44 (Maryknoll, N.Y.: Orbis Books, 1991); idem, "War," *The New Dictionary of Catholic Social Thought*, ed. Judith A. Dwyer, 977–82 (Collegeville, Minn.: The Liturgical Press, 1994); Joseph Cardinal Bernardin, "*The Challenge of Peace* Revisited," in Coleman, *One Hundred Years of Catholic Social Thought*, 273–85; and Brian Wicker, "War," in *The Oxford Companion to Christian Thought*, ed. Adrian Hastings, Alistair Mason, and Hugh Piper, 746–48 (Oxford: Oxford University Press, 2000).

[20] The conditions for a just war are of two kinds: those concerning the going to war (*jus ad bellum*) and those regarding the conduct of war (*jus in bello*). The former include just cause, comparative justice, legitimate authority, peaceful intention, proportionality, last resort, and probability of success; the latter include noncombatant immunity, right intention, proportionality, humane treatment of prisoners, and observance of international treaties and conventions. As far as just cause is concerned, traditionally the church has recognized three appeals: to vindicate rights, to repel unjust attack, and to avenge injury. Pope Pius XII, because of his experiences of the Second World War, restricted the appeals to just one: defense against aggression.

[21] D. Christiansen, "Whither the 'Just War?'" *America* 188/10 (March 24, 2000), 8. Christiansen summarizes here the position of the November 1993 document of the U.S. Catholic bishops *The Harvest of Justice Is Sown in Peace*. This deep commitment to the use of nonviolent means to resolve international conflicts needs constant repeating in light of the Bush administration's immoral doctrine and policy of "preemptive war."

[22] For a recent official statement of the National Conference of Catholic Bishops of the United States, see *The Harvest of Justice Is Sown in Peace*. The current position of the Catholic church on war is well summarized by Clarke E. Cochran and David Carroll Cochran, *Catholics, Politics, and Public Policy: Beyond Left and Right* (Maryknoll, N.Y.: Orbis Books, 2003), 189–99: "First, a basic presumption against war and its moral condemnation in general have become much more prominent. . . . Second, the requirements for a war to be deemed just have become more strict. Only defense against unjust aggression, or coming to the aid of others suffering such aggression, justifies going to war, and only then as a last resort. . . . Third, rejection of war in favor of nonviolence, though not replacing the just war framework, has been elevated to the position of a legitimate alternative within the church, to the point that the American bishops, writing in their 1993 statement *The Harvest of Justice Is Sown in Peace*, refer to the church's 'dual tradition.'"

Even if one continues to hold on to the just-war doctrine, it is important to recall that it was not developed to justify war but to promote peace by curbing violence and limiting as far as possible the damages of warfare. Indeed, one of the conditions for a just war is the "right intention," with which the combatants must aim at achieving a genuine peace as soon as possible. Hence, the second theoretical task incumbent upon Christians is to develop a comprehensive theology of peace, which is still in its infancy. Since peace is not just the absence of war but an "enterprise of justice" and the "fruit of love," as Vatican II affirms (*GS*, no. 78), a full-fledged theology of peace must be related to the theology of economic and social rights, justice, liberation, and ecology.

As a preliminary step, such a theology must unmask what Walter Wink calls the "Domination System," that is, the network of what the New Testament calls the "principalities and powers" (Eph 6:12) that conspire to subjugate humans by means of violence. This Domination System is constituted by, in Wink's description, "unjust economic relations, oppressive political relations, biased race relations, patriarchal gender relations, hierarchical power relations, and the use of violence to maintain them all."[23] At the heart of this system is the "myth of redemptive violence," that is, the belief that "violence saves, that war brings peace, that might makes right."[24] This myth is the hidden message of the Babylonian story of creation, according to which the cosmos is fashioned out of the dismembered body of a goddess (as René Girard reminds us with his notion of mimetic desire and scapegoating); of children's cartoon shows; of comics, video and computer games, and action movies; of the national security state. This same myth of redemptive violence also lurks behind the just-war doctrine, with its seductive assumption that when all else fails, violence is still the savior. To counteract this myth of redemptive violence, it is useful to recall that pacifism understood as nonviolent resistance is an authentic heritage of the gospel tradition, much more so than the just-war doctrine.[25]

The next step in a theology of peace is to construct what Mary Evelyn Jegen calls "a revisionist history of peace,"[26] that is, a rereading of human history not as a succession of conflicts and wars, punctuated by brief periods of truce, but as humanity's continuous collective effort at creating culture and a civilization of love. As John Paul II has said:

Let us . . . learn to reread the history of peoples and of mankind, following outlines that are truer than those of the series of wars and revolutions.

---

[23] Wink, *The Powers That Be*, 39.

[24] Ibid., 42.

[25] As Kenneth R. Himes correctly points out, according to the Catholic tradition pacifism is an individual's right, based on the dignity of the conscience, to reject violence as a means to achieve peace. It is an option for individuals and not a duty for all. It requires a clear commitment to resist injustice and an effort to promote human rights and the common good. It does not invalidate the state's right to engage in war as the last resort for self-defense (see Himes, "Pacifism and the Just War Tradition," 329–44).

[26] Mary Evelyn Jegen, "Peace and Pluralism: Church and Churches," in Coleman, *One Hundred Years of Catholic Social Thought*, 288.

Admittedly the din of battle dominates history. But it is the respites from violence that have made possible the production of those lasting cultural works which give honor to mankind. Furthermore, any factors of life and progress that may have been found in wars and revolutions were derived from aspirations of an order other than that of violence.[27]

An essential part of this theology of peace is a retelling of the lives and work of peacemakers and peacebuilders, saints and martyrs of our time.[28] In addition, careful attention must be paid to the success stories of nonviolent resistance in solving national and international conflicts (in places as diverse as the Philippines and Eastern Europe), as well as to the achievements, often unknown and unsung, of various organizations, both religious and secular, in reconciliation and peacebuilding. Lessons should then be drawn from their visions and strategies to be applied, with appropriate modifications, to other situations in the future. R. Scott Appleby has documented in detail the contributions to world peace that have been made by the "militants for peace," in particular the Mennonite Central Committee, the World Conference on Religion and Peace (an NGO affiliated with the United Nations), and the Comunità di Sant'Egidio in Rome.[29] Appleby has also shown that the Catholic church in particular, thanks to its world view, its hierarchical organization, and its multinational and multicultural resources, is in a privileged position to contribute to peacebuilding.[30]

On the practical level, the American bishops have recommended the following actions to build up peace: (1) strengthening global institutions (for example, the United Nations); (2) securing human rights; (3) assuring sustainable and equitable development; (4) restraining nationalism and eliminating religious violence (respect for the right of self-determination, respect for minority rights, commitment to tolerance, solidarity, dialogue, and reconciliation); and (5) building cooperative security to face challenges such as stopping nuclear proliferation and promoting nuclear disarmament, general global demilitarization, economic sanctions, humanitarian intervention, and global responses to regional conflicts.[31]

This agenda, which highlights the intrinsic connection between peace and justice, can be fully achieved only if religions are harnessed to the task in conjunction with secular organizations, both governmental and nongovernmental.

---

[27] John Paul II, "To Reach Peace, Teach Peace," message for the World Day of Peace, 1979, quoted in Jegen, "Peace and Pluralism," 288.

[28] See, for instance, the books by Michael True, *Justice Seekers, Peace Makers* (Mystic, Conn.: Twenty-Third Publications, 1985), and *To Construct Peace* (Mystic, Conn.: Twenty-Third Publications, 1992).

[29] See Appleby, *The Ambivalence of the Sacred*, 121–65.

[30] R. Scott Appleby, "Catholic Peacebuilding," *America* 189/6 (September 2003), 12–15. Appleby mentions the recent formation of a Catholic peacebuilding network whose initial members include Catholic Relief Services, the United States Conference of Catholic Bishops, the Center for Mission Research and Study at Maryknoll, Pax Christi, the Comunità di Sant'Egidio, and several Catholic colleges and universities.

[31] See NCCB, *The Harvest of Justice Is Sown in Peace*, section II ("The Challenges of Peace in a New World: An Agenda for Peacemaking").

Whether religions, despite their legacy of violence, can today contribute to peacemaking and peacebuilding is no longer a moot point. The fact is that in many parts of the world they have demonstrably done so, and against facts there is no gainsaying *(contra factum non datur argumentum)*.[32] Even the ambivalent legacy of religions, it may be argued, opens a window of opportunity for them to be an effective player in the construction of peace and justice, provided that the religious leadership and religious actors are willing to use their power and resources, in collaboration with their secular counterparts, to resist forces of extremism and to train the local grassroots members and the middle management in the skills required for peace education, conflict prevention, mediation, conflict resolution, reconciliation, and social reconstruction. As R. Scott Appleby has insightfully remarked:

> The ambivalence of religion toward violence, toward the sacred itself, is actually good news for those who recognize, correctly, that religion will continue to be a major force in determining the quality and kind of relations among disparate peoples. Ambivalence provides an opening, an opportunity to cultivate tolerance and openness toward the other; indeed, religions, despite the shameful record of a minority of their adherents, are strikingly accomplished in developing their own traditions of peace-related practices and concepts. Lifting up, celebrating, and empowering those elements of the religious community are acts of civic responsibility in today's world.[33]

But is Christianity, with its revelation of a God who is the innocent victim, the only religion that can break the cycle of violence, the vicious triangle of mimetic desire–violence–scapegoating, as René Girard has claimed, and build up reconciliation and peace? If not, must it not learn from the experiences and teachings of other religions?

Asian Non-Christian Religions and Peacebuilding

In his detailed study of violence and religions, in particular Judaism and Christianity, Leo D. Lefebure notes that many earlier biblical scholars, especially those of the Biblical Theological Movement, sought to identify the originality of the revelation in the Hebrew and Christian religions by sharply *contrasting* it with that of other religions, often arguing for the former's difference from and superiority to the latter and ignoring their mutual historical connections. Recent scholarship has shown that this contrasting method, which tends to highlight the Hebrew-Christian revelation as God's acts in history in opposition to the other religions as ahistorical and purely human quests for philosophical

---

[32] For a brief exposition of the contribution of all major religions to justice and peacebuilding, see, besides the work by Appleby cited above, Francis Arinze, *Religions for Peace* (New York: Doubleday, 2002).

[33] Appleby, *The Ambivalence of the Sacred*, 306–7.

wisdom, does not do justice to the complexity of the relationship between Hebrew religion and other ancient traditions, especially in their wisdom traditions. This mutual relationship is well described by Lefebure: "Israel did not simply reject the religions of its neighbors; it frequently drew elements of other religious traditions into a new synthesis of its own. The originality of Israel's religion often lay not in formulating absolutely new ideas, but in reconfiguring ideas and practices of other traditions into a new whole."[34]

Unfortunately, the contrasting method is implicitly operative in René Girard's analysis of biblical traditions on violence. While it is true that the Hebrew-Christian God rejects the violence of the scapegoating system and takes sides with the victims, this conception of the deity is neither unique nor the only one present in the Bible. Girard has ignored or played down the many "texts of terror" of both the Old and New Testaments, whose embarrassing violence later theologians will attempt to attenuate by an allegorical interpretation. Raymond Schwager points out that there are six hundred passages of explicit violence in the Hebrew Bible, one thousand verses where God's own violent actions of punishment are described, a hundred passages where Yahweh expressly commands others to kill, and several stories where God irrationally kills or tries to kill for no apparent reason.[35] Michel Desjardins notes that while there is an insistent call to peace in the New Testament, there are in it many aspects, especially the apocalyptic notion of a cosmic war, that cannot easily be reconciled with the call to peace.[36] Indeed, it must be honestly acknowledged that in the Hebrew-Christian imagination the Crucified God stands side by side with God the Warrior.

Nor can Girard's claim for the uniqueness of the Hebrew-Christian God's identification with victims and God's rejection of victimization and violence be sustained. Nonviolence and the call for peace are also present in non-Christian religions, as I will show by focusing on the concept of harmony in Confucianism and of "mindfulness" as proposed by the Vietnamese Buddhist monk Thich Nhat Hanh in his teaching on "Engaged Buddhism."

Peace as Universal Harmony

Harmony is arguably the central concept of Asian cultures and religions in general.[37] It is said to constitute "the intellectual and affective, religious and

---

[34] See Lefebure, *Revelation, the Religions, and Violence*, 31.

[35] See Raymond Schwager, *Must There Be Scapegoats?* (San Francisco: HarperSanFrancisco, 1987).

[36] See Michel Desjardins, *Peace, Violence, and the New Testament* (Sheffield, England: Sheffield Academic Press, 1997).

[37] Given the centrality of harmony in Asian religions, it has been made the theme of a lengthy document of the Theological Advisory Commission of the Federation of Asian Bishops' Conferences entitled *Asian Christian Perspectives on Harmony* (1996). This text is available in *For All Peoples of Asia: Federation of Asian Bishops' Conferences*, vol. 2, *Documents from 1992 to 1996*, ed. Franz-Josef Eilers (Quezon City, Philippines: Claretian Publications, 1997), 229–98.

artistic, personal and social soul of both persons and institutions in Asia."[38] Harmony was the overriding concern of Confucius (ca. 551–479 B.C.E.) and of Confucianism as an ethical, social, political, and religious system of thought.[39] Having witnessed the disintegration of the feudal order, an era characterized by a constant internecine warfare among the states and the tyranny and venality of the rulers, Confucius urged a system of morality and statecraft that would preserve peace and produce a just and stable government. He believed that such a moral and political order could be achieved by returning to the way of virtues practiced by the sage emperors of antiquity.

To appreciate the central role given to harmony by Confucianism, it is necessary to place it within Confucian metaphysics according to which there are three ultimates or three powers of the universe: Heaven *(t'ien)*, Earth *(di)*, and Humanity *(jen)*. Heaven stands for a variety of things: the universe or the cosmos (in this sense, it includes Earth); the complex of ethical principles governing and sanctioning human behavior (comparable to natural law); and most important, the Lord or Supreme Being or the Ultimate Reality, who governs the material and spiritual worlds and to whom humans are answerable for their destiny. Earth stands for the material world in which humans live and act as responsible beings. Humanity stands for both the individual person and the human society (that is, the family, the state, and the international community).

According to Confucius, in trying to achieve harmony with Heaven, Earth, oneself, and others, humans must follow the Way *(Tao)*, which originates from Heaven and Earth and is the universal source of the meaning and value of human life. The Way is the foundation of a harmonious universe, a peaceful society, and a good life. It brings about the realization of the fundamental Confucian principle, namely, the harmonious unity of Heaven and Humanity *(t'ien-jen ho-yi)*. Since the Way brings about the harmony between Heaven and Humanity, it may be distinguished into three: the Way of Heaven, the Way of Humanity, and the Way of Harmony.

What is of immediate interest to us is the Way of Harmony. In Confucianism, the Way of Harmony is not merely a collection of ethical rules and norms

---

[38] Ibid., 2:232.

[39] The literature on Confucius and Confucianism is immense. An excellent introduction is Xinzhong Yao, *An Introduction to Confucianism* (Cambridge: Cambridge University Press, 2000), with an extensive bibliography. In this essay I use *Confucius* and *Confucianism* interchangeably, without making a distinction between what can be established as belonging to the historical Confucius and the later developments of his thought. Yao has helpfully distinguished five stages of Confucianism: in formation (Confucius and his immediate disciples, in particular Mengzi and Xunzi), in adaptation (during the Han and Wei-Jin dynasties), in transformation (Neo-Confucianism during the Song-Ming dynasties), in variation (Confucianism as appropriated and modified by other countries of East Asia, in particular Korea, Vietnam, and Japan), and in renovation (Confucianism as developed in contact with Western philosophies and Christianity) (see Yao, *An Introduction to Confucianism*, 7–9). For an extensive account of the evolution and transformation of Confucianism, see ibid., 68–137. For a collection of Chinese philosophical texts, see *A Source Book in Chinese Philosophy*, trans. and comp. Wing-Tsit Chan (Princeton, N.J.: Princeton University Press, 1963).

for conflict resolution and peacebuilding. As a central theme running through Confucian doctrine and its culmination, it is the point where the Way of Heaven and the Way of Humanity converge. In a word, it is a spirituality, a total way of living. Xinzhong Yao expresses succinctly how harmony penetrates all levels and dimensions of Confucian discourses:

> In terms of metaphysics, a harmonious relation between Heavens and humans refers to harmony between spirit and material, between form and matter, between mind and body, and between the one (the universal) and the many (the particular). In a religious sense, it indicates a continual process between this life and the life hereafter, between the divine and the secular, and between heavenly principles and human behavior. In the area of naturalism, it points to the unity between humans and Nature, between beings (the living) and things (the existent), and between the social and the natural. From the perspective of politics, it affects the unity between the ruled and the ruling, between the government and the mandate to govern, and inspires the people to correct disorder and chaos in order to attain peace and harmony.[40]

Originally a musical term, harmony indicates first of all a person's inner state, in which all feelings and emotions are properly expressed. As the book *Doctrine of the Mean* puts it: "Before the feelings of pleasure, anger, sorrow, and joy are aroused, it [the emotional state] is called equilibrium (*chung*, centrality, mean). When these feelings are aroused and each and all attain due measure and degree, it is called harmony. Equilibrium is the great foundation of the world, and harmony its universal path."[41]

The way to harmony within oneself must be built, according to Confucius, on the virtue of *jen*, variously translated "benevolence," "humaneness," "human-heartedness." Confucius views humans as essentially social beings, constituted by various relationships, and *jen* is the virtue by which these relationships are lived out correctly and properly. There are basically five reciprocal relationships: sovereign and subject, parent and child, husband and wife, elder and younger sibling, and friend and friend. Each of these relationships brings with it duties and obligations proper to each person in the relationship. The duties and obligations are mutual, and their performance is governed by the Golden Rule.

Jen is achieved through the observance of a complex of rituals, ceremonies, and proper social behaviors called *li*. The knowledge of *li* is obtained through the study of ancient poetry, rituals, and music. Though basically concerned with regulating human behavior, *li* has a magical quality associated with ritual, music, and incantation. It has the power to induce people to do the right thing without strenuous efforts. In such moral self-cultivation, a person will acquire the five basic Confucian virtues: beside *jen* and *li*, these are righteousness *(yi)*,

---

[40] Yao, *An Introduction to Confucianism*, 173.
[41] Chan, *A Source Book in Chinese Philosophy*, 98.

wisdom *(chih)*, and faithfulness *(hsin)*. In practicing *jen* any person, irrespective of his or her social class, can become a *chün-tzu*, that is, a "gentleman." Originally, *jen* designated a member of the aristocracy. Confucius used it to refer to character rather than birth. The gentleman is one who never loses sight of virtue; in everything he does, he does not look for profit but does what is right. Virtue stands as its own reward.

It is of extreme importance to note that for Confucianism, the cornerstone of all harmony, peace, and order is the intellectual, moral, and spiritual self-cultivation of the individual. The book *The Great Learning* delineates the achievement of universal harmony and peace in eight successive steps. The first five concern the total and comprehensive cultivation of the self: investigation of things, extension of knowledge, sincerity of the will, rectification of the mind, and cultivation of personal life. The sixth step is the regulation of the family. The seventh step is the ordering of the state. The eighth step is the peacebuilding or pacification of the world. The progressive order is from the individual to the family to the state and to the world: "From the Son of Heaven to the common people, all must regard cultivation of the personal life as the root and foundation."[42]

Though primarily a personal ethics, Confucian ethics is essentially social and political.[43] This is so because, for Confucius, the human person is constituted by a network of relationships, such that the family is merely an extension of the individual, the state an extension of the family, and the international order an extension of the state. Consequently, only a ruler who sincerely and truly practices the virtues is worthy to rule and is able to bring prosperity and peace to his subjects. For Confucianism, the real task of the political ruler is promoting morality, not establishing legislation, much less using force.[44] Confucianism offers three measures to bind the ruler to morality. The first is the doctrine of the Mandate of Heaven, according to which a ruler's government is legitimate only if it is supported by the people; it is a version of the doctrine of the "sovereignty of the people." The second is the ruler's obligation to venerate his ancestors and to preserve ancient culture; in this way the ruler must show himself worthy of the blessings, including the power to rule, he has received from his ancestors. The third is the doctrine of the loss of the Mandate of Heaven, by which it is said that Heaven withdraws its mandate from an immoral ruler and hence his subjects are no longer required to show loyalty and obedience.

---

[42] Ibid., 87.

[43] For a discussion of Confucian social and political ethics with extensive quotations from the Confucian classics, see Li Fu Chen, *The Confucian Way: A New and Systematic Study of 'The Four Books,'* trans. Shih Shun Liu (London and New York: KPI Ltd., 1987), 412–580; and David L. Hall and Roger T. Ames, *Thinking Through Confucius* (Albany, N.Y.: State University of New York Press, 1987), 131–92.

[44] Confucianism rejected the so-called School of Law or Legalism *(fa jia)*, which advocated the use of laws (the penal code) and military force to establish social order. During the Ch'in dynasty (221–206 B.C.E.), the School of Law overwhelmed Confucianism and all other schools by helping the first emperor of the Ch'in dynasty to unify the whole of China.

Because it relies on the practice of virtues by both the ruler and his subjects as the foundation for social order and harmony, Confucianism rejects violence and the use of lethal force. In particular, it condemns capital punishment and war. It regards punishment as an inferior way of governing; indeed, resorting to killing in order to maintain order is considered a failure on the part of the ruler. When asked if it is lawful to execute people for their crimes, Confucius categorically denied its legitimacy and argued that there was no need to kill those who fail to follow the Way since if "your evinced desires be for what is good, the people will be good."[45] War destroys people's lives, because in war the warring rulers, as Mencius puts it, "rob their people of their time, so that they cannot plough and weed their fields, in order to support their parents. Their parents suffer from cold and hunger. Brothers, wives, and children are separated and scattered abroad."[46] For Confucius, the most effective way to defend one's country from aggression is not to build up arms but to strengthen the people's trust. Asked which of the three things is most important for the well-being and security of the people, food, arms, or trust, Confucius replied: "The requisites of government are that there be sufficiency of food, sufficiency of military equipment, and the confidence of the people in their ruler. . . . But if the people have no faith in their ruler, there is no standing for the State."[47]

Despite its insistent appeal to the ruler to govern by moral self-cultivation and virtue and not by force and violence, and despite its strong opposition to war and killing, Confucianism does not advocate strict pacifism. Confronted with the brutal reality of unjust aggression, it has developed a version of the just-war theory: "A just war is the one waged by righteous people, for good causes, and for 'punishing the tyranny and consoling the people.'"[48] Nevertheless, it is still true that Confucianism vastly prefers to secure peace and harmony by means of virtue rather by means of law and violence: "Lead the people with administrative policies and organize them with penal law, and they will avoid punishments but will be without a sense of shame. Lead them with *te* [virtue] and organize them with ritual actions, and they will have a sense of shame and moreover will order themselves harmoniously."[49]

Finally, with regard to rituals and sacrifices, which occupy a central position in the Confucian practice of *li*, it is to be noted that there is no place for violence and scapegoating. In the three major sacrifices offered to Heaven, to the ancestors, and to Confucius himself, there is no killing of victims as scapegoats for the sins of the community. Rather, as the *Book of Rites* declares of the offerings: "The fruits and grains presented in the high dishes of wood and bamboo were the product of the harmonious influences of the four seasons. The tribute of

---

[45] Confucius, *The Analects,* XII, 19. The English translation is by James Legge in *Confucius: Confucian Analects, the Great Learning and The Doctrine of the Mean* (New York: Dover Publications, 1971), 258.

[46] *The Works of Mencius*, Part I, chap. V, 4, trans. James Legge (New York: Dover Publications, 1970), 135–36.

[47] Confucius, *The Analects*, XII, 7.

[48] Yao, *An Introduction to Confucianism*, 187.

[49] Confucius, *The Analects*, II, 3.

metal showed the harmonious submission (of the princes). The rolls of silk showed the honour they rendered to virtue."[50] Furthermore, Confucianism insists that the primary purpose of sacrifices is not to obtain material benefits but rather to attain moral perfection, with a sincere attitude, a reverential heart, and a virtuous motive. Indeed, only persons who have gained moral perfection or have made a great contribution to the spiritual and material well-being of the people are entitled to perform sacrificial rituals.[51]

Engaged Buddhism and Peacebuilding

To Confucians, especially the Neo-Confucians of the Sung-Ming dynasties (960–1644), Buddhism, which was introduced from India into China in the first century C.E., appeared to be otherworldly and to shirk social and political responsibilities. To them, Buddhism was solely concerned with the liberation of the individual from the cycle of rebirth and suffering and neglected the task of contributing to a more peaceful and just society.

Buddhists, of course, rebut such accusations by showing how the Buddha's way of wisdom and compassion has intrinsic social and political implications. The Buddha's teaching on non-self *(anatta* or *anatman)*, that is, on the illusion of a separate, independent existence, which is the central tenet of Buddhism, is another way of affirming the essential interdependence of all beings (what René Girard calls "interdividuals"). According to this doctrine, no being is an independent, isolated, self-contained unit. On the contrary, each and every being is constituted by an ongoing and constant process of interaction with all other beings, past, present, and future. This metaphysics of non-self led the Buddha to reject the caste system inherent in Hinduism, with its unjust social divisions. He also rejected the Vedic system of sacrifices, which perpetuated violence and social apartheid. Instead, he advocated the alternative practice of compassion and generosity toward all living beings, which excludes any form of mimetic desire, rivalry, and violent scapegoating. Furthermore, the Eightfold Path that the Buddha prescribed demands moral behavior (right speech, right action, and right livelihood), meditation (right effort, right mindfulness, and right concentration), and wisdom (right insight and right thought) that will bring about a new social and political order based on nonviolence and compassion.

These socio-political insights and teachings of the Buddha have recently been retrieved and put into practice in the service of justice and peace by the proponents of Engaged Buddhism.[52] This last part of the chapter will examine the

---

[50] *The Li Ki or the Collection of Treatises on the Rules of Propriety or Ceremonial Usages*, trans. James Legge, vol. 27 of *The Sacred Books of the East* (Oxford: Clarendon Press, 1885), 413.

[51] On sacrifices in Confucianism, see Yao, *An Introduction to Confucianism*, 191–209.

[52] On Engaged Buddhism, see Kenneth Kraft, ed., *Inner Peace, World Peace: Essays on Buddhism and Nonviolence* (Albany, N.Y.: State University of New York Press, 1992); Kenneth Kraft, ed., *The Wheel of Engaged Buddhism: A New Map of the Path* (New York: Weatherhill Press, 2000); Christopher S. Queen, ed., *Engaged Buddhism in*

contribution of Buddhism to peacemaking and peacebuilding by studying the life and work of the Vietnamese Buddhist monk Thich Nhat Hanh.[53]

Thich Nhat Hanh is the name given to Nguyen Xuan Bao (b. 1926) at his ordination as a Buddhist monk in 1949. He soon left Central Vietnam for Saigon (now Ho Chi Minh City) and took part in the development of the South Vietnam School of Buddhist Studies. In 1955 Nhat Hanh became editor of the journal *Vietnamese Buddhism* and began advocating the unification of the different branches of Vietnamese Buddhism into a single organization. His ideas were not acceptable to the Buddhist leaders, and the journal was closed down. With some friends Nhat Hanh bought a piece of land in the highlands, about a hundred miles from Saigon, where he established a contemplative community called Fragrant Palm Hamlet. As his writings became better known, they met with opposition from both Buddhist leaders and the Ngo Dinh Diem government. In 1962 Nhat Hanh left for the United States to study at Princeton University, and a year later he was invited to teach at Columbia University. In November 1963 Ngo Dinh Diem was assassinated, and at the beginning of the following year Nhat Hanh returned to Vietnam.

Toward the end of 1964 Nhat Hanh saw his dream of a unified Buddhist organization realized. He also founded the School of Youth for Social Services as an example of what he called Engaged Buddhism in the service of the war victims, especially in the villages, in the areas of health, organization, education, and

---

the West (Boston: Wisdom Publications, 2000); Fred Eppsteiner, ed., *The Path of Compassion: Writings on Socially Engaged Buddhism* (Berkeley, Calif.: Parallax Press,1988); Christopher S. Queen and Sallie B. King, eds., *Engaged Buddhism: Buddhist Liberation Movements in Asia* (Albany, N.Y.: State University of New York Press, 1996); Christopher Queen et al., *Action Dharma: New Studies in Engaged Buddhism* (Richmond, Surrey, Great Britain: Curzon Press, 2003); Arnold Kotler, ed., *Engaged Buddhist Reader: Ten Years of Engaged Buddhist Publishing* (Berkeley, Calif.: Parallax Press, 1997); and Susan Moon, *Not Turning Away: The Practice of Engaged Buddhism* (Boston: Shambhala Press, 2004).

[53] Among Thich Nhat Hanh's prolific writings, the following are to be noted: *Being Peace* (Berkeley, Calif.: Parallax Press, 1987); *Present Moment Wonderful Moment* (Berkeley, Calif.: Parallax Press, 1990); *Cultivating the Mind of Love: The Practice of Looking Deeply in the Mahayana Buddhist Tradition* (Berkeley, Calif.: Parallax Press, 1996); *The Heart of the Buddha's Teaching: Transforming Suffering into Peace, Joy and Liberation: The Four Noble Truths, The Eightfold Path, and Other Buddhist Basic Teaching* (Berkeley, Calif.: Parallax Press, 1998); *Interbeing: Fourteen Guidelines for Engaged Buddhism* (Berkeley, Calif.: Parallax Press, 1998); *Living Buddha, Living Christ* (New York: Riverhead Books, 1995); *Love in Action: Writings on Nonviolent Social Change* (Berkeley, Calif.: Parallax Press, 1993); (with Daniel Berrigan), *The Raft Is Not the Shore: Conversations toward a Buddhist-Christian Awareness* (Boston: Beacon Press, 1975; Maryknoll, N.Y.: Orbis Books, 2001); *The Sun My Heart: From Mindfulness to Insight Contemplation* (Berkeley, Calif.: Parallax Press, 1988); *Teachings on Love* (Berkeley, Calif.: Parallax Press, 1998); *The Heart of Understanding: Commentaries on the Prajnaparamita Heart Sutra* (Berkeley, Calif.: Parallax Press, 1998); *Touching Peace* (Berkeley, Calif.: Parallax Press, 1992); *Transformation and Healing: The Sutra on the Four Establishments of Mindfulness* (Berkeley, Calif.: Parallax Press, 1990). A very useful selection of Thich Nhat Hanh's writings is found in *Thich Nhat Hanh: Essential Writings*, ed. Robert Ellsberg (Maryknoll, N.Y.: Orbis Books, 2001).

economic development. Meantime, Nhat Hanh combined social activism at the School of Youth for Social Services with scholarly research and teaching at the Institute of Higher Buddhist Studies, which he had helped found in Saigon.

To promote this union of action and wisdom characteristic of Engaged Buddhism, Nhat Hanh composed a set of fourteen "guidelines" for "mindfulness trainings" to be practiced by the new community he founded, called *Tiep Hien* (translated into English as "Interbeing"). In 1966 Nhat Hanh left for the United States to attend a conference on Vietnamese Buddhism, to be followed by a speaking tour organized by the Fellowship of Reconciliation, a pacifist organization. It was during this trip that Nhat Hanh met Trappist monk Thomas Merton (who wrote an introduction to his book *Lotus in a Sea of Fire*) and Martin Luther King Jr. Nhat Hanh's peace activism earned him the hostility of the Saigon government, which accused him of communist sympathies and refused him permission to return.

Barred from returning home, Nhat Hanh went to Paris in 1967. In 1969 he was asked by the Unified Buddhist Church of Vietnam to set up the Buddhist Peace Delegation in Paris and to present the Buddhist voice to the peace talks between the United States and North Vietnam. Even after the communist victory over South Vietnam in 1975, Nhat Hanh was not allowed to return. Now settled into his life in exile, Nhat Hanh founded in 1982 a permanent community in the southwest of France near Bordeaux, named the Plum Village as a center for the practice of mindfulness in the service of Engaged Buddhism. In 1988, at the request of his disciples, Nhat Hanh allowed them to receive monastic ordination in the community of the Order of Interbeing.

Just as in Confucianism, the starting point and center for social activism is, for Nhat Hanh, individual self-cultivation. In his case it is achieved through mindfulness. By mindfulness he means the deep consciousness of oneself as living and acting in the present moment. By a series of physical exercises, such as conscious breathing in and breathing out as well as sitting and walking in meditation, one becomes conscious of what one is doing and of the fact that one is existing in the present moment. Through this awareness the present moment becomes a gateway to enlightenment, a "wonderful moment":

> We have within us a miraculous power, and if we live our daily lives in mindfulness, if we take steps mindfully, with love and care, we can produce the miracle and transform our world into a miraculous place to live. Taking steps slowly, in mindfulness, is an act of liberation. You walk and you free yourself of all worries, anxieties, projects, and attachments. One step like this has the power to liberate you from all afflictions. Just being there, you transform yourself, and your compassion will bear witness.[54]

Once one acquires the capacity to be aware of the present, one becomes aware of one's essential connection with everything else. Because of "non-self,"

---

[54] *Cultivating the Mind of Love*, in Ellsberg, *Thich Nhat Hanh*, 43.

everything is interdependent, everything penetrates everything else; the one is the all and the all are the one. This is what Nhat Hanh means by *interbeing*. In a striking elaboration of the Buddhist concept of emptiness, Nhat Hanh shows how a piece of paper "inter-is" with the sun, the cloud, the logger, the onlooker, and anything that has existed, exists, and will ever exist: "'To be' is to inter-be. You cannot just *be* by yourself alone. You have to inter-be with every other thing. This sheet of paper is, because everything else is. . . . As thin as this sheet of paper is, it contains everything in the universe in it."[55] Interbeing means that we bear responsibility for others: "The truth is that everything is everything else. We can only inter-be, we cannot just be. And we are responsible for everything that happens around us."[56] This "everything" includes the material world: "We must learn to practice unconditional love for all beings so that the animals, the air, the trees, and the minerals can continue to be themselves. Our ecology should be a deep ecology—not only deep, but universal."[57]

But how does mindfulness lead to peace and harmony and compassion? Following Buddhist psychology, Nhat Hanh notes that like a house with the ground floor and the basement, human consciousness is made up of a "mind consciousness" and a "store consciousness." Both the mind consciousness and the store consciousness can be likened to a plot of land where all kinds of seeds can be planted, seeds of suffering, happiness, joy, sorrow, fear, anger, and hope. Practicing mindfulness allows us to cultivate the good feelings as they arise and thus to strengthen them and to transform the bad ones as they emerge: "Practicing mindfulness helps us get strong enough to open the door to our living room and let the pain come up. Every time our pain is immersed in mindfulness, it will lose some of its strength, and later, when it returns to the store consciousness, it will be weaker."[58] In addition, mindfulness allows us to realize ultimate reality. Using the metaphor of wave and water, the former for historical phenomena and the latter for Ultimate Reality (nirvana), Nhat Hanh suggests that in mindfulness we touch the present, which contains all the past and all the future, and thus touch nirvana itself.

Finally, mindfulness facilitates the healing of anger and leads to compassion. Nhat Hanh suggests that we heal our anger by focusing on its root causes in ourselves rather than in others: "Our anger is rooted in our lack of understanding of ourselves and of the causes, deep-seated as well as immediate. . . . Anger is also rooted in desire, pride, agitation, and suspiciousness. . . . The chief roots of our anger are in ourselves. Our environment and other people are only secondary roots."[59] To heal our anger at others, we must, Nhat Hanh says, practice the meditations on love and compassion. These meditations consist in looking deeply into the suffering of others, especially those who have caused us to

---

[55] *The Heart of Understanding*, in Ellsberg, *Thich Nhat Hanh*, 56.
[56] Ibid., 58.
[57] *The Sun Our Heart*, in Ellsberg, *Thich Nhat Hanh*, 69.
[58] *Touching Peace*, in Ellsberg, *Thich Nhat Hanh*, 85.
[59] *Transformation and Healing*, in Ellsberg, *Thich Nhat Hanh*, 99.

suffer, and in sincerely wishing happiness to our enemies: "Meditate on someone you consider to be your enemy, someone whom just thinking about makes you angry. Put yourself in his place and give rise to the thought, 'May he be peaceful, happy, and light in body and spirit. . . . ' As soon as you see that the person you call your enemy is also suffering, you will be ready to love and accept him."[60]

To make compassion and love an effective force for societal transformation, Thich Nhat Hanh founded his *Tiep Hien* monastic community or the Order of Interbeing as a "community of resistance,"[61] for which he has set up, as mentioned above, fourteen "guidelines." The Vietnamese word *tiep* means "to be in touch" and "to continue," and *hien* means "the present time" and "to realize or manifest." The Order of Interbeing, then, is aimed at helping people to get in touch with themselves as well as with the Buddha and the bodhisattvas through mindfulness exercises and to continue their work of peacemaking and peacebuilding. As a community of resistance, the Order of Interbeing achieves this twin goal by resisting fanaticism, intolerance, narrow-minded attachment to views and doctrines and by practicing compassionate dialogue, compassion for those who suffer, simple living, mindful breathing and walking, deep awareness of the present moment, truthful and constructive speech. With regard to nonviolence in particular, the guidelines say:

> Aware that much suffering is caused by war and conflict, we are determined to cultivate nonviolence, understanding, and compassion in our daily lives, to promote peace education, mindful meditation, and reconciliation within families, communities, nations, and in the world. We are determined not to kill and not to let others kill. We diligently practice deep looking with our Sangha to discover better ways to protect life and prevent war.[62]

Clearly, then, just as in Confucianism, personal practices of mindfulness in Thich Nhat Hanh's Engaged Buddhism, far from detracting from social and political commitments, offer an alternative way, that is, nonviolence, to bring about harmony and peace to our war-torn world.[63] It is also clear that, despite their tragic record of violence and hatred, all religions can and must reexamine their

---

[60] *Teachings on Love*, in Ellsberg, *Thich Nhat Hanh,* 105.

[61] *The Raft Is Not the Shore*, 130. Nhat Hanh says: "If in many monastic communities people are praying and meditating but do not resist, maybe it's because they do not pray and meditate properly. Because, I think, the proper object of praying and meditating is life—life in the most beautiful, glorious meaning of the word" (134).

[62] *Interbeing*, in Ellsberg, *Thich Nhat Hanh,* 155. For the complete text of the fourteen guidelines and the five mindfulness trainings, see 152–60.

[63] Another example of Buddhist nonviolent engagement for peace and reconciliation is the work of the Buddhist primate of Cambodia, Samdech Preah Maha Ghosananda, since 1993 in his native country. For a brief presentation of Ghosananda and his activities, see Appleby, *The Ambivalence of the Sacred*, 123–36.

teachings and practices and collaborate together to bring about world peace and harmony, because, as Hans Küng puts it, there is "no peace among the nations without peace among the religions, no peace among the religions without dialogue between the religions, no dialogue between the religions without investigation of the foundations of religions."[64]

---

[64] Hans Küng, *Global Responsibility: In Search of a New World Ethics*, trans. John Bowden (New York: Crossroad, 1991), xv.

PART THREE

Worship
in the
Postmodern World

13

Liturgical Inculturation

UNITY IN DIVERSITY IN THE POSTMODERN AGE

There is little doubt that one of the thorniest challenges for Catholic theology and in particular for liturgy for some time to come is inculturation. Inculturation is the double process of inserting the gospel into a particular culture and inserting this culture into the gospel so that both the gospel and the culture are challenged and enriched by each other.[1] The process itself, albeit not the term and the theoretical reflection upon it, has been a constant preoccupation of Christianity from its very inception, of course, as it attempted to make its message and way of life, which had been framed within the Jewish matrix, intelligible to the Greco-Roman world and subsequently to the peoples of different parts of the globe outside Europe, especially following its massive missionary movement in the sixteenth century.[2]

That inculturation in general and liturgical inculturation in particular are extremely complex is a theological truism. Inculturation, John Paul II warned, is "a slow journey" (*RM,* no. 52).[3] But this journey, arduous as it was in the past, is made even more so by the contemporary cultural context that has been dubbed

---

[1] John Paul II, quoting the 1995 Extraordinary Assembly for the Synod of Bishops, says: "Inculturation means the intimate transformation of authentic cultural values through their integration in Christianity and the insertion of Christianity in the various human cultures" (*RM,* no. 52). For the English text of this encyclical, see *Redemption and Dialogue: Reading* Redemptoris Missio *and* Dialogue and Proclamation, ed. William Burrows (Maryknoll, N.Y.: Orbis Books, 1993), 5–55. The book also contains a commentary on the encyclical by Marcello Zago (ibid., 56–90).

[2] As Vatican II puts it: "The Church learned early in its history to express the Christian message in the concepts and language of different peoples and tried to clarify it in the light of the wisdom of their philosophers: it was an attempt to adapt the Gospel to the understanding of all men and the requirements of the learned, insofar as this could be done. Indeed, this kind of adaptation and preaching the revealed Word must ever be the law of all evangelization. In this way it is possible to create in every country the possibility of expressing the message of Christ in suitable terms and to foster vital contact and exchange between the Church and different cultures" (*GS,* no. 44). English translation from Austin Flannery, ed., *Vatican Council II: The Conciliar and Post-Conciliar Documents* (Collegeville, Minn.: Liturgical Press, 1984).

[3] "Inculturation is a slow journey, which accompanies the whole of missionary life. It involves those working in the Church's mission *ad gentes,* the Christian communities as

213

postmodern. Since inculturation by definition must take into account the cultural context into which the gospel is to be inserted, it is imperative to inquire how this postmodern sensibility, widely assumed to be the hallmark of contemporary culture, affects the nature and process of inculturation itself.

This chapter focuses on liturgical inculturation and begins with a brief description of postmodernism and the challenges it poses to inculturation. The second part presents and evaluates the Fourth Instruction of the Congregation for Divine Worship and the Discipline of the Sacraments on liturgical inculturation in the light of the challenges of postmodernism. The last part makes some proposals for liturgical inculturation from the perspective of mission history in Asia and Asian theologies.

INCULTURATION IN THE POSTMODERN AGE

My intention is not to present even a cursory overview of postmodernism, nor is it possible within the narrow compass of this chapter.[4] Rather, the focus is on the postmodern understanding of culture and how this understanding challenges the process of liturgical inculturation. Conventionally, the overarching term *postmodernism* refers to the cultural and social shift that has emerged since the 1930s and has been making its way from the West to the other parts of the world through the process of globalization.[5] Three or four decades later, during the 1960s, this phenomenon made its influence felt first in architecture and the arts, then invaded literature, philosophy, and theology, and by the 1980s became a general characteristic of popular culture.[6] It is

---

they develop, and the Bishops, who have the task of providing discernment and encouragement for its implementation." In his Discourse to the Bishops of Zaire, April 12, 1983, John Paul II said that "satisfactory progress in this domain [inculturation] can only be the fruit of a progressive growth in faith, linked with spiritual discernment, theological clarity, a sense of the universal Church" (no. 5).

[4] The theological literature on postmodernity, not to mention the literary, artistic, and philosophical literature, has grown by leaps and bounds. For our purposes two introductions are especially helpful: Stanley J. Grenz, *A Primer on Postmodernism* (Grand Rapids, Mich.: Eerdmans, 1996); and Paul Lakeland, *Postmodernity: Christian Identity in a Fragmented Age* (Minneapolis: Fortress Press, 1997). The former work contains a useful bibliography on postmodernity (197–202). Generally, the term *postmodernism* refers to the cultural mood and intellectual ideas that are contrasted to those of modernism (here the prefix *post* is taken not only in the chronological sense but also as a rejection—at least partial—of modernism). *Postmodernity* refers to the epoch or era in which postmodern ideas and values shape the outlook of a particular society.

[5] For the early uses of the term *postmodernism*, see Margaret Rose, "Defining the Post-Modern," in *The Post-Modern Reader*, ed. Charles Jencks, 119–36 (New York: St. Martin's Press, 1992).

[6] The following reflections on postmodern architecture, art, theater, fiction, and various expressions of popular culture are derived from Grenz, *A Primer on Postmodernism*, 22–38, and Lakeland, *Postmodernity*, 1–7. For general descriptions of postmodern culture, see Steven Connor, *Postmodernist Culture: An Introduction to Theories of the Contemporary* (Oxford: Basil Blackwell, 1989); and Walter Truett Anderson, *Reality Isn't What It Used to Be: Theatrical Politics, Ready-to-Wear Religion, Global Myths, Primitive Chic, and Other Wonders of the Post-modern World* (San Francisco: Harper & Row, 1990).

helpful to see briefly how postmodernism has affected some of the cultural expressions of our times.

The Postmodern World and Its Cultural Expressions

In contrast to modern architecture, which in the wake of Frank Lloyd Wright emphasizes organic unity and practical functionality and is typified by the nearly universal pattern of glass-and-steel boxes, postmodern architecture celebrates "multivalence" by making use of a variety of incompatible historical styles, forms, techniques, and materials. By accentuating pluriformity and hybridity postmodern architecture wants to show that behind the principle of organic unity and practical functionality of modern architecture lies the dehumanizing uniformity of standardized mass production, aided and abetted by the powers of science, technology, and industry.[7]

Similarly, postmodern art rejects the stylistic integrity and "purity" of modernity and embraces multivalence and heterogeneity. It favors the technique of juxtaposition, which assembles cheek by jowl seemingly contradictory styles of diverse origins. By adopting this "impure" composition, it subtly and ironically rejects modernity's claim to universal rationality and the myth of a single artistic author or creator. Two popular techniques of juxtaposition are collage and bricolage, the former bringing together incompatible source materials, and the latter reconfiguring various traditional objects. The result is pastiche, which by means of its eclectic mixture of disjointed and contradictory elements calls into question the modern fiction of objective reality and meaning invested in dominant institutions and canonical traditions.

The same drive toward diversity and pluralism reigns in theater too. In theatrical performance, following Antonin Artaud's protest against the idolatry of classical art and his proposal of the "theater of cruelty,"[8] the postmodern theater celebrates transience instead of temporal permanence. Perceiving what it takes to be the repressive power of a script and a director, practitioners of postmodern theater experiment with immediate performance without a script, thus making each performance unique and unrepeatable, and with improvisation, group authorship, and audience participation. They reject modernity's "aesthetics of presence" and advocate the "aesthetics of absence," which highlights the lack of any permanent, underlying truth. Life, like the story performed on the stage, is but an eclectic assemblage of intersecting, disconnected, and impermanent narratives.

In postmodern fiction, as well, juxtaposition is practiced so that it is difficult to tell the real character from the fictitious, the author from the fictional work,

---

[7] On postmodern architecture, see Charles A. Jencks, *The Language of Post-Modern Architecture* (London: Academy Editions, 1984).

[8] See Antonin Artaud, "The Theater of Cruelty: Second Manifesto," in *The Theatre and Its Double*, trans. Victor Corti (London: Calder & Boyers, 1970), 81–87. Artaud called for an abandonment of the older script-centered style of theatrical performance and the distinction between actors and the audience. He advocated free performance that includes improvisation of light, color, movement, gesture, and space.

the author's voice from the fictional story. By means of this technique postmodern fiction blurs the line between reality and unreality, between temporality and atemporality, so that the reader is no longer able to view the world from a privileged and secure vantage point of eternal truths. The two representative genres of postmodern fiction are the spy novel and science fiction. In contrast to the typically modern genre of the detective story, in which a seemingly disjointed series of events becomes a unified whole at the end, the spy novel juxtaposes two radically different worlds, the one real in appearance that turns out to be illusory at the end, and the other sinister in appearance but turning out to be more real than the former. In science fiction reality is by definition eliminated, and an alternative world is depicted as possible.[9]

On the level of pop culture, which postmodernism refuses to distinguish from "high art," the film world is paradigmatic of the postmodern world—a realm in which truth and fiction merge. The cinematic reality is largely an illusion. Filmmaking technology allows the viewer to perceive as a unity in time and space what was disjointed in both time and space. The unity of a film does not reflect the real world but is imposed by the editor, who assembles into a unified product footage shot at different times and at various locations. Even the characters may not be the same, as stunt doubles replace them in dangerous scenes. With advanced techniques of computer-generated images and special effects, it is not possible to tell the real from the fantastic, the historical from the fictional.

An extension of the film industry, television (and cable and direct satellite broadcasts with an almost infinite variety of viewing options) brings the postmodern ethos of the film world into the living room and day-to-day life. But television can go beyond film by offering live broadcasting so that viewers can see for themselves events as they are happening anywhere in the world. In this way the world *as* presented by television, with its interpretation, commentary, and editing—often with bias—becomes the real world for most people, and consequently, what is not presented on television does not appear real to them. Indeed, as the advertising tag "as seen on TV" implies, the television world guarantees the reality and truth of the real world! Furthermore, by juxtaposing serious news with commercials, sitcoms, and docu-dramas, television, like other postmodern artistic expressions, blurs the boundaries between truth and fiction, between the important and the trivial.

Add the personal computer to television, with the unlimited possibility of surfing the Web, and reality becomes virtual reality and vice versa. In virtual reality one has "been there and done that," and yet need not be there and do that at all!

Perhaps the power of postmodernism to blur reality and fiction is best epitomized by the screen—whether the movie, television, or computer screen. What happens on the screen is neither objective reality out there nor subjective reality

---

[9] On postmodern literature, see Ihab Hassan, *The Dismemberment of Orpheus: Towards a Postmodern Literature* (New York: Oxford University Press, 1971); and Brian McHale, *Postmodernist Fiction* (New York: Methuen, 1987).

within the viewer; rather, it is somewhere in between, blurring the distinction between object and subject, the very thing postmodernism advocates.

The Postmodern Ethos

From this cursory overview several characteristics of postmodernism have emerged. In his description of the postmodern ethos Stanley Grenz mentions pessimism, holism, communitarianism, and relativistic pluralism as its main characteristics.[10] Pessimistic, because postmodernism abandons the Enlightenment myth of inevitable progress and highlights the fragility of human existence; holistic, insofar as it rejects the modern privileging of rationality and celebrates emotions and intuition; communitarian because it eschews modernity's individualism and its quest for universal, supracultural, and timeless truth, and emphasizes the role of the community in creating the truth; and relativistic and pluralistic, because since there are many different human communities, there are necessarily many different truths.

These characteristics, however, do not constitute a coherent philosophical world view. Indeed, for postmodernism, there is not a "world" about which one can construct a unitary true "view"; there is not a single objective world to which our knowledge must correspond. What we call the real world is, for postmodernism, nothing more than our ever-shifting social creation. Ours is a symbolic world, which we create through our common language. Hence, knowledge is replaced by interpretation. As Stanley Grenz has pointed out, postmodern epistemology is built on two basic assumptions: it views "all explanations of reality as constructions that are useful but not objectively true" and denies that "we have the ability to step outside our constructions of reality."[11] With this constructivist rather than objectivist outlook, postmodernism rejects the correspondence theory of truth and adopts a pluralistic view of knowledge.[12]

---

[10] Grenz, *A Primer on Postmodernism*, 15. Lakeland describes the postmodern sensibility as "nonsequential, noneschatological, nonutopian, nonsystematic, nonfoundational, and, ultimately, nonpolitical" (*Postmodernity*, 8).

[11] Grenz, *A Primer on Postmodernisn*, 43.

[12] Here is not the place to discuss postmodern philosophy. For a survey of postmodern philosophy, beginning with the critiques of René Descartes and Immanuel Kant, through Friedrich Nietzsche's nihilistic rejection of the Enlightenment concepts of truth and value, the emergence of hermeneutics in replacement of metaphysics (Friedrich Schleiermacher, Wilhelm Dilthey, Martin Heidegger, and Hans-Georg Gadamer), the "linguistic turn" (language as game in Ludwig Wittgenstein, language as social construction in Ferdinand de Saussure, the dissolution of the self in structuralism), to the philosophers of postmodernism (Michel Foucault's theory of knowledge as power, Jacques Derrida's deconstruction of logocentrism, and Richard Rorty's pragmatic utopia), see Grenz, *A Primer on Postmodernism*, 83–160. Paul Lakeland distinguishes three types of postmodern philosophy—"radical postmoderns" (e.g., Foucault, Derrida, Rorty, Georges Bataille, Julia Kristeva, and Luce Irigaray); "nostalgic postmoderns" (e.g., Heidegger, Allan Bloom, Theodor Adorno, and Alasdair MacIntyre); and "late moderns" (e.g., Jürgen Habermas, Charles Taylor, and Jean-François Lyotard)—and discusses how postmodernism approaches the issues of subjectivity, relativism, and otherness (*Postmodernity*, 12–38).

In terms of culture, postmodernism spells the demise of metanarratives, to use Jean-François Lyotard's expression.[13] *Metanarrative* refers to the system of myths that binds a society together and by which it legitimates itself. Not only do postmoderns no longer cling to the modern metanarrative of progress, which is itself founded on the Christian narrative and is at best a "useful fiction," but they also reject any appeal to metanarratives as social legitimation. The age of the grand narrative is over; what is left are *local* narratives that one constructs in one's particular community.

Together with the death of metanarratives, Lyotard points out, came the end of modern science, which had been based on the political myth of freedom and the philosophical myth of the progress of knowledge. The loss of credibility of the grand narratives of scientific progress does not mean the death of science, however, but only of a particular model of science, namely, that of Newtonian mechanistic understanding. Not science as such but only the modern assumption that the universe contains an internally consistent order from which a quantitative analysis will yield universal laws permitting the prediction of other natural occurrences has been questioned. In the post-Newtonian science, other physical theories have been formulated that have fundamentally undermined our previous way of viewing the world, such as quantum theory, the relativity theory, chaos theory, and the Heisenberg Uncertainty Principle.

All together, these theories suggest that the universe is not something that can be fully and completely described by science but is ultimately an unfathomable mystery. The ever-changing universe not only *has* a history but *is* a history that cannot be controlled or predicted by scientific methods. Moreover, these theories contend that science is not a culturally neutral fact, as modernity has assumed. Rather, it is a social construction of reality, a paradigm, that controls what the scientist sees. Every experiment ultimately rests on a networks of interests, theories, opinions, and traditions, often buttressed by money and power, and the resulting knowledge is not a collection of objective universal truths but a formulation of research traditions done within a particular cultural community.[14]

Postmodern Theory of Culture:
Culture as a "Ground of Contest in Relations"

This leads to the question of how, in contrast to modernity, postmodernism understands culture. The modern concept of culture is represented by the anthropological concept of culture that emerged as a theoretical construct after the 1920s, especially on the American scene.[15] This concept was used to account

---

[13] See Jean-François Lyotard, *The Postmodern Condition: A Report on Knowledge*, trans. Geoff Bennington and Brian Massumi (Minneapolis: University of Minnesota Press, 1984).

[14] For reflections on postmodern science, see Lakeland, *Postmodernity*, 36–38.

[15] For a history of the concept of culture, see Alfred A. Kroeber and Klyde Kluckhohn, *Culture: A Critical Review of Concepts and Definitions* (Cambridge, Mass.: Papers of the Peabody Museum of American Archeology and Ethnology, Harvard University, 1952). For a brief overview, see Kathryn Tanner, *Theories of Culture: A New Agenda*

for differences in customs and practices of a particular human society. These differences are explained in terms of cultures rather than in terms of God's will, racial or generational variations, environmental factors, or differences in origin. Furthermore, in this understanding of culture, no evaluative judgment is made as to whether a particular culture represents a less noble or less developed stage of human evolution.

This anthropological approach to culture tends to view it as a human universal. This universal is realized, however, in particular forms by each social group as its distinct way of life. Culture is constituted by the conventions created by the consensus of a group into which its members are socialized. Given this notion of culture as group differentiating, holistic, non-evaluative, and context dependent, anthropologists commonly perceive the culture of a social group as a whole, as a single albeit complex unit, and distinguish it from the social behaviors of its members. Culture is seen as the ordering principle and control mechanism of social behaviors without which human beings would be formless. Above all, culture is seen as an integrated and integrating whole whose constituent elements are functionally interrelated to one another. These elements are thought to be integrated because they are perceived as expressing a fundamental, overarching theme, style, or purpose. Or they are thought to be consistent with or imply one another. Or they are supposed to operate according to laws or structures, not unlike the grammatical rules in a language. Or, finally, they are supposed to function with a view to maintaining and promoting the stability of the social order. Thanks to this non-evaluative approach to culture, anthropologists can avoid ethnocentrism, concentrating on an accurate description of a particular culture, rather than judging it according to some presumed norms of truth, goodness, and beauty.[16]

The modern anthropological concept of culture has its advantages. As Robert Schreiter has noted, the concept of culture as an integrated system of beliefs, values, and behavioral norms has much to commend it. Among other things, it promotes holism and a sense of coherence and communion in opposition to the fragmentation of mass society; is congenial to the harmonizing, both-and way of thinking prevalent in oral cultures and many Asian cultures; and serves as an antidote to the corrosive effects of modernity and capitalism.[17] Religion as a quest for meaning and wholeness is seen as a boon to these positive aspects of culture.

---

for Theology (Minneapolis: Fortress Press, 1997), 3–24. Tanner surveys the meaning of *culture* as it was used in France, Germany, and Great Britain before its current usage in anthropology. For a presentation of Vatican II's understanding of culture and its development, including the notion of culture in John Paul II, see Michael Paul Gallagher, *Clashing Symbols: An Introduction to Faith and Culture* (New York: Paulist Press, 1998), 36–55.

[16] For a development of this concept of culture, see Tanner, *Theories of Culture*, 25–37.

[17] See Robert Schreiter, *The New Catholicity: Theology between the Global and the Local* (Maryknoll, N.Y.: Orbis Books, 1997), 49–50.

In recent years, however, this modern concept of culture has been subjected to a searing critique.[18] The view of culture as a self-contained and clearly bounded whole, as an internally consistent and integrated system of beliefs, values, and behavioral norms that functions as the ordering principle of a social group and into which its members are socialized, has been shown to be based on unjustified assumptions.[19] Against this conception of culture it has been argued: (1) that it focuses exclusively on culture as a finished product and therefore pays insufficient attention to culture as a historical process; (2) that its view of culture as a consistent whole is dictated more by the anthropologist's aesthetic need and the demand for synthesis than by the lived reality of culture itself; (3) that its emphasis on consensus as the process of cultural formation obfuscates the reality of culture as a site of struggle and contention; (4) that its view of culture as a principle of social order belittles the role of the members of a social group as cultural agents; (5) that it privileges the stable elements of culture and does not take into adequate account its innate tendency to change and innovation; and (6) that its insistence on clear boundaries for cultural identity is no longer necessary because it is widely acknowledged today that change, conflict, and contradiction are resident *within* culture itself and are not simply caused by outside disruption and dissension.[20]

Rather than as a sharply demarcated, self-contained, homogeneous, and integrated whole, culture today is seen as "a ground of contest in relations"[21] and as a historically evolving, fragmented, inconsistent, conflicted, constructed, ever-shifting, and porous social reality. In this contest of relations the role of power in the shaping of cultural identity is of paramount importance, a factor that the modern concept of culture largely ignores. In the past anthropologists tended to regard culture as an innocent set of conventions rather than as a reality of conflict in which the colonizers, the powerful, the wealthy, the victors, the dominant can obliterate the beliefs and values of the colonized, the weak, the poor, the vanquished, the subjugated, so that there has been, in Serge Gruzinski's expression, "la colonisation de l'imaginaire."[22] The role of

---

[18] For the following reflections on the postmodern concept of culture, see Peter C. Phan, "Religion and Culture: Their Places as Academic Disciplines in the University," in *The Future of Religions in the Twenty-first Century*, ed. Peter Ng, 321–53 (Hong Kong: Centre for the Study of Religion and Chinese Society, 2001).

[19] See Pierre Bourdieu, *Outline of a Theory of Practice* (Cambridge: Cambridge University Press, 1977); James Clifford, *The Predicament of Culture* (Cambridge, Mass.: Harvard University Press, 1988); George Marcus and Michael Fischer, *Anthropology as Cultural Critique* (Chicago: University of Chicago Press, 1986); Ulrich Beck, *Risk Society: Toward a New Modernity* (London: Sage, 1992); Homi K. Bhabha, *The Location of Culture* (London: Routledge, 1994); Jonathan Friedman, *Cultural Identity and Global Process* (London: Sage, 1994); and Mike Featherstone, *Undoing Modernity: Globalization, Postmodernism, and Identity* (London: Sage, 1995).

[20] For a detailed articulations of these six objections to the anthropological concept of culture, see Tanner, *Theories of Culture*, 40–56.

[21] The phrase is from Schreiter, *The New Catholicity*, 54.

[22] Serge Gruzinski, *La Colonisation de l'imaginaire: Sociétés indigènes et occidentalisation dans le Mexique espagnol XVIe-XVIIIe siècle* (Paris: Gallimard, 1987). English translation, *The Conquest of Mexico,* trans. Eileen Corrigan (Cambridge: Polity, 1993).

power is, as Michel Foucault and other masters of suspicion have argued, central in the formation of knowledge in general.[23] In the formation of cultural identity the role of power is even more extensive, since it is constituted by groups of people with conflicting interests, and the winners can dictate their cultural terms to the losers.

This predicament of culture is exacerbated by the process of globalization, in which the ideals of modernity and technological reason are extended throughout the world (globalization as *extension*), aided and abetted by a single economic system (neoliberal capitalism) and new communication technologies.[24] In globalization geographical boundaries, which at one time helped define cultural identity, have collapsed. Even our sense of time is largely compressed, with the present predominating and the dividing line between past and future becoming ever more blurred (globalization as *compression*). In the process of globalization a homogenized culture is created, consolidated by a "hyperculture" based on consumption, especially of goods exported from the United States, such as clothing (for example, T-shirts, denim jeans, athletic shoes), food (e.g., McDonald's and Coca Cola), and entertainment (e.g., films, video, and music).

Such a globalized culture is not accepted by local cultures hook, line, and sinker. Between the global and the local cultures there is a continuous struggle, the former for political and economic dominance, the latter for survival and integrity. Because of the powerful attraction of the global culture, especially for the young, local cultures often feel threatened by it, but they are far from powerless. To counteract its influence, they have devised several strategies of

---

[23] See Michel Foucault, *The Archaeology of Knowledge*, trans. A. M. Sheridan Smith (New York: Pantheon Books, 1972); idem, *Discipline and Punish: The Birth of Prison*, trans. Alan Sheridan (New York: Vintage Press, 1975); Michael Kelly, ed., *Critique and Power: Recasting the Foucault/Habermas Debate* (Cambridge, Mass.: MIT Press, 1994); Michel Foucault, *Madness and Civilization: A History of Insanity in the Age of Reason*, trans. Richard Howard (New York: Vintage Books, 1988); idem, *Language, Counter-Memory, Practice: Selected Essays and Interviews*, ed. Donald Bouchard. Donald Bouchard and Sherry Simon (Ithaca, N.Y.: Cornell University Press, 1977); idem, *Power/Knowledge* (New York: Pantheon Books, 1987); idem, *Politics, Philosophy, Culture: Interviews and Other Writings*, ed. Lawrence D. Kritzman, trans. Alan Sheridan (New York: Routledge, 1988).

[24] For a discussion of the historical development of globalization, see Immanuel Wallerstein, *The Modern World-System I: Capitalist Agriculture and the Origins of the European World-Economy in the Sixteenth Century* (New York: Academic, 1974); idem, *The Modern World-System II: Mercantilism and the Consolidation of the European World-Economy, 1600–1750* (New York: Academic, 1980); Anthony Giddens, *Modernity and Self-Identity: Self and Society in the Late Modern Age* (Stanford, Calif.: Stanford University Press, 1991); and Roland Robertson, *Globalization: Social Theory and Global Culture* (London: Sage, 1992). In general, Wallerstein attributes an exclusively economic origin to globalization, while Giddens sees it rooted in four factors, namely, the nation-state system, the world military order, the world capitalist economy, and the international division of labor. Robertson highlights the cultural factors in globalization.

resistance, subversion, compromise, and appropriation. And in this effort religion more often than not has played a key role in alliance with local cultures.[25]

Like the anthropological concept of culture as a unified whole, the globalized concept of culture as a ground of contest in relations has its strengths and weaknesses. On the positive side, it takes into account features of culture that are left in shadow by its predecessor. While recognizing that harmony and wholeness remain ideals, it views culture in its lived reality of fragmentation, conflict, and ephemerality. Cultural meanings are not simply discovered ready-made but are constructed and produced in the violent cauldron of asymmetrical power relations. It recognizes the important role of power in the formation of cultural identity. Furthermore, it sees culture as a historical process, intrinsically mutable, but without an a priori, clearly defined *telos* and a controllable and predictable synthesis. On the debit side, this postmodern concept of culture runs the risk of fomenting fundamentalistic tendencies, cultural and social ghettoization, and romantic retreat to an idealized past.[26]

Postmodern Challenges to Liturgical Inculturation

What challenges does postmodernism in all its cultural expressions (from architecture to theater, fiction, cinema, television, and the Internet), with its concept of culture as a ground of contest in relations, pose to inculturation, in particular liturgical inculturation? Here I highlight only a few of these challenges.

The first challenge regards the concept of inculturation itself. If the gospel, and more specifically, the liturgy, must be regarded as a cultural, symbolic "world," a social construct with its own interests and idiosyncrasies, then inculturation is not an "incarnation" of a timeless, unchanging, and acultural reality (such as the eternal Logos) into a particular culture, but an *intercultural* encounter or dialogue between at least two cultures. What are the dynamics and rules of intercultural communication that liturgical inculturation must attend to in order to be successful?

---

[25] For a brief discussion of globalization, see Schreiter, *The New Catholicity*, 4–14. Social scientist Arjun Appadurai lists five factors that have contributed to the "deterritorialization" of contemporary culture: "ethnoscape" (the constant flow of persons such as immigrants, refugees, tourists, guest workers, exiles), "technoscape" (mechanical and informational technologies), "finanscape" (flow of money through currency markets, national stock exchanges, commodity speculation), "mediascape" (newspapers, magazines, TV, films), and "ideoscape" (key ideas such as freedom, welfare, human rights, independence, democracy). See his "Disjuncture and Difference in the Global Economy," *Public Culture* 2/2 (1990): 1–24.

[26] On these three tendencies or cultural logics, dubbed antiglobalism, ethnification, and primitivism, see Schreiter, *The New Catholicity*, 21–25. For a lucid exposition and critique of postmodernism, see Dale T. Irvin, "Christianity in the Modern World: Facing Postmodern Culture and Religious Pluralism," in Ng, *The Future of Religions in the Twenty-first Century*, 253–66. For Irvin, postmodernism is liable to three temptations: facile acceptance of the processes of consumerism and commodification, disdain for tradition and memory, and reduction of the historical past to its Western cultural form.

Second, in this intercultural encounter, according to postmodernism, the issue of power is of paramount importance. It concerns, first of all, the relation between Roman authorities and the local churches. How does power play out in liturgical inculturation, especially if the process of liturgical inculturation must preserve "the *substantial unity* of the Roman rite,"[27] which is itself a cultural world? Or if it is conceived mainly as translation into the vernaculars of "the [Latin] typical editions of liturgical books,"[28] which themselves embody a particular culture (for example, Latin-Roman)? Or if these books "must be translated integrally and in the most exact manner, without omissions or additions in terms of their content, and without paraphrases or glosses"?[29] Why should Latin be used as the official language of the Roman liturgy (incidentally, *which* Latin?)—which itself forms and is formed by a cultural world? Why can't the liturgical texts be composed in the vernaculars in the first place? Why should translation of culturally foreign texts be resorted to? Is the unity of the church maintained and promoted by a common liturgical text? Finally, why should translations, which have been approved by the national episcopal conferences, still need to be given the *recognitio* by the Congregation for Divine Worship and the Discipline of the Sacraments, which more often than not has minimal linguistic skills, if any, in the languages concerned?[30] In the process of inculturation carried out in this way, is not the Latin/Roman culture imposed on other churches?

Third, the question of power emerges again in the choice of the culture into which the Roman liturgy is to be inculturated. The culture of a particular country or ethnic group is not an integrating and integrated whole, equally and fairly encompassing the beliefs, values, and practices of all the people constituting that country or ethnic group. Rather, the economically, politically, and religiously dominant elements will exclude or subjugate the weaker ones, whose cultures will be marginalized as a consequence. To take an example, which culture will the liturgy dialogue with in India: the Hindu culture or that of the *Dalits*, who make up the larger membership of the church?

---

[27] Congregation for Divine Worship and the Discipline of the Sacraments, *Inculturation of the Liturgy within the Roman Rite*, no. 36. The official Latin text is "De Liturgia romana et inculturatione. Instructio quarta ad exsecutionem Constitutionis Concilii Vaticani Secundi de Sacra Liturgia recte ordinandam (ad Const. Art. 37–40)," published in *Notitiae* 30 (1994): 8–115, dated March 29, 1994. Its English text, under the title *Inculturation of the Liturgy within the Roman Rite*, was published by Vatican Press, 1994. Henceforth, *Varietates legitimae.*

[28] *Varietates legitimae*, no. 36.

[29] Congregation for Divine Worship and the Discipline of the Sacraments, *On the Use of Vernacular Languages in the Publication of the Books of the Roman Liturgy*, no. 20. The official Latin text of this Fifth Instruction is: "De usu linguarum popularium in libris liturgiae romanae edendis," published on March 28, 2001. Its English translation is available from the NCCB/USCC. Henceforth, *Liturgiam authenticam.*

[30] It is interesting to note that *Liturgiam authenticam* affirms that this *recognitio* "is not a mere formality, but is rather an exercise of the power of governance, which is absolutely necessary" (no. 80). The instruction says that the *recognitio* "expresses and effects a bond of communion between the successor of blessed Peter and his brothers in the Episcopate" (ibid.). The question is, of course, whether there is not a better and more collegial way to express communion between the pope and the bishops.

Fourth, the issue of power looms large again in the question of the place and role of popular religion in liturgical inculturation. Popular religion has often been depicted as the religion of the poor and dispossessed, a form of identity-affirmation and resistance of the "subaltern class" (Antonio Gramsci) against the ruling class. In liturgical inculturation the official liturgy will inevitably have to deal with popular religion, not only as it has already been Christianized (for example, Marian piety) but also as it is practiced in non-Christian religions (for example, the cult of ancestor). How should popular religion with its myriad devotional practices be viewed vis-à-vis the official religion? Is popular religion to be seen as the "small traditions" as opposed to the "great traditions"? Should the practices of popular religion be introduced into liturgical worship? How are they to be evaluated theologically?

Fifth, Christian liturgy reenacts the great biblical narratives of God's acts in history, especially in Jesus Christ. With the death of metanarratives in postmodernity, such reenactment faces difficult challenges, particularly in places where Christianity has to compete with other religious metanarratives. Can liturgical inculturation be carried out without an effective dialogue with these religious metanarratives? What is the connection between liturgical inculturation and interreligious dialogue? Can liturgy be fully inculturated without making use of religious rituals and sacred texts of other religions?

Sixth, the scope of liturgical inculturation includes not only the sacred texts and rituals but also the music, songs, musical instruments, gestures, dance, art, and architecture of the local culture. May and should liturgical inculturation embrace the postmodern preference for juxtaposition, bricolage, and collage, with pastiche as the result, and the "aesthetics of absence"? How far can and should it go in adopting classical or traditional art forms without falling into archaeologism and nostalgia? On the other hand, how much of postmodern art forms can it adopt without succumbing to ephemeral fads and passing trends? If liturgical celebrations are performances, how far can the community and the presider experiment with improvisation, group authorship, and audience participation, and still preserve the unity of faith and worship?

Finally, liturgical inculturation cannot be divorced from theology. How then can it meet the major challenges of postmodernism to such theological themes as God, Christ, and church? How can liturgy justify its pervasive use of anthropomorphic and anthropocentric (and most often sexually exclusive) language for God and God's agency in the world against the postmodern decentering of the human person? How can inculturated Christian worship preserve and proclaim the truth of Jesus Christ as the universal and unique Savior against the postmodern affirmation of radical religious pluralism that decenters Christ? How can inculturation, through liturgical celebrations, build up a church that is truly local against the globalizing trend of postmodernity, which homogenizes everything with its "hyperculture"?[31]

---

[31] For a critical survey of postmodern theology, especially under the themes of God, Christ, and church, see Lakeland, *Postmodernity*, 39–86.

LITURGICAL INCULTURATION ACCORDING TO *VARIETATES LEGITIMAE* IN THE POSTMODERN CONTEXT

Before exploring how mission history in Asia and Asian theologies can help us meet some of the postmodern challenges to liturgical inculturation, it is useful to examine how the Fourth Instruction of the Congregation for Divine Worship and the Discipline of the Sacraments, *Varietates legitimae,* envisions the scope and process of liturgical inculturation. My intention here is not to offer a comprehensive analysis and critique of the instruction but only to highlight those points that appear to have a particular relevance for inculturation in the postmodern context.[32]

Liturgical Adaptation according to *Varietates Legitimae*

Any fair evaluation of *Varietates legitimae*'s program of liturgical inculturation must take into account the fact that it is only intended to be an authoritative guide to the "right application of the Conciliar Constitution on the Liturgy (nn. 37–40)," as the subtitle of the instruction stipulates, and not a comprehensive manual on inculturation as such. Within this limited scope *Varietates legitimae* states that "the work of inculturation does not foresee the creation of new families of rites; inculturation responds to the needs of a particular culture and leads to adaptations which still remain part of the Roman rite" (no. 36). Earlier, the instruction has expressed its preference for the neologism *inculturation* instead of the traditional term *adaptation (aptatio),* which was used by *Sacrosanctum concilium,* because the latter term suggests "modifications of a somewhat transitory and external nature" (no. 4), whereas inculturation signifies, according to the instruction, quoting Pope John Paul II's *Redemptoris missio* (no. 52), "an intimate transformation of the authentic cultural values by their integration into Christianity and the implantation of Christianity into different cultures" (no. 4).

The instruction clearly differentiates between two types of liturgical adaptation, namely, those that are "provided for in the liturgical books" (as envisaged by nos. 38–39 of *Sacrosanctum concilium*) and those which are "more radical" (as contemplated by no. 40 of the same constitution). While detailed procedures are laid down for both kinds of adaptation, the overwhelming focus of the instruction is on the former, which, in contrast to the latter, is presumably less radical and pervasive. After outlining the principles regarding the goal, the limit,

---

[32] For general evaluations of *Varietates legitimae,* see Nathan Mitchell, "The Amen Corner," *Worship* 68 (1994): 369–77; Julian Saldanha, "Instruction on Liturgical Inculturation," *Vidyajoti* 60 (1996): 618–21; David Power, "Liturgy and Culture Revisited," *Worship* 69 (1995): 225–43; and D. Reginald Whitt, "*Varietates Legitimae* and an African-American Liturgical Tradition," *Worship* 71 (1997): 504–37.

and the competent authority of liturgical inculturation,[33] the instruction enunciates norms governing the first kind of liturgical adaptation in language, music and singing, gesture and posture, art, the veneration of sacred images, and popular devotion (nos. 39–45).

The instruction goes on to show how adaptations of this kind may be carried out with regard to the liturgical books (no. 53), the Eucharist (no. 54), the rites of Christian initiation (no. 56), the marriage rite (no. 57), funerals (no. 58), the blessings of persons, places, and things (no. 59), the liturgical year (no. 60), and the Liturgy of the Hours (no. 61). In all these areas it is presumed that the official liturgical texts are composed by the Congregation for Divine Worship and the Discipline of the Sacraments, known as "the Latin typical editions," which are then to be translated into the vernaculars, with possible adaptations indicated therein as belonging to the competence of the episcopal conferences and to the individual bishops.

As to the "more radical" adaptations of the liturgy, *Varietates legitimae* describes them as involving "more than the sort of adaptations envisaged by the general instructions and the praenotanda of the liturgical books" (no. 63). The instruction does not give examples of such adaptations, but it says that they should be undertaken only after "an episcopal conference has exhausted all the possibilities of adaptation offered by the liturgical books" (no. 63). These "more profound" or "more far-reaching" adaptations can be made in any of the eight areas mentioned above—liturgical texts; the Eucharist; the rites of Christian initiation; the marriage rite; funerals; the blessings of persons, places, and things; the liturgical year; and the Liturgy of the Hours—if there are still "problems about the participation of the faithful" after adaptations of the first kind have been introduced (no. 63). Nevertheless, the instruction stipulates that "adaptations of this kind do not envisage a transformation of the Roman rite, but are made within the context of the Roman rite" (no. 63).[34]

---

[33] *Varietates legitimae* sees the goal of inculturation as a clear expression of the meaning of the "holy things" in both texts and rites so as to enable the faithful "to understand them with ease and to take part in the rites fully, actively and as befits a community" (no. 35). The limit of inculturation is set by the necessity to "maintain the *substantial unity* of the Roman rite" (no. 36). The authorities overseeing liturgical inculturation are the Apostolic See (that is, through the Congregation for Divine Worship and the Discipline of the Sacraments), and "within the limits fixed by law," episcopal conferences and the diocesan bishop (no. 37).

[34] What *Varietates legitimae* affirms is that liturgical inculturation should not result in "the creation of new families of rites" (no. 36). The Latin original says "novas familias rituales," so a better translation would be "new ritual families." By "ritual families" are meant the three canonically recognized liturgical traditions, namely, the *Ambrosian*, the *Hispano-Mozarabic*, and the *Roman* ritual families of the liturgical patrimony of the canonical Latin rite. Thus there should not be a new "ritual family" in addition to the three current ones. Any liturgical innovation of the Roman ritual family through inculturation, even the "more radical" one, must remain within the Roman ritual family. It is to be noted that Vatican II left open the possibility of the development and recognition of new *ritual families* that can appear within any of the twenty-one recognized

Varietates Legitimae in the Postmodern Context

At this point it may be asked how well *Varietates legitimae* meets the seven challenges of postmodernity to inculturation mentioned above. Clearly, undergirding the instruction is the modern notion of culture as an integrated and integrating whole, which is also that of Vatican II and of most papal documents, including those of John Paul II.[35] Being an instruction on the implementation of *Sacrosanctum concilium, Varietates legitimae* simply assumes Vatican II's concept of culture and offers no discussion, by way of acceptance or rejection, of the extensive developments in the understanding of culture in the last thirty years. It appears not to be aware of the momentous cultural shift from modernity to postmodernity, even though, as will be shown shortly, there surface here and there in the document concerns that may be described as postmodern.

Perhaps the most striking deficiencies in the instruction are its lack of the understanding of inculturation as an *intercultural* encounter and its failure to attend to the dynamics of intercultural communication (challenge 1). As has been correctly pointed out by Julian Saldanha, in spite of its preference for *inculturation,* the instruction repeatedly lapses into using *adaptation,* thus perpetuating the older, inadequate understanding of the process of inculturating the Christian faith.[36] The document is impervious to the fact that the Roman rite, however it is understood, *is* itself a cultural form, embodying a particular and local way of seeing the world, performing divine worship, and living the Christian faith, especially through its linguistic medium and the theology enshrined in its texts and rituals. By insisting on the necessity of maintaining "the *substantial unity* of the Roman rite" in liturgical inculturation, as stipulated by Vatican II, and by holding that "this unity is currently expressed in the typical editions of liturgical books, published by authority of the Supreme Pontiff, and in the liturgical books approved by the episcopal conferences for their areas and confirmed by the Apostolic See" (no. 36), and by requiring the use of translations of the "typical editions of liturgical books" (ibid.) composed by experts chosen by the Congregation for Divine Worship and the Discipline of the Sacraments, the instruction in practice imposes the Roman/Latin cultural and religious expressions on the other local churches.

A comparison with the secular strategies dealing with multiculturalism highlights the strengths and weaknesses of the instruction's approach to inculturation.

---

canonical rites forming the six basic liturgical traditions of the universal church (Alexandrine, Antiochene, Armenian, Chaldean, Constantinopolitan, and Roman) and even of a new *canonical rite*, although since 1963 no new canonical rite has been recognized. For helpful clarifications, see Whitt, "*Varietates legitimae* and an African-American Liturgical Tradition," 248–54.

[35] For a brief discussion of Vatican II's concept of culture, see Gallagher, *Clashing Symbols*, 36–43. For discussions of John Paul II's understanding of culture, see Stephen B. Bevans, *Models of Contextual Theology* (Maryknoll, N.Y.: Orbis Books, 2002), 42–46; and Schreiter, *The New Catholicity*, 22–23, 52–53.

[36] See Saldanha, "Instruction on Liturgical Inculturation," 619.

John Coleman, an American Jesuit sociologist, speaks of eight ways in which culturally pluralistic societies have historically dealt with ethnic group differences. Four seek to eliminate differences, ranging from the injustice of (a) genocide and (b) forced massive population transfer to the more acceptable strategies of (c) partition or secession and (d) assimilation. The other four seek to manage differences without eliminating them: (e) hegemonic control, (f) territorial quasi-autonomy in a federalist system, (g) territorial autonomy (consocialism), and (h) multicultural integration.[37]

Varietates legitimae clearly does not intend to eliminate cultural differences, as was often done in the pre–Vatican II era; on the contrary, it seeks to maintain and promote the "legitimate differences" of the local churches. But its approach to inculturation lies somewhere between assimilation and hegemonic control. The assimilationist strategy proposes an eventual eradication of cultural differences: immigrants are allowed to keep their cultural heritages in the transitional stage but they are expected eventually to "become like one of us." Hegemonic control honors cultural differences but insists on some common culture among different ethnic groups, and the culture of the dominant or hegemonic group is imposed on all as such common culture, no matter what lip service is given to the rhetoric of equality and the right of a people to its own culture and language. In stipulating that the typical Latin editions of liturgical books composed by outside experts be the normative texts of which translations into the vernaculars of the local churches will have to be made, with limited and strictly controlled "adaptations" and/or new compositions by the episcopal conferences allowed, *Varietates legitimae* is still operating on the assimilationist model at worst and on the hegemonic control model at best. In either case a genuine inculturation that is modeled on "multicultural integration" is forfeited. On this model of "affirmative multiculturalism" culture is acknowledged, as is done in postcolonialism and postmodernism, to be a site of struggle and a ground of contest in relations. In the intercultural encounter that constitutes inculturation, the two cultures—in our case, the local Latin/Roman culture embodied in the Roman rite and another local culture—ideally should engage with each other as equal partners, challenging, modifying, and enriching each other in a two-way exchange.

Unfortunately, as many sociologists and historians have pointed out, most multicultural societies, even those with a strong democratic tradition such as the United States, are at bottom monocultural and assimilationist, exclusive of cultural minorities. Sadly, the encounter among different cultures within the same country has been achieved, as Coleman has put it tersely and accurately, "always imperfectly, never without conflict and almost never with full equality."[38] This being the case, it is all the more incumbent upon the church, given its catholicity, to be more committed to genuinely equal partnership in inculturation.

---

[37] See John Coleman, "Pastoral Strategies for Multicultural Parishes," *Origins* 31/30 (January 2002): 498–501.

[38] Ibid., 498.

This brings us to another challenge of postmodernity to inculturation, namely, the use of power. This power play, as is indicated above, occurs between the Roman authorities and the other local churches in the choice of cultures to enter into dialogue with and in matters of popular religion. I will shortly discuss how *Varietates legitimae* regards the choice of cultures into which liturgy should be inculturated. Here I briefly reflect on the instruction's view of the relationship between the Roman authorities and the other local churches and popular religion.

That liturgical inculturation is not a private affair to be left to the initiatives and fancies of individuals, whether bishop, priest, or lay person, is not disputed. On the other hand, the well-founded need for hierarchical supervision should not be allowed to stifle genuine collaboration and the application of the principle of subsidiarity (challenge 2). In this respect *Varietates legitimae* does at times go overboard in its stipulations of the various procedures to be followed in both the normal and more radical forms of inculturation. For example, at the Special Assembly of the Synod of Bishops for Asia (1998), questions were raised about the necessity of a *recognitio* by the Congregation for Divine Worship and the Discipline of the Sacraments for translations of liturgical books already approved by the local episcopal conferences. Likewise, it may be asked why "concessions granted to one region cannot be extended to other regions without the necessary authorization, even if an episcopal conference considers that there are sufficient reasons for adopting such measures in its own area" (no. 37).[39] In either case it appears that the instruction is motivated by an excessive desire for control and does not respect the relative autonomy of the local churches.

With regard to popular religion (challenge 4), *Varietates legitimae* sees it mainly as "popular devotion" or "devotional practices" and decrees that their "introduction into liturgical celebrations under the pretext of inculturation cannot be allowed 'because by its nature, (the liturgy) is superior to them'" (no. 45). According to the instruction, it is the duty of the local bishop to "organize such devotions, to encourage them as supports for the life and faith of Christians, and to purify them, when necessary, because they need to be constantly permeated by the Gospel" (no. 45). Clearly, from the postmodern perspective of popular religion and the history of the development of popular Catholicism, the instruction's understanding of "popular devotion" is too superficial and constricted.[40]

---

[39] Note the condescending expression of "concessions granted" in the quotation.

[40] On popular religion and liturgy, see Peter C. Phan, "The Liturgy of Life as the 'Summit and Source' of the Eucharistic Liturgy: Church Worship as the Symbolization of the Liturgy of Life?" in *Incongruities: Who We Are and How We Pray*, ed. Timothy Fitzgerald and David A. Lysik, 5–33 (Chicago: Liturgy Training Publications, 2000); idem, "Culture and Liturgy: Ancestor Veneration as a Test Case," *Worship* 76/5 (2002): 403–30; idem, "Popular Religion and Liturgical Inculturation: Perspectives and Challenges from Asia," *Proceedings*, North American Academy of Liturgy, Annual Meeting, Reston, Virginia (January 3–6, 2002), 23–58; and the whole issue of *Liturgical Ministry* 7 (Summer 1998), which is devoted to popular religiosity, with informative essays by James L. Empereur ("Popular Religion and the Liturgy: The State of the Question"); Patrick L. Malloy ("Christian Anamnesis and Popular Religion"); Mark R. Francis ("The Hispanic Liturgical Year: The People's Calendar"); Keith F. Pecklers ("Issues of Power and Access in Popular Religion"); and Robert E. Wright ("Popular Religiosity: Review of Literature").

As to the remaining challenges of postmodernity, *Varietates legitimae* does not seem to look upon them favorably. For example, with regard to the need to conjoin interreligious dialogue with inculturation (challenge 5), the instruction's position is somewhat ambiguous.[41] On the one hand, it is open to the use of "expressions from non-Christian religions" in the liturgy (no. 39). On the other hand, its attitude toward them is largely negative and defensive:

> The liturgy is the expression of faith and Christian life, and so it is necessary to ensure that liturgical inculturation is not marked, even in appearance, by religious syncretism. This would be the case if the places of worship, the liturgical objects and vestments, gestures and postures let it appear as if rites had the same significance in Christian celebrations as they did before evangelization. The syncretism will be still worse if biblical readings and chants or the prayers were replaced by texts from other religions, even if these contain an undeniable religious and moral value" (no. 47).[42]

Any admission of rites and gestures from the local customs into the Christian liturgy must be "accompanied by purification and, if necessary, a break with the past. . . . Obviously the Christian liturgy cannot accept magic rites, superstition, spiritism, vengeance or rites with a sexual connotation" (no. 48).

As to the various expressions of culture in their contemporary, postmodern forms of collage and bricolage, *Varietates legitimae* has little to say (challenge 6). Regarding music and singing, gesture and posture, art and architecture, it focuses almost exclusively on the local and popular forms,[43] and is in favor of them, provided that they accord with the sacred character of worship (no. 40) and "are always the expression of the communal prayer of adoration, praise, offering and supplication, and not simply a performance" (no. 42).

Lastly, with regard to the larger issue of the relationship between liturgy and theology, especially in the context of postmodern relativism and pessimism (challenge 7), *Varietates legitimae* is aware that in countries, even those with a Christian tradition, there exists "a culture marked by indifference or disinterest in

---

[41] Nathan Mitchell has noted this "schizophrenic atmosphere" of *Varietatis legitimae*—"appearing to *affirm* a principle while later *rescinding* it"—in at least three areas: in its position regarding inculturation as a double movement of mutual enrichment, in its attitude toward central supervision and episcopal collegiality, and in its affirmation of the necessity of the Roman rite and the diversity of liturgical families (see "The Amen Corner," 375–76).

[42] Note that the instruction opposes only the *replacement* of biblical readings, chants, or prayers by texts from other religions. It does not pronounce on the *addition* of these to the liturgy. As Julian Saldanha suggests, "The rescinding of the prohibition of the use of non-biblical readings in the liturgy in India is long overdue" ("Instruction on Liturgical Inculturation," 621). As to the necessity to avoid, "even in appearance," any suggestion of religious syncretism, it must be pointed out that the danger can be avoided by enlightened catechesis and not the refusal to make use of places of worship, liturgical objects and vestments, gestures and postures that are found in other religions.

[43] "Preference should be given to materials, forms and colors which are in use in the country" (no. 43).

religion" (no. 8).[44] To meet the challenges of this type of culture, the instruction, strangely enough, judges that liturgical inculturation is not the appropriate approach since inculturation "assumes there are preexistent religious values and evangelizes them" (no. 8). Rather, it suggests the use of "liturgical formation" and "finding the most suitable means to reach spirits and hearts" (no. 8). In this context it is worth noting that postmodernism is not hostile to religion as such but only to religions with absolute claims to truth and universal validity. As mentioned earlier, postmodernism and even postmodern science have an acute sense of reality as an unfathomable mystery. Only now the mystery is located elsewhere than in religious institutions and official worship. Hence, to dismiss inculturation as an inappropriate means to recover the sense of the sacred in postmodernism because of the alleged lack of "preexistent religious values" is a shortsighted policy. Inculturation may turn out to be one of the "most suitable means to reach spirits and hearts" in postmodernity.

On the positive side, as has been mentioned above, in spite of the fact that *Varietates legitimae* seems not have been aware of the challenges of the postmodern understanding of culture, it does contain here and there statements that reflect some of the concerns of postmodernism. For example, the instruction explicitly acknowledges the historical evolution of the Roman rite, which "has known how to integrate texts, chants, gestures and rites from various sources and to adapt itself in local cultures in mission territories, even if at certain periods a desire for liturgical uniformity obscured this fact" (no. 17). Again, with regard to the choice of cultures into which the liturgy is to be inculturated (challenge 3), the instruction notes that "in a number of countries, there are several cultures which coexist, and sometimes influence each other in such a way as to lead gradually to the formation of a new culture, while at times they seek to affirm their proper identity, or even oppose each other, in order to stress their own existence" (no. 49). In these places, the instruction warns, the episcopal

---

[44] *Varietates legitimae* distinguishes three situations for liturgical inculturation. (1) The first is that of countries that do not have a Christian tradition or countries where the use of the Roman rite, brought in by missionaries, is recent (presumably Asia and Oceania). Here liturgical inculturation is said to bring to the peoples the riches of Christ and welcome their cultural riches into the liturgy so that a mutual enrichment may result. (2) The second is that of countries with a longstanding Western Christian tradition and with a well-established use of the Roman rite (presumably Europe and the Americas). Here liturgical inculturation is said to be limited to the measures of adaptation already envisaged in the liturgical books and considered sufficient. (3) The third is that of countries, both with and without a Christian tradition, where there is a growing culture marked by indifference or disinterest in religion. Here it is said that inculturation is not the appropriate approach but rather "liturgical formation" and finding the "most suitable means to reach spirits and hearts" (nos. 6–8). Given the fact that postmodernism, with its indifference (not necessarily hostility) to religion, is the hallmark of contemporary Europe and North America, and is rapidly spreading throughout the world through globalization, for *Varietates legitimae* to say that the inculturation of the Christian faith is not the appropriate means of evangelization for the third situation is either to have a very jejune notion of inculturation (akin to adaptation, which it has in principle rejected) or to restrict it to a very small geographical area.

conference "should respect the riches of each culture and those who defend
them, but they should not ignore or neglect a minority culture with which they
are not familiar" (no. 49).[45] In these statements one can hear the echo of the
postmodern understanding of culture as a site of struggle and a ground of contest in relations.

LITURGICAL INCULTURATION: PERSPECTIVES FROM THE ASIAN CHURCHES

Despite its many positive contributions to liturgical inculturation, *Varietates
legitimae* still falls short of offering an adequate strategy for this task, especially in view of the challenges of postmodernism.[46] For a fuller view of
inculturation, we now turn to the Asian churches, whose greatly varied cultural
and religious contexts pose the most difficult challenges to inculturation, on the
one hand, and which, on the other hand, from their experience of colonialism,
their missionary history (in particular, the so-called Chinese Rites Controversy),
and their own spiritual traditions, seem to offer a rich trove of resources to meet
the challenges of inculturation in the postmodern context. I examine below the
contribution of the Benedictine Filipino liturgist Anscar J. Chupungco, whose
works deal extensively with liturgical inculturation, as well as the theology of
the Federation of the Asian Bishops' Conferences.

Anscar J. Chupungco and Liturgical Inculturation

A former president of the Pontifical Liturgical Institute and Rector Magnificus
of the Pontifical Athenaeum of Sant' Anselmo in Rome and founder of the Paul
VI Institute of Liturgy in the Philippines, Chupungco is internationally known
for his works on liturgical inculturation.[47] My intention here is not to present

---

[45] Earlier, the instruction drew attention to the need to take into account the problems
posed by the coexistence of several cultures, especially as the result of immigration (no.
7).

[46] Nathan Mitchell recognizes eight valuable points in *Varietates legitimae*: It affirms
that inculturation is a two-way street, enriching a culture by inculturating the gospel
into it and enriching the gospel with the insights of that culture; it sees parallels between
the incarnation and inculturation; it affirms that faith does not require renunciation of
one's culture; it affirms that liturgical inculturation is a gradual process; it highlights
the historical evolution of the Roman rite; it promotes the preservation of all liturgical
families of both East and West; it affirms the radical inclusiveness of worship; and it
sees the Sunday assembly's full eucharistic worship as the normative ritual ("The Amen
Corner," 374).

[47] For his bibliography up to 1997, see "Bibliography of Anscar J. Chupungco," in
*Liturgy for the New Millennium: A Commentary on the Revised Sacramentary. Essays
in Honor of Anscar Chupungco*, ed. Mark Francis and Keith Pecklers, 165–68
(Collegeville, Minn.: Liturgical Press, 2000). The most important works for our purpose are: *Toward a Filipino Liturgy* (Manila: Benedictine Abbey, 1976); *Cultural Adaptation of the Liturgy* (New York: Paulist Press, 1982); *Liturgies of the Future: The
Process and Methods of Inculturation* (Mahwah, N.J.: Paulist Press, 1989); *Liturgical
Inculturation: Sacramentals, Religiosity, and Catechesis* (Collegeville, Minn.: Liturgical Press, 1992); *Shaping the Easter Feast* (Washington, D.C.: The Pastoral Press, 1992);

Chupungco's theology as a whole; rather, the focus is only on his understanding of liturgical inculturation. One significant strength of Chupungo's reflections on the relationship of the liturgy and its cultural context is their rootedness in the history of the development of the Roman rite and the teaching of Vatican II.[48] His knowledge of liturgical history impresses upon him the necessity of inculturation and gives him the freedom for liturgical innovation since all liturgies are culture-dependent. As he puts it later, "Perhaps the root of our woes in inculturation is the failure to recognize the basic fact that all liturgical rites are vested in culture, that no liturgy is celebrated in a cultural vacuum."[49] On the other hand, Vatican II's *Sacrosanctum Concilium* provides the *terra firma* from which he can sally forth into liturgical inculturation.

Undergirding inculturation, according to Chupungco, are three principles which he calls theological, liturgical, and cultural. Theologically, it is the mystery of the Incarnation that demands that the church incarnate itself in every culture. Inculturation is "an incarnational imperative, rather than a concession of Vatican II."[50] Liturgically, inculturation is governed by the following principles: (a) the liturgy is worship of God; (b) it is centered on Christ; (c) in it God's written word obtains primacy; (d) it must be actively participated in by the people; and (e) it is composed of unchangeable and changeable elements. Culturally, Chupungco distinguishes three types of liturgical adaptation. The first is *accomodatio*, which affects liturgical celebrations *hic et nunc* by the assembly and need not involve cultural adaptation. The second is *acculturation*, which is "the process whereby cultural elements which are compatible with the Roman liturgy are incorporated into it either as substitutes or illustrations of euchological and ritual elements of the Roman rite."[51] Acculturation may be achieved in both the formal or the theological elements of the Roman rite and may be carried out by dynamic translation or by assuming the rituals and traditions of the local cultures as substitutes or illustrations of the ritual elements of the Roman rite. The third is *inculturation*, which is "the process whereby a pre-Christian rite is endowed with Christian meaning."[52]

In his later writings Chupungco seems to prefer *inculturation* to *adaptation*, as the titles and subtitles of his books indicate; in these works he elaborates in

---

Worship: Beyond Inculturation (Washington, D.C.: The Pastoral Press, 1994); reissued as *Worship: Progress and Tradition: A Church Caught between Tradition and Progress* (Notre Dame, Ind.: Notre Dame Center for Pastoral Liturgy, 1995); as editor, *Handbook for Liturgical Studies*, 5 vols. (Collegeville, Minn.: Liturgical Press, 1997–2001).

[48] See the first two chapters of *Cultural Adaptation of the Liturgy*, titled "A History of Liturgical Adaptation" (3–41) and "The Magna Carta of Liturgical Adaptation" (42–57), respectively. See also the first chapter of *Liturgies of the Future*, and the first four chapters of *Worship: Beyond Inculturation* on the early cultural settings of baptism, Eucharist, orders, and music.

[49] Anscar Chupungco, "Liturgy and Components of Culture," in *Worship and Culture in Dialogue*, ed. S. Anita Stauffer (Geneva: Lutheran World Federation, 1994), 153.

[50] Chupungco, *Cultural Adaptation of the Liturgy*, 62.

[51] Ibid., 81.

[52] Ibid., 84.

greater detail what the process of inculturation entails.[53] Following Aylward Shorter, he now explains more clearly that *acculturation* is the encounter between two cultures in which they are juxtaposed side by side on a footing of mutual respect and tolerance but without producing an internal change in either. Put in a formula, acculturation is A+B=AB. In inculturation, the encounter between the two cultures occurs in three processes, namely, interaction, mutual assimilation, and transculturation. Its formula is A+B=C. Culture A is no longer simply A but becomes C; likewise, culture B is no longer simply B but becomes C. However, culture A does not become culture B, nor does culture B become culture A; each culture retains its essential elements, but both cultures are nevertheless internally transformed to constitute a new culture.[54] Liturgical inculturation, for Chupungco, is the process whereby "the liturgy is inserted into the culture, history, and tradition of the people among whom the Church dwells. It begins to think, speak, and ritualize according to the local cultural pattern."[55] Chupungco argues that the Roman rite is the example par excellence of liturgical inculturation understood in this sense.

Describing the process of liturgical inculturation, Chupungco explains that it consists in the meeting of two elements, namely, the typical editions of the liturgical books, presumably composed in Rome, and the patterns of the local culture. In Chupungco's interpretation of culture, the cultural patterns form one of the three components of culture, the other two being values and institutions. The values (for example, hospitality, community spirit, and leadership) are the principles shaping the life and activities of the community. The institutions are the community's rites, with which it celebrates the different phases of human life from birth to death. And the cultural patterns are "the typical ways members of a society think or form concepts, express their thoughts through language, ritualize aspects of their life, and create art forms. The areas covered by cultural patterns are thus: thought, language, rites and symbols, literature, music, architecture, and all other expressions of the fine arts."[56]

As to the method of liturgical inculturation, Chupungco expands the two ways of dynamic translation and finding cultural equivalents into three: dynamic equivalence, creative assimilation, and organic progression. By "dynamic equivalence," which includes translation, he means "replacing an element of the Roman liturgy with something in the local culture that has an equal meaning and value."[57] By "creative assimilation," which for Chupungco "should not be regarded as the ordinary method of liturgical inculturation,"[58] he means "the integration of pertinent rites, symbols, and linguistic expressions, religious or

---

[53] Chupungco studies the use of various terms such as *indigenization, incarnation, contextualization, revision, adaptation,* and *inculturation* (see *Liturgical Inculturation,* 13–26). He even suggests that one should go "beyond inculturation," as the subtitle of his later book *Worship: Beyond Inculturation* seems to imply.

[54] Chupungco, *Liturgical Inculturation,* 27–31.

[55] Ibid., 30.

[56] Chupungco, "Liturgy and the Components of Culture," 157.

[57] Chupungco, *Liturgical Inculturation,* 37.

[58] Ibid., 45.

otherwise, into the liturgy."[59] "Organic progression" is not so much a method of inculturation as the necessity of going beyond both dynamic equivalence and creative assimilation (or "acculturation" and "inculturation," as Chupungco uses these terms). The reason for this further step is that neither Vatican II nor the post-conciliar typical editions can foresee and provide for all the particular circumstances of the local churches, which must create new forms of worship to meet their own needs:

> The work of organic progression should continue on the level of the local churches. The typical editions normally offer a wide range of options and possibilities. But the breadth of inculturation should not be hemmed in by the provisions contained in a document. The typical editions cannot possibly envisage for the local Church all the options and possibilities of inculturation. Thus their provision will prove insufficient and at times also deficient when placed vis-à-vis the demand for a truly inculturated liturgy.[60]

Liturgical inculturation, then, is only an intermediate step; one must move beyond it to what Chupungco calls "liturgical creativity." As confirmation, he cites the statement of the instruction "On the Translation of Liturgical Texts for Celebrations with a Congregation": "Texts translated from another language are clearly not sufficient for the celebration of a fully renewed liturgy. The creation of new texts will be necessary" (no. 43).[61] This does not mean a total disregard for tradition or any preexisting liturgical material, Chupungco clarifies, but only "new liturgical forms not based on the Roman typical editions."[62] He cites as examples the symbolic dance at the offertory procession, the mimetic interpretation of the gospel reading, and the use of audiovisuals at the general intercessions. Cautiously he calls for *alternative liturgies*, "whose aim is to give expression to those facets of liturgical tradition or modern life that are not considered by the Roman rite."[63] In this context he urges the creation of new sacramentals by the local churches,[64] cross-fertilization between liturgy

---

[59] Anscar Chupungco, "Two Methods of Liturgical Inculturation," in *Christian Worship: Unity in Cultural Diversity*, ed. S. Anita Stauffer (Geneva: Lutheran World Federation, 1996), 78–79. There seems to be a slight change of emphasis in Chupungco's later writings. In this essay, some four years after *Liturgical Inculturation*, Chupungco places creative assimilation before dynamic equivalence and no longer says that it is not the ordinary method of liturgical inculturation. On the contrary, the method of creative assimilation is "ideal in those instances where the liturgical rite is too austere and sober, if not impoverished. In the liturgy people need to see, feel, touch, taste, act" (81). Which is to say, most of the instances, and therefore the Roman rite, which is characterized by "sobriety, directness, brevity, simplicity, and practical sense" (*Liturgical Inculturation*), is totally inappropriate outside of the Latin/Roman world!

[60] Chupungco, *Liturgical Inculturation*, 50.

[61] Ibid., 51.

[62] Ibid., 52.

[63] Ibid., 53.

[64] Ibid., 94: "There will be occasions when a local Church will experience the need for new sacramentals, for new forms of God's continuing presence in the rhythm of daily life outside the sphere of the sacraments."

and popular religiosity,[65] and a liturgical catechesis based not only on the typical editions but also on the rituals created by the local church.[66]

From this brief survey it is clear that Chupungco's theology of and proposals for liturgical inculturation as symbolized by the formula A+B=C goes far beyond *Varietates legitimae*. He explicitly states that translations of the typical editions (in acculturation) and adoption of local traditions (in inculturation), though necessary and useful steps, are insufficient and calls for "liturgical creativity" in devising new texts and "alternative liturgies" by the local churches. Furthermore, though he does not discuss postmodernism as such, Chupungco does address, albeit indirectly, some of its challenges. For example, for him inculturation is necessarily an intercultural encounter, and more specifically, an encounter between the Roman culture, with its typical patterns of sobriety, brevity, directness, and practicality, and the culture of another local church with its own distinct and often very different patterns (challenge 1). Briefly he notes cultural pluralism and warns that a power play is at stake in inculturation (challenges 2 and 3): "Monoculturalism . . . is often the arm of conquest and domination."[67] In addition, he recognizes the irreplaceable and significant role of popular religion in an adequately inculturated liturgy (challenge 4). Finally, he avers to the existence of contemporary expressions of culture (though not necessarily postmodern) for which the Roman rite and its typical editions prove largely inadequate (challenge 6). Indeed, if A+B=C is carried to its logical conclusion, the result of liturgical inculturation can no longer be the Roman rite as it currently exists.

The Federation of Asian Bishops' Conferences: A Triple Dialogue as a Way of Being Church

While Chupungco's insights are helpful for a truly inculturated theology, they could be strengthened by the ecclesiology of the FABC. If, as Chupungco says, an inculturated catechesis presupposes an inculturated liturgy, a fortiori the latter presupposes an inculturated ecclesiology, or better, a new way of being church. This is what the FABC offers.[68]

---

[65] Ibid., 99–100: "Through the process of inculturation, liturgy and popular religiosity should enter into the dynamic interaction and mutual assimilation in order to be enriched with each other's pertinent qualities. For local Churches with long-standing popular religious practices it would seem that inculturation is the only available solution to the problem of liturgical alienation and also the best method to transform popular religiosity into an authentic vehicle of the gospel."

[66] Ibid., 169–71. Chupungco puts it pithily: "An inculturated catechesis presupposes an inculturated liturgy" (169).

[67] Chupungco, "Liturgy and Its Components of Culture," 155.

[68] The FABC was founded in 1970 during the visit of Paul VI to Manila, Philippines. It is a voluntary association of episcopal conferences in South, Southeast, East, and Central Asia. It functions through a hierarchy of structures consisting of the Plenary Assembly, the Central Committee, the Standing Committee, and the Central Secretariat with its seven offices (evangelization, social communication, laity, human development, education and student chaplaincy, ecumenical and interreligious affairs,

By historical accident, Christianity was and continues to be a foreign religion for Asians. Even Pope John Paul II points out the paradoxical fact that "most Asians tend to regard Jesus—born on Asian soil—as a Western rather than an Asian figure" (*EA*, no. 20). Furthermore, the church in Asia is still burdened by its past connections with colonial powers. Consequently, the FABC emphasizes that the most urgent task for the Asian churches is to become churches not only *in* but also *of* Asia, in other words, to become local churches.

This new way of being church in Asia demands a different ecclesiology, one that decenters the church in the sense that it makes the center of the Christian life and worship not the church but the reign of God. This sort of Copernican revolution in ecclesiology sees the goal and purpose of the mission of the church to be not the geographical and institutional expansion of the church (the *plantatio ecclesiae*) but a transparent sign and effective instrument of the saving presence of the reign of God, the reign of justice, peace, and love of which the church is a seed.

This theme has been repeatedly emphasized by the FABC, especially in its first and fifth plenary assemblies in Taipei, Taiwan, 1974, and Bandung, Indonesia, 1990, respectively.[69] In Taipei the FABC affirmed categorically: "To preach the Gospel in Asia today we must make the message and life of Christ truly incarnate in the minds and lives of our peoples. The primary focus of our task of evangelization then, at this time in our history, is the building up of a truly local church."[70] In Bandung the FABC spoke of "alternative ways of being Church in Asia in 1990s" and envisioned four specific ways. The church in Asia, it said, must be a "*communion of communities*, where laity, Religious and clergy recognize and accept each other as sisters and brothers," " a *participatory* Church where the gifts that the Holy Spirit gives to all the faithful—lay, Religious, and clerics alike—are recognized and activated," "a church that faithfully and lovingly *witnesses* to the Risen Lord Jesus and reaches out to the people of other faiths and persuasions in a dialogue of life towards the integral

---

and theological concerns). The decisions of the FABC are without juridical binding force; their acceptance is an expression of collegial responsibility. For the documents of the FABC and its various institutes, see Gaudencio Rosales and C. G. Arévalo, eds., *For All the Peoples of Asia: Federation of Asian Bishops' Conferences*, vol. 1, *Documents from 1970 to 1991* (Maryknoll, N.Y.: Orbis Books; Quezon City, Manila: Claretian Publications, 1992); Franz-Josef Eilers, ed., *For All the Peoples of Asia: Federation of Asian Bishops' Conferences,* vol. 2, *Documents from 1992 to 1996* (Quezon City, Manila: Claretian Publications, 1997); and Franz-Josef Eilers, ed., *For All the Peoples of Asia: Federation of Asian Bishops' Conferences,* vol. 3, *Documents from 1997 to 2002* (Quezon City, Manila: Claretian Publications, 2002). Other documents of the FABC after 1997 are available from FABC, 16 Caine Road, Hong Kong.

[69] See *For All the Peoples of Asia*, 1:12–25, 53–61, and 274–89.

[70] Ibid., 1:14. It says further: "The local church is a church incarnate in a people, a church indigenous and inculturated. And this means concretely a church in continuous, humble and loving dialogue with the living traditions, the cultures, the religions—in brief , with all the life-realities of the people in whose midst it has sunk its roots deeply and whose history and life it gladly makes its own" (ibid.).

liberation of all," and a Church that "serves as a *prophetic sign* daring to point beyond this world to the ineffable Kingdom that is yet fully to come."[71]

This necessity to be local churches was reiterated by the seventh plenary assembly (Samphran, Thailand, January 3–12, 2000). Speaking of "an Asian vision of a renewed Church," the assembly's final statement declares that the church in Asia is moving toward a "'truly local Church,' toward a Church 'incarnate in a people, a Church indigenous and inculturated' (2 FABC Plenary Assembly, Calcutta, 1978)."[72] In this way the church in Asia will become a "communion of communities," that is, a community of local communities, which, as Vatican II teaches, image the universal church and in which and out of which the one and only Catholic Church exists (*LG,* no. 23).[73]

The mode in which this process of becoming the local church is dialogue. It is important to note that dialogue is understood here not as a separate activity, for example, ecumenical or interreligious dialogue, but as the *modality* in which everything is to be done by and in the church in Asia, including liberation, inculturation, and interreligious dialogue. It is through this triple dialogue—with the Asian people, especially the poor, their cultures, and their religions—that the church in Asia carries out its evangelizing mission and thus becomes the local church. Hence, dialogue is not a substitution for proclamation or evangelization, as Asian theologians are sometimes accused of doing; rather, it is the way and indeed the most effective way in which proclamation of the good news is done.

The reason for this modality is the presence in Asia of the many living religions and rich cultures, among whom Christians are but a tiny minority and therefore must, even on the purely human level, enter into dialogue with other believers, in an attitude of respect and friendship, for survival. But more than the question of number there is the theological doctrine today, at least in the Roman Catholic Church, that, as John Paul II says, "the Spirit's presence and activity affect not only individuals but also society and history, peoples, cultures and religions. Indeed, the Spirit is at the origin of the noble ideals and undertakings which benefit humanity on its journey through history" (*RM,* no. 28). In light of this divine presence in people's cultures and religions, and not just in individuals, and in view of the socio-historical nature of human existence, it is possible to say, as some Asian theologians have done, that the followers of other religions are saved not in spite of them but in and through them, though it is always God who saves, and, Christians will add, in and

---

[71] Ibid., 1:287–88. For a development of this ecclesiology, see Peter C. Phan, "*Ecclesia in Asia*: Challenges for Asian Christianity," *East Asian Pastoral Review* 37/3 (2000): 220–26. See also S. J. Emmanuel, "Asian Churches for a New Evangelization: Chances and Challenges," *East Asian Pastoral Review* 36/3 (1999): 252–75.

[72] The final statement of the seventh plenary assembly of the FABC, *A Renewed Church in Asia: A Mission of Love and Service.* FABC papers, no. 93 (Hong Kong: FABC, 2000), 3.

[73] For a clear exposition of the communion ecclesiology in Vatican II, see Joseph Komonchak, "The Theology of the Local Church: State of the Question," in *The Multicultural Church*, ed. William Cenkner, 35–49 (Mahwah, N.J.: Paulist Press, 1996).

through Jesus. At least in this restricted sense, then, religions are "ways of salvation."[74]

Given this religious pluralism, it is only natural that dialogue is the preferred mode of proclamation. As Michael Amaladoss puts it:

> As soon as one no longer sees the relationship of Christianity to other religions as presence/absence or superior/inferior or full/partial, dialogue becomes the context in which proclamation has to take place. For even when proclaiming the Good News with assurance, one should do it with great respect for the freedom of God who is acting, the freedom of the other who is responding and the Church's own limitations as a witness. It is quite proper then that the Asian Bishops characterized evangelization itself as a dialogue with various Asian realities—cultures, religions and the poor.[75]

It is important to note also that dialogue as a mode of being church in Asia does not refer primarily to the intellectual exchange among experts of various religions, as is often done in the West. Rather, as we have noted several times before, it involves a fourfold presence:

> a. The *dialogue of life*, where people strive to live in an open and neigh-borly spirit, sharing their joys and sorrows, their human problems and preoccupations. b. The *dialogue of action*, in which Christians and others collaborate for the integral development and liberation of people. c. The *dialogue of theological exchange*, where specialists seek to deepen their understanding of their respective religious heritages, and to appreciate each other's spiritual values. d. The *dialogue of religious experience*, where

---

[74] The Declaration of the Congregation for the Doctrine of the Faith *Dominus Iesus* (August 6, 2000) warns that "it would be contrary to the faith to consider the Church as *one way* of salvation alongside those constituted by the other religions, seen as comple-mentary to the Church or substantially equivalent to her, even if these are said to be converging with the Church toward the eschatological Kingdom of God" (no. 22). The operative words here are "complementary" and "substantially equivalent." Obviously, it is theologically possible to hold that non-Christian religions are "ways of salvation" without holding the view implied in those two expressions. Furthermore, it does not seem necessary to affirm, as the declaration does, that "if it is true that the followers of other religions can receive divine grace, it is also certain that *objectively speaking* they are in a gravely deficient situation in comparison with those who, in the Church, have the fullness of the means of salvation" (ibid.) since (1) what is ultimately important, from the point of view of salvation, is that the person receives divine grace, no matter where and how, and (2) it does not do the Christians much good to have "the fullness of the means of salvation" and not in fact make effective use of them. As Augustine has observed, there are those who are in the church but do not belong to the church, and those who are outside of the church but do belong to it. At any rate, such expressions as used by the declaration are nowhere found in Vatican II.

[75] Michael Amaladoss, *Making All Things New: Dialogue, Pluralism, and Evangeli-zation in Asia* (Maryknoll, N.Y.: Orbis Books, 1990), 59.

persons, rooted in their own religious traditions, share their spiritual riches, for instance, with regard to prayer and contemplation, faith and ways of searching for God or the Absolute (*DP*, no. 42).

As noted above, the FABC suggests that this dialogue take place in three areas: dialogue with the Asian poor, their cultures, and their religions.[76] In other words, the three essential tasks of the Asian churches are liberation, inculturation, and interreligious dialogue.[77] For our discussion on liturgical inculturation, it is vital to note that for the FABC these are not three distinct and separate activities of the church; rather, they are three intertwined dimensions of the church's one mission of evangelization. As the FABC's seventh plenary assembly puts it concisely:

These issues are not separate topics to be discussed, but aspects of an integrated approach to our Mission of Love and Service. We need to feel and act "integrally." As we face the needs of the 21st century, we do so with Asian hearts, in solidarity with the poor and the marginalized, in union with all our Christian brothers and sisters and by joining hands with all men and women of Asia of many different faiths. Inculturation, dialogue, justice and option for the poor are aspects of whatever we do.[78]

Liturgical Inculturation as Dialogue

It is only in light of the Asian church's attempt to find a new way of being church, of becoming a fully local church, a church that is a participatory "communion of communities," integrally engaged in the triple, intrinsically interconnected dialogue with the Asian poor, their cultures, and their religions, that, in my judgment, liturgical inculturation can be correctly understood. It is very interesting to note that in the thirty years of its existence and its abundant theological production, the FABC has devoted very few pages to the explicit theme of liturgical inculturation.[79] This lacuna, I believe, is not an oversight. Rather, it is due to the FABC's overarching and fundamental insight that inculturation, liturgical or otherwise, is not something to be pursued for its own sake, or to make worship palatable to Asian aesthetic and religious tastes. It must be subordinated

---

[76] See *For All the Peoples of Asia*, 1:14–16, 22–23, 34–35, 107, 135, 141–43, 281–82, 307–12, 328–34, and 344; *For All the Peoples of Asia*, 2:196–203.

[77] As Archbishop Oscar V. Cruz, secretary general of the FABC, said at the seventh plenary assembly: The Asian churches are engaged in "the triple dialogue with the poor, with cultures, and with peoples of other religions, envisioned by FABC as a mode of evangelization, viz., human liberation, inculturation, interreligious dialogue" (*A Renewed Church in Asia: Pastoral Directions for a New Decade*, FABC papers, no. 95 [Hong Kong: FABC, 2000], 17).

[78] FABC, *A Renewed Church in Asia: A Mission of Love and Service*, 8.

[79] One of the FABC's important texts on liturgical inculturation is found in *Theses on the Local Church: A Theological Reflection in the Asian Context*, thesis 8, FABC papers, no. 60 (Hong Kong: FABC, 1991).

to the task of becoming an Asian church through the essential mode of dialogue with the Asian poor, their cultures, and their religions.

Of course, it is not the task of the FABC to devise concrete forms or programs of liturgical inculturation. These fall within the competence of each bishop and each conference of bishops. The FABC recognizes that the church in Asia still "remains foreign in its lifestyle, in its institutional structure, in its worship" and that "Christian rituals often remain formal, neither spontaneous nor particularly Asian."[80] Hence it urges, in general terms, a renewal of all aspects of the church's prayer life, including "its liturgical worship, its popular forms of piety, prayer in the home, in parishes, in prayer groups."[81] One step of this renewal is the use of "venerable books and writings" of other religions for prayer and spirituality.[82]

With regard to Asian popular religion in particular, the FABC recognizes that its world view is heavily influenced by Confucian and Taoist thought, which emphasizes that "the human person is a spiritual being living in a spirit-filled, mutually interacting and interdependent world" and that "the underlying aim of customs, ritual, worship, etc. is the maintenance of harmony between humankind and the natural world."[83]

In spite of these rather general indications, the FABC does provide two very useful guidelines for an authentic liturgical inculturation. First, liturgical inculturation must be undertaken always in conjunction with and as an intrinsic component of interreligious dialogue and the work for human liberation. Without interreligious dialogue, liturgical inculturation would operate in the void, at least in Asia, since it would lack the context into which it can insert Christian worship, on the one hand, and it would have nothing to bring into Christian worship, on the other, as the twofold movement of inculturation implies. This inculturation of Christian liturgy must be carried out in two areas, namely, the metacosmic religions or soteriologies (Hinduism, Buddhism, Taoism, Confucianism, Islam, Shintoism, and so on) with their official forms of worship and prayer, and the cosmic religion that is often embodied in popular devotions commonly practiced at home and in the family. Even in the United States, where the prevalent context is not yet religious pluralism, although it is a rapidly growing phenomenon, liturgical inculturation must still take into account the American culture and its civil religion, not to mention the black and Hispanic/Latino cultures and their religious traditions. At any rate, the separation of religion from culture, which is often made in the West and which permits an inculturation of

---

[80] *For All the Peoples of Asia,* 2:195.

[81] Ibid., 1:34.

[82] Ibid., 1:35: "We believe that with deeper study and understanding, with prudent discernment on our part and proper catechesis of our Christian people, these many indigenous riches will at last find a natural place in the prayer of our churches in Asia and will greatly enrich the prayer-life of the Church throughout the world." For the FABC's theology of liturgical inculturation, see Jonathan Tan Yun-ka, "Constructing an Asian Theology of Liturgical Inculturation from the Documents of the Federation of Asian Bishops' Conferences (FABC)," *East Asian Pastoral Review* 36/4 (1999): 383–401.

[83] *For All the Peoples of Asia,* 2:163.

liturgy into culture without facing the religious issues, makes no sense in Asia, where culture and religion form an indivisible whole.

Furthermore, as a form of interreligious dialogue, liturgical inculturation will not be undertaken simplistically as the "incarnation" of a culture-free gospel or culture-free liturgy into another culture, which at times the model of incarnation for inculturation seems to suggest. As Michael Amaladoss and Aylward Shorter have reminded us, inculturation is always *interculturation*. It is an encounter among at least three cultures—of the Bible, of the Christian tradition, and of the people to whom the gospel is proclaimed.[84] I will broach the dynamics of power play in this intercultural encounter in the last part of my essay; here suffice it to note that liturgical inculturation without an adequate sensitivity to its intercultural dimension runs the risk of imposing a particular culture, for example, that implicit in the Roman rite, onto others.

Without the struggle for human liberation, liturgical inculturation runs the risk of being an elitist enterprise, perhaps with purely aesthetic and archeological interest.[85] Worse, it may be a disguised form of cultural chauvinism, especially when the culture into which the liturgy is inculturated is that of the dominant class.[86] For instance, *Dalit* and Tribal theologians in India have consistently argued that Brahminic Hinduism is not the only culture and religion of India, and therefore liturgical inculturation cannot assume it as the only partner with which it must dialogue.[87] Similarly, *minjung* theologians of Korea have chosen the "people"—that is, the mass that is politically oppressed, economically exploited, socially alienated, religiously marginalized, and culturally kept uneducated by the dominant group of the society—as the embodiment of the Messiah.[88] Among

---

[84] See Michael Amaladoss, *Beyond Inculturation: Can the Many Be One?* (Delhi: Society for Promotion of Christian Knowledge, 1998), 20–23; and Aylward Shorter, *Toward a Theology of Inculturation* (Maryknoll, N.Y.: Orbis Books, 1988), 13–16.

[85] For the FABC's theology of human liberation, see Peter C. Phan, "Human Development and Evangelization: The First to the Sixth Plenary Assembly of the Federation of Asian Bishops' Conference," *Studia Missionalia* 47 (1998): 205–27.

[86] *Varietates legitimae* has reminded the bishops that "they should not ignore or neglect a minority culture with which they are not familiar" (no. 49).

[87] The *Dalits* (literally, "broken") are considered too polluted to participate in the social life of Indian society; they are the untouchable. Between two-thirds and three-quarters of the Indian Christian community are *Dalits*. On *Dalit* theology, see Sathianathan Clarke, *Dalit and Christianity: Subaltern Religion and Liberation Theology in India* (New Delhi: Oxford University Press, 1998); James Massey, *Dalits in India: Religion as a Source of Bondage or Liberation with Special Reference to Christians* (New Delhi: Mahohar, 1995); and M. E. Prabhakar, *Towards a Dalit Theology* (Madras: Gurukul, 1989). On tribal theology, see Nirmal Minz, *Rise Up, My People, and Claim the Promise: The Gospel among the Tribes of India* (Delhi: ISPCK, 1997). See also R. S. Sugirtharajah, ed., *Frontiers in Asian Christian Theology: Emerging Trends* (Maryknoll, N.Y.: Orbis Books, 1994), 11–62.

[88] On *minjung* (literally, "people") theology, see Jung Young Lee, ed., *An Emerging Theology in World Perspective: Commentary on Korean Minjung Theology* (Mystic, Conn.: Twenty-Third Publications, 1988); and Peter C. Phan, "Experience and Theology: An Asian Liberation Perspective," *Zeitschrift für Missionswissenschaft und Religionswissenschaft* 77/2 (1993): 118–20.

Asian theologians no one has argued more forcefully for the unity between inculturation and liberation than the Sri Lankan Jesuit Aloysius Pieris, who insists that the church *in* Asia, in order to be *of* Asia, must undergo a double baptism in the river of the "religiousness of the Asian poor" and the "poverty of religious Asians."[89]

If this coupling of liturgical inculturation with liberation and interreligious dialogue is objected to on the ground that it is made into an exceedingly complicated affair, then my point has been understood. Indeed, we should disabuse ourselves of the notion that liturgical inculturation consists mainly in the adaptation of local language, music and singing, gesture and posture, and art while maintaining the *"substantial unity* of the Roman rite," as *Varietates legitimae* insists. In fact, in such a strategy there is a serious danger of what Aloysius Pieris calls "theological vandalism," that is, picking and choosing elements of non-Christian religions and "baptizing" them for Christian use, with no reverence for the wholeness of non-Christians' religious experience.[90]

The second important insight of FABC on liturgical inculturation concerns popular religion. By focusing on dialogue with the Asian poor, the FABC see popular religion primarily as the religion of the poor people. This popular religion or cosmic religiosity in Asia is characterized, according to Pieris, by seven features: it has a this-worldly spirituality, it is animated by a sense of total dependence on the divine, it longs for justice, it is cosmic, it accords women a key role, it is ecological, and it communicates through story.[91] By engaging with and retrieving this popular religion, liturgical inculturation will tap into its potential for human liberation. In popular religion believers seek immediate satisfaction of physical and material needs, they feel God as a close liberating presence, they appeal to the spirits for protection and deliverance, they accord equal roles to women and men in their rituals, and their religious symbols can function as rallying points for the masses. An example of this liberative power of popular religion, from the Christian perspective, is People Power in the Philippines, which has demonstrated the power of popular devotions to unite

---

[89] See Aloysius Pieris, *An Asian Liberation Theology* (Maryknoll, N.Y.: Orbis Books, 1988), 45–50.

[90] See ibid., 41–42, 53, 85.

[91] See Aloysius Pieris, "An Asian Paradigm: Inter-religious Dialogue and Theology of Religions," *The Month* 254 (1993): 131–32. Michael Amaladoss offers a comprehensive discussion of popular Catholicism in "Toward a New Ecumenism: Churches of the People," in *Popular Catholicism in a World Church: Seven Case Studies in Inculturation*, ed. Thomas Bamat and Jean-Paul West, 272–301 (Maryknoll, N.Y.: Orbis Books, 1999). He sees popular Catholicism to be characterized by the desire for a good earthly life, a concern to ward off evil, a connection with the world of spirits and ancestors, an inclination toward sacramentality and community, and a suspicion of modern ideologies. For a presentation of Catholic popular devotions with respect to Asia, see José M. de Mesa, "Primal Religion and Popular Religiosity," *East Asian Pastoral Review* 37/1 (2000): 73–82; Kathleen Coyle, "Pilgrimages, Apparitions and Popular Piety," *East Asian Pastoral Review* 38/2 (2001): 172–89; and Peter C. Phan, "Mary in Vietnamese Piety and Theology: A Contemporary Perspective," *Ephemerides Mariologicae* 51/4 (2001): 457–71.

the people in their effort to overthrow dictatorship, and recently, to remove a corrupt president.

In conclusion, in the postmodern age with its manifold challenges to the Christian faith, a truly inculturated liturgy capable of meeting these challenges can no longer, it seems to me, be conceived mainly as a transposition of the Roman rite with its inherited rituals and centrally composed typical editions, even in the "accommodated" and "inculturated" forms, by way of both "dynamic equivalence" and "creative assimilation." This method of inculturation will be regarded, and rightly so in an age deeply suspicious of power play, as an unjustified imposition of a particular culture with its patterns and institutions onto another culture and will inevitably fail to respond fully to the needs of the local churches. The starting point of a genuine inculturation must be a vibrant new way of being church, characterized by the triple dialogue as advocated by the FABC, out of which a new ritual family, with its own texts, rites, sacramentals, forms of popular religiosity, and various expressions of worship will eventually be constituted. Only in this way is the unity of faith preserved and promoted amid cultural pluralism. This is no revolutionary approach; after all, that is what the Roman rite did, in its own way.

14

How Much Uniformity Can We Stand? How Much Unity Do We Want?

WORSHIP IN A MULTICULTURAL AND MULTI-RELIGIOUS CONTEXT

The place is a parish mission in Dalat, a mountainous region in South Vietnam. The time is Sunday. The people who have gathered for worship, clad in their multicolored costumes, belong to the Co Ho, a group of the Mon-Khmer tribal peoples that populate the southern highlands of the country. The leader of the community is a woman, because the Co Ho society is matriarchal. She has been leading the congregation in prayer, as she does every day, to prepare them for the Mass. There is a palpably festive mood in the air because this is the first time in months that the priest has paid the community a visit. While the assembly is reciting devotional prayers, the priest sits in a corner listening to confessions. When he finishes with the last penitent, he dons the alb over his black cassock, ties a cord around his waist, puts the stole over his shoulders, and tops it all with a chasuble. He then places the white hosts in a ciborium and pours a little wine into the chalice, with extreme care, to prevent waste, because both the flour with which the hosts are made and the wine are imported from Europe at great cost. He proceeds to the rectangular altar to celebrate the Mass, accompanied by boys carrying the book of readings and the *Roman Missal,* the translations of which into Vietnamese have been duly approved by the Vatican. The people attend to his words and gestures with rapt attention and deep devotion, despite their strangeness. When the time comes for communion, almost all of them line up to receive the hosts, so happy that they can welcome into their hearts what their faith teaches is the very body and blood of the Lord Jesus Christ. After the Mass the priest visits the sick people who were unable to come to Mass, and then he leaves, to return perhaps in a few months. Meanwhile, the woman who is the leader of the community resumes her day-to-day ministry of teaching, building up, and caring for the community during the priest's absence.

This scene, which I witnessed on my recent visit to my country after twenty years' absence, is not limited to an isolated parish in Vietnam. With the steadily increasing shortage of priests and the rapidly growing number of priestless parishes, the Sunday Mass is being enacted in similar fashion throughout the world— in Asia, Australia, Africa, South America, and recently even in the United States.

This scenario serves as a springboard to broach the theme of this chapter, namely, unity and uniformity in worship in the Roman Catholic Church, especially in its third millennium. In fact, in my judgment the celebration of the Mass as described above embodies, poignantly, what is best and what is worst in current liturgical practices, canonical determinations, administrative policies, and theological reflections of the Roman Catholic Church.

I first examine these "worsts" and "bests" under two questions: How much uniformity can we stand? How much unity do we want? I then delineate the shape that the church of this new millennium must assume if its forms of worship are to become life-giving for those who participate in them.[1]

HOW MUCH UNIFORMITY CAN WE STAND?

To understand the import of this question, imagine for a moment that you are the Co Ho Christian woman who is the leader of her community at that Mass. A young Co Ho woman does not stay at home, demurely waiting for a man to ask her to marry him. She actively looks for one, and when she has found the man she wants, she informs her parents of the fact. With a go-between, the parents visit the young man's family to propose the marriage, with offerings of a copper bracelet and a glass bead necklace. Acceptance of the gifts means agreement to the marriage. After the wedding the bridegroom comes to live with his wife's family, and their children take the name of the maternal family, Co Ho families being bound by matrilineal ties. The *Khmer* term *mêkhlôt*, meaning "head of the household," indicates the woman in the family.

Now you have become a Catholic Christian. At the heart of your faith life is the Eucharist. But to celebrate it, several anomalies have been forced upon you and your people. The service of someone from outside the tribe is required because no man of your people is willing to be trained for the priesthood, one of the many reasons being the celibacy requirement. Furthermore, the priest is a man, something foreign to the structure of your matriarchal society. And he comes to the community only rarely, whenever time and circumstances permit, so that your community is regularly deprived of what you are taught and feel to be the most powerful sustenance of your faith life. Spiritually, your people are being starved.

And when this male priest celebrates, he is dressed in the strangest of clothes. In his sacred garb he definitely looks like one of those Europeans who colonized your country for almost two hundred years, though he is a Vietnamese, similar to you in complexion and race. Surely, the festive costumes of your tribe express much better the solemnity and joyousness of the occasion.

---

[1] In general terms this essay may be said to be concerned with the issue of liturgical inculturation. However, my intention here is not to discuss inculturation in the abstract or to relate my reflections to various theories of liturgical inculturation, the literature on which is extensive. For my reflections on inculturation, see Chapter 1 herein and my "Contemporary Theology and Inculturation in the United States," in *The Multicultural Church: A New Landscape in U.S. Theologies*, ed. William Cenkner (New York: Paulist Press, 1996), esp. 109–30, 176–92.

The rituals and gestures of the priest also look weird. The priest genuflects, presumably to express respect, extends his hands above his head as a sign of prayer, and even washes his hands in the middle of the celebration. That is not the way your people express veneration for and pray to God. When your tribespeople celebrate sacred rituals, they dance and dance, dressed in costumes of variegated colors and accompanied by musical instruments such as copper gongs, trumpets, bamboo flutes, bamboo oboes, buffalo horns, and string instruments. Surely God's eyes and ears must be more aroused and delighted by such colorful vestments, melodious sounds, and vigorous movements than by the timid ringing of a tinny bell by the altar boy!

Furthermore, the prayers the priest recites sound foreign. Presumably, they were composed by a committee of liturgical experts in Rome, then sent to a committee of Vietnamese experts to be translated into the local language, and sent back to Rome for approval by another committee whose knowledge of your tribe's language and culture is highly questionable. Yet this committee will have a final say in deciding whether the translation is accurate and appropriate. Meanwhile, the rich religious heritage of your people, the sacred texts of your indigenous religions, and their sacred rituals, which have nourished the souls of your people for centuries, are left unexploited.

But what is stranger still is how the tiny white hosts and wine are supposed to symbolize food and drink for your people. You understand that they are *symbols* of spiritual nourishment; still, your people don't eat bread made of wheat or drink wine made out of grapes. These things are all imported, and only the rich, surely not your tribe, can afford them. Somehow the truth of Christ's body and blood as food and drink for your people, especially for the poor for whom he had a preferential love, is largely obscured. And the very parsimonious way the priest doles out the hosts and measures the wine belies the generosity and abundance of God's love and God's desire to share divine life with us.

Another thing that strikes you as extremely sad is that what is most sacred and central to the religious traditions of your tribe is barely given a place in the most sacred ritual of your church. There is, of course, a brief prayer for "those who have died in the peace of Christ," but that hardly counts as veneration of ancestors. The Co Ho tribe, like many other Asian peoples, worship their ancestors. Their names and histories are written on a finely carved piece of wood that is placed above the entrance door or at the most honored place in the house. On the anniversaries of their deaths and on any important occasion for the family, such as the New Year, the birth of a child, an engagement or wedding, graduation, or the death of a member of the family, foods and flowers are offered to the ancestors in gratitude for their love, and prayers are addressed not only *for* but also *to* them to ask for their continued protection.[2]

Finally, something anomalous catches your eye. The male priest comes and goes, like a sacramental salesman. You have been told that priestly ministry is

---

[2] For a discussion of the Vietnamese cult of ancestors and an attempt to construct a Christology on it, see Peter C. Phan, "The Christ of Asia: An Essay on Jesus as the Eldest Son and Ancestor," *Studia Missionalia* 45 (1996): 25–55.

leadership of the community by which you teach, build up, care for, and share life with the believing community. The priest is not just one who has the power to "confect" the sacraments, especially to consecrate the eucharistic species and to forgive sins.

It has come to your attention that, contrary to this Counter-Reformation sacral model of priesthood, the East Asian Pastoral Institute in Manila, Philippines, has published a report entitled "Priests for the Twenty-first Century," in which the kind of priest needed, at least for Asia, in the new millennium is described as

> a loving person aware of his gifts and sinfulness, someone who recognizes the reality of change as an invitation rather than a threat; a disciple ready to listen and learn from any person and any experience; someone alive to the reality of society, to the challenges of biocide, poverty, injustice; a person who can accompany and guide people in their search for God in the everyday realities of their lives and who can lead the community in celebration of that reality and of God's presence in it.[3]

Ironically, you, the lay woman who leads this community both during the Mass and the priest's prolonged absence, seem to fill this job description far better than the male priest who, through no fault of his, occasionally pops in with his Mass kit to confect the Eucharist and then departs.

What is the root cause of all these lamentable anomalies? It is, I submit, the lust for uniformity. Other names for it are fear of otherness, libido for power, mania for control, bureaucratic centralization, Eurocentrism, cultural imperialism, and theological colonialism. These aberrations need not be conscious, nor are they undertaken necessarily for evil reasons. Indeed, perniciously, they often are unconscious and may be motivated by a sincere concern for doctrinal orthodoxy, correct praxis, and ecclesial unity. Pernicious, especially when divine sanction is invoked to justify church policies, because any attempt at questioning this presumably well-intentioned imposition of uniformity will be condemned, at least by some, as deviation from the true faith, cultural relativism, and disloyalty to the hierarchy. This is not to say that such a critique is never liable to degenerate into these evils. The question is whether it can and should be done in an atmosphere of mutual respect and trust so that the unity of the faith and Christian charity are not endangered.

HOW MUCH UNITY DO WE WANT?

This brings us to the second question: How much unity do we want? Again, to understand the import of this question, let us return to the scene of the Mass described above. Despite its strangeness and anomalies, the Mass achieves something unimaginable. It creates a profound unity, a union of mind and heart among the people of the Co Ho tribe that transcends time, space, race, gender, and

---

[3] Quoted in Joseph F. Eagan, *Restoration and Renewal: The Catholic Church in the Third Millennium* (Kansas City: Sheed & Ward, 1995), 344.

class. It effects a union that binds them to the Vietnamese priest who celebrates the Mass with them, to the pope and the local bishop for whom they pray, to the Jews whom they have never met and probably never will but from whose scripture they read, to the early church of the apostles whose gospels and letters are proclaimed to them, to the present church worldwide, to the living and the dead, to the angels and saints, and to the persons of the divine Trinity themselves.

It is a mind-shattering miracle that a group of humble, poor, and uneducated tribespeople in a thatch-roofed church nestled in the highlands of a Communist country can achieve that indescribable universal communion. And this same communion is realized at every eucharistic celebration in every corner of the world.

What brings about this communion? It is the assembly's celebration of the Eucharist and, most powerfully, the body and blood of Christ, the gift of God the Father, brought forth by the power of the Holy Spirit. That is why the Co Ho people are excited and filled with joy that the Vietnamese priest brings them this gift. They eagerly line up at communion to receive it, to feast their minds and hearts on it, to let their lives be transformed by what they have been taught to call "a sacrament of love, a sign of unity, a bond of charity, a paschal banquet . . . a pledge of future glory" (*SC,* no. 47). That is why it is atrocious that, for whatever manmade reasons (the word *man* is used advisedly), they and so many other Christians around the world are being deprived of the Eucharist. It is an ironic tragedy as well that the church, which prides itself on its sacramentality, is losing, through its own making, its most essential characteristic.

To feel the pains of eucharistic deprivation and the power that the Eucharist has in achieving unity, allow me to tell you two stories I was privileged to hear, the first from a priest, and the second from a lay man, both of whom have come to the United States after years of imprisonment. The priest was an army chaplain, who, after the 1975 victory of the Communists over South Vietnam, was imprisoned along with hundreds of other chaplains, Catholic, Protestant, and Buddhist. The government forbade the priests to celebrate Mass; furthermore, it was impossible to do so due to the lack of proper "matter." Sometimes, however, their relatives succeeded in smuggling in the hosts and wine, and so the priest would celebrate the Mass, silently, in the dead of night. I was told by this priest, who spent thirteen years in prison, that it was then that he felt a profound sense of unity and communion with the church.

Not only priests but the laity achieved that sense of communion with the church through the Eucharist. During a recent lecture at a Vietnamese parish, I asked the audience when they had had a vivid sense of God's presence for the first time. After many had recounted their religious experiences, a man in his late fifties raised his hand. He had been a military officer, he said, and had been imprisoned by the Communists for eight years. During those years he longed for the Eucharist, and once he secretly received from a fellow prisoner a tiny fragment of the consecrated host. In ecstatic terms and with deep conviction he described how he had felt at that moment, as never before, the burning nearness of God. Communion with Christ brought him peace and joy, he added, and as a result he could forgive his enemies.

Admittedly these historical vignettes, each in its own way a desperate cry for the universal availability of the Eucharist, only tell us what creates our unity with God and among ourselves, but they have not settled the question of what kind of unity we should want, the kind of unity that is diametrically opposed to deadening and alienating uniformity. Before we examine this question, however, let us not lose sight of the enormous irony that in the very one and same act of worship, oppressive uniformity produced by humans is overcome by liberating unity wrought by God. The fact that God can and does write straight with crooked lines should bolster our hope as we enter a new century and a new millennium, even when a realistic assessment of the signs of the times does not forecast a significant change in church policies in the near future.

But what kind of unity should we want? In his encyclical *Ad Petri cathedram (On Truth, Unity, and Peace in a Spirit of Charity),* Pope John XXIII repeats a well-known dictum: "Let there be unity in what is necessary, freedom in what is doubtful, and charity in everything."[4] In light of this principle the answer to our question must be that we should want unity only in things that are necessary or essential to our faith and Christian living. Unfortunately, the wisdom and simplicity of this principle is deceptive, since there is a heated debate precisely about what constitutes the "necessaria" in which there must be "unitas." Indeed, what appears to be, for many theologians and lay Catholics, still doubtful or at least open to debate, has been of late declared by the Magisterium to be definitively held. Church teachings on the "artificial" contraception and the ordination of women come to mind.

The question then turns on how the church goes about determining what is necessary and essential. The answer to this question, too complex to be dealt with here, falls within the purview of theological methodology and ecclesiology. At any rate, however this determination is carried out, clearly it cannot be done by the Magisterium alone or by the theologians alone or by the laity alone. It must be a *common* and *concerted* effort by the church as a whole, in which all voices and experiences, even those of non-Catholics and non-Christians, are respectfully and carefully listened to and evaluated, in which the *ecclesia docens* is also the *ecclesia discens* and vice versa.

If after this open, honest, and extensive learning process a consensus does not emerge among committed, practicing, and well-qualified Christians, perhaps it is a sign that a doctrine is still doubtful, and therefore freedom should be allowed, as John XXIII teaches us. To impose a doctrine or a practice when there is still widespread debate about its rootedness in the scripture, in the creed, and in the tradition is to risk "non-reception" by the people of God.

But there is another criterion by which the necessity of a doctrine and practice can be gauged: its practical consequences for the life of faith and worship. The question to be kept in mind is: To what extent does this doctrine or practice allow Christ's saving grace to be most effective for the greatest number of people? Here the matter is somewhat less murky than theoretical considerations. For it

---

[4] *Acta Apostolicae Sedis* 51 (1959), 513. This principle was reiterated by Vatican II (*GS,* no. 92).

is not difficult to answer the questions of whether it is worth preserving certain ecclesiastical policies when they end up preventing, by the law of unintended consequences, millions of Catholics from receiving the eucharistic gift of life, daily or on Sundays; Catholic women from living out their baptismal vocation and dignity in its fullness; priestly ministry from achieving its full potential; or cultures from manifesting the active but hidden presence of God in them. These questions sound ludicrously rhetorical, for there can be, from the perspective of the principle of *sacramenta propter homines* and of practical wisdom, only one reasonable answer to them. Framed in the context of salvation, the issues of married clergy and the ordination of women, insofar as they affect the availability of the Eucharist, do not seem to be overly complex at all. If the Son of God emptied himself and became human "for the sake of our salvation," who are we to stand in the way, preventing him from feeding millions of humans who are being starved spiritually?

THE SHAPE OF THE CHURCH TO COME

If practical wisdom and concern for salvation seem to afford a reasonable answer to many currently debated issues in the church, why is it that the Catholic church, at least in the United States, seems to be torn apart by polarization and even mutual hatred, forgetting John XXIII's injunction about "charity in all things"? Why do we need a special project to reestablish a "common ground" among Catholics, such as the one initiated by the late Cardinal Joseph Bernardin?

It seems to me that the problem of division in the church does not lie much more in a particular "mood" in the church than in particular decisions or structures taken by church authorities, on the one hand, and vocal opposition to them by some groups in the church, on the other. Of course, certain church policies do anger or alienate people, especially if they are perceived to commit an injustice against certain groups. But far deeper than policies and structures lies a fundamental "mood" that gives a certain "shape" to the church. By *mood* I do not mean simply a psychological posture, a sort of *fin-de-siècle* or end-of-millennium malaise. I mean a theological and ecclesiological vision that shapes the life of the church, a vision that, ironically, is common to both conservatives and liberals.

This mood can be characterized as, to use an old label, Pelagian. I call it a mood because it is not explicitly articulated but seems to undergird the two opposing camps in the church equally. It is Pelagian because it consists in thinking that the church stands or falls on one's success in imposing on the entire church one's ideologies and agenda. It is, when all is said and done, a form of righteousness. Both conservatives and liberals are sincerely convinced that they are the last bastion in the cosmic battle for the survival of the church. Needless to say, in the end-of-millennium apocalyptic fervor, this sense of one's indispensability and this messianic complex can be brought to a feverish pitch.

One needs not be a Vatican basher to recognize that in the last two decades there has been a concerted effort on the part of influential Vatican officials, sometimes with the powerful support of right-wing and fundamentalist lay Catholics, to stop or at least slow down the reform movement undertaken by Vatican II. In their view, the church, because of the liberals' tendentious interpretations of Vatican II, has traveled on a wrong track. The list of "interventions" by the Vatican in order to "save" the church is too well known to require recounting here.

On the other hand, in response to these authoritarian measures, groups of liberal Catholics have attempted, sometimes through pressure, to "rescue" the church from what they perceive as destructive actions of the conservatives. They agitate and apply pressure for such structural changes as a more genuine exercise of episcopal collegiality (for example, deliberative vote for the synod of bishops, respect for the voices of the local churches in the appointment of bishops, greater autonomy for the national episcopal conferences), married clergy, the ordination of women, academic freedom, and a greater role for the laity in the life of the church.

In this struggle for control of the church's future, the conservatives no doubt gain an advantage over the liberals because they often have church authorities on their side to whom they urge obedience and loyalty. They accuse their adversaries of heresy and disloyalty, and of making use of political means, especially the media of communication, to further their goals. The truth of the matter is that these conservatives are no less ready to resort to power and pressure of whatever sort to achieve their ends. Often it is impossible to distinguish between the strategies and tactics of conservatives and of liberals. Common to both the right and left wings is, as I have suggested, the conviction that without them and their actions the church will perish.

It is this mood that is at the root of so much division and polarization in the church. Of course, it may be inspired by heartfelt sincerity and spiritual zeal. But however subjectively blameless it may be, it is nevertheless destructive of church unity because it is fundamentally arrogant, self-righteous, and intolerant. Worst of all, it is contrary to the gospel. In the first place, it is forgetful of the parable of the weeds among the wheat, which warns against separating the weeds from the wheat while they are still growing (Mt 13:24–30). It dismisses Jesus' injunction not to attempt to anticipate God's final judgment by excluding anyone, even sinners, from the kingdom in its present stage. Similarly, it is forgetful of Jesus' parable of the net thrown into the sea and catching all kinds of fish, of which the bad ones will be thrown away only at the end of the age (Mt 13:47–49).

Second, it is forgetful of the extremely wise warning of Gamaliel, who told his colleagues in the Sanhedrin about persecuting the apostles: "So now I tell you, have nothing to do with these men, and let them go. For if this endeavor or this activity is of human origin, it will destroy itself. But if it comes from God, you will not be able to destroy them; you may even find yourselves fighting against God" (Acts 5:38–39). Gamaliel's counsel, though not necessarily inspired by God, contains an all-important distinction between activities of human origin and those coming from God, and an urgent call for careful discernment between the two. Such a discernment is indeed a matter of life and death, since one might be fighting against a particular cause in vain, and much more terrifying, one might be fighting against God!

Third, and most important, it is forgetful of Jesus' promise that he will be with the church always, "until the end of the age" (Mt 28:20), and that "the gates of hell will not prevail against it" (Mt 16:18). Even if conservatives and liberals regard each other as "the gates of hell," however interpreted, they should be convinced by Jesus' own words that their enemies can never destroy the church. They should also realize that the church will survive not because of whatever good actions they do but because of Jesus' promise that he will be with his church until the end of time.

My critique of the Pelagian mood of conservatives and liberals alike in the church is not a call for passivism and quietism. Nor is it a version of the doctrine of *sola fide* justification. On the contrary, both faith and work are necessary, or better still, good work is required as response to and imperative of justification by faith alone. What is demanded, then, is neither mere passivism nor mere activism but a healthy dose of self-criticism and even self-doubt, a willingness to admit not only that one's opponents may be inspired by the same (or better) love for God and the church as oneself, but also that one's motives may be not entirely noble and pure, that one's policies and actions may not produce uniformly good results, and that one's tactics may be a source of scandal for the people of God and persons of good will.

That such a measure of intellectual honesty and humility is in tune with the postmodern age, which has grown skeptical of claims to universal validity, is not the only or first reason for adopting it, though to do so may help make the Christian message more credible to people of our times. Rather, the most compelling reason for such a posture of honesty and humility is theological, for it has to do with the nature of God as Absolute Mystery, ever elusive of human attempts to encapsulate God. It is also christological, for it has to do with Jesus' promise to abide with us and not with the success of our work. Our work may at best be the condition but never the cause of the coming of the reign of God which is always only God's deed. The conviction that God's reign will come in spite of what humans can do against the church should fill us with confidence, courage, and hope in our work; and the knowledge that it comes not because of our planning, strategies, and implementation of these but by the power of the Holy Spirit should imbue us with a good measure of self-questioning and humility.

How does this attitude affect the shape of the church to come and its worship? It is impossible, of course, to delineate in detail the ecclesiological and liturgical implications of this non-Pelagian theology. In terms of John XXIII's dictum, it may be said that there should be as much charity as possible and as much freedom as feasible. Or, in terms of the two questions of our essay, we stand as little uniformity as possible and we want as much unity as possible. To put it differently, in church and worship there should be unity-in-diversity.

The general principle of unity-in-diversity may be further specified by saying that we should be united with one another in doing everything possible to enable God's *salvation* in Christ to reach as many persons as possible (with which conservatives are rightly concerned), while we should be as diverse as possible in choosing the *ways* and *means* to achieve this goal (with which liberals are rightly concerned). The question and criterion to keep in mind is the pragmatic one I have suggested above: To what extent does this doctrine or practice allow Christ's saving grace to be most effective to the greatest number of people? In everything it is the soteriological question that holds sway; after all, it is "for us and for our salvation" that the Son of God is made human. It is this soteriological focus that will fire our imagination to invent all possible ways to make Christ's saving word and grace accessible to all people, in worship and out of it.

Perhaps a brief reflection on artistic representations of the Last Supper will illustrate what I mean.[5] Among the paintings of the Last Supper no doubt that of Leonardo de Vinci has exerted the most powerful pull on the imagination of Western theologians. Jesus is represented as seated at a long rectangular table, with his twelve male disciples on either side of him. It looks as if the Last Supper were a private banquet in an elite male-only club. There was no one else present, not Jesus' mother, not the many women who had followed and supported him (and who probably had cooked the dinner!), not the poor, the sick and the oppressed people to whom Jesus had proclaimed the good news with preferential love, not the children whom he had blessed and held up as model of discipleship and whom he had been delighted to play. It was simply Jesus and twelve *men!*

Furthermore, the table was rectangular. Because of this shape, not every disciple was within equal reach of Jesus; the men nearest to Jesus could talk to him directly, whereas the ones at the two ends of the table had to lean sideways and strain their necks to see and hear him. It is not difficult to imagine how theologians contemplating this painting would develop the theology of the Eucharist, the sacrament of orders, and the role of women in the church.

Suppose a Vietnamese artist tries to represent the Last Supper for his or her people. The first thing the artist would do is to change the shape of the table from rectangular to round.[6] Most Asian homes have round dinner tables, probably because, Asian families being normally large, round tables can accommodate as many people as necessary; you just add more chairs and squeeze in a little bit. Furthermore, at a round table everyone has equal access to the food; if necessary, a "lazy susan" (what a chauvinistic phrase!) will make the foods available to everyone. A rectangular table sets up a hierarchy among the diners, with the most important one at the head of the table. With sharp edges and corners, rectangular tables create separation rather than union. At a round table,

---

[5] I am indebted to C. S. Song for the following reflections on the Eucharist at a round table (see his *Jesus, The Crucified People* [New York: Crossroad, 1990], 188–207).

[6] In a recent visit to the Accademia dell'Arte in Venice, I saw a fourteenth-century painting of the Last Supper. The table is round, and Jesus and the apostles sit around it. There was no information on who the painter was, and my persistent attempts to identify the artist have been fruitless.

everyone—woman, man, child, host, guest—is equal; the circle begins with anyone and ends with anyone. At a round table everyone sees and hears everyone else. Its circularity bespeaks inclusiveness and harmony. Metaphysically, this inclusiveness is expressed by the symbols of *yin* and *yang* forming a circle in which opposites are united to achieve cosmic harmony.

Because of its roundness, the dinner table symbolizes communion par excellence. Not only does it create and express equality among the diners, host, guests, and family members, but it also brings about and manifests unity in the way the food is served and taken. Usually, at dinner in an Asian family, each member is not served portions of food on a separate plate. Rather, the food is placed on common plates in the middle of the table, and the diners extend their arms and use chopsticks to take the food. The physical act of reaching out to a common food makes manifest and at the same time deepens the communion of minds and hearts that binds those who sit at the table together.

Finally, in Vietnamese religious traditions the circle symbolizes heaven. In eating at a round table the Vietnamese remember the Lord of heaven who makes rain fall to fertilize the earth so that rice can grow and feed all. They also remember their ancestors, who have given them life and to whom they offer foods as symbols of thanks and communion with them. Thus, in sharing food with one another, the Vietnamese achieve communion with God and with one another, both living and dead.

Now construct a theology of the church and of the Eucharist on the basis of a round rather than a rectangular table at the Last Supper. What shape will the church have, rectangular or round? Will the emphasis be placed on hierarchy, power, and distinction? Or on equality, communion, and inclusiveness? Will only men be present, perhaps sitting at the head of the table? Or will there also be women, extending their arms equally, with equally long chopsticks, to share in the common foods? Will only one voice be heard, which people have to crane their necks to hear, or will everyone be seen and heard equally? Will the host at the head of the table dominate the gathering, dictating what his fellow diners are to eat and drink and how they are to think and speak and behave, or will the host and guests, family members and strangers, be equal participants in the festival of communion and sharing, where everyone is duly recognized and every voice respectfully listened to?

Plan a Mass with a round rather than a rectangular altar. Will the focus be placed on someone (normally a male) "presiding" over the rituals and all other participants, or on the common and equal participation of children, women, and men in the act of worship? Will the readings be taken exclusively from the Christian Bible, or will they also include the sacred writings of the local people? Will the eating and drinking be of bread made from flour and wine made from grapes, expensive items imported from faraway countries, or will the local people eat foods made from what their own "earth has given" and their own "hands have made"? Will the prayers and songs be translated from previous compositions of foreign experts in Rome, or will they come from the depths of the people's cultural and religious traditions? Will the rituals be rigidly patterned on rubrics determined from above, or will they incorporate the native sacred celebrations?

In thinking through all these questions and others, the guiding norm will always be: How can we make Christ's saving grace as accessible and effective as possible for these people here and now? It is this faith, hope, and love for Christ and this single-mindedness in proclaiming his good news and his saving love that keep us all united with one another in our myriad diversities.

The new millennium for the church can be a propitious occasion for spiritual renewal and transformation. Most important, it can be a moment to take stock of who we are, where we are going, and how to get there. It is a time for humility, courage, and hope. The church, in these early years of the third millennium, is faced with numerous challenges and opportunities, some of which have been mentioned above. It is also evident that it has wonderful spiritual riches to offer to the world, both in its beliefs and practices. The question is whether we can help the church make use of its riches to meet its challenges, knowing all the while that it is the Lord, and not we, who will bring the church to its fulfillment. It is the Lord's deed that will make all the tribes of the earth, from the twelve tribes of Israel to the Co Ho tribe, into the one people of God and mold their diverse tongues into a harmonious symphony to the honor of God.

15

Liturgy of Life as Summit and Source of Eucharistic Liturgy

CHURCH WORSHIP AS SYMBOLIZATION OF LITURGY OF LIFE?

The question mark at the end of the subtitle of the chapter is not a cheap rhetorical flourish to attract the reader's attention. Rather, it is intended to highlight the tentative and controversial character of the thesis proposed in this chapter, namely, that the "liturgy of life" itself is the "summit and source" of the Christian liturgy and worship. The phrase "summit and source" *(culmen et fons)* is of course taken from Vatican II's Constitution on the Liturgy *(SC)*. The word *liturgy* is used here not univocally but analogously. What liturgy and Eucharist are has been explained by the council; what is meant by *liturgy of life* and *symbolization* will be elucidated in due course.

The thesis that the liturgy of life is the "summit and source" of the eucharistic liturgy and not the other way around is presented not as a straightforward assertion but as a genuine *questio disputata* regarding the relationship between worship and life. Needless to say, this issue is not irrelevant speculation for ivory-tower theologians; rather, it entails far-reaching implications for the pastoral task of preparing the church for worship. In what follows I first discuss Vatican II's teaching on the liturgy as *culmen et fons* of all the church's activities as well as possible theological misinterpretations and pastoral misapplications of it. Second, I explore the theological basis for the alternative thesis that the liturgy of life is the summit and source of the eucharistic liturgy. Finally, in the light of this thesis I examine the nature and function of one of the celebrations of the liturgy of life, namely, popular religion.

THE CHURCH LITURGY AS SUMMIT AND SOURCE

The Teaching of Vatican II

The liturgy as *culmen et fons* has become something of a mantra among post–Vatican II liturgists. The full text of article 10 of *SC*, in which the phrase occurs, reads:

257

The liturgy is the summit [*culmen*] toward which the activity of the Church is directed; it is also the fount [*fons*, "source"] from which all her power flows. For the goal of apostolic endeavor is that all who are made sons of God by faith and baptism should come together to praise God in the midst of his Church, to take part in the Sacrifice, and to eat the Lord's Supper.

The liturgy, in its turn, moves the faithful filled with "the paschal sacraments" to be "one in holiness"; it prays that "they hold fast in their lives to what they have grasped by their faith." The renewal in the Eucharist of the covenant between the Lord and man draws the faithful and sets them aflame with Christ's insistent love. From the liturgy, therefore, and especially from the Eucharist, grace is poured forth upon us as from a fountain [*ut e fonte*], and the sanctification of men in Christ and the glorification of God to which all other activities of the Church are directed, as toward their end [*uti ad finem*], are achieved with maximum effectiveness [*maxima cum efficacia*].

Article 10 of *SC* should be read in the context of articles 9–13 which, *taken as a whole*, explain the relation of the liturgy to the whole of church life and activities. On the one hand, against those who so exaggerate the importance of the liturgy as to identify it with the whole church life, article 9 affirms that "the sacred liturgy does not exhaust the entire activity of the Church" and mentions, as examples of other kinds of necessary church activities, missionary preaching to unbelievers, spiritual preparation of believers for the sacraments by means of catechesis, and the works of charity, piety, and apostolate. On the other hand, against those who minimize the importance of the liturgy, article 10 asserts that it is both the "summit toward which the activity of the Church is directed" and the "fount [source] from which all her power flows." However, for liturgical celebrations to achieve their full effects, article 11 urges that participants come to them "with proper dispositions" and that pastors aim not only to ensure a valid and licit celebration but also to enable the faithful to "take part fully aware of what they are doing, actively engaged in the rite and enriched by it." Once again, against liturgical enthusiasts, article 12 warns that "the spiritual life, however, is not limited solely to participation in the liturgy" but includes also community prayers, private prayer, and spiritual discipline. Article 13 singles out popular devotions *(pia exercitia)* for special consideration as a "highly recommended" means for spiritual life.

It is interesting to note that of the five articles of *SC* that elucidate the relationship between the liturgy and church life, only one affirms that the liturgy is the summit and source of the church's life, and even that affirmation is carefully qualified by the other four. This fact alone demands that we keep the statement about the liturgy as summit and source in proper perspective and balance. This refusal to absolutize the liturgy is confirmed by the history of the composition of article 10. During the council many fathers expressed their misgivings against the affirmation that the liturgy is "the summit toward which the activity of the Church is directed and the fount from which all her power flows" and proposed amendments to it during the final vote on the constitution. In the text

that the Central Commission submitted to the council, the sentence was modified to say that "in its center, that is, in the divine sacrifice of the Eucharist" the
liturgy is the summit and source. But even this milder formulation aroused objections during the assembly. It was pointed out that not even the Eucharist can
be said to be that to which everything is ordered and from which everything
proceeds. However, Bishop Henri Jenny, who had been a member of the Prepa-
ratory Commission, insisted on retaining the original version with its comprehensive statement. The Central Commission approved his proposal, and article
10 as it now stands in the constitution was accepted by the council by 2004
votes to 101.

But even those who endorsed the formula in the final vote explained in their
proposed amendments why there was resistance to it. The summit and goal of
the activity of the church, they argued, is not the liturgy but the salvation of
souls and the glory of God. Furthermore, the highest virtue is not religion, which
is realized in worship, but love. Moreover, the liturgy is a means and not the end
of the church life. Finally, it was pointed out, the source of the church life is not
the liturgy but Christ and the Holy Spirit.[1] These various observations serve as
useful cautions against taking the affirmation about the liturgy as *culmen et fons*
of the church's activities *sic et simpliciter*. Rather, the statement, like any other
theological affirmation, must be taken *cum grano salis*.

What are then the theological reasons for affirming that the liturgy is both
the summit and the source of all the church's activities? Though not providing a
comprehensive justification for its statement, *SC* does offer elements for an
answer to this question. The first reason for the exalted dignity of the liturgy (as
culmen) lies no doubt in its very nature. Liturgy is

> an exercise of the priestly office of Jesus Christ [*veluti Iesu Christi
> sacerdotalis muneris exercitatio*]. It involves the presentation of man's
> sanctification under the guise of signs perceptible by the senses and its
> accomplishments in ways appropriate to each of these signs. In it full
> public worship [*integer cultus publicus*] is performed by the Mystical Body
> of Jesus Christ, that is by the Head and his members.
>
> From this it follows that every liturgical celebration, because it is an
> action of Christ the Priest and of his Body which is the Church, is a sacred
> action surpassing all others [*actio sacra praecellenter*]. No other action of
> the Church can equal its efficacy by the same title and to the same degree
> [*eodem titulo eodemque gradu*] (*SC*, no. 7).

Here the liturgy's unsurpassed value is said to derive from the fact that it is a
sacred action performed by the mystical body of Jesus Christ, which includes
himself as the head and the church as his members. But in what sense is the
liturgy the summit toward which the activities of the church are directed? Is it in

---

[1] For a summary presentation of the composition of article 10, see Josef Andreas
Jungmann, "Constitution on the Sacred Liturgy," in *Commentary on the Documents of
Vatican II*, ed. Herbert Vorgrimmler, vol. 1 (New York: Herder and Herder, 1967), 15–
16.

the sense that the liturgy constitutes the *end* of the church's life? It seems not, since article 10 further specifies that all the activities of the church are directed not to the liturgy but to "the sanctification of humanity in Christ and the glorification of God . . . *as toward their end*" (emphasis added). Hence, it is only *indirectly* that the liturgy can be said to be the *culmen* to which the activities of the church are directed, insofar as it is the action by which the church accomplishes its twin tasks of glorifying God and being the sacrament of salvation to all humanity. Well taken, therefore, is the point of the above-mentioned amendments of many council fathers who objected to the original formula on the ground that the liturgy is a means and not the end and that the goal and summit of the church's activities is not the liturgy but the glory of God and the salvation of souls.

Intimately connected with the nature of the liturgy is, according to *SC*, the second reason for the liturgy's unsurpassed excellence, and that is its "efficacy." No other action of the church is said to equal its efficacy "by the same title and to the same degree." "By the same title" means that the efficacy of the liturgical celebrations is brought about by Christ himself who is their agent so that "when anyone baptizes it is really Christ himself who baptizes" (*SC*, no. 7). "To the same degree" refers to the fact that in the liturgical celebrations the glorification of God and the salvation of souls "are achieved with maximum effectiveness" (*SC*, no. 10). In theological parlance, the efficacy of the liturgy is said to be by way of *ex opere operato* and not *ex opere operantis*. It is for this reason that the constitution says that the liturgy is "far superior" to any popular devotion (*SC*, no. 13).

With reference to the Eucharist in particular, *SC* describes it as "a memorial of his [Jesus'] death and resurrection: a sacrament of love, a sign of unity, a bond of charity, a paschal banquet in which Christ is consumed, the mind is filled with grace, and a pledge of future glory is given to us" (no. 47). Because of what it is, the Eucharist has been declared in *Lumen gentium* to be "the source and summit of the Christian life [*totius vitae christianae fontem et culmen*]" (*LG*, no. 11). In the *Decree on the Ministry and Life of Priests (PO)* the council powerfully affirms the centrality of the Eucharist for the life of the church and explains the reason for it:

> The other sacraments, and indeed all ecclesiastical ministries and works of the apostolate are bound up with the Eucharist and are directed toward it [*cum Eucharistia cohaerent et ad eam ordinantur*]. For in the most blessed Eucharist is contained the whole spiritual good of the church, namely Christ himself our Pasch and the living bread which gives life to humanity through his flesh—that flesh which is given life and gives life through the Holy Spirit. Thus human persons are invited and are led to offer themselves, their works and all creation with Christ. For this reason the Eucharist appears as the summit and source of all preaching of the Gospel [*ut fons et culmen totius evangelizationis*]" (*PO*, no. 5).

The reason for the supreme excellence of the Eucharist, then, lies in the special presence of Christ "in the eucharistic species" (*SC*, no. 7), although this "real presence" is to be understood together with Christ's presence in the person of his minister, the word of God, and the assembly of the worshiping faithful.

The Liturgy and Eucharistic Celebrations in Church Life: Theological Interpretations and Pastoral Applications

Vatican II's ringing affirmation of the liturgy and especially the Eucharist as the summit and source of the church's life and activities has not remained empty rhetoric. On the contrary, it has deeply influenced the theological interpretation of the faith and shaped the pastoral practices of the church. On the theological level the Eucharist has served as a lens through which almost all the doctrines of the faith are systematically reexamined and elaborated, from the Trinity through ecclesiology to eschatology.

On the pastoral side, Sunday Masses are the focal point around which the life of the parish revolves. Pastors, associate pastors, permanent deacons, ushers, the choir, musicians, altar boys and altar girls, lectors, eucharistic ministers, members of the parish council, catechists, youth ministry directors, parish bulletin writers, collections receivers and counters, sacristans, nobody who is anybody in the parish is left out of the all-consuming production of the Sunday liturgy. The parish building complex, which is relatively deserted on weekdays, wakes up from its slumber on Sunday mornings to become the gathering point of the parish community, with the pastor nervously timing the length of his homily so as not to create a traffic jam in the parking lot among those who leave one Mass and those driving in for another. Those who come from countries such as those of Europe, where attendance at Sunday Mass is often minimal and where liturgical celebrations are more often than not dingy affairs, will recognize that the Catholic church in the United States truly practices what the council has said about eucharistic celebrations as the summit and source of the life of the church.

While the centrality and vibrancy of eucharistic celebrations in American parishes is a source of legitimate pride for American Catholics, it may be asked whether the doctrine that the liturgy is the summit and source of the church life, though theologically justified, has not led to one-sided theological interpretations and skewed pastoral practices. I would like to mention three areas where distortions may occur. They have to do with the two metaphors *culmen* and *fons* themselves.

First, the image of "summit" suggests a mountain or a pyramid and is symptomatic of the kind of epistemology that Ian Barbour identifies as the medieval paradigm. This way of knowing emphasizes fixed order, teleology, substance, hierarchy, anthropocentrism, dualism, and kingdom in contrast to the postmodern paradigm, which stresses evolution and historical emergence, structure and openness, mutual relation and interdependence, systems and wholes, organicism, multileveled composition, and community.[2] Viewing the liturgy and in particular the Eucharist as the summit toward which all the life of the church is ordered

---

[2] See Ian Barbour, *Religion in an Age of Science* (New York: Harper & Row, 1997), 219.

sets up a scale of values and willy-nilly devalues all other activities, ecclesial or otherwise, that do not qualify as liturgical and sacramental. This has happened, as we shall see, with popular devotions, which are placed at the bottom of the ladder of spiritual activities because their efficacy is said to be not *ex opere operato*, not even *ex opere operantis ecclesiae*.

Within sacramental theology itself, even if it is granted that the Eucharist is the *culmen* and *fons* of the church life, it has been debated whether it is more fundamental than, for example, baptism. Interestingly enough, it is not by accident that those who favor baptism over the Eucharist often regard the universal priesthood conferred by baptism on all Christians as the basis for the possibility of the ordination of women to the ministerial priesthood, whereas when the Eucharist is granted primacy, the celebration of which implies hierarchical distinction with the priest alone acting *in persona Christi*, an argument is made to justify the exclusive reservation of the ministerial priesthood to males. The question here is not to deny the centrality of the Eucharist for the church life but to search for a metaphor that fosters fundamental equality, mutual relationship, reciprocal dependence, openness, change, and novelty in the way the liturgy and the Eucharist interact with the other activities of the church.

Second, the metaphor *fons* underlines the one-way relation between the original source and the body of water that flows out of it. However small the source and however large the river flowing down from it, there is only one way in which the two are related to one another, and that is, from the top to the bottom, never from the bottom to the top. The water of the mighty river and its tributaries never flows backward, much less upward, to its source at the top of the mountain for which the image of *culmen* stands. Thus, the metaphor of source or fountain systematically excludes any possibility of fecundation and enrichment of the liturgy and the Eucharist by other forms of worship or sacramental celebration, let alone popular devotions and daily life in general. Unlike the artificial fountains that grace our cities and buildings whose water gushes upward reflecting the colors of the spectrum only to fall back down to the basin and then be driven upward again to feed a continuous and perpetual watery arch, the image of the liturgy and the Eucharist as *fons* in *SC* conjures up no visions of returning movement, helpful feedback, mutual confrontation, and reciprocal enrichment between worship and life. The movement is exclusively downstream, or as *SC* puts it, "from the liturgy, therefore, and especially from the Eucharist, grace is poured forth upon us as from the fountain" (no. 10). Once again, the point is not to deny the fact that the liturgy and the Eucharist are the conduit of divine life for us but to devise a metaphor that intimates a continuous dynamics of mutual correction and fertilization between worship and life.

Third, and more important, underlying these two metaphors and their conceptions of liturgy and the Eucharist is, I suggest, a particular theology of the relationship of God to the world (theology of grace) and of human beings (anthropology) that dominated the Catholic theological scene during the post-Tridentine era, residues of which still lingered in Vatican II's documents. With unavoidable over-generalization, it may be said that this theology views Christians as living in two different and separate worlds, the secular and the sacred. The larger world, the world of everyday life, the world of Monday through Saturday and even the greater part of Sunday, is secular and devoid of grace because it is only "nature" and worse, fallen and sinful. Only occasionally, at discrete points in time and space, by means of the sacraments and through worship, is it possible for Christians to encounter God and grace. This encounter, however, requires that Christians leave the secular world behind, at least for a while, and enter the sacred temple to experience God's grace, and then, fortified by God's gracious intervention, return to the fallen and unredeemed world. In this view nature and grace are seen as forming the two separate levels of a two-story house, with grace on top of nature, and even building on it, but never quite belonging to it and penetrating it.

In this view it is possible to establish a hierarchy whereby things of the world can be graded according to the degree of their proximity to the sacred temple. This scale of value is implied in the statement that the liturgy, especially the Eucharist, is the summit and source of the church life. The Eucharist is pictured as the fountain from which streams of grace cascade over the different regions of the spiritually parched world, more or less distant from it. Though watered by grace, the secular world is never brought into the sacred temple, nor is the temple built in the midst of the world. The assumption is that grace is an absolutely free gift of God only if it is parsimoniously and sporadically given to the sinful world, which otherwise is normally deprived of it.

These three distortions are no innocuous musings; on the contrary, they have deleterious effects on spiritual and pastoral practices. Three areas may serve as examples. In all three there is a gaping dichotomy. The first is the dichotomy between liturgy and spirituality, the second between spirituality and socio-political involvement, and the third, to close the circle, between socio-political involvement and liturgy.[3]

In spite of Vatican II's efforts to integrate spirituality and liturgy, in the post-conciliar years the old dualism and of late the old clericalism have crept back, sometimes with a vengeance. The reason for this unexpected turn of events is, as has been shown above, the metaphors of *culmen* and *fons* and their implicit theology separating church and world, worship and life, liturgy and spirituality, clergy and laity. In the immediate post–Vatican II era liturgical experts were busy rearranging the altars, composing new liturgical texts, introducing the vernaculars, devising new rituals, and so on, all very useful things, indeed, but only on the condition that they are rooted in the liturgy of life, which alone, as I will show in the next part of the chapter, provides them with meaning and effectiveness. Uprooted from the liturgy of life, these reforms appear as no more than clever gimmicks concocted by the Vatican and imposed on the rest of Christendom

---

[3] For an analysis of these dichotomies, see Aloysius Pieris, *An Asian Theology of Liberation* (Maryknoll, N.Y.: Orbis Books, 1988), 3–14. Pieris argues that only a genuine liberation theology can break this triple dichotomy that keeps these three elements apart from each other. This it does, he suggests, by refocusing the church's attention on the liturgy of life, the theology of the cross, and the historical Jesus and his humanity.

to cover up the vast irrelevance of the liturgical celebrations for everyday, real life. The famous phrase *ubi Christus, ibi ecclesia* (Where Christ is, there is the church), or to apply it to our context, where the liturgy of life is, there is church worship, is reversed to read *ubi ecclesia, ibi Christus* (Where the church is, there is Christ), or to apply it again to our context, where church worship is, there is the liturgy of life, which, of course, is not necessarily true.

The second dichotomy, between spirituality and socio-political involvement, shatters the synthesis that Ignatius of Loyola elaborated between contemplation and action. Rather than permanently yoked to action and nourished by it, contemplation is elevated to being a God-experience reserved to the few elite mystics, mostly clerics and religious, and confined to the sacred temple or the monastery, and is set in opposition to action that is equated exclusively with concern for the world. The result is that contemplation is turned into a leisurely, harmless exercise in an ashram or retreat center to which those who can afford the luxury withdraw to commune with nature and soothe their bruised egos, and action is cut off from the source of its effectiveness and Christians become nothing more than social workers.

The third dichotomy completes the circle. It isolates socio-political commitment from the liturgy and vice versa. The liturgy then becomes mere aesthetic performances, redolent with incense and dazzling with colorful vestments, perhaps accompanied by a full orchestra (or guitars to accommodate more plebeian tastes) and a polyphonic choir, and even Gregorian chant. The body and blood of Jesus are then reduced to being the spiritual nourishment for the soul and cease to be the bread and the rice and the drink feeding and slaking the thirst of the poor and the hungry. On the other hand, separated from the church liturgy, socio-political involvement loses its religious dimension and ceases to be the "secular liturgy" that it is.

With these dichotomies playing havoc with church life and church worship, no wonder those responsible for preparing the parish for the liturgy spare no time, money, and labor to make it a meaningful and relevant event. No wonder also that on Sundays, after the "shows" are over, all those involved in the liturgy—from the pastor to the lowliest minister—breathe a collective sigh of relief, if not collapse in utter exhaustion, only to begin again on Monday mornings the rounds of preparation for the next Sunday liturgy.

And yet, despite the gargantuan efforts, the long-term effects of Sunday worship on the lives of the faithful seem like a momentary "high" at best and a blob on the screen at worst. The reason for this is, as we have seen, the chasm separating the church liturgy from the liturgy of life. Perhaps it is precisely this separation, and not any profound theological underpinning, that makes the Eucharist appear as the summit and source of the church life for most people. Ironically, continuing to talk about eucharistic celebrations as the summit and source perpetuates and widens this chasm. Contemporary secular culture offers interesting parallels to this irony. Because the parents' lives are so much disconnected from those of their children, there is emphasis on parents spending "quality time" with their offsprings, whereas such a need scarcely arises when their lives are deeply intertwined. Because the human body has lost its sexual appeal due to overexposure, "intimate apparel" stores can make millions with their minimalist sartorial creations, advertising them to our saturated imagination as "sexy outfits," which would scarcely be necessary for those for whom the body is charged with innate erotic power. Because our daily meals are no longer occasions for sharing and friendship and communion, pricey restaurants can lure us with their promises of "a candle-lit, romantic dinner for two," which would hardly be a necessity for real lovers. Quality time, sexy outfits, romantic dinners are the secular equivalents of the Eucharist as "summit and source" that our consumerist culture attempts to purvey as substitutes for genuine care, authentic appreciation of the erotic, and committed love. Only in a culture that has lost the sense of the liturgy of life can these ersatz products pass as genuine articles.

THE LITURGY OF LIFE AS SOURCE AND SUMMIT: CHURCH WORSHIP AS SYMBOLIZATION OF THE LITURGY OF LIFE

To revitalize church worship something akin to a Copernican revolution in theology and pastoral practice is called for. Rahner used this expression to describe the transition from the post-Tridentine theology of the relation between God and the world as explained above to the theology of worship he proposed, though he later recanted and thought it to have been an exaggeration.[4] Exaggeration or not, there is no doubt that a paradigm shift has occurred. What is being advanced here is the reverse of Vatican II's adage: it is the liturgy of life that is the summit and source of the church liturgy and not the other way round. It is impossible, of course, to offer a full theological justification of this thesis here; only an outline of Rahner's most important theological reflections in support of this position can be presented.[5]

The Whole World as Graced by the Self-Communication of God

One of Rahner's fundamental theological principles is that God's grace has embraced and pervaded the world since its very beginning in the form of God's self-communication.[6] This gift not *from* but *of* God is present in our history in

---

[4] See Karl Rahner, "On the Theology of Worship," in *Theological Investigations*, vol. 19 (New York: Crossroad, 1983), 149.

[5] For Rahner's two most important essays in this respect, see "Considerations on the Active Role of the Person in the Sacramental Event," in *Theological Investigations*, vol. 14 (New York: The Seabury Press, 1976), 161–84; and "On the Theology of Worship," 141–49. For a helpful study of Rahner's theology of worship, see Michael Skelley, *The Liturgy of the World: Karl Rahner's Theology of Worship* (Collegeville, Minn.: Liturgical Press, 1991).

[6] For Rahner's most important writings on grace, see "Concerning the Relationship between Nature and Grace," in *Theological Investigations*, vol. 1 (Baltimore: Helicon, 1961), 297–317; "Some Implications of the Scholastic Concept of Uncreated Grace," in *Theological Investigations*, 1:319–46; "Nature and Grace," in *Theological Investigations*, vol. 4 (New York: Crossroad, 1982), 165–88; and *Foundations of Christian Faith: An Introduction to the Idea of Christianity*, trans. William Dych (New York: The Seabury Press, 1978), 116–33.

two modes. First, God's gift of self is present by way of being *offered* to our freedom. This offer of God's self-gift, which belongs to us as human beings constitutively, has truly transformed our nature by making us capable of being united with God in grace. Second, the same God's gift of self is present by way of being *accepted* or *rejected* by us. If accepted, it brings us into specifically distinct relationships with each of the three divine persons. If rejected, it is not withdrawn but still remains as an offer. In either mode, whether as an offer or as an accepted (or rejected) gift of God's self, grace is present always and everywhere in our history.

According to Rahner, as spirits we humans are essentially oriented to God as the ever-recessive horizon of all our acts of knowing and loving. In every act of knowledge and love we necessarily transcend ourselves beyond the concrete objects that we know and love and reach out toward and anticipate the infinite horizon against which these objects are known and loved and which is therefore the condition of possibility of our knowledge and love, but which forever eludes our grasp.[7] This self-transcendence in knowledge and love makes us capable of hearing a word of revelation from God if God chooses to speak to us (our *potentia obedientialis*).[8]

However, because of his actual self-communication to us in history, God, who is the absolute, ever-elusive, and distant Mystery, has come near us, irrevocably and supremely in Jesus Christ, becoming for us not only the Absolute but also the Holy Mystery, the God not only of infinite distance but also absolute closeness and immediacy. As a result of this divine self-gift, there is in us, as an intrinsic and constitutive part of our concrete being, what Rahner calls the "supernatural existential," that is, a real, ontological modification of our concrete, historical nature that orients us toward union with God and the beatific vision. It is existential (the term is borrowed from Martin Heidegger) because it is something not extrinsic but intrinsic to and constitutive of our nature, and it is supernatural because it is a gratuitous gift of God that cannot be demanded by our nature and therefore is not part of our essence abstractly conceived. It is an a priori condition, preexisting every act of choice of ours, which disposes us for a personal union with the triune God. Rahner writes:

> The world is permeated by the grace of God. . . . The world is constantly and ceaselessly possessed by grace from its innermost roots, from the innermost personal center of the spiritual subject. It is constantly and ceaselessly sustained and moved by God's self-bestowal even prior to the question (admittedly always crucial) of how creaturely freedom reacts to this "engracing" of the world and of the spiritual creature as already given and "offered," the question, in other words, of whether this creaturely freedom accepts the grace to its salvation or closes itself to it to its perdition.[9]

---

[7] See Karl Rahner, *Spirit in the World*, trans. William Dych (New York: Herder and Herder, 1968).

[8] See Karl Rahner, *Hearers of the Word*, trans. Joseph Donceel (Milwaukee, Wis.: Marquette University Press, 1982).

[9] Rahner, "Considerations on the Active Role of the Person in the Sacramental Event," 166.

In Rahner's view, then, human history and the world are totally and completely permeated by God's grace. Strictly speaking, therefore, there are no secular and sacred zones in human history, no profane marketplace and holy temple, but only the saved (where God's self-gift is accepted) and the damned (where it is rejected). This does not mean that Rahner compromises the gratuitousness of God's grace. He still maintains the logical necessity of the concept of "pure nature" to preserve the gratuitousness of grace, though "pure nature" has never existed in fact. Grace does not cease to be grace, even when it is poured out upon everybody, always and everywhere, lavishly and abundantly.

Experience of God and Mysticism of Everyday Life

One important corollary of this theology of grace is that experiences of God and even mystical experiences are not seen as rare, much less confined to liturgical celebrations. On the contrary, since in every act of knowing and loving a particular object we necessarily transcend ourselves and reach out toward the absolute horizon of being and value, and since this self-transcendence is permeated by the supernatural existential, experiences of God and grace are inescapable to everyone and everywhere. These experiences of God do not occur *in addition to* or *apart from* our acts of knowing and loving particular objects; rather, they lie hidden within them as their very condition of possibility. To distinguish these two levels of experiences, Rahner calls our knowledge and love of particular things "categorical," "thematic," "explicit," and "objective," and the experience of God "transcendental," "unthematic," "implicit," and "unobjective." Because of the hidden character of experiences of God we are normally not aware of them, but our chronic inability to see God in everyday life is no indication that God is absent from it; rather, God is *radically* present in it, in the literal sense of the word, that is at the root, so that we who are habituated to perceiving life only at its surface cannot see God at its depth.

By the same token, for Rahner, mystical experiences are not the preserve of the spiritual elite but are available to everyone. They can occur in extraordinary phenomena such as visions, glossolalia, prophecies, ecstasies, dreams, and the like, and these are not given to everyone. But mysticism has fundamentally to do with our self-transcendence and is basically an experience of the absolute mystery of God. So, says Rahner,

> if we want to describe as "mysticism" this experience of transcendence in which humans in the midst of ordinary life is always beyond themselves and beyond the particular object with which they are concerned, we might say that mysticism always occurs, concealed and namelessly, in the midst of ordinary life and is the condition of the possibility for the most down-to-earth and most secular experience of ordinary life.[10]

---

[10] Karl Rahner, "Experience of the Holy Spirit," in *Theological Investigations*, 18:197.

What are the kinds of experiences in which mysticism, that is, the graced encounter with God, occurs? The following long passage from Rahner deserves full quotation for its marvelous richness and lyrical beauty:

> But one point must be emphasized about this grace to the extent that it proceeds from the innermost heart and center of the world and of the human person: it takes place not as a special phenomenon, as one particular process *apart from* the rest of human life. Rather it is quite simply the ultimate depths and the radical dimension of all that which the spiritual creature experiences, achieves and suffers in all those areas in which it achieves its own fullness, and so in its laughter and tears, in its taking responsibility, in its loving, living, and dying, whenever the person keeps faith with the truth, breaks through egoism in one's relationships with one's fellows, whenever one hopes against all hope, whenever one smiles and refuses to be disquieted or embittered by the folly of everyday pursuits, whenever one is able to be silent, and whenever within this silence of the heart that evil which a person has engendered against another in his or her heart does not develop any further into external action, but rather dies within this heart as its grave— whenever, in a word, life is lived as we would seek to live it, in such a way as to overcome our own egoism and the despair of the heart which constantly assails us. *There* grace has the force of an event, because all this is of its very nature (i.e. precisely through God's grace which has all along broken mere "nature," leading it beyond itself and into the infinitude of God) no longer has any limits or any end but (as willingly accepted) loses itself in the silent infinitude of God, is hidden in his absolute unconditionality in the future of the fullness of victory which in turn is God himself.[11]

It is clear, therefore, that for Rahner, experiences of God and mysticism are given to us in both positive and negative experiences, perhaps more in the latter than in former, because then we are confronted with our own limitations and brought face to face with the infinite mystery. This means that there is nothing in life so profane and secular, so negative and evil, that God cannot be experienced in it.

Liturgy of Life

These universal experiences of God and mystical encounters with God's grace in the midst of everyday life, made possible by God's self-gift embracing the

[11] Rahner, "Considerations on the Active Role of the Person in the Sacramental Event," 167–68. See also Rahner's other essays: "Reflections on the Experience of Grace," in *Theological Investigations*, vol. 3 (New York: Crossroad, 1982), 86–90; "The Experience of God Today," in *Theological Investigations*, vol. 11 (New York: Crossroad, 1982), 149–65; "Experience of the Spirit and Existential Commitment," in *Theological Investigations*, vol. 16 (New York: Crossroad, 1979), 24–34; "Religious Feeling inside and outside the Church," in *Theological Investigations*, vol. 17 (New York: Crossroad, 1981), 213–38; "Experience of Transcendence from the Standpoint of Catholic Dogmatics," in *Theological Investigations*, vol. 18 (New York: Crossroad, 1983), 173–88; "Experience of the Holy Spirit," 189–210.

whole human history, always and everywhere, Rahner calls the "liturgy of the world" *(Liturgie der Welt)* or the "Mass of the world" *(Messe der Welt)*.[12] To underline its dynamic and personal character, one may prefer to call it the liturgy of life. Rahner describes this liturgy of the world or liturgy of life as follows:

> The world and its history are the terrible and sublime liturgy, breathing of death and sacrifice, which God celebrates and causes to be celebrated in and through human history in its freedom, a history which God sustains in grace by his sovereign disposition. In the entire length and breadth of this immense history of birth and death, complete superficiality, folly, inadequacy, and hatred . . . on the one hand, and silent submission, responsibility even to death in dying and in joyfulness, in attaining the heights and plumbing the depths on the other, the true liturgy of the world is present. To this liturgy of the world the liturgy which the Son has brought to its absolute fullness on his Cross belongs intrinsically, emerges from it, that is, from the ultimate source of the grace of the world, and constitutes the supreme point of *this* liturgy. All else draws its life from this supreme point, because everything else is always dependent upon the supreme point as upon its goal and is supported by it. This liturgy of the world is as it were veiled to the darkened eyes and the dulled human heart which fails to understand its true nature. This liturgy, therefore, must, if the individual is really to share in the celebration of it in all freedom and self-commitment even to death, be interpreted, "reflected upon" in its ultimate depths when one celebrates that which we are accustomed to call liturgy in the more usual sense. But there is a further point, just as valid and indeed still more radical: We can understand this liturgy in the usual sense and can achieve a genuine enactment of it . . . only if we draw our strength from this liturgy of the world, from the existential liturgy of faith which is identical with the history of the world rightly enacted.[13]

From this description four characteristics of the liturgy of life emerge. First, the liturgy of life consists of experiences of God, available to all human beings, in the midst of life and in all concrete situations, from the most sublime to the most mundane, both positive and negative. It is called "liturgy" because these experiences are always sustained by God's self-gift to the world. It is called "of the world" because it takes place in the universal history of the world, which, according to Rahner, is "coextensive" (though not identical) with the history of salvation.[14] This "general" history of salvation is to be distinguished from the

---

[12] Rahner, "Considerations on the Active Role of the Person in the Saramental Event," 174.

[13] Ibid., 170. For the idea of the liturgy of life, Rahner refers to the works of Pierre Teilhard de Chardin, especially his *Hymn of the Universe* (New York: Harper & Row, 1965). The expression "Mass of the world" is derived from Teilhard de Chardin.

[14] For Rahner's discussion of the relationship between the general and special histories of revelation and salvation, see Rahner, *Foundations of Christian Faith*, 138–61, 170–75.

"special" history of revelation and salvation (that is, the history of the Old and New Testaments), just as the liturgy of life is different from church liturgy and worship. Though less easily identifiable than the special history of salvation and church worship, the general history of salvation and its liturgy of life are no less real and important.

Second, this liturgy of the world has a christological character, for two reasons. The first is that Jesus' sacrifice on the cross or his liturgy derived its origin or emerged from the liturgy of the world. For Rahner, the incarnation of the Word in Jesus, though a unique event, is "an intrinsic moment within the whole process by which grace is bestowed upon all spiritual creatures."[15] In other words, the incarnation of the Logos forms an intrinsic part of the process of God's self-communication to the world, the dynamic power of which prepared for it and without which it could not have happened: "Grace in all of us and hypostatic union in the one Jesus Christ can only be understood together, and as a unity they signify the one free decision of God for a supernatural order of salvation, for God's self-communication."[16] This thesis not only provides unity to the doctrines of creation and redemption but also coheres with an evolutionary view of the world in which matter is conceived of as actively transcending itself toward and becoming spirit. If humanity as the unity of matter and spirit can be considered as the goal of the cosmic evolution, then the incarnation of the Logos can rightly be said to be the highest actualization of the essence of human reality.[17] The second reason for the christological character of the liturgy of life is the fact that the incarnation, death, and resurrection of the Logos brought it to its fullest fulfillment and constitute its supreme point. Through these events God's self-communication in history became definitive, irrevocable, irreversible, insofar as it is now both *offer* and *acceptance* indissolubly united as one in the person of Jesus (which is what *hypostatic union* means). In this sense Rahner suggests that Christ can be called the "Absolute Savior."[18]

Third, the liturgy of life is necessarily diffuse, unstructured, and therefore easily unnoticed. This characteristic flows from the transcendental nature of our experiences of God. The presence of God—silently present and silencing his presence—occurs as a nameless mystery in the depths of our everyday experiences and hence is frequently ignored, misinterpreted, and even suppressed. Even when this divine presence is attended to, it can never be fully captured and communicated in conceptual categories. What is needed, according to Rahner, is mystagogy, that is, the spiritual discipline whereby we are guided and formed to perceive beyond the surface of life the abiding presence of the Absolute and Holy Mystery.[19] One place where this mystagogy should be carried out in particular is church liturgical celebrations.

---

[15] Ibid., 201.

[16] Ibid.

[17] For Rahner's proposal of a Christology within an evolutionary world view, see ibid., 178–203.

[18] See ibid., 193–95.

[19] On mystagogy in Rahner, see James Bacik, *Apologetics and the Eclipse of Mystery: Mystagogy according to Karl Rahner* (Notre Dame, Ind.: University of Notre Dame Press, 1980).

Fourth, though less visible than church liturgy, this liturgy of life is the very source of fecundity and effectiveness of the liturgy of the church. Indeed, humanity's ongoing communion with God in grace in daily life is, according to Rahner, the primary and original liturgy. It is this liturgy of life that we must first think of when we speak of worship. Worship is not primarily the explicit act of praise and thanksgiving that we perform within the walls of the church away from the secular arena but the daily, silent, unobtrusive surrendering of ourselves to the infinite Mystery in our everyday action: "The Church's worship is not the installation of a primarily sacramental sphere in a profane, secular world, it is not an event otherwise without roots in reality, but the explicit and reflex, symbolic presentation of the salvation event which is occurring always and everywhere in the world; the liturgy of the Church is the symbolic presentation of the liturgy of the world."[20]

Church Liturgy as "Real Symbol" of the Liturgy of Life

With the last quotation we have broached the issue of how to articulate the relationship between the liturgy of life and church liturgy, in particular eucharistic celebrations. We have seen above the validity as well as the theological and pastoral limitations in the use of the metaphors *culmen* and *fons* to express this relationship. One alternative way of conceiving it that retains the important role of liturgy and sacramental celebrations for church life and yet eschews the distortions to which the metaphors of summit and source are liable is by way of Rahner's theology of the symbol.[21]

According to Rahner, a real symbol, in contrast to an artificial sign, is a reality in which and by means of which another reality comes to be, to be real, to be effective, to be present. This real symbolization occurs whenever a being comes to be by means of the unity of its several intrinsic dimensions. In this being, unity and plurality do not annul each other; rather, they come to be by means of each other. Its unity grows out of and depends upon the plurality of its constitutive dimensions; conversely, the plurality of its dimensions is resolved into and at the same time retains its plural character in the unity of the one being. Rahner uses the term "self-expression" to refer to this coming of a being's plural dimensions into unity and the converse movement of the thus unified being's unfolding itself into its plural dimensions. In spiritual beings this self-expression takes place by acts of knowledge and love. In this sense, says Rahner, "a being is in itself and for itself symbolic, and hence (and to this extent) symbolic for another."[22] In short, a symbol is "the reality, constituted by the thing symbolized as an inner moment of itself, which reveals and proclaims the thing

---

[20] Rahner, "On the Theology of Worship," 146.

[21] For Rahner's theology of symbol, see his "The Theology of the Symbol," in *Theological Investigations*, vol. 4 (Baltimore: Helicon, 1966), 221–52; and "The Concept of Mystery in Catholic Theology," in *Theological Investigations*, vol. 4 (Baltimore: Helicon, 1966), 36–73.

[22] Rahner, "The Theology of the Symbol," 231.

symbolized, and is itself full of the thing symbolized, being its concrete form of existence."[23]

Rahner applies this concept of real symbol to the doctrine of the Trinity, in which the Logos is said to be the symbol of the Father; to ecclesiology, in which the church is said to be the symbol of Christ; to sacramentology, in which the sacraments are said to be the symbols of the church; and to anthropology, where the body is said to be the symbol of the soul.[24]

Rahner also uses his theology of the symbol to explicate the relationship between the liturgy of life and the liturgy of the church. To put it in a nutshell, for Rahner, the liturgy of the church is the "real symbol" of the liturgy of life. There are several theological and pastoral implications in this thesis. First, as the thing symbolized and its symbol constitute an ontological and indissoluble unity, so the liturgy of life and the liturgy of the church constitute the one worship that humanity renders to God and whose center and supreme fulfillment is Jesus Christ. Conversely, just as the symbol and the thing symbolized preserve their irreducible distinctiveness and difference, so the liturgy of life is not identical with the liturgy of the church and vice versa. The one is not and should not be absorbed into the other.

Second, just as the thing symbolized comes to be real, present, and effective in the symbol, so the liturgy of life comes to be real, present, and effective in the liturgy of the church. Because the liturgy of life is diffuse and hidden in everyday ordinary experiences in the midst of life and therefore runs the risk of being ignored, it needs to be brought to our consciousness by being symbolized in the concrete and explicit rituals and prayers of the church worship and sacraments. The sacrament then "constitutes a small sign, necessary, reasonable and indispensable, within the infinitude of the world as permeated by God. It is the sign that reminds *us* of this limitlessness of the presence of divine grace, and *in this sense* and in no other, precisely in *this particular* kind of anamnesis, is to be intended to be an event of grace."[25]

Third, just as the symbol does not exist by itself but derives its being from the thing symbolized, so the liturgy of the church does not exist by itself and is not effective except as symbolization of the liturgy of life. The original liturgy is not the church liturgy but the liturgy of life. In its liturgical celebrations the church does not perform a worship *in addition to* the liturgy of life or unconnected with it. Rather, it makes explicit and intensifies through words and rituals the liturgy of life that takes place unceasingly through God's self-gift and humanity's acceptance of this divine self-gift. The value of the church liturgy is precisely in not identifying itself with or replacing the liturgy of life as the original and exclusive liturgy but in being its symbol by making it concretely present here and now in the consciousness of the faithful. The church liturgy is important not because what happens there does not happen elsewhere, not

---

[23] Ibid., 251.
[24] Ibid., 235–49.
[25] Rahner, "Considerations on the Active Role of the Person in the Sacramental Event," 169.

because what happens supremely there happens only as a shadow elsewhere. Rather, it is because what happens in the church liturgy happens always and everywhere in the world, but here it is explicitly celebrated, announced, and appropriated. Consequently, says Rahner, "to anyone who has (or might have had) absolutely no experience in his own life of this history of grace in the world, no experience of the cosmic liturgy, the Church's liturgy could only seem like a strange ritualism, as strange as the sacrificial action of a Vedic priest who feeds the gods and thinks that by his action he is keeping the world on its track."[26]

Fourth, just as the thing symbolized and its symbol are not related to each other by a hierarchical, one-way, top-to-bottom, static order, as implied in the metaphors of summit and source, but by a dynamic, two-way, mutual interdependence, so the liturgy of life and the liturgy of the church interact with each other as two intrinsic dimensions of the one reality, correcting and enriching each other. Contrary to Vatican II, which speaks of the liturgy of the church as the summit and source of all the activities of the church, the theology of the church liturgy as symbol of the liturgy of life does not speak of it as summit and source. If these metaphors are used of it at all, they are used only in a very attenuated sense, that is, in the sense that there the faithful are brought to explicit awareness of and celebrate in tangible forms God's universal and transcendental self-communication to us in Christ and by the power of the Holy Spirit. On the contrary, just as the thing symbolized is in a certain sense more original than its symbol, so it is the liturgy of life that is the more original and more fundamental, and in this sense could be said to be the summit and source of the church liturgy. To be more precise, the true summit, center, and source of both the liturgy of life and the liturgy of the church is Jesus Christ, who in his incarnation, ministry, death, and resurrection brought God's self-communication to the world to its irrevocable, irreversible, and victorious fulfillment. Consequently, with the liturgy of the church as the symbol of the liturgy of life, there is no dichotomy but rather mutual inclusion between spirituality and liturgy, between liturgy and socio-political involvement, and between socio-political involvement and spirituality.

Finally, it is to be noted that between the thing symbolized and its symbol there is no relation of efficient causality by means of which the one brings the other into existence, externally as it were, by its own power. Rather, there is between them a relation of formal or "symbolic" causality by which the one comes into being either by being symbolized by the other or by being the symbol of the other, that is, by the self-expression of the other in this symbol. Similarly, between the liturgy of life and the liturgy of the church there is no relation of efficient causality by which one brings the other into existence *ex nihilo*, as if the one were totally dependent on the other without the other being in some measure also dependent on it. Rather, between them there is a relationship of mutual dependence and reciprocal origination by which the one comes into being, being

---

[26] Rahner, "On the Theology of Worship," 147.

real, being effective through the other, the thing symbolized by expressing itself in the symbol, and the symbol by being the concrete embodiment of the thing symbolized. Indeed, this kind of formal causality is proper to the sacraments as *signum efficax* of grace: the liturgy of the church is the sign of the original liturgy of life, and insofar as it is the sign of the liturgy of life that is sustained by the ever-present grace of God, it "causes" grace, that is, makes the grace of the liturgy of life concretely effective here and now for the worshiping community.

POPULAR RELIGION:
PARALLEL SYMBOLIZATION OF THE LITURGY OF LIFE

In the light of the theology of the liturgy of life as the original liturgy it is useful to revisit the complex and controverted issue of popular religion or popular religiosity *(religiosidad popular)*. It is impossible to offer within the remaining space anything remotely approaching an adequate theological treatment of popular religion, especially its relationship to the church liturgy. In the following reflections it is suggested that popular religion can be best understood if it is viewed as a real symbol of the liturgy of life, in much the same way as the church liturgy symbolizes the liturgy of life.

Whether under the rubric of popular religion, or folk religion, or common religion,[27] it is well known that nonliturgical, nonofficial, popular expressions of religiosity (*popular* not in the sense of "in fashion" but in the sense of "the people in general") received scant attention from Vatican II. Article 13 of *SC* treats it only under the aspect of popular devotions *(pia exercitia)* and declares:

Popular devotions of the Christian people, provided they conform to the laws and norms of the Church, are to be highly recommended, especially where they are ordered by the Apostolic See.

Devotions proper to individual churches also have a special dignity if they are undertaken by order of the bishops according to customs or books lawfully approved.

But such devotions should be so drawn up that they harmonize with the liturgical seasons, accord with the sacred liturgy, are in some way derived from it, and lead the people to it, since in fact the liturgy by its very nature is far superior to any of them.[28]

---

[27] For a helpful discussion of these terminologies and of popular religion in general, see Robert Schreiter, *Constructing Local Theologies* (Maryknoll, N.Y.: Orbis Books, 1985), 122–43. Popular religion is often contrasted to official religion, elite religion, and esoteric religion. Schreiter rightly notes the inadequacy of these approaches and calls for an adherence in the studies of popular religion to the following principles: "trying to listen to the culture on its own terms; adopting a holistic pattern of description; remaining attentive to the audience and the interest of the questioner in each event" (126).

[28] This relative neglect of and suspicious attitude toward popular religion by Vatican II was one of the results of the triumph of the liturgical movement, spearheaded by Dom Prosper Guéranger, at the council. The liturgical movement saw popular religion as

In the immediate post–Vatican II era, as the liturgical reform went into full swing, popular religion suffered a serious decline. All its four forms, as classified by Domenico Sartore, were affected: first, devotions to Christ, the Blessed Virgin, and the saints in the forms of pilgrimages, patronal feasts, processions, popular devotions, and novenas; second, the rites related to the liturgical year; third, traditional practices in conjunction with the celebrations of the sacraments and other Christian rites like funerals; and fourth, institutions and religious objects connected with various forms of popular religiosity.[29]

Recently, however, there has been a noticeable resurgence of popular religion not only among the churches of the Third World, in particular Latin America and Asia,[30] but also among Christians of the First World.[31] One of the contributing factors to this comeback is the widespread dissatisfaction with the classical form of Vatican II's reformed rites characterized by Roman *sobrietas, brevitas, simplicitas,* and linear rationality, which do not respond to the people's need for emotional and total involvement in liturgical celebrations.[32] This need is met by

---

rooted in subjective and emotional piety, thus favoring the Enlightenment's individualist tendencies, which it wanted to combat. This belittling of "subjective" or "personal" piety and consequent rejection of "all other religious exercises not directly connected with the sacred Liturgy and performed outside public worship" were criticized by Pope Pius XII as "false, insidious, and quite pernicious" (*Mediator Dei,* no. 30). Papal condemnations notwithstanding, the liturgical movement's negative assessment of popular religion found its way into article 13 of *SC.* See Patrick L. Malloy, "The Re-Emergence of Popular Religion among Non-Hispanic American Catholics," *Worship* 72/1 (1998): 2–4.

[29] See Anscar Chupungco, *Liturgical Inculturation: Sacramentals, Religiosity, and Catechesis* (Collegeville, Minn.: Liturgical Press, 1992), 102, summarizing Domenico Sartore, "Le manifestazione della religosità popolare," *Anamnesis* 7 (Genoa, 1989): 232–33.

[30] For a study of Latin American theology's evaluation of popular religion, see Michael R. Candelaria, *Popular Religion and Liberation: The Dilemma of Liberation Theology* (Albany, N.Y.: SUNY Press, 1990); and Cristián Parker, *Popular Religion and Modernization in Latin America: A Different Logic,* trans. Robert Barr (Maryknoll, N.Y.: Orbis Books, 1996). For studies of Hispanic-American popular religion, see Orlando Espín, *The Faith of the People: Theological Reflections on Popular Catholicism* (Maryknoll, N.Y.: Orbis Books, 1997); and C. Gilbert Romero, *Hispanic Devotional Piety* (Maryknoll, N.Y.: Orbis Books, 1991).

[31] See Malloy, "The Re-Emergence of Popular Religion among Non-Hispanic American Catholics," 5–8. Just to have an idea of how this reemergence has spawned a veritable avalanche of literature on popular religion, a bibliography composed in 1979 showed that in the previous decade there had been 528 titles. See F. Trolese, "Contributo per una bibliografia sulla religiosità popolare," *Ricerche sulla religiosità popolare* (Bologna, 1979), 273–535. For other bibliographies, see Chupungco, *Liturgical Inculturation,* 95.

[32] It is these characteristics that lie behind *SC*'s insistence on a "full, conscious, and active participation in liturgical celebrations" (no. 14). For a presentation of the critique of Vatican II's liturgical reform by four ideologically diverse theologians (Joseph Ratzinger, David Power, Francis Mannion, and Matthew Fox), see Malloy, "The Re-Emergence of Popular Religion among Non-Hispanic American Catholics," 12–20.

popular religion with its emphasis on spontaneity, festivity, joyfulness, and community.[33]

Besides the inadequacy of the Roman rites, *SC*'s approach to popular religion is heavily legalistic. Popular devotions are said to be "highly recommended" only on condition that "they conform to the laws and norms of the Church" and "especially ordered by the Apostolic See." They have a special dignity "if they are undertaken by order of the bishops according to customs or books lawfully approved." More importantly, the four norms that *SC* formulates for drawing up devotions, namely that "they harmonize with the liturgical seasons, accord with the sacred liturgy, are some way derived from it, and lead the people to it" are all derived from the principle that the liturgy is the summit and source of all activities of the church.[34] This principle, as we have seen above, can and does lead to distortions in both theology and pastoral practice.

Rather than seeing popular religion in direct relationship to the church liturgy which functions as its exclusive norm, I suggest we view it as the symbolization of the liturgy of life, a symbolization that is parallel to the symbolization of the liturgy of life by the church liturgy, and therefore needs to be assessed on its own terms and not in dependence on the church liturgy. The function and value of popular religion lie not in their requisite ability to "harmonize with the liturgical seasons," "accord with the sacred liturgy," be "in some way derived from it," and "lead people to it." Nor should popular religion be ranked at the bottom of spiritual activities on the basis of its alleged efficacy on mere *ex opere operantis*, as opposed to *ex opere operato* (the liturgy and sacraments) and *ex opere operantis ecclesiae* (the sacramentals)[35] or

---

[33] For a description of the general traits of popular religion, see Chupungco, *Liturgical Inculturation*, 109–11. Chupungco quotes C. Valenziano's characterization of popular religion: "It is festive, felt, spontaneous; it is expressive, immediate, human; it is communitarian, collective, joyful, symbolic, traditional, alive" (109–10). See C. Valenziano, "La religiosità popolare in prospettiva antropologica," in *Liturgia e religiosità popolare* (Bologna, 1979), 83–110. Chupungco, in his analysis of Filipino popular religion, identifies the principal features of popular religion as follows: "These are, first, their literary genre, which is marked by discursive and picturesque quality; second, their use of sacred images; third, their preference for such devices for participation as repetitiveness and communal recitation; and fourth, their use of dramatic forms that are often strongly mimetic or imitative" (*Liturgical Inculturation*, 119).

[34] The same legalistic approach to popular religion is maintained in the Congregation for Divine Worship and the Discipline of the Sacraments' instruction *The Roman Liturgy and Inculturation* (Rome, 1994): "The introduction of devotional practices into liturgical celebrations under the pretext of inculturation cannot be allowed 'because by its nature, (the liturgy) is superior to them.' It belongs to the local Ordinary to organize such devotions, to encourage them as supports of the life and faith of Christians, and to purify them, when necessary, because they need to be constantly permeated by the Gospel. He will take care to ensure that they do not replace liturgical celebrations or become mixed up with them" (no. 45).

[35] Such a theological distinction is rendered quite fuzzy by the fact that even for the sacraments to produce their effects the "proper dispositions" of the recipient are necessary; after all, the sacraments are *sacramenta fidei*. Furthermore, in real life, sometimes kissing a statue, going on a pilgrimage, or making a novena can bring more spiritual transformation than celebrating the sacraments.

on its alleged "private" character as opposed to the "public" character of church worship.[36]

As symbol of the liturgy of life, popular religion is related to it in very much the same way as the church liturgy is related to it. I have explained above the five ways in which the liturgy of life and the church liturgy are related to each other. There is no point in repeating them here with regard to popular religion. In brief, the liturgy of life and popular religion form the one worship rendered to God, though each retains its distinctive identity. The liturgy of life becomes real, effective, and concrete in and through popular religion, just as popular religion achieves its effectiveness by being the real symbol of the liturgy of life. Between them there is a mutual causal relationship characterized not by efficient causality but by formal or symbolic causality.

In this understanding of popular religion the two negative approaches, which regard popular religion as mere superstitious practices (the elitist interpretation) and as the false consciousness imposed upon the proletariat by the ruling class (the Marxist interpretation), are discounted. On the other hand, this symbolic approach does not fall into romanticism by regarding popular religion as the genuine religion that has been skewed by official religion or that now resides in the majority of the people who lead a poor and simpler life (the romanticist interpretation). Nor does it see popular religion as the residue of the previous, pre-Christian religion that now survives in a transformed and improved state in Christianity (the remnant interpretation). Nor does it look upon popular religion mainly as articulation of the social-psychological needs of individuals in their interaction with the economic, social, and political patterns of the environment (the social-psychological approach). Positively, this approach is similar to the baseline approach proposed by Robert Towler, which recognizes that every culture has its own religious symbolization that takes place in two parallel forms, popular religion and organized world religions with their own official liturgy and worship. Both popular religion and official liturgy are distinct symbolizations of the liturgy of life; the one should not be identified with the other, or replaced by the other, or reduced to the other. Finally, this approach is sympathetic to the subaltern approach inspired by the Italian Marxist Antonio Gramsci, which sees popular religion as having an identity of its own, independent from the official religion, with its own public worship, capable of forging the identity of the oppressed people over against the ruling class.[37]

Needless to say, this view of popular religion entails important implications for the issue of liturgical inculturation.[38] While it is impossible to spell out the details of this process of inculturation here, one thing is clear: Vatican II's

---

[36] The distinction between "private" and "public" is also very fuzzy. Saying Mass in a hotel room or an individual reciting of the breviary is no more "public" worship than a procession through the streets of the city. This distinction depends on the view that the church is more "sacred" than the public square.

[37] For a helpful explanation of these seven approaches to popular religion, two negative (elitist and Marxist) and five positive (baseline, romanticist, remnant, subaltern, and social-political), see Schreiter, *Constructing Local Theologies*, 131–39.

[38] On the liturgical inculturation of popular religion, see Chupungco, *Liturgical Inculturation*, 95–133. Chupungco favors the method of dynamic equivalence (121–

wholesale and one-way reduction of popular religion to liturgy is no longer viable. Rather there should be a mutual and enriching exchange between the liturgy and popular devotion,[39] in the composition of the texts as well as the establishment of rituals, because both are equally valid symbolizations of the liturgy of life. The liturgy of life is the first seed sown by God's gracious love that grows up and blossoms in the vicissitudes of human history, a seed not unlike the one celebrated by the Irish-American poet William D. Carroll as he recalled the wild grass and the wild flowers that grow in acres and acres of rock called the Burren in County Clare, Ireland:

A Seed

A seed did fall upon the ground
Where desolation did abound
A crack within a rock it found
And waited.
For winds that came from off a hill
With flecks of dust the crack to fill
And rain from out the sky did spill
And sated.

The little seed's great appetite.
And nurtured through long Winter's night
It waited for the Spring's sunlight
As fated.

The Winter melded into Spring
Bringing new life to everything
And nature's elemental sting
Abated.

Out from the rock a plant did sprout
Midst degradation all about
And to the universe did shout
Elated.

"I am the vanguard of a breed."
And as nature had decreed,
Upon the ground did fall a seed
And mated.[40]

---

33). He distinguishes the method of dynamic equivalence (which he acknowledges is not "officially the exclusive method of inculturation" [125]) from the method of introducing the various forms of popular religion into the liturgy (the method of acculturation) and from the method of raising certain forms of popular religiosity to the status of a liturgical rite (the method of aggregation).

[39] CELAM, *Evangelization in Latin America's Present and Future*, final document of the third General Conference of the Latin American Episcopate, Puebla de Los Angeles, Mexico, 1979, no. 465. For an English translation, see John Eagleson and Philip Scharper, eds., *Puebla and Beyond* (Maryknoll, N.Y.: Orbis Books, 1979), 188.

[40] William D. Carroll, *Songs Poems Perceptions* (Washington, D.C.: Semone West Publishing Company, 1998), 72–73. Used with permission.

Index

Abraham, 148, 151–52
acculturation, 233–34, 236
Acts, Book of, 68
Acts of Thomas, 163–64
adaptation, 227, 233–34
Addai (missionary), 163–64
Ad gentes, xxii, 139
Ad Petri cathedrum, 250–51, 253
advaita (non-dual) experience, 74–75
Ai Tan, 164
Alopen (missionary), 165
anthropology, 39–40, 190–93, 218–19
anti-Semitism, 145, 153, 156–71, 178, 190
Apostles' Creed, 93–94
Appleby, A. Scott, 198
Aquinas, Thomas, 97
Asian religions: concepts of God in, xxv, 119–26; harmony concept in, 123–25, 199–204; liturgical inculturation and, 232–44; multiple religious belonging in, 62–64, 68–78; peacebuilding in, 198–209
Asian Synod of Bishops, 122, 128, 229

Balthasar, Hans Urs von, 30, 39
Beeck, Frans Jozef van, 58–59
Buddha, the: on non-self, 204; relation to Jesus, xxv, 99–100, 128–46
Buddhism: and Christianity, 118–19, 128–36; Eightfold Path in, 119, 204; and multiple religious belonging, 6, 63nn7–8; and peacebuilding, xxvi, 204–9

capitalism, 122
Cappadocians, the, 13–14
Carroll, William D., 278
catechesis: doctrines in, 29–32; and identity, 52–53; method in, 24–29; Trinity in, 32–41

Catechism of the Catholic Church, xxv, xxvi, 23–24, 33–41, 36–37nn54–59, 44, 53, 147–60
catholic, as term, 43–44
Catholic Church: conservatives vs. liberals in, xxvi, 53, 78, 251–53; and Judaism, xxvi, 147–60; Eurocentrism of, xix; identity in, xxv, 42–59, 58–59n36; liturgy in, xxvi, 213–78; moral teachings of, 53–55, 57; and other religions, xxii–xxiv, 67–81; and peacebuilding, 187, 195–98; uniformity of worship in, 245–56
Catholic Identity after Vatican II (van Beeck), 58–59
Christ: church of, 46–47, 50–51; in Eucharist, 260–62, 264; experience of, 58–59; as marginal person, 178–87; in Trinity, 34–41; uniqueness and universality of, xxv, 64–67, 89–91, 93–98, 137–46
Christianity: in Asia, 116–20, 125–27; early, 68; and Judaism, xxvi, 68, 77, 156–60; and other religions, 66–67, 93–101, 139–41; and war, 186–98; Western vs. other cultures in, 61–62
Christology, 93, 141–46, 154–56, 178–80
Chung Hyun Kyung, 177–79
Chupungco, Anscar, xxvi, 232–36, 235n59
Co Ho people, 245–48
Cobb, John B. Jr., 77
Code of Canon Law 1917, 46
Cohen, Arthur, 173
Cohn-Sherbrook, Dan, 162–63
coincidentia oppositorum, unification of contradictions, 15–19
"communal Catholic," the, xxv, 48–49, 51–52

279